Caste and Capitalism in Colonial India

Caste and Capitalism in Colonial India

The Nattukottai Chettiars

DAVID WEST RUDNER

University of California Press

BERKELEY LOS ANGELES LONDON

University of California Press
Berkeley and Los Angeles, California

University of California Press, Ltd.
London, England

Parts of chapters 3 and 10 of this book were previously published in "Banker's Trust and the Culture of Banking among the Nattukottai Chettiars of Colonial South India," *Modern Asian Studies* 23, part 3 (1989): 417–458. Reproduced by permission of Cambridge University Press.
Part of chapter 7 was published in "Religious Gifting and Inland Commerce in Precolonial South India," *Journal of Asian Studies* 46, no. 3 (1987): 361–379. Reproduced by permission of the Association for Asian Studies, University of Michigan.

Library of Congress Cataloging-in-Publication Data

Rudner, David West.
Caste and capitalism in colonial India: the Nattukottai Chettiars / David West Rudner.
p. cm.
Includes bibliographical references and index.
ISBN 0-520-07236-7 (alk. paper).—ISBN 0-520-08350-4 (alk. paper)
1. Nattukottai Chettiars. 2. Caste—India—Tamil Nadu. 3. India—Commerce—History. I. Title.
DS432.N38R84 1994
305.5′54′095482—dc20 92-38124
CIP

Printed in the United States of America
9 8 7 6 5 4 3 2 1

The paper used in this publication meets the minimum requirements of American National Standard for Information Sciences—Permanence of Paper for Printed Library Materials, ANSI Z39.48-1984. ∞

Contents

Illustrations

Tables

Acknowledgments

When not describing Nakarattar business practice and social organization, much of this book engages friends and colleagues in a conversation about the nature (or natures) of Indian society. I acknowledge my debt to a wide range of scholars in the context of this discussion. But I would like to make special acknowledgment to a few individuals and institutions without which this book could not have been written. First of all, I wish to thank all my friends in India for hospitality and help in a project that they must long since have despaired of seeing in print. In Madurai, I owe a debt of gratitude to Mr. and Mrs. Sv. Arunachalam, Mr. and Mrs. Al. Periyannan Shunmugum, Mr. and Mrs. S. Sundaramurthi, Mr. and Mrs. M. Vaidyalingam, Mr. and Mrs. M. Salim, R. Ramamurthy, P. Karuthammal, V. Somasundaram, and V. Narayanan. In Madras, I was greatly helped by Dr. K. M. and Debbie Thiagarajan and by M. V. Subbiah. It is impossible for me to name all the Nakarattars who extended hospitality to me in Chettinad. None of my work would have been possible without my Tamil teachers and guides, V. S. Rajam (who tried to teach my tongue to dance at the University of Pennsylvania), K. Paramasivam, Muthu Chidambaram, V. Vijayavenugopal, V. Saraswathi and Raja Sekhar, who tried not to wince in Madurai. Much of my understanding of Nakarattar ritual comes from S. S. Sundaram Chettiar, a visionary poet and orator as well as accountant. I owe my systematic view of Nakarattar history and social organization to my principal informant, S. M. L. Lakshmanan Chettiar (Somalay). I deeply regret that he did not live to see the effort he expended on my behalf repaid by publication of this book. My field work was made possible by language and junior fellowships from the American Institute of Indian

Studies between 1979 and 1981. The Social Science Research Council provided me with the funds and the opportunity to explore the India Office Library and reflect more deeply about my research in 1986–87. By a stroke of good fortune, Peter Nabokov (whose past research focuses more on American Indians than Asian Indians) visited India in 1991. Peter fell in love with the vernacular architecture of Chettinad. On his return to America, he read my doctoral dissertation, contacted me, and allowed me to see his beautiful photographs of Chettinad houses and temples. Some of them now grace this book. I look forward to seeing the results of his further researches into Chettinad architecture. Finally, I would like to mention the following special friends who never gave up on me and who never lost an opportunity to ask if I was ever going to finish: Arjun Appadurai, Chris Bayly, Carol Breckenridge, Val Daniel, Nick Dirks, Chris Fuller, Doug Haynes, Jim Heitzman, Stephen Inglis, John Loud, David Ludden, Johnny Parry, Lee Schlesinger, Burt Stein, and David Washbrook. For the last decade, you have made up my intellectual family, enriched my thoughts, and sustained my vocation.

Note on Transliteration and Spelling of Non-English Words

The non-English vocabulary in this study draws on Tamil, Sanskrit, Urdu, and Anglo-Indian sources. Many terms used in written documents vary in their original transcription. In cases where a word occurs in a Tamil document or was spoken by a Tamil informant, I severely modify the transliteration system of the Madras University Lexicon, stripping terms of diacritical marks that would be useful only for Tamil scholars. In addition, plural forms of these terms, when used in the text rather than mentioned in a quotation from Tamil, are formed by adding the English morpheme *s* (e.g., *panams* rather than *panankal*). In cases where a word occurs in governmental or other documents from the colonial period, I adopt its most frequent Anglo-Indian spelling. In cases where a word occurs in both contexts, I generally follow the Anglo-Indian conventions, especially with regard to proper names. For variant transcriptions of the terms and for diacritical marks providing a precise indication of non-English orthography or phonology, see the glossary.

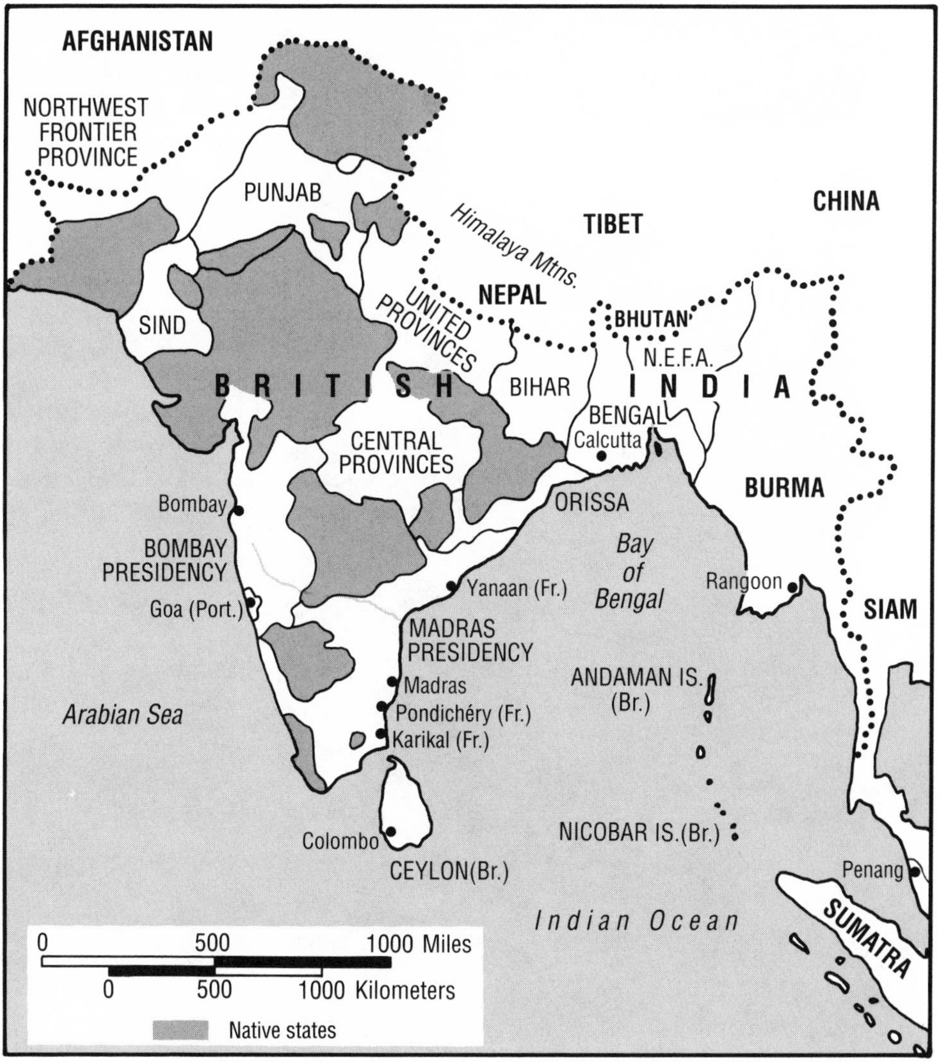

Map 1. British India, 1900

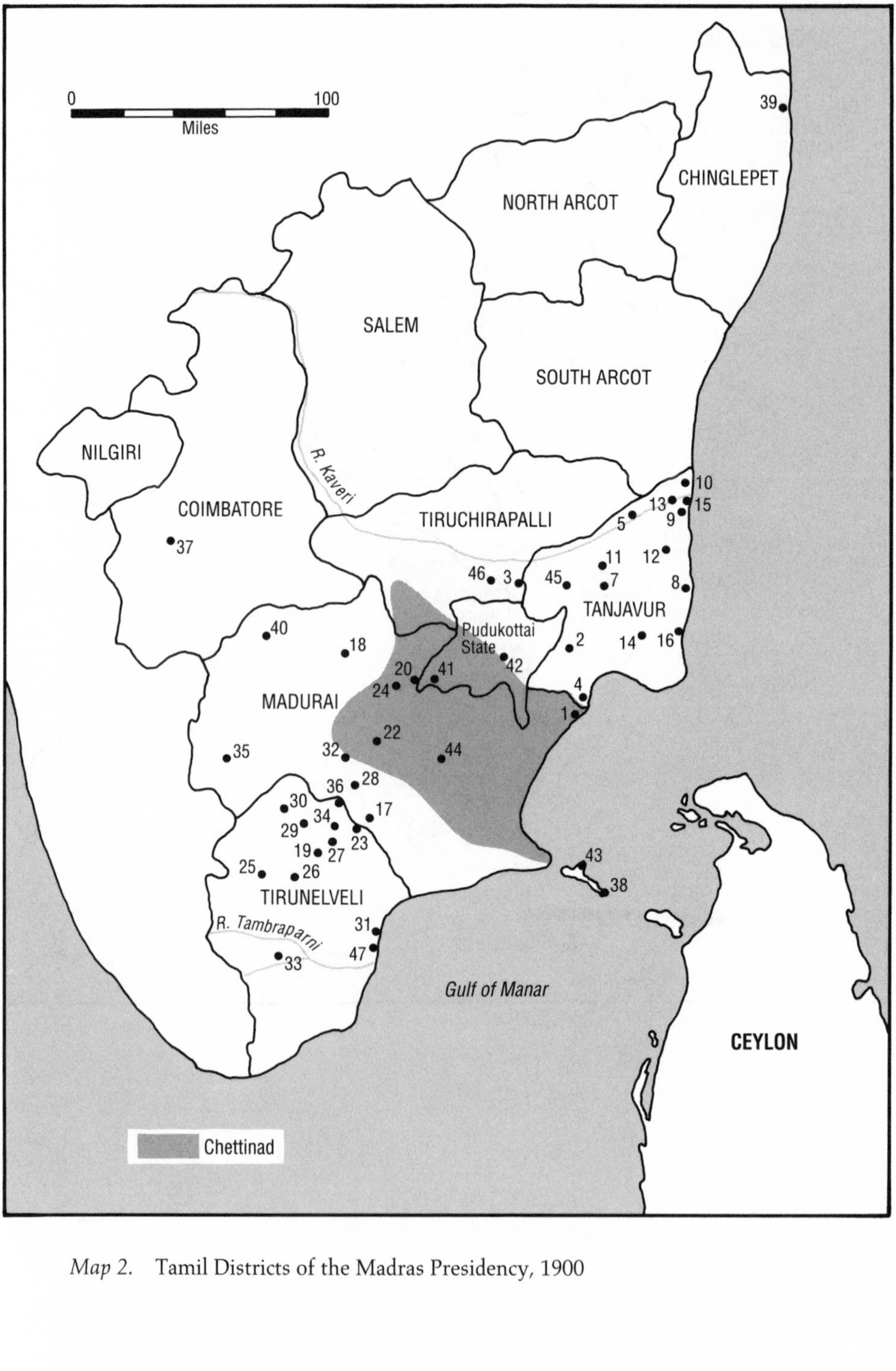

Map 2. Tamil Districts of the Madras Presidency, 1900

Early nineteenth-century Nakarattar sites of trade in Chola country (Ramanathan Chettiar, 1953)

1. Avudaiyapuram
2. Kalugumalai (Kalugapullikadu)
3. Kangeyanpattana (Kangeyampatti)
4. Karampaikkudi (Karambarkoil)
5. Kutalam
6. Manchakkolai*
7. Mannarkovil (Mannarkudi)
8. Nagapattinam
9. Nagoor
10. Pillaiyarpatti
11. Porulvaitaceri or Puravaceri
12. Sikkal
13. Sirkali
14. Tirutturaippundi
15. Tirumullaivasal
16. Velippalayam (Vellapallam)

Early nineteenth-century Nakarattar sites of trade in Pandya country (Ramanathan Chettiar, 1953)

17. Aruppukkottai
18. Dindigul
19. Elayiramapannai
20. Kottampatti
21. Madavilagam*
22. Madurai
23. Mannarkottai
24. Natham
25. Sankaralingapuram
26. Sankaranayanarkovil
27. Sattur
28. Sennampatti
29. Chinnakkarampatti
30. Srivilliputtur
31. Thavalaikulam
32. Tirumangalam
33. Tirunelveli
34. Tulukkapatti
35. Uthamapalayam
36. Virudhunagar

Other major cities in Madras

37. Coimbatore
38. Dhanuskodi
39. Madras
40. Palani
41. Piranmalai
42. Pudukottai
43. Rameswaram
44. Sivaganga
45. Tanjavur
46. Tiruchirapalli
47. Tuticorin

*Could not be located—not shown on map.

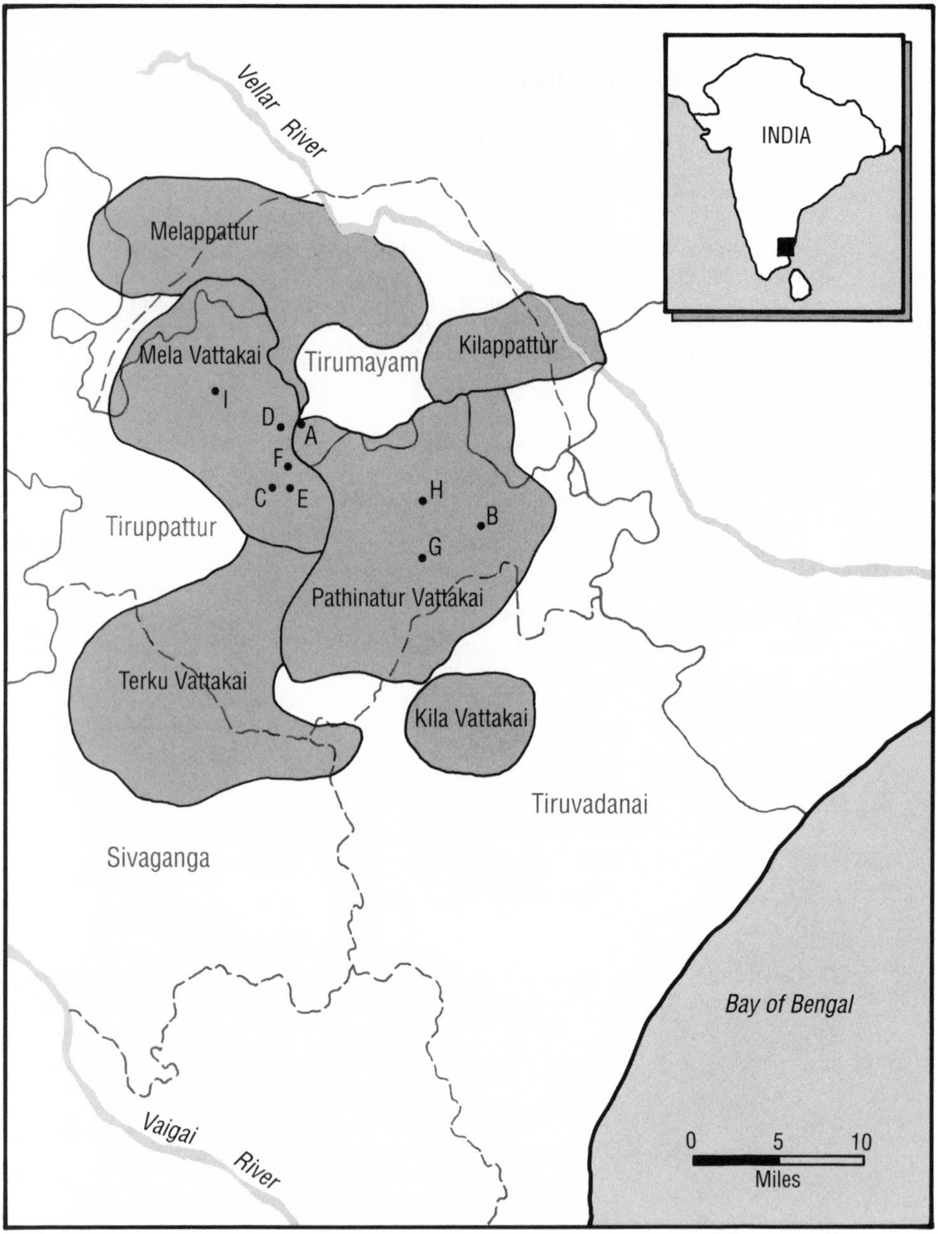

Map 3. Clan temples and *vattakais* of Chettinad

Nakarattar Clan Temples in Chettinad

A. Ilayathakudi Temple
B. Mattur Temple
C. Vairavan Temple
D. Iraniyur Temple
E. Pillaiyarpatti Temple
F. Neman Temple
G. Iluppaikudi Temple
H. Soraikudi Temple
I. Velankudi Temple

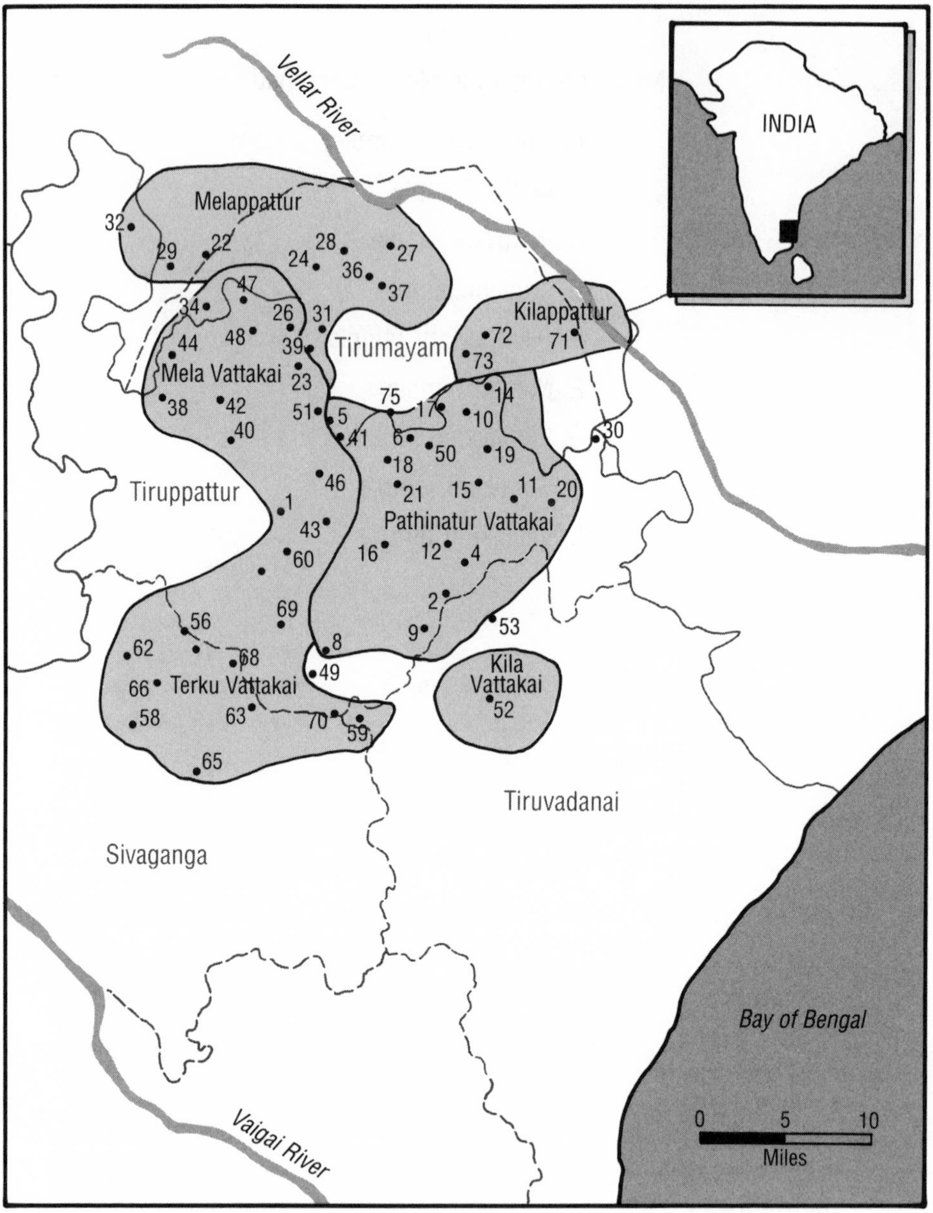

Map 4. Villages of Chettinad. (Some villages are not shown. *Vattakais* are shown on Map 2.)

Villages by Vattakai and Pirivu (Vattakai Divisions)

Pathinattur Vattakai

1. Alagapuri
2. Amaravathiputhur
3. A. Muthupattanam*
4. Ariyakkudi
5. Athankudi
6. Chokkalingamputtur
7. Jeyankontapuram*
8. Kallal
9. Kallappatti
10. Kanadukathan
11. Kandanur
12. Karaikudi
13. K. Lakshmipuram*
14. Kothamangalam
15. Kottaiyur
16. Managari
17. Nemuthupatti
18. Palavankudi
19. Pallattur
20. Puduvayal
21. U. Siruvayal

Melappattur

22. Goppanapatti
23. Guruvikkondanpadi
24. Kulipirai
25. Melasivapuri*
26. Mithivaippatti
27. Nachanthupatti
28. Panaiyappatti
29. Ponnamaravatti
30. Puthuppatti
31. Rangiyam
32. Ulakanpatti
33. Valaiyapadi*
34. Vekuppatti
35. Venthanpatti*
36. Varaiyachilai
37. V. Lakshmipuram

Mela Vattakai

38. Athekkur
39. Avinippatti
40. Kandavarayanpatti
41. Kilasivalpatti
42. Mahipalanpatti
43. Nachiyapuram
44. Nerkuppai
45. Pariyamirthappatti*
46. Pillaiyarpatti
47. Puvankurichi
48. Sevur
49. Siravayal
50. Sirukutarpatti
51. Viramatti

Kila Vattakai

52. Devakottai
53. Shanmuganathapuram
54. Dhanishavurani*

Terku Vattakai

55. Alavakkottai*
56. Chokkalingapuram
57. Chokkanathapuram*
58. Cholapuram
59. Kalaiyarmangalam
60. Kandaramanickam
61. Karunkulam*
62. Kilappungudi
63. Nadarajapuram
64. N. Alagapuri*
65. Nattarasankottai
66. Okkur
67. Panangudi*
68. Paganeri
69. Sembanur
70. Vetriyur

Kilappattur

71. Arimalam
72. Rayavaram
73. Ramachandrapuram
74. Thenippatti*

Nindakarai Pirivu

75. Konapattu

*Could not be located—not shown on map.

1 Introduction

The Nakarattars of Tamil Nadu

This book examines a vital component in the South Indian economy, the merchant-banking caste: a corporate organization of men and families that has been crucial to processes of capital accumulation, distribution, and investment. My focus of study is the well-known Nattukottai Chettiar caste or, as they call themselves, the Nakarattars. They represent the major banking caste of South India during the period from 1870 to 1930. I present an analysis of the commercial organization and activities of the caste during the period of their preeminence. I also demonstrate the precolonial roots of Nakarattar commercial practices and commercially oriented social institutions extending back to the beginning of the seventeenth century. I do not argue that the caste was unchanged during this period. I do argue, however, that many of the activities and institutions of merchant-banking castes in the colonial era had a deep historical dimension.

My study is based, in part, on field research carried out in the state of Tamil Nadu, South India, from October 1979 to November 1981. My primary residence and base of operations was the city of Madurai, located close to the Nakarattar homeland of Chettinad and one of the many sites of substantial Nakarattar philanthropy and investment. I did not initially plan to focus my research on the Nakarattar caste. In fact, when I first arrived in Madurai, I planned to study the interaction between elite Indian merchants and political authority in this traditional, inland, urban center. Two findings emerged during the course of investigation that fundamentally altered my research topic. In the first place, it soon became apparent that—contrary to the claims of most publications on Indian commerce—elite merchants and businessmen in Madurai had relied in important ways on their participation in corporate caste activities for the conduct of commerce. Secondly, it became evident that the most powerful members of Madurai's mercantile elite were Nakarattars and that the caste organization in which they participated operated beyond the local limits of the city, beyond even the limits of South India, and instead operated throughout the macroregion of British Southeast Asia. The implication for my study was clear: to understand the activities of elite Nakarattar businessmen in Madurai, it was necessary to consider the activities of both elite and nonelite Nakarattars and to consider their interaction over the entire sphere of their coordinated economic activities.

The Nakarattar caste numbered perhaps ten thousand in 1896, forty thousand in 1920, and, by 1980–81, when I carried out my field research, approximately one hundred thousand people.[1] Their lifestyle combined qualities common to settled agriculturalists, urban industrialists, and itinerant merchants. Accordingly, I did not have the option of confining my study of Nakarattars to a single village, or even to a single urban center. But I grew to know a core of Nakarattar families living in Madurai and Madras. And during the last four months of my field research I toured extensively through the villages of Chettinad, staying with Nakarattar families in their homes or at pilgrim rest houses connected with Nakarattar temples.

Since my focus is historical, I rely primarily on oral and documentary evidence rather than firsthand observation. The documentary evidence available to me included both Tamil and European materials. The former comprise temple inscriptions carved in stone, palm-leaf manuscripts, caste journals, family genealogies, and account books from Nakarattar banking houses. Among documents I label as "European," I include documents such as English-language newspapers written by Indians and documents from different branches of the Indian colonial government as well as documents written specifically by or for Europeans. The oral evidence consists of interviews with Nakarattar informants who described what they knew of their caste and family histories, and the details and rationale for a variety of Nakarattar customs. A few key informants proved especially informative and cooperative. They provided a disproportionate amount of the information reported in the book. But I have checked the data supplied by individuals for its internal consistency, for its agreement with data supplied by other knowledgeable persons, and for its agreement with relevant documentary sources.

Historical Overview

Records of Nakarattar activities are scanty until the middle of the nineteenth century, when they finally blossom under the fertile hands of colonial bureaucrats. Specific information about banking practice comes only in the second and third decades of the twentieth century, in the form of account books and reports from government inquiry committees (although these sources are supplemented by the memories of retired Nakarattar bankers). Interestingly, it is information about the connection between business and religion that recurs most reliably, not only for the period from 1600 to 1930, but also for the period extending back to the early Chola empire (A.D. 900–1200, cf. Abraham 1988; Hall 1980; Spencer 1968; Stein 1980). Although it is possible to trace many Nakarattar commercial practices back to the Chola period, the caste itself does not appear in the historical record until the seventeenth century,[2] when they were involved primarily in small-scale, itinerant salt-trading activities in the interior regions of Tamil-speaking South India. By the eighteenth century, some individuals had extended their business operations as far south as the pearl, rice, cloth, and arrack trade of Ceylon; others, as far north as the rice and wheat trade in Calcutta. As in the case of other mercantile groups, trade was inseparable from money lending and other credit-extending operations.

By the nineteenth and early twentieth centuries, especially after the opening of the Suez Canal, Nakarattars were the major sources of finance for myriad agrarian transactions between Burma, Ceylon, Malaya, and the Madras Presidency. They dominated the role of mercantile intermediary between foreign British rulers and local populations by monopolizing important components of the credit, banking, and agrarian systems of Southeast Asia, and by remitting huge amounts of capital from Southeast Asia back to their South Indian homeland for industrial investment and large-scale philanthropy. During the twentieth century, the Nakarattar business environment was altered in crucial ways by the development of nationalistic movements in Southeast Asian countries, by the general growth of legislation restricting indigenous forms of banking, and by the increase in industrial opportunities within India for non-British businessmen. The consequences were significant. The caste organization of the Nakarattars began to unravel in the face of multigovernmental interference with traditional banking practices. Elite members of the Nakarattar caste began a gradual transfer and "freezing" of investment capital from mercantile to industrial ventures. Nonelite Nakarattars—perhaps 80 to 90 percent of the caste—were forced to scramble for new employment opportunities, often working as employees in government and business offices, although many of these are owned or managed by Nakarattars.

Being a Nakarattar in Colonial India

To be a Nakarattar in the period from 1870 to 1930 was to belong to one of the great "country fort" houses (*nattukottais*) of Chettinad and to worship one's family's deity (*kula teyvam*) in one of Chettinad's seventy-six villages. As young Nakarattar boys grew up (I have very little information about young girls), their families trained them in the ways of business and, when they were old enough, apprenticed them to family firms with agency houses located in far-flung business stations throughout South and Southeast Asia. After a three-year tour of duty, the boys would return to Chettinad, to their families, to their neighbors, and to their temples. There, they would rest briefly, perhaps no longer than the three-month summer, during which most Nakarattar marriages and temple ceremonies occur. Then they would return to work in the outside world as young men. On his second tour of duty, a young man might return to the employ of the same firm for which he had worked before, perhaps even working as the principal agent (*mudali*) in its agency house. Alternatively, he might take over as resident proprietor or partner in an agency house for his own family firm. Eventually, a Nakarattar businessman would retire to Chettinad, where he would direct the activities of agents for his own family firm and join the round of ceremonies with the women, children, and other retirees who resided permanently in Chettinad.

Long before this, when family and financial circumstances permitted, a young man's joint family (*kutumpam, valavu*) would take advantage of his periodic return to Chettinad and arrange a marriage with an auspicious bride from another family. The ceremony initiated an elaborate pattern of gift giving and potential business cooperation within a kindred formed by patrilineal relatives (*pankalis*) of the husband and wife. This pattern of gifting and cooperation continued until all children born to the couple were established in alliance-forming marriages of their own. Alternatively, it might be continued beyond the marriage of offspring if two joint families of (what anthropologists call) "cross-relatives" within the kindred chose to renew the alliance begun with the original marriage. In either case, candidate families for marriage alliance were chosen from within the same territorial division (*pirivu, vattakai*) of Chettinad. Both families would register the marriage at their respective clan temples (*nakara-k-kovils*).

Many Nakarattars loaned money to agriculturalists and artisans within the Madras Presidency, especially within their Chettinad homeland and within the rice-growing regions and coastal ports of Tirunelveli and Thanjavur. But business in the Presidency was risky and paid a poor return on financial investment. As a consequence, the majority of Nakarattar business dealings took place overseas, in Southeast Asia. There, supported by the British colonial administration, Nakarattar business firms supplied credit to all who required it, at interest rates that were exorbitant by today's standards but generally far lower (in some cases, by an order of magnitude) than those supplied by their competitors.

This is not to say that Nakarattar business dealings were undertaken as acts of selfless charity, although Nakarattars in hearings by the colonial government did occasionally suggest a rather lofty motivation (just as bankers do today). Certainly their clients were under no such misapprehension (Adas 1974). Under the colonial government, Southeast Asian agriculturalists lacked the legal rights and the local organization that made money lending in Madras so risky. And, in an economic environment in which agricultural return on borrowed money was marginal, they often lost the land that they had improved as much by the labor of their hands as by inputs of Nakarattar capital. Nevertheless, it was Nakarattar bankers who provided the financial wherewithal for many Southeast Asians to make a living and who ultimately made possible the tea and coffee plantations in Ceylon, the rich rice frontier of lower Burma, and the tin and rubber industries of Malaya.

Within the Madras Presidency, a few of the wealthiest Nakarattars involved themselves with the largest peasants in the Indian countryside: the *zamindars* ("landlords") descended from Tamil chieftains who, during the last two hundred years, had lost a millenial struggle for local autonomy to the emerging British colonial regime. Nakarattars regarded these "little kings" with a very British attitude of scornful sympathy for irresponsible natives who wasted money on useless ceremonial expenditures. Nakarattars often interceded on their behalf, lending money to cover revenue arrears in return for a permanent lease on the most productive villages in a *zamindar*'s domain. These villages might, with help from the goddess, show a profit in the gradually improving commodities market of Madras in the latter part of the nineteenth century. In other cases, borrowers were unable to pay their debt, and Nakarattar lenders gained clear title to land. In the process, some Nakarattars even gained ceremonial rank in colonial society as they became *zamindars* themselves, or received other titles such as *Rao Bahadur* or Raja Sir.

The major sources of Nakarattar pride and honor, however, were their families, their business acumen, and their devotion to their gods: three indissociable components of Nakarattar life. Nakarattars gave generously to Siva temples in their *ur* (residential village) and in their *nakara-k-kovil* (clan temple). They contributed to temples for Siva, Aiyyanar, and the goddesses for the villages in their leased land. And they made contributions for the construction of Murugan temples with the other Nakarattar bankers in their *nakaravituti* (Nakarattar "rest houses" or choultries) wherever they did business. As recently as 1980, a wealthy Nakarattar textile mill owner reported to me that he proposed to give one hundred thousand rupees to each of the twenty-three major Saivite temples in India. He fully expected Siva to bless his family and his business in order to make this possible.

Nakarattar Studies

A central theme of this book is that it is impossible to understand Nakarattar business practices without understanding Nakarattar kinship. The focus on kinship, however, poses an evidentiary problem since kinship constitutes the least-documented domain of historical Nakarattar practices. Accordingly, my description of Nakarattar kinship during the colonial period is based primarily on personal observation of contemporary Nakarattar rituals in Chettinad and on field interviews with Nakarattars about their family histories and about the histories of their clan and village temples. Despite the absence of concrete historical documentation, I believe the picture I present of Nakarattar kinship is reasonably accurate as far back as the beginning of the seventeenth century. Certainly, documents from that early period indicate that the basic units of Nakarattar kin organization were all in place (Rudner 1987), including its hearthholds (*pullis*), joint families (*valavus*), lineages (*kuttikkira pankalis*), residential villages (*urs*), clans or temple groups (*nakara-k-kovils*), affinal kindreds, and territorially bounded "microcastes" (*vattakais*).

Aspects of Nakarattar history and customs have been addressed in a variety of publications.[3] Of these, Thurston (1909), Krishnan (1959), Tun Wai (1962), and authors of various papers contained in reports of the Madras, Burma, and Ceylon Banking Enquiry Committees (MPBEC 1930, BPBEC 1930, CBEC 1934) constitute the basic sources of information for most of the more recent work. Thurston provides a standard account of Nakarattar social organization and custom. Krishnan, Tun Wai, and the banking enquiry committee papers present useful information on the operation of Nakarattar financial instruments and banking practices. It was my impression that, due to reliance on these sources of data, most scholars know Nakarattars primarily in their capacity as money lenders. Their involvement in and contributions to Asian industrialization were almost unrecognized. To remedy this bias, a great deal of my field investigation was devoted to tracing Nakarattar involvement in South and Southeast Asian industry by consulting native documents collected by one of my principal informants, the late Nakarattar writer and publicist Somalay (S. M. Lakshmanan Chettiar). After I had carried out considerable research, however, I became aware of Raman Mahadevan's (1976) thesis on precisely this topic, which changed the direction of my own research.

Among other publications concerning Nakarattars, Adas (1974) and Siegelman (1962) make use of information contained in reports of the Burma Provincial Banking Enquiry Committee (BPBEC) and various Burmese settlement reports to describe the role of the Nakarattars in Burma. Christopher Baker's 1984 study draws on the Madras Provincial Banking Enquiry Committee (MPBEC) report (1930) and other useful publications, such as Krishnan's (1959) study of indigenous Tamil banking, and offers an insightful and contextualized appreciation of Nakarattar commercial practices in the financial markets of inland Madras.[4] Other writers have concentrated on legal, political, or ritual activities of members of the community. Weersooria (1973) points out that Nakarattar litigation was responsible for significant developments in Ceylonese legal precedent and focuses his study primarily on this topic. Breckenridge (1976) and Price (1979) make use of information contained in legal briefs to explore the interaction of specific Nakarattar individuals with South Indian temples and kingdoms. Moreno (1981, 1984; Marriott and Moreno 1990) makes use of observations and interviews obtained during recent anthropological field work to formulate a cultural account of a Nakarattar pilgrimage.

To date, however, there has been no systematic effort to synthesize the various kinds of information emphasized in the work of these Nakarattar scholars. Moreover, none of these scholars really address the unique blend of Nakarattar caste organization, religious custom, and business practice or the implications of this blend for understanding Indian culture and society. As a result, their findings about Nakarattars have had little effect on South Asian scholarship. In fact, outside the circle of anthropologists and historians mentioned above, most South Asian scholars know of the Nakarattars primarily through acquaintance with Thurston (1909 V:249–271).

Nakarattars and the Anthropological Study of Caste

The present study of Nakarattars, then, explores two aspects of South Indian commerce and society. On one hand, I examine the way a specific caste acted as an institution of banking and trade. On the other hand, I examine the way a specific financial institution functioned as a caste. My findings have implications for issues presently at the forefront of research in Asian history and anthropology, including the nature of noncapitalist economic formations and protoindustrialization, the impact of colonial rule on indigenous commercial systems, and variety and change in India's caste and ethnic groups. These considerations shape the organization of this book, guiding it from an initial survey of the study of commerce in

Indian society to a critical revision of standard anthropological and historical conceptions of caste.

My approach to the last topic deserves some preliminary comment. To begin with, I have deliberately undertaken an analysis of the social organization of the Nakarattar caste as well as the business practices of individual Nakarattars. In anthropology, such a focus has become increasingly unfashionable during the last twenty-five years, along with studies of social organization in general. I return to it, not out of a fetishistic love for the anthropology of days gone by, but because the focus on collective institutions holds potential for bringing together scientists and humanists, who, in various incarnations, have polarized anthropological discourse since its inception as a formal discipline. The "scientists" of the field have generally been interested in large-scale, diachronic, "macro" phenomena; the "humanists," in small-scale, synchronic, "micro" phenomena. There are, of course, exceptions. One need only think of work by such humanistic stalwarts as Dumont, Geertz, or Tambiah to recognize that the scientists have not yet acquired a monopoly on macro perspectives. Nor are psychological and cognitive anthropologists—not to mention economic anthropologists employing microeconomic theory in non-Western societies—willing to cede microanalysis to the humanists. Despite these qualifications, it seems to me that anthropology has flown outward in two different directions from its older focus on institutions. In doing so, it has lost track of institutional structures that mediate between individuals and their historical environments. Economic anthropologists and political economists have moved onward and upward in their analyses; interpretive and postmodern anthropologists have sunk downward and inward. One reason —though certainly not the only one—that the two groups don't talk to each other is that they are no longer interested in understanding the same kinds of phenomena. Those parts of the present study that focus on institutional analysis are offered in the belief that they provide a neutral ground for cooperative action.

Although my study of the Nakarattars requires that standard conceptions of caste be drastically qualified, even a cursory glance through the pages of this essay reveals how much I owe to scholars who have preceded me. The first is Louis Dumont. But it is Dumont the ethnographer and author of *Une Sous-Caste de l'Inde du Sud* (1957a) rather than Dumont the grand theorist and author of *Homo Hierarchicus* (1980 [1970]) who has been most influential. The brilliance of Dumont's (1957a, 1957b) work on the Pramalai Kallars established the importance of status hierarchy and affinity or marriage alliance as twin principles complementing the principle of descent in South Indian kinship relations. Although in his most recent (1983) work Dumont alters the way in which he presents his theory—speaking of values held by South Indian actors rather than of principles ordering anthropological models—he has not altered his view that descent, hierarchy, and affinity are all crucial for understanding South Indian kinship, whether one is a South Indian or an anthropologist. Nor does Dumont's shift in formulation allow an anthropologist working in this area the luxury of ignoring his insights.

My quarrel with Dumont is that he tends to see the general Indian landscape through Kallar'ed glasses. It seems to me, as it has to others, that Dumont has closely observed forms of descent, marriage alliance, and hierarchy, as exhibited by the Kallars and other dominant agrarian castes, but that he overgeneralizes this pattern to all South Indian castes. Many caste groups do not structure their lives around an elaborate formation of descent groups, even if they do exhibit marriage alliance and hierarchy. Other castes do not exhibit perpetual marriage alliance even if they make use of Dravidian kin terms to classify their caste mates. Still other castes exhibit structural equality rather than hierarchy among their constituent segments, yet they do not fail to exhibit a holistic, many-place ordering of all their constituents that is irreducible to the single-place predication of individuals.[5] In other words, it seems to me that Dumont's generalizations about all castes actually represent caste-specific values for variables that range over many more possibilities. Some of these values are apparently instanced by the Pramalai Kallars. But other castes exemplify different values, including the polar opposites of Kallar values.

McKim Marriott is the second anthropologist whose influence is prominent in my argument. Whereas Dumont is a French structuralist (even when appealing to values rather than structures), Marriott is an influential theorist among American cultural anthropologists. Perhaps more importantly, whereas Dumont's theory emphasizes unifying themes that run through wildly differing caste groups, Marriott focuses precisely on the dimensions along which they differ. Without necessarily subscribing to their most elaborated and still evolving formulations (cf. Marriott 1990), I have found some of Marriott's most general concepts to be useful in developing a model of South Indian kinship that encompasses caste groups ranging from Nakarattars and Kaikkolars to Kallars, Maravars, Vellalars, and Brahmans. In particular, I have found it useful to modify Marriott's (1976) preliminary formulations about Hindu gross and subtle substances and about maximal and minimal transactional strategies as part of a theory of caste as symbolic capital that complements my treatment of caste as an institution. Nakarattars maximized transactions of subtle substances, especially money, *hundis* (bills of exchange), and credit. They minimized transactions of gross substances, especially wives and the "seed" of their descent lines.[6]

Brenda Beck's (1972) analysis of left-hand and right-hand castes in Kongunad, Tamil Nadu, links together the structuralism of Dumont and the systematic study of variation of Marriott. Like Dumont, however, she tends to overgeneralize from the data of her field study. It is not the case that all regions of Tamil Nadu are like Kongunad: they do not at present, nor did they in the past, exhibit a bifurcate social structure split between mercantile and agrarian castes. However, like Dumont and Marriott, Beck explores the structural dimensions of caste organization in ways that define a research agenda for my own study. This is particularly true with respect to her focus on caste histories, marriage alliance, and the linkage between descent, territorial control, and cult membership.

A fourth anthropological contribution to my own understanding of caste traces its lineage to A. M. Hocart's (1950) theory of caste as an institution based not on kinship but on kingship. More recent ethnohistorical studies by Appadurai and Breckenridge (1976; Appadurai 1981; Breckenridge 1976), Dirks (1988), and Price (1979) extend Hocart's interpretation by showing how South Indian kingship was articulated with South Indian temples and religious endowments. Together, all three institutions provided an arena for the interaction of worship and politics in South Indian society.

The importance of this perspective lies not merely in its expansion of the anthropological gaze on India but also in its correction of a broadly Western orientalist and colonial bias that viewed indigenous institutions of governance as merely "hollow crowns," devoid of power or authority.[7] In my study, I focus on the further articulation of kings, temples, and endowments with a variety of commercial institutions (formal and informal) that, like institutions of kingship, have been excluded from the Western image of India. Again, my concern here lies in the characteristic ways in which different castes integrate themselves at any of these points of institutional articulation.

The blind spots in orientalist visions of caste are symptomatic of a pervasive essentialism and totalism common to anthropological treatments of cultures. Although my own understanding of caste rests on the shoulders of my disciplinary elders, my approach reflects the last decade's historiographically conditioned discontent with any search for timeless cultural essence, whether of hierarchy and hollow crowns in India; mud, blood, and semen in New Guinea; shame and honor in Mediterranean cultures; or alienated individuals in Western civilization (Appadurai 1986; Bourdieu 1977; Ortner 1984). Certainly, my analysis of the Nakarattars is directed not at distilling the essence of caste or of the caste system but at exploring the structure of variation among different castes located throughout India's social and historical landscapes.

Accordingly, historiographic treatments of caste influence my analysis as much as do the anthropological treatments reviewed above. Indeed, the various anthropological approaches to conceiving of caste provide only one vertex of a triangular discourse in which I have tried to act as mediator. The other vertices consist of a discourse on caste by historians and a reflexive discourse on their own identity by Nakarattars themselves. I rather fear that some anthropologists may find my tale overburdened with historical detail, while some historians will find my history underdocumented and, what's worse, deflected by digressions into the trivia of kinship terminology and ritual. I am sure that my Nakarattar friends will consider that I have barely touched the rich texture of their lives and histories. To all these likely complaints, I must agree. My excuse in steering this preliminary investigation of Nakarattar history between three sets of interests is to provide a platform for future studies of a people whose practices can teach us much about the political economy of South and Southeast Asia.

Outline of the Book

My study is broken into four parts. The first provides a theoretical orientation based primarily on empirical studies—ethnographic and historical—of caste and capitalism, the two focal concepts of this book. Chapter 2 reviews central themes in standard and revisional theories of caste, setting the stage for my reconstruction of a system of continuous linkage between Nakarattar business practice, kinship organization, and religion. My guiding assumption here is that it is possible to examine the internal social organizations of different caste groups, contrast features found within their organizations, and explain these differences as adaptive responses to the occupational specializations of the castes. Chapter 3 discusses the range of theoretical perspectives developed by anthropologists and historians for interpreting Indian commerce and discusses the blindness of these perspectives to major components in Indian commerce, such as castes specialized around the business of banking.

In the second part of this book, I present three chapters exploring the history, practice, and organization of Nakarattar business. Chapter 4 provides a historical context for analyzing Nakarattar social organization in the colonial period. It traces the explosive growth of the Nakarattar Southeast Asian financial empire from early, scattered references to it in nineteenth-century East India Company documents to the prominent role it plays in the banking enquiry committee reports of 1930. Chapter 5 describes the formal organization of financial cooperation between caste members, especially in regard to their activities of deposit banking, exchange banking, collective decision making about interest rates, and accounting. These activities are shown to depend on careful reckoning and bookkeeping of degrees of trust, especially among the Nakarattars themselves. Chapter 6 continues to explore the formal apparatus of Nakarattar finance, shifting attention to the institutions devoted explicitly to business activities. Alternative interpretations of Nakarattar business institutions are evaluated in light of information gathered during my field study.

The third part of this book explores the informal bases of Nakarattar business organization. Three chapters focus on elite philanthropy, marriage alliance, and descent-based cults in Chettinad, respectively. Each chapter places its discussion in the context of relevant anthropological literature concerning the relationship of religion to kinship, on the one hand, and to business practice, on the other.

The conclusion of this book returns to the theoretical issues that were framed in Part 1: the nature of caste and commerce. Specifically, in Chapter 10, I summarize my findings about Nakarattar kinship organization as an adaptive response to financial occupational specialization, explore their implications for standard models of Dravidian kinship, and begin a project of systematic comparison between Nakarattars and nonmercantile forms of caste organization.

PART ONE

CONCEPTS

2 Conceiving Caste

Capitalism and Caste

The nineteenth and twentieth centuries witnessed a sea change in India's commercial and political relations with the rest of the world—a change that, in Wallerstein's (1974, 1980) terms, "incorporated" and "peripheralized" India in a British-dominated world system. To say this, however, is not to accept auxiliary allegations about the noncapitalist qualities of India's precolonial political economy or other allegations about the locus of agency and the role of Indian class interests in the colonial transformation. All such claims seem to me to deserve a thorough rethinking. Yet, although much of what I have to say in the present book bears on these topics, I will not take the opportunity to comment on them. Instead, I shall focus on an additional claim, rooted in the classic sociological theories of Marx, Weber, and Simmel: namely, the claim that any capitalist transformation entails (as cause, consequence, or both) a form of commodity fetishism and objectification of labor that brings about the dissolution of social groups and the creation of alienated individuals.

The exploitative essentialism and evolutionism inherent in these and most comparisons between modern Western society and every other society remain dominant in the social sciences and have recently received considerable critical attention (Chandravarkar 1985; Fabian 1983; Fuller 1989; Inden 1986, 1991; Said 1978). This book participates in that criticism by taking issue with the underlying assumptions behind orientalist interpretations of Indian political economy—whether classic or contemporary, Marxist or a product of modernization theory. Toward this end, the present chapter considers the implications of Nakarattar caste structure and role in

Indian society both for standard theoretical treatments of caste and for generalizations about caste drawn from case studies of other castes.

The Standard View of Caste

"Standard" anthropological views of caste were well established by the 1950s and 1960s. By and large, they were shaped by studies of dominant agrarian castes. Some studies focused their attention on peasant cultivating castes, others on warrior or robber castes, and still others on nondominant, landless laboring castes. Almost no studies focused on mercantile castes. From the standard but agrarian perspective, castes were held to be commensal, endogamous groups, ritually ranked with other castes in consideration of local standards of relative purity. They were also held to be economically specialized with respect to their members, who were, therefore, interdependent with members from other, differently specialized castes (Dumont 1980 [1970]; Leach 1960; Marriott 1976; Srinivas 1962). Indigenous conceptions about *varna* (the religious ideal of the caste order) were seen, in Geertz's (1973) terms, to act as models of and for interaction between members of different castes within villages (Dumont 1980 [1970]; Marriott and Inden 1974; Rocher 1975). Concomitant conceptions about kinship were seen to regulate interaction between members of the same caste who lived in different villages (Dumont 1980 [1970]; Mayer 1960). All of these characteristics were supposed to be maintained by the corporate organization of castes within traditional, politically defined regions referred to as chiefdoms or "little kingdoms"—at least in South India (Dumont 1980 [1970]; Miller 1954; Srinivas 1962). Each corporate caste was governed by the operation of its own caste *panchayat:* a decision-making body composed of elder caste members whose purpose was to establish and sanction castewide standards of behavior.

Within this standard view there were disagreements about the relative importance of economic interdependence versus competition, of politico-economic power versus religious ideology, of attributional versus interactional systems of ritual ranking, and of other important considerations in the understanding of Indian society. Despite these disagreements, there was broad agreement that castes played a fundamental role in the lives of Indian people. For most social scientists, caste was the characteristic unit of Indian social organization: Indian society was caste society.[1]

With this general tenet, I have no disagreement. Nevertheless, it is a central theme of the present study that recent studies of mercantile castes including the Nakarattars require a radical revision of the standard concept of caste. No such proposal occurs in a vacuum. On the contrary, a general dissatisfaction with the standard view has given rise to various calls for its revision during the last few decades. The remainder of this chapter reviews an important segment of this revisionary work, setting the stage for the substantive analyses of Nakarattar caste organization to follow.

Caste as Symbolic Capital in Political Ethnicization

Recent historical studies of caste groups carry out a radical reconceptualization of the institution of caste and, by implication, raise serious questions about the adequacy of the standard social science view. I refer, in particular, to analyses that fall under such rubrics as the "substantialization," "ethnicization," or "racialization" of caste: the alleged twentieth-century transformation of caste from one kind of social formation into another. Research on this phenomenon raises questions, both about the kind of social formation caste is taken to have been prior to its transformation and about the kind of social formation it is said to be in the process of becoming. In both cases, the most frequent answers reflect a distinctive analytic bias.

Historical treatments of the changing nature of caste appear most prominently in connection with more broadly defined historiographic concerns about the growth of Indian self-rule prior to independence (Gallager, Johnson, and Seal 1973). Within this context, it is not surprising that historians have focused their attention on the twentieth-century emergence and role of caste associations: sodalities that seem to integrate aspects of caste organization with aspects of organization in Western-style political parties. The growth of these sodalities marks an apparent watershed in the way members of subcastes sharing a common name interact with one another, and this change has led influential historians of South India (including Baker 1976; Stein 1980; and Washbrook 1975, 1976, 1982) to raise important doubts about the putative corporate status of castes, the collective action of castes, and sometimes, it almost seems, the very relevance of caste groups within South India, at least for any level of territorial organization larger than a village.[2]

As an alternative, these radical historians argue that, prior to the late nineteenth century, South Indian castes constituted unintegrated clusters of localized, endogamous subcastes that had little in common except name. This view of caste is one that follows in the wake of an anthropology that emphasized village studies without giving adequate attention to extravillage and regional social phenomena. Because of the absence of regional caste studies, and because of their predisposition to look for the impact of caste in the Indian independence movement, some radical historians have based their findings on investigations of the twentieth-century development of caste associations formed for political purposes (e.g., Hardgrave 1969; Rudolph and Rudolph 1967).[3]

If I understand the arguments of these historians correctly, South Indian caste identity has gradually been shaped into a vague umbrella concept that covers a range of *potential* practical and moral linkages, but that entails no specific rights or obligations among people who share a common caste name. Rather, caste identity defines a category of people who are candidates for alliance in virtually any common cause. They do not exist as permanent corporate groups, but they can be mobilized in temporary political factions (Boissevain 1968) or quasi groups (Mayer 1966) on an occasional basis by powerful politicians pursuing individual ends. Caste identities, in this view, constitute a form of what Bourdieu (1977) called *symbolic capital*, available for investment by politicians with the skill to manipulate its meanings.[4]

The most elaborated version of this position is represented in a series of papers and books by David Washbrook (1975, 1976, 1982, 1984). Developing a sophisticated comparative model of ethnicity and social stratification, Washbrook carefully orients himself within the luxuriant literature about Indian castes. For example, with respect to sociological and historical theories about the "modernity of tradition" (Rudolph and Rudolph 1967), Washbrook sees postconquest and colonial caste associations as the results of novel manipulations of traditional symbols. At the same time, Washbrook is too good a historian to posit a timeless tradition. Rather, along with scholars such as Cohn (1960, 1983, 1987) Carroll (1978), and Dirks (1987), he theorizes that "traditional" Indian symbols and ideas about caste may themselves have been recent inventions, born out of interaction between European conquerors and indigenous elites. In this view, the apparent nineteenth- and twentieth-century modernization of caste represents a continuation of seventeenth- and eighteenth-century processes.

Washbrook is also careful to place his viewpoint in relation to more culturally based theories of caste. Thus, despite a sustained critical attack against the theories of Dumont (1980), he shares a number of Dumont's interpretations of Indian society, especially as elaborated by Stephen Barnett (1973). Like Dumont and Barnett, Washbrook finds that precolonial caste identity fits more or less closely with what I have characterized as the standard model of caste society. In particular, he holds that precolonial caste membership applied only disjointedly to distinct social identities within localized caste hierarchies. The social obligations of membership were wholly specified by the local situation and were not generalized to caste members belonging to regionally disbursed subcastes sharing nothing other than a common name. By contrast, the "substantialized," "ethnicized," or (in Washbrook's terms) "racialized" systems of caste identity in colonial and independent India have reversed this emphasis. That is to say, subcastes have come to be identified on the basis of kinship within a commonly named caste cluster; clusters as wholes are ranked with respect to legal and ritual prerogatives that are sanctioned by pan-regional, governmental authorities; and finally, interactions between members of the same local subcaste and between members of different subcastes sharing a common caste name are free from all caste-defined regulations, except those preserving endogamy.[5]

Washbrook marshals a number of arguments that complement those of Dumont and Barnett. These, however, are incidental to his primary interest in explaining "the rise of ethnic and racial sentiment" as "a characteristic response to certain kinds of economic and political instability" (1982: 153). In his view, the evolution of a caste cluster into an ethnic group within a racially stratified system reflects a complex political process. Elite cluster members create and "sell" a myth of cluster solidarity to the emerging colonial government, position themselves as brokers of political influence for members of their caste clusters, and employ these newly created patronage resources to build a base of political support.[6] As the multicaste members of caste clusters cooperate to support an elite member, they create temporary political factions whose memberships change with the political fortunes of their leaders. Such cluster-based factions exemplify regional caste units that never existed in precolonial India. Their members disregard local variation and conceive of themselves in substantialized, ethnicized, and racialized terms that are equally novel and that, in fact, resemble Western-style ethnic or racial groupings. In Washbrook's apt restatement of Srinivas, "the djinn (of caste) was released from the bottle [of little kingdoms]. . . . All hell broke loose as society began to form itself into 'castes' which, so far from accepting the hierarchy of the *varna* scheme, began furiously to contest their own places within it" (1988: 26–27).[7]

"Where's the Rest of Me?" The Case of the Komatis

My own research persuades me that the caste-as-symbolic-capital interpretation of Indian political society has considerable merit, but that it also has a markedly distortive Western accent. In the first place, it restricts its focus to the way that *Western*-style political activities are structured by, and structure, ideas of caste. In the second place, it dichotomizes social organization into Western-style corporate groups and Western-style political factions in a way that is quite insensitive to a variety of *South Indian*, caste-based social forms that fit neither category. In other words, the doubly accented, Western interpretation of caste fails to consider the likely possibility that non-Western, caste-based social forms might occupy South India's social landscape. A closer look at some of the details in Washbrook's conception of caste as a politically mobilized ethnic group will illustrate my concerns.

To begin with, Washbrook's elaborated discussion significantly qualifies the basic ethnicization thesis by applying it primarily to case studies of various mercantile and service castes. According to Washbrook (1975: 164) these castes exhibited important organizational differences from the castes of their agrarian brothers, differences that made factional organization at the provincial level an attractive and feasible political strategy that was unworkable for agriculturalists.

Washbrook illustrates his model of the ethnicization of merchant castes by analyzing the historical transformation of the Komati Chettiars, a merchant-banking caste whose members dominated South Indian commerce in their role as European/Indian brokers until the mid-nineteenth century (Suntharalingam 1974). The Komatis constituted a highly segmented caste cluster split by religious-sectarian, occupational, territorial, and affinal boundaries (Thurston 1909 III:306–348; Washbrook 1975: 152–159). Washbrook cites some meager evidence for inter-regional cooperation, such as use of a common trade language (Thurston 1909 III:308) and a common cross-cutting system of exogamous clans which, in principle, could have allowed inter-subcaste marriage exchanges (312–314). But the only hard evidence that suggests inter-subcaste cooperation within the cluster as a whole is the presence of a few elite families operating throughout the Madras Presidency from the sixteenth to the nineteenth century.

It would clearly be wrong to argue from the absence of information about Komati organization that the Komatis therefore lacked pan-regional organization, especially without any systematic effort to establish what kinds of cooperation may have existed. Yet, having asserted that Komatis were commercially organized throughout South India, Washbrook proceeds to reject every possible social mechanism for making such organization work and, in so doing, contradicts his thesis that mercantile castes were distinctively preadapted to twentieth-century ethnicization. According to Washbrook's model, Komati marriage was restricted to localized subcastes; collective worship of the caste goddess at a shrine in the Komati homeland, north of Madras, had no economic, political, or other discernible social implications; and, finally, the only Komatis who truly conducted commerce on a pan-regional scale were elites, who, according to Washbrook, had separated themselves from specialized commercial interaction with their fellow Komatis in order to pursue alternative and somehow incompatible commercial opportunities offered by the developing British East India Company and colonial economies.

These propositions, as I have said, run contrary to Washbrook's important insight about the preadaptive qualities of mercantile caste organization for twentieth-century caste associations. Yet, because issues outside the politicized organization of castes are secondary to his major arguments, Washbrook does not explore the possibilities for nonpolitical forms of subcaste cooperation or the possibilities for elite-nonelite interaction. As a consequence, it seems to me that it is premature to judge the case of the Komatis. Although Washbrook claims that they and other mercantile and service castes successfully form caste associations because of pre-twentieth-century organizational characteristics unique to mercantile and service castes, in the end, he never really identifies the relevant preadaptive organizational features and therefore implicitly suggests that they may not have been distinctive after all.[8] The present study agrees with Washbrook's original suggestion that mercantile caste organization was distinctive. And although I am unable to offer any further information about the Komatis, my study of the Nakarattars, the merchant-banking caste who succeeded the Komatis as dominant players in the Indo-European credit market, explores precisely those properties of caste organization that were characteristic of a mercantile specialization. There remains, however, one more lesson about caste that I wish to draw from Washbrook and from one of his critics.

Segmentary Structure and Structural Variation

The criticism I have just made of Washbrook's treatment of caste-based political formations in the twentieth century bears a superficial similarity to criticism that Michael Roberts (1982) has also aimed at Washbrook. According to Roberts, Washbrook is guilty of a "sociological naivete" that imparts a "misplaced concreteness" to the study of caste (1982: 194). Roberts means by this that Washbrook ignores the social implications of "cultural typifications" about caste (1982: 194, 202–204). In particular, Roberts argues that Washbrook fails to consider the fluid, segmentary organization manipulated by a caste's membership (1982: 197).

I agree with Roberts that Washbrook does not give adequate consideration of non-Western forms of pan-regional social organization. I disagree with Roberts's claim that Washbrook is unaware of the "cultural"—in contrast to the sociological—nature of typifications about caste. On the contrary, the central point of Washbrook's interpretation is precisely the flexible political use of cultural typifications. Where Washbrook goes wrong, or so it seems to me, is *not* in any failure to appreciate either the cultural nature of caste as cultural typification or the fluidity of caste-based political structures, but in limiting attention narrowly to a single use of typification: the construction of Western-style political coalitions. In Washbrook's restricted view, symbols of caste identity simply fail to operate in the organization of pan-regional social groups, except in temporary nineteenth- and twentieth-century political coalitions. In other words, although both Roberts and I agree that Washbrook does not adequately appreciate the segmentary nature of caste formations, my criticism of Washbrook is that he ignores important social variables, not that he ignores cultural variables.

From my view, caste identity has been and continues to be an important (though certainly not the exclusive) form of symbolic capital invested in the segmentary production of a variety of South Indian social formations. To recognize the segmentary nature of caste-based formations, however, marks the beginning of investigation—not, as Roberts seems to suggest, the end. Different castes face different opportunities, constraints, and threats in different regions and at different times. They invest their caste identities accordingly, producing no uniform segmentary structure but instead varieties of segmentary structures, structured by—and structuring in turn—the actions of their members.

The "Corporacy" of Castes: Kayasths and Nakarattars Compared

Interpreting caste as a form of symbolic capital raises a number of definitional questions about the nature of corporate and quasi-corporate groups in which the capital of caste is invested.[9] To this end, it is helpful to consider Karen Leonard's (1978) important study of the Kayasths of Hyderabad. Less radical in its position than those of Baker, Stein, or Washbrook, Leonard's study argues that although castes may not constitute corporate wholes in themselves, their membership may nevertheless be organized in a variety of supervillage and even superregional corporate units. In particular, Leonard indicates that actively cooperating caste members most commonly form corporate units at the level of families, lineage segments, marriage networks, or restricted bilateral kindreds, all of them operating within multiple urban contexts. She points out that, in any given historical period, a caste is characterized by a typical constellation of such component kin groups, each of which conducts distinctive economic and political activities. These constellations of kin groups vary according to the conditions of the wider politico-economic environment. She describes (1978: 15) the following progression of constellations in the case of the Kayasths:

> In the eighteenth century military aristocracy, an individual and his immediate family were the important social unit. In the nineteenth century, kin groups formed, and these small groups of closely related families controlled hereditary positions within the Muglai administration. Due to the educational and administrative changes of the late nineteenth century, some Kayasths organized on the basis of common sub-caste membership; in the twentieth century, they have organized on the basis of common caste membership.

Notice that, in at least one important respect, Leonard's view of caste supports those of Baker, Stein, and Washbrook. Excepting only a brief period of political organization at the beginning of the twentieth century, Leonard claims that not even Kayasths have operated in a corporate fashion on a caste level (i.e., by organizing the unrestricted kindreds comprising the Kayasth caste cluster). She differs from the three South Indian historians in presenting a much richer picture of multilocale, intracaste organization. Nevertheless, not even her enriched model of caste organization alters the unified picture of internal caste politics presented by all of the historians under review. In particular, no constellation of kin groups seems determined by any decision-making body acting in the interests of the whole. Nor does there exist any such body having powers or rights to act with regard to any other matter of collective concern. The caste cluster as a whole is simply a culturally distinguished set of individuals and groups—a kindred of recognition in contrast to a kindred of cooperation (cf. Mayer 1966). It is a cultural category designating an aggregate of people with the potential for participating in useful but less inclusive forms of social organization.

It should be pointed out (Leonard's conclusions notwithstanding) that even if our analysis is confined to political organization, the absence of a centralized, decision-making body operating within either the kindred of cooperation or the kindred of recognition is not a sufficient condition for withholding recognition of a subcaste's or a caste cluster's corporate status. This is especially the case when subunits of a caste (such as the Kayasths) exhibit traits of segmentary organization similar to those that have been well analyzed in anthropological studies of African political systems. Without further study of what may prove a wide variety of political mechanisms, the absence of effective castewide *panchayats* should not be taken as conclusive.

Nevertheless, assuming that Leonard's evidence would have reflected Kayasth corporate organization if it had existed, her study offers us an important contrast with the Nakarattars of colonial south India. To begin with, Nakarattar identity was unexceptionably based on jural principles of kinship and was regulated by the operation of temple-clan committees (see Chapter 9). Secondly, Nakarattars as a body made a variety of economic, ritual, and political claims upon each other in virtue of their common caste identity. Moreover, they traditionally and often successfully claimed special rights in the administration and execution of government in those states in which they played a commercial role. Finally, Nakarattars exercised a variety of collective rights over their ancestral homeland of Chettinad. It is true that the Nakarattars were politically acephalous—that they were not organized by any single institution such as kingship or a caste *panchayat*. But this did not prevent the caste from making collective decisions about a wide variety of issues and disputes through a system of institutions that embodied both a nonhierarchical, crosscutting form of segmentary organization and also considerable centralization of power vested in the hands of a relatively small body of elite Nakarattars (*adathis*).

All this, however, may be besides the point, for Nakarattar caste organization is best viewed as primarily economic in orientation rather than political. For individual Nakarattars, for their families, and for the caste group as a whole, it was commerce, not politics, that dominated almost every consideration and every action. Commercial considerations affected institutions that regulated practices ranging from philanthropy and politics to marriage and adoption. Conversely, the net effect of institutional adaptation to the needs of business was to render the caste especially efficient in the task of capital accumulation and distribution. In the case of the Nakarattars—particularly in their nineteenth- and twentieth-century incarnation as merchant-bankers—there is little room for doubt concerning the putative corporate status and collective action of the *jati* across village, regional, and even international boundaries.

In sum, although I endorse many recent historiographic interpretations of caste in its modern and flexible embodiment as a form of political coalition, I disagree that ethnicized and substantialized caste factions are the only forms that caste groups take outside the level of the village. At the very least, for Nakarattars and other large-scale merchant-banking castes (and I suspect for many landholding and military castes as well), such relatively recent interpretations of caste, like the more standard anthropological views they superceded, ignore a variety of corporate institutional arrangements between caste members. This conclusion in no way contradicts political analyses of castes as constituting—among other things—potential factions occasionally mobilized by politicians. It does indicate that factional mobilization represents only part of the organization and functioning of caste in Indian society; in particular, an exclusive focus on factional politics ignores the economic resources that castes provide their members and the ways in which these resources are organized. By contrast, if economic variables are taken into account, I suggest that castes will typically emerge as complex, multilayered, multifunctional corporate kin groups with enduring identities, a variety of rights over property, and crucial economic roles, often within large regions. This is precisely the conclusion that can be drawn from recent historical analyses of agrarian castes, as will be addressed in the following section.

Ecologically Qualified Views of Caste

The standard view of caste society deals spectacularly poorly with the on-the-ground diversity of India's caste systems. No "little kingdom" in India has ever been the same as any other. Some have been governed by authentic kings. Others have been governed by assemblies representing important clans of a dominant caste. Some little kingdoms incorporate as many as fifty castes and include a substantial "untouchable" population. Others comprise only a single caste and structure their social relationships primarily in terms of kinship. The importance of ritual purity as an ordering principle for social relations varies widely; and so does its concrete expression in articulated prescriptions and sanctions on behavior. All of these variables, and many more as well, threaten to render the standard view of caste meaningless, unless some order can be found that links the cultural capital embodied in the structure of historically specific castes to the opportunities for investing this capital available in specific historic environments.

Two recent works on South Indian rural history make significant progress in such an inquiry: David Ludden's *Peasant History in South India* (1985), and Christopher Baker's *An Indian Rural Economy* (1984). Ludden's and Baker's descriptions of the agrarian castes of South India arise in the context of an inquiry into agricultural production and land revenue, and they are only indirectly concerned with the conceptualization of caste. Nevertheless, I have found their treatment of caste enormously helpful in my own work. Using statistical information culled from early revenue reports, censuses, and government reports on land, climate, soils, agricultural techniques, rural credit, and innumerable other topics, Ludden and Baker construct a socioecology of caste. Baker's regional division of Tamil Nadu into valleys, plains, and Kongunad is inspired by Ludden's regional subdivision of Tirunelveli District into wet-farming, dry-farming, and mixed-farming zones. Both map the distribution of dominant agrarian castes onto their respective rural landscapes and suggest a link between modes of production and modes of political domination: namely, that kinship-based "tribal" formations control resources in the dry-farming plains, and kingship-based "ritual state" formations control resources in the wet-farming valleys. To put this another way, they link differences in the segmentary structures of different castes to the goals of caste members as they try to exploit their natural and social environments.

Ludden and Baker are, perhaps, somewhat insensitive to variations in caste segmentation that social anthropologists have found significant throughout the world and that seem operative in the Tamil countryside. They contrast the structure of royal honors and service in the wet-farming valleys with the segmentary lineage structure of the dry-farming plains, but they fail to consider the kinship structure of the valleys and the kingship structure of the plains—an omission all the more remarkable since the best available studies of Tamil kingship concern precisely the little kingdoms of the plains and their integration with kinship organization (Dirks 1988; Dumont 1957a, 1957b; Price 1979). Nevertheless, the lesson that I draw from their studies concerns, again, adaptive variability in the social organization of different castes. My analysis of the Nakarattars attempts to complement their findings by characterizing a mercantile caste that is territorially dominant in its residential homeland, but which has a resource base that lies neither in agrarian production nor in military control.

Mercantile Caste Variation: Some South Indian Dimensions

To say that a particular caste functions as a regional or pan-regional commercial organization is not to claim that all commercially organized castes function in the same way. Different castes specialize in different forms of trade, characterized by location, geographic scope, and types of commodities traded. The geographic distribution, internal organization, standards for behavior, and resource opportunities of the castes vary accordingly. In other words, however much Indian businessmen might exhibit class resemblances, they differ from one another with respect to the resources available to them through their castes, the roles they play in their castes, and the roles their castes play in Indian society. Put concretely, Nakarattars did business differently than Komatis, who did it differently than Nadars, who did it differently than did the multiple species of South Indian Chettis.

The exact nature of these differences is still very much at issue. The two best-known studies directed at the historical roles of mercantile castes throughout India—Hardgrave's (1969) study of Nadars, and Timberg's

(1978) study of Marwaris—do not provide the kind of information needed to carry out a systematic comparison of the forms of mercantile organization in question. Hardgrave focuses on politics and cultural identity; Timberg, on the historic and geographic diaspora of the Marwaris. Neither provides a detailed analysis of social organization. Under the circumstances, results from my own investigation can only suggest avenues for future comparative research. Nevertheless, even such preliminary observations indicate important dimensions of variation between the differently specialized commercial groups located, in this case, on South India's historical, commercial landscape.

On one hand, for example, Nakarattars were unlike many of their brethren Chettis, who conducted small-scale wholesale and retail trade in groceries, edible oils, jewelry, and other commodities. Such "petty" Chetti castes tended to operate their businesses within a small radius around their native towns or villages.[10] By contrast, Nakarattars conducted their business activities well beyond their residential homeland. In this respect they resembled some other pan-regional mercantile castes—including, for example, both the merchant-weaving Kaikkolars (or Sekuntar Mudaliars) and the grain-trading Nadars.

On the other hand, Nakarattars differed from both of these large-scale mercantile castes in a variety of other respects. To begin with, Nakarattars carried out their commercial activities over a much larger territory than that covered by even the Kaikkolars or Nadars. Both of these were confined by and large to the Tamil-speaking regions of South India. Nakarattars, however, conducted business as far north as Calcutta, and the bulk of their dealings actually took place in British Southeast Asia. In addition, unlike the merchant-artisan Kaikkolars or the grain-trading Nadars, Nakarattars acted primarily as bankers, extending financial credit, discounting bills of exchange, and receiving deposits—in short, performing all the functions of a modern bank. In other words, unlike the other two pan-regional mercantile groups, Nakarattars kept themselves relatively free from the requirements of commodity production or processing, especially the necessity imposed by activities of production to tie up resources in relatively fixed capital investments. Nakarattars much preferred to keep their resources liquid and thus concentrated their activities primarily in financial operations.[11]

A Closer Look at Merchant-Artisans: The Case of the Kaikkolars

It was not feasible for me to collect detailed information about concomitant variation in the social organization of most of the differently specialized commercial castes. Fortunately, the Kaikkolar caste, as the subject of an ethnohistorical study by Mattison Mines (1984), represents an unusual exception to the general lack of scholarly attention given the organization of commercial castes. Accordingly, it becomes possible to contrast Kaikkolar organization with that of the Nakarattars. In his study of Kaikkolars, Mines is primarily concerned with the spatially segmented organization of their "seventy-two-*natu*" system extending throughout Tamil Nadu, and the contrast between this form of organization and that of agrarian castes.[12] Within the seventy-two-*natu* system, interaction between Kaikkolar caste members tended to be territorially segmented into *natus:* small local regions where sites of descent group formation and marriage alliance coincided with the sites of business activity. In fact, notwithstanding the pan-regional scope of commerce represented by the Kaikkolar caste as a whole, individual traders operated within their local territories much as did the small-scale Chettis, forming what amounted to microcastes, sub-*jatis,* or even segmented, endogamous *jatis* within the Kaikkolar caste cluster. They extended the total range of their caste's operation by maintaining a network of ties between different local segments: in pre-twentieth-century days through their ancient seventy-two-*natu* system, and more recently through the operation of a modern caste association (Mines 1984). Thus it was the caste as a whole that conducted business beyond the range of the disbursed and discrete residential homelands of its individual members. Caste members as individuals, however, tended to merge residential and business domains.[13]

As clearly demonstrated by Mines, the difference between Kaikkolar and agrarian castes is based on their differing economic specializations. Kaikkolars produced textile commodities that were easily transportable and that, in fact, have been the object of international trade for a thousand years or more. By contrast, agrarian castes specialized in production for local consumption. Only recently have they had the means for transporting their bulky and perishable produce. For agriculturalists, there was never any question of combining production with long-distance commerce. For the Kaikkolars, without long-distance commerce there would have been no justification for production. The pan-regional Kaikkolar *natu* system established standards of quality for textile goods, provided its members with market intelligence, adjudicated conflicts over production and market monopolies, and interceded with local governments on behalf of its members. There was no comparable corporate organization that tied together agricultural castes across spatially dispersed residential communities.

Mines views the division of Indian society into agriculturalists and merchant-artisans as breaking down in the twentieth century under the impact both of technological innovations that facilitate transport of agrarian produce and of an altered political system that discourages caste organization in favor of organization by industrial sector. But, he argues, the kind of dual organization exemplified by agriculturalists and Kaikkolars represented the norm for all of South Indian society for at least a thousand years prior to the 1920s.

The Merchant-Banker Nakarattars Contrasted

On the whole, I believe Mines is premature in constructing a simple dual model of agriculturalists and merchant-artisans for the entire range of South Indian society. In particular, such a model ignores important variations in the conduct of South Indian commerce. My study of the Nakarattars, for example, identifies aspects of their social organization that directly contradict the central features of Mines's mercantile model. I emphasize, however, that my findings with regard to the Nakarattars do not have implications for Mines's analysis of the Kaikkolars, but only for his generalizations to all mercantile organization. Notwithstanding any disagreement over the scope of Mines's conclusions, I remain in total agreement with his identification of the topic of commercial organization as a crucial and neglected topic in Indian studies. His study represents an important contribution to the field and provides useful comparative material for understanding variation between mercantile castes.

For example, there are important organizational differences associated with differences in the economic specializations of Kaikkolars and Nakarattars. In contrast to Kaikkolars, Nakarattars conducted their business activities in "business stations" that could lie hundreds of miles beyond their Chettinad homeland. Why the two groups should differ in this regard is not clear. It seems reasonable, however, to suppose that there was a functional link between occupation and organization. The production and processing of trade commodities such as textiles was conducted more efficiently with the participation of the domestic group (the wives and children) of merchant-producers than it could have been without the group's participation. At the same time, Kaikkolar concern for ritual purity of the endogamous group operated to restrict the distance that the combined domestic and producing unit could travel. By contrast, Nakarattar merchant-bankers traveled long distances to strange lands. But their banking operations could operate just as efficiently with paid male employees as with labor supplied by the merchant's family (see Chapter 6). Concomitantly, Nakarattars satisfied their ritual concerns with purity by leaving the domestic group behind in the circumscribed homeland of Chettinad.

Whatever the truth of these speculations, the presence of pan-regional commercial groups, organized in the ways I have ascribed to, respectively, merchant-producing castes and merchant-banking castes, extends back in history to a period when guilds rather than castes were the primary institutions for long-distance trade. A thousand years ago, guilds termed *manigrammams* exhibited a split between their residential homelands and their circuits of trade that is similar to the more recent organizational pattern of the Nakarattar caste. In the same period, other guildlike groups, functioning as municipal councils for market towns, exhibited the territorial segmentation of present-day merchant-producing castes such as Kaikkolars or Nadars.[14]

In other words, the different organizational patterns exemplified by Nakarattars and Kaikkolars cannot be interpreted as modern adaptations to South Indian involvement in the colonial economic system. Rather, my proposal is that longstanding cultural concerns with status purity combined with the exigencies of business operations and the political influence of local and regional rulers to produce two separate organizational structures. Moreover, these two distinct structures transcend the institutional differences between castes and guilds.

Other differences in the internal organization of mercantile castes cannot be traced back in history to the same extent, but they are no less significant. For example, not even within their homeland of Chettinad did the Nakarattar *jati* develop a territorially segmented system of microcastes like the one developed by the Kaikkolars. There did exist what might be recognized as incipient microcastes in the division of Chettinad into subterritories called *vattakais* (Chapter 8). But membership in temple-clans created links of association that cut across tendencies toward *vattakai* endogamy and precluded segmentation of the caste into localized kin groups beyond the level of village-bound lineage segments. (Chapters 9 and 10). Similarly, commercial activities in Nakarattar business stations reflected the crosscutting divisions of their kinship and territorial organization in Chettinad. That is, Nakarattars from the same village, *vattakai,* or temple-clan might conduct business in different business stations. Conversely, Nakarattars operating in the same business station might belong to entirely separate villages, *vattakais,* or temple-clans.

Again, it seems reasonable to suppose that Nakarattar social organization represented an adaptation to the exigencies of their specialization in banking activities. In particular, the crosscutting nature of different Nakarattar kin groups may have operated to maximize the flow of information and credit extension throughout the entire caste, without any impediment from a noncrosscutting, segmentary system like the Kaikkolar system, which fostered a corresponding division in the production of specialized textiles.

All of these suggested associations between business specialization and social organization are highly speculative and require systematic comparative study before they can be accepted with certainty. Moreover, the issue becomes more problematic the farther one looks back in time. For example, only two to three hundred years ago, Nakarattars specialized in a geographically localized salt trade rather than in colonial-era banking operations. But this change in occupation may not have involved adaptations to the kinds of considerations suggested above. In particular, as far as we can tell, Nakarattars were never involved in the production of salt, but only facilitated its transport between producers and consumers. Furthermore, it seems as though the social organization which underpinned the Nakarattars' colonial banking operations was already in place. Yet both of these conclusions are based on indigenous records (in the form of palm-leaf manuscripts) maintained at a Nakarattar site of pilgrimage and trade (cf. Chapter 7). And these records deal only briefly and indirectly with the topic of trade and social organization.

Symbolic Capital and the Cultural Ecology of Caste

What implications do these various reflections about diverse castes have for anthropological and historical conceptions about caste in general? Perhaps the ultimate implication is that although India is a caste society, requiring (even today) analysis in terms of its constituent castes, there is no single thing properly identified as a caste. There are individual castes formed by unique histories of investments and transactions in symbolic capital. There are local configurations joining several different castes, similarly formed. Each caste and each configuration bears some family resemblance to every other caste and configuration. But as Srinivas (1952) showed us long ago, the similarity in the relationships between castes and their local configurations covers an enormous range of diversity: from the elaborate, multicaste villages of rice-growing river valleys to the single-caste villages of "tribal" groups in the hills. More recently, as studies by Dumont, Barnett, the Rudolphs, and Washbrook have shown, castes have become ethnic groups subject to manipulation by regional politicians and mass media. Within this diversity, some castes and configurations are undoubtably more similar, in important respects, to social groupings and configurations outside India than they are to local caste systems several steps removed in the Indian chain of resemblances.

Yet, if there is no single thing that can properly be called 'caste' in India, there are, perhaps, factors of mind and society that influence the social and cultural ecology of different castes, including factors that consist of opportunities for economic investment in a capitalist world. The existence of such factors is what I try to suggest in this book by looking at an Indian caste both like and unlike other castes from which we have tried to abstract a unitary definition in the past. The following chapter, however, takes up another conceptual difficulty no less problematic than that provided by Western definitions of caste—one that, in fact, complicates and is complicated by those definitions.

3 The Study of Commerce in Indian Society

Giants on Our Shoulders

A major difficulty standing in the way of adequate historical understandings of Indian commerce is that we labor under the burden of past misunderstandings.[1] For example, despite contemporaneous and near-contemporaneous accounts to the contrary (Buchanan 1870; Crawfurd 1971[1837]), most studies of India's precolonial economy have, until recently, simply assumed an agrarian and noncommercial system. Historians who were concerned with economic issues at all directed their efforts to a debate about India's economic development (or underdevelopment) during the nineteenth and twentieth centuries. On the one hand, nationalist historians of India argued that colonialism stifled Indian development through unfair taxation and trade regulations. On the other hand, proponents of Western modernization theories argued that colonialism fostered development by providing a peaceful environment and by promulgating the growth of efficient transportation, communication, education, and government. But both sides shared the standard social science models of precolonial Indian economy developed by Marx and Weber. These classic models divide India into autonomous peasant villages and oriental despots who siphon off agricultural surplus. They characterize India as lacking a commercial life worthy of study, except insofar as she provides an example of a "premodern" society incompatible with commerce. They deny the existence of commerce and hence of institutional involvement in commercial activities.[2]

More recent scholars place India's nineteenth-century economy into perspective by examining seventeenth- and eighteenth-century documents connected with mercantile and "protocapitalist" systems of the period (Bayly 1983; Das Gupta 1967, 1970; Habib 1969, 1980; Leonard 1979; Mendels 1972; Pearson 1976; Perlin 1983; Subrahmanyam 1990). The result is a developing revisionist view of India's precolonial economy. It envisions a significant manufacturing power, producing perhaps a third of the world's manufactured goods—principally textiles (Washbrook 1984). In this view, the colonial transformation had two major effects. It destroyed India's textile and other manufacturing industries, and it subverted her "traditional," noncommercial systems of agricultural production by forcing agriculturalists to produce exportable crops at the expense of food crops and subsistence agriculture (Habib and Raychaudhuri 1982; Neale 1957; Thorner 1960). In other words, some scholars now see colonialism as having destroyed India's precolonial industrial capabilities and created a colonial economy whose narrow basis in agricultural production was, ironically, to become the model for mythical reconstructions of her precolonial past.

Despite considerable progress in demythologizing the concept of the traditional Indian economy, most of the revisionist work directs its attention toward aggregate measures—of trade volume, terms of trade, or quantity of money. (Deyell 1970; Habib 1982; Hasan 1969; Moosvi 1980; Prakash 1976; Prakash and Krishnamurty 1970). Excepting only some of the most recent studies, such as those by Baker (1984), Bayly (1983), and Subrahmanyam (1990), almost no one addresses the specific institutions that were agents of Indian commercial activity in the colonial or precolonial periods.[3] For the most part, our understanding of India's precolonial social formations retains many traditional assumptions about India's noncommercial character. This conservative perspective is particularly noticeable in work influenced by formulations of neo-Marxist and substantivist economic anthropologists. By and large, proponents of these schools of historical interpretation arrive at their conclusions deductively, through evolutionary or dialectical theories about the rise of capitalism. From their perspectives, only evolutionarily advanced societies whose economic activities are organized by contract law, commodities markets, stock markets, central banking systems, and other institutions characteristic of Western commerce are capable of conducting commercial activities. Conversely, the absence of Western institutions is seen as the hallmark of a precapitalist society and as logically equivalent to—or at least providing prima facie evidence for—incompatibility with activities oriented around private property, market production, capital investment, and credit extension for long-distance trade.

None of these revisionist perspectives diverge from the basic premise that India lacked indigenous commercial systems. Excepting the subversive intrusion of the capitalist system into commodity production, no other remotely commercial activity figures in neo-Marxist and substantivist accounts of the colonial period. Any precolonial evidence of commercial activity is interpreted by a Procrustean set of categories whose chief characteristic is that they are the opposite of commerce. If goods are produced, it is for purposes of "subsistence" rather than exchange. If goods are exchanged, it is a transaction of "prestations" rather than a buying and selling of commodities. If commodities are bought, it is for purposes of "consumption" rather than investment. If commodities are valued, they are said to have a "use value" rather than an exchange value. If profits from an exchange are saved, the savings constitute a "primitive hoard" rather than an accumulation or reserve of capital.

Neo-Marxist and substantivist analyses of Indian economy share an additional property besides their doctrinal similarity. They are remarkably ahistorical. Pitting their analyses of contemporary or colonial India against an idealized model of "traditional" India, proponents ignore evidence of extensive commercial activity extending back to the third or fourth century B.C. (Maloney 1970; Thapar 1966). Perhaps this is only to be expected. Only recently has there been any progress in addressing the powerful and complex non-Western commercial apparatus that underlay the Indian economy. Yet, despite growing recognition that India has long maintained itself as a formidable commercial society, we still understand very little about the people who engaged in commerce, the institutional structures by which they controlled credit and money, the ways they used these structures for investment, and the values that underlay these uses.

Three Stereotypes of the Indian Moneylender

The powerful influence of nineteenth-century sociological theory is most clearly seen in three widely occurring stereotypes about Indian moneylenders and their relationships with agricultural producers. Perhaps the most prominent of these stereotypes is illustrated by the wonderfully evocative descriptions in R. K. Narayan's *The Financial Expert* (1952), a novel about a twentieth-century moneylender who guides his actions more with an eye to the goddess Lakshmi than with any consideration of economic rationality. Margayya, the moneylender of Malgudi, begins his business life by assisting peasants in dealing with the town's Central Cooperative Land Mortgage Bank. He collects some fees for this service. More importantly, he actively creates money for his clients. If a peasant requires a loan for marriage expenses, Margayya persuades a better-off peasant to borrow money from the bank and loan it to the first peasant. The better-off peasant pays the interest he owes the bank from the slightly higher interest paid him by the first peasant. Margayya receives a fee for his assistance in the transaction on the occasion of the initial bank loan, which is made at no risk to himself. Money is plentiful. Only the interest is repaid, never the principal. Everybody is happy.

Irrationality enters the picture when Margayya steps beyond the role of broker and begins to loan money that he himself has borrowed or has received on deposit. By loaning money on outrageously large margins, Margayya plants the seeds of his own downfall. For he has neither the reserves of the cooperative bank nor any guarantee of government intervention in a crisis. As the book reaches its climax, Margayya's clients start a run on his money-lending operation, and he is forced into insolvency. Mystical, befuddled, and irrational, Margayya never comprehends the potential for disaster until it is too late.

A second and even more prevalent stereotype portrays Indian moneylenders as all too rational: coldly preying upon their cultivator clients, luring them further and further into debt, and finally sucking them dry of surplus, savings, property, and liberty. A classic ethnographic depiction of the usurious moneylender may be found in Darling's (1947) account of Punjabi peasantry (for a literary illustration of the stereotype, see Raja Rao's Gandhian indictment of village moneylenders in his 1939 novel *Kanthapura*).[4] In this stereotype, it is peasant cultivators who take over the burden of irrationality, while moneylenders emerge as rational but immoral.

Some of the excesses in these stereotypes have been addressed in an article by Michie (1978), who explores the blend of rationality and morality that actually characterizes interaction between moneylenders and peasant farmers. Unfortunately, even such a welcome corrective essay perpetuates one further stereotype: the image of the moneylender as an independent, strictly small-scale entrepreneur whose business activities are confined to credit transactions with his client agriculturalists. For example, even though Michie mentions the ability of moneylenders to manipulate links between villages and wider market networks (1978: 50), he pays no attention to the kinds of organization these links presuppose. His focus is tightly confined to the moneylender/cultivator relationship, defined by an exchange of loans and repayments. His primary concern is the organization of production. Missing from Michie's account is any description of market networks and moneylender/moneylender relationships, defined by exchanges of deposits, letters of credit, bills of exchange, and other financial instruments. In other words, he does not address the organization of finance and trade. By default, Michie assigns moneylenders to small-scale operations limited by the assets they can generate from their cultivator clients.

Legal Stereotypes and Historical Myopia

It is this final stereotype about the scale of Indian finance that invariably colors the writing of colonial administrators, of economists during the colonial period, and of historians today. In general—to the extent that Indian credit operations are recognized at all—Indian moneylenders are taken as unreliable and irrational, or rational to the point of usurious immorality, but in any case as strictly small scale in the size of their assets and the scope of their credit extension activities. For example, it is easy to find reports devoting large amounts of space to efforts to distinguish between petty moneylenders (representing the Indian stereotype) and large-scale bankers (operating in the fashion of Western banks).

Reflecting this distinction, the legal history of the period is replete with judicial efforts to define indigenous financial instruments such as the *hundi* (a kind of bill of exchange used by moneylenders but not by "true bankers"). Ultimately, the courts concluded that such instruments lacked explicit statements stipulating conditions for certain kinds of transactions between multiple trading partners. Accordingly, their negotiability could not be appealed to a court of law (Krishnan 1959; Weersooria 1973). The implication of such a finding is that instruments such as *hundis,* which lack legal standing, could not possibly function effectively outside of a specific local community's ability to apply customary sanctions; therefore, *hundis* must be ineffective instruments for any kind of large-scale or long-distance trade.

Such a conclusion might be appropriate for a jurist or administrator who looks only to the courts for sanctions on contracts or authoritative judgment of disputes. On the other hand, it is certainly inappropriate for any person dealing with the day-to-day operation of an Indian commercial enterprise. The difficulty is that it simply ignores customary sanctions on *hundi* transactions that are rigorously enforced by multilocale, multiregional, and even multinational communities of businessmen. Indeed, the considerable negotiability established by *hundis* is a testament to the adequacy of these customary sanctions (see discussion in Chapter 5). When jurists' failure to appreciate these important financial instruments is placed in the context of stereotypic views about Indian bankers as merely clever (and sometimes irrational or usurious) moneylenders, it is clear that British and British-trained jurists never really comprehended the systematic operation of Indian financial institutions.

Stereotypes of the Indian moneylender even affect scholars who explicitly recognize indigenous systems of trade and banking during the colonial period. A. K. Bagchi (1972), for example, cites the monopolistic access of British entrepreneurs to "organized" banking systems as one of their important advantages in preempting Indian investment in industrial opportunities well into the twentieth century. Apparently, Bagchi has in mind characterizations of the Indian banking system in which Madras Presidency and British exchange banks, which made credit available to the British, are compared with the developing Indian joint-stock banks of the early twentieth century, which made credit available to Indians. An example is provided by Vakil and Muranjan (1927: 532), whose analysis of capital within the "organized" banking system for the period from 1913 to 1917 indicates a ratio of British credit to Indian credit of approximately five to two.[5]

Buried in Bagchi's own footnotes is evidence that he unconsciously discounts (perhaps "devalues" is the better term) indigenous credit markets—presumably the "unorganized" banking sector. Compare the following two passages quoted by Bagchi from official government reports about British investment credit and the Nakarattars or Nattukottai Chettiars, the focus of the present book. The passages were published in 1901 and 1930, on either side of the period characterized by Vakil and Muranjan; nevertheless, they illustrate the point.

> It was established in 1901 by Sir Edward Law [the member in charge of finance in the Viceroy's Council] that [British] banking capital available in India for trade purposes was less than £10 million [approximately Rs. 80 million], after making allowances for the share of the capital of the exchange banks which was held outside India; the amount required was estimated as £12 million [Rs. 96 million].[6]

By contrast:

> According to [Chettiar evidence in the Report of the Madras Provincial Banking Enquiry Committee], the capital of the Chettiars had increased from Rs. 100 million in 1896 to Rs. 800 million in 1930, and the capital employed by them (including borrowed capital) at home and in Madras came to Rs. 750 million, which is equal to what Furnivall claimed to be the capital employed by them in Burma alone.[7]

Notice that the Chettiars' own estimate of Chettiar capital in 1896 — not to mention Furnivall's (1956) less conservative estimate originally made during the same period — are both far in excess of the amount that the colonial government claimed was available for British trade in 1901; an amount which, according to Bagchi, represented superior British access to investment capital. And this estimate does not even begin to take into account the capital controlled by non-Chettiar banking castes such as Marwaris, Parsis, or Baniyas. Yet none of this capital enters into calculations about the credit available to Indians (or Europeans) in India's organized banking sector. Thus, even modern economic historians such as Bagchi continue to accept Western colonial views that India lacked an institutional system capable of providing the large-scale finance necessary for industrial investment.8

Lacking in all such views of Indian credit resources is any appreciation for the complex network of financial debts, opportunities, and possibilities that indigenous moneylenders and bankers could activate outside of Western-style banks through relationships of kinship and caste or through common participation with potential investors and lenders in a variety of religious and secular institutions. It is scarcely surprising that the scale and scope of Indian financial operations have been denied, when the very mechanisms for their transaction have gone unrecognized.

What are we to make of colonial administrators who regularly denied the existence of large-scale Indian commerce while interacting with its institutions on a daily basis? How are we to account for the strange myopia of British administrators and the historians who study them? On one hand, I suspect that verbal denial constituted a device by British banking interests for attaining special treatment from the emerging government-regulated banking systems in South and Southeast Asia (e.g., Buchanan 1870; Crawfurd 1971[1837]). On the other hand, as we have seen, anticolonial historians may give too much credit to claims made by colonial administrators in pronouncements on commercial policy while failing to consider the massive capital controlled and invested by Indian financiers. But these provocative assertions are themes for another essay. The present book attempts to modify the existing stereotypes (whatever their basis) by examining aspects of a large-scale system for credit provision—a non-Western banking system—operated by a South Indian caste during the colonial period.

Village Studies of Indian Commerce

One reason for the longevity of nineteenth-century biases about Indian society is that there have been remarkably few studies of the operation of even contemporary Indian commercial and other economic systems. Anthropologically, the focus has tended to fall on operations of the so-called *jajmani* system, a putatively India-wide redistributive system that operates within strictly local village contexts. According to standard models of *jajmani,* members of occupationally specialized castes exchange their services for shares of agricultural produce controlled by members of the dominant landed caste in a village.[9]

But there is growing reason to believe that the entire anthropological orientation toward and emphasis on *jajmani* models of village economic life merely reflect an untenable presumption about the noncommercial autonomy of precapitalist peasant villages. Recent systematic and detailed studies of village economic transactions have begun to show that the *jajmani* does not represent a pan-Indian phenomenon and that where *jajmani* or *jajmani*-like systems do operate, they make up only part of the total village economy (Commander 1983; Fuller 1989; Good 1982, 1991). Perhaps the most frustrating aspect of anthropological emphasis on *jajmani* is the impression it gives of India's economy as consisting of nothing else. Against any such misapprehension, it must be remembered that throughout Indian history, 40 percent to 60 percent, and under extreme circumstances perhaps as much as 80 percent, of village produce has left the village (Habib 1969; *MBPEC* 1930 I:35–85; Nicholson 1895; Rajayyan 1964–65; Robert 1983; Thorner 1960).

A large part of this exported village surplus takes the form of taxes in kind or money levied by various governmental institutions. Although not studied by anthropologists, such expropriation of village surplus has received attention from historians attempting to understand the financial basis of the great Indian empires, Mughal and British (Chandra 1966; Chaudhuri 1971; Habib 1969; Ludden 1985; Marshall 1976; Stokes 1978). Other historians, strongly influenced by anthropological concerns with indigenous ethos and world view, have attempted to integrate values believed to underlie village *jajmani* transactions with values believed to underlie the interactions between regional kings and local peasants (Dirks 1988; Greenough 1983; Price 1979). This last set of important studies identifies hierarchical values of "royal generosity" and "indulgence" as structuring the behavior of two sets of roles, as Greenough puts it: "the first set comprising powerful, resource controlling 'parents,' the second set comprising helpless needy 'children.' The roles in each set are equivalent in the sense that those in the first (kings, gods, masters) are all destined providers of subsistence . . . while those in the second (devotees, subjects, dependents) are all persons requiring nurture" (1983: 841).

Studies such as these break down the artificial boundaries that existed between village geography and Indian economy. But they still ignore a major sector of the Indian economy not governed by parent/child values of hierarchical indulgence and generosity. What they miss are the relatively egalitarian values governing commercial relationships. Role sets of persons engaged in a commercial transaction are not split into two asymmetrical categories of "subsistence providers" and "nurture requirers." Instead, they involve elaborate chains of lenders and debtors who are often mutually lenders and debtors to each other. For example, on one occasion, an agriculturalist may borrow money to purchase land, seed, or fertilizer. On another occasion, he may deposit excess profits from his harvest with a banker for investment on his account.[10] Moreover, a landholder or trader who borrows money from a moneylender may loan out that money himself. And the original moneylender may easily borrow up to 90 percent of the monies he loans out (Robert 1983). In such relationships, values taken to underlie behavior cannot be understood as any simple transformation of generosity and indulgence from holders of parental roles to holders of child roles. Rather, the operative values seem to entail nonhierarchical relationships of trust and trustworthiness, often created and symbolized by religious gifting on the part of those engaged in commerce.

In other words, anthropologists and historians have paid little attention to an entire range of significant economic activities occurring beyond the level of the village. This observation applies to trade at a variety of periodic markets and especially to money-lending and banking activities involved in sophisticated indigenous systems for providing credit to farmers, traders, and governments. Without institutions of credit extension, India could not have maintained either its notorious tax levies or its extensive system of medium- and long-distance trade in agricultural and nonagricultural commodities.

Beyond the Village Moneylender

Another explanation for the continuing influence of stereotypes about Indian moneylenders may lie simply in the failure to consider implications of financial transactions beyond the level of the village. This omission, in turn, may be due to a marked bifurcation between money-lending peasants in village contexts and merchant-banking firms in urban contexts.[11] This is not to say that social scientists have totally ignored nonvillage India, but only to indicate that nonvillage studies have failed to have any impact on prevailing views about the organization of Indian finance.

To the extent that scholars have addressed Indian financial organization beyond the village, their studies seem to fall into two categories: (1) studies of bazaar economy, and (2) studies of major commercial centers, sometimes referred to as "burgher cities" (Bayly 1978, 1983), and of Indian "burghers," sometimes called "portfolio capitalists" (Subrahmanyam 1990). Analyses of Indian bazaars look explicitly at sources of capital for petty shopkeepers, retail traders, and moneylenders operating within regional markets.[12] In contrast to studies of village-based credit markets, these bazaar studies explicitly raise questions about the scale of moneylender resources and the kind and degree of financial cooperation between moneylenders acting as insurers for and investors in one another. But the change in venue does not alter the analytic bias. By and large, the focus of these studies is confined to small-scale activities of moneylenders oriented toward what Fox (1969: 302)—drawing a parallel with putatively risk-aversive peasants—calls "subsistence trade." In keeping with prevailing stereotypes, moneylenders and shopkeepers of the bazaar are portrayed as irrational, as requiring only small amounts of capital, as lacking permanence, as conservative or even stagnant, and so forth.[13] Bazaar studies perform an important service in broadening our understanding beyond agrarian production in the village. But they scarcely scratch the surface of Indian commerce. The role, operation, and even existence of large-scale merchant-bankers remains, with few exceptions, unknown or unconsidered.

The major exception to this general indictment consists of studies focused on coastal entrepôts and port cities extending from Saurastra through Gujarat, down the Malabar Coast and up the Coromandel to Golconda.[14] In addition, a relatively small amount of attention has been paid to the role of merchants in inland cities such as Allahabad or Benares (Bayly 1978, 1983). Subrahmanyam's (1990) work on late precolonial South India and Baker's (1984) work on "modern" South India (1984) provide two additional examples of a focus that extends to inland commerce. With the exception of the last three writers, however, the predominant concern of these studies remains the working of empires—or, more recently, the working of local or regional polities. Their strength lies in their focus on politics; their weakness, in their lack of attention to commerce. In effect, they constitute analyses of political power in cities which happen to have a marked mercantile orientation. But the implications of mercantile organization and values as opposed to royal, professional, or administrative organization and values are not seriously examined.[15]

Indian Burghers and Portfolio Capitalists

The recent studies by Bayly and Subrahmanyam require additional comment, for, as I have already indicated, they represent a major turning point to the general trends I have just described, and at first glance their findings seem to stand in radical contradiction to the conclusions presented in the present study.[16] I begin with Bayly, who explicitly joins the issue and, in this respect, provides the best opportunity to scout out potential differences and agreements in our views. In several places Bayly presents detailed historical data and interpretations about North Indian commercial towns and cities that correct largely unfounded, Weberian stereotypes about Indian commerce (Gadgil 1959; Lamb 1959; Sjoberg 1970). In particular, he is concerned with the organization of commerce in so-called burgher cities, such as Allahabad or Benares, which exhibit long histories of financial, commercial, and industrial activity and an elite, multicaste commercial community. Among other topics, Bayly addresses Weberian ideas concerning the relationship between caste and commerce within these burgher cities. In a concluding section of one paper on the topic, he points out that

> caste at the level of geographically extended kin groups had an important role in the organization of trading diasporas; at the level of the commensal jati group it was relevant to the social and economic organization of artisan groups; at the level of varna it had some implications for general mercantile status. Nevertheless, it is difficult to see how caste in any sense could have been the prime parameter of mercantile organization in complex cities. Forms of arbitration, market control, brokerage, neighborhood communities, and above all conceptions of mercantile honor and credit breached caste boundaries, however construed, and imposed wider solidarities on merchant people. (1978: 192)

In this passage, Bayly's primary argument is directed against the tendency to reduce all merchant organization to caste organization. Unfortunately, the argument is put so strongly that a casual reader might conclude that Bayly sees little or no commercial role for caste at all. The polemical issue of whether caste is a prime parameter of mercantile organization overshadows potentially interesting questions about its role as a nonprime but still significant parameter, not to mention questions about the systematic interaction of various parameters of mercantile organization. The trick is to avoid an all-or-nothing view of the significance of caste.17

The positive contributions of Bayly's research are too rich for detailed comment in the present context. Along with work by a small number of fellow historians (e.g., Habib 1960, 1973; Leonard 1979; Pearson 1976; Perlin 1983; Subrahmanyam 1990), it represents an important correction to views limiting Indian financial operations to those of small-scale moneylenders. In particular Bayly identifies an upper stratum of powerful merchant-bankers who maintain interregional trade in various commodities and credit notes and who provide important treasury and remittance facilities for regional and imperial authorities. The point I wish to make about Bayly's studies, however, is that they are open to serious misinterpretation. Bayly's focus on complex organizational networks that crosscut ties of caste or neighborhood, combined with his historically specific analyses of urban commercial groups who elevate ties of class over ties of caste, are designed (among other things) to counter the classic view that castes are uniformly specialized with respect to occupation. It does not follow from this observation, however, that no castes were ever specialized. In particular, it does not follow that no caste ever specialized in commercial activities. Moreover, any such conclusion flouts the spirit of Bayly's work, which emphasizes the diversity of principles operating in the organization of Indian commerce, including principles of caste (Bayly, personal communication).

It may indeed be the case that the commercial elites of Allahabad and Benares gave no special precedence to relationships of caste. But this was not the case for all commercial magnates, especially those belonging to the Marwari caste (Timberg 1978) or the Kaikkolar caste (Mines, 1984). Nor was it the case for the Nakarattars, whose caste organization constituted a corporate financial institution in Indian society. Nevertheless, given the potential for misunderstanding, it is worth emphasizing that my approach to these issues is resolutely anti-Weberian: it no more forecloses the possibility for caste-neutral studies of elite businessmen than caste-neutral studies foreclose studies of the commercial role of caste. On the contrary, both kinds of study are needed. Chapter 7 outlines one way of beginning such a larger project.

The Historiographic Gap

Before presenting my analysis of the collective character of the commercial practice and social organization of the Nakarattars, it is worth commenting about a peculiar historiographic blind spot concerning their important role in colonial Asian society. By 1870 (and, perhaps, for some time before this) the Nakarattars had no contemporary South Indian competitors within the region comprising South India and British Southeast Asia. They were the premier merchant-banking caste of the region. Moreover, individual Nakarattars were among the first Tamil businessmen to divert their assets from banking and trade to capital-intensive industry. Nakarattars also played major roles in providing financial support and management for temples and charitable institutions wherever they did business. Finally, prominent Nakarattars wielded considerable political influence in a variety of local arenas throughout the Madras Presidency and Southeast Asia and, from 1920 onward, held important political offices in the city of Madras and the provincial government.

Despite the important role the Nakarattars played in Indian society, despite the availability of relevant information, even despite the publication of a handful of books and papers about Nakarattars, most accounts of

Indian commerce scarcely acknowledge them. Part of this omission follows in the wake of Weberian pronouncements about the putative incompatibility of Hinduism and capitalism, noted above. Another part may be attributed to too narrow a focus on village economy, or to stereotypic views of Indian moneylenders, which have also been discussed. But part of the problem arises from two further sources of historiographic bias. On one hand, scholars who focus explicitly on the activities of merchants in the seventeenth and eighteenth centuries tend to focus only on Indian-European connections in the organization of the textile export trade, especially as these connections were established in Madras and other port cities. As a consequence, they tend to look only at specific groups who were prominent in these port cities, such as Telugu Chettis and Brahmans or Tamil Vellalas. They do not explore the inland "country trade" of internal South India during the sixteenth and seventeenth centuries.[18]

Nor do they address the growth of new economic actors in commercial activities during the late eighteenth and early nineteenth centuries.[19] Rather, the dominant historiographic emphasis on the rise of Indian nationalism in the nineteenth century raises another difficulty. In post-1850s Madras, mercantile political power seems to have given way to growing influence by administrative and professional elites. And scholars whose research focuses on political developments in the period after 1850 tend to give mercantile and commercial elites only passing attention (Appadurai 1981; Lewandowski 1976; Suntharalingam 1974). In fact, the literature barely touches on them except in their capacity to bankroll politicians and ideologues (both the anti-Brahmans and those in Congress). Moreover, even here little attention is given to the source of the funds expended by the bankrollers.

Apart from such disciplinary biases, the whole issue seems to be conditioned by early European interactions with and efforts to master the Indian economic system. From the seventeenth to the nineteenth century, much of the European trade depended on financing by Indian capital under the control of large-scale merchants (Appadurai 1974; Arasaratnam 1980; Basu 1982; Brennig 1977; Chaudhuri 1978; Furber 1951; Lewandowski 1976; Subrahmanyam 1990). Not surprisingly, the relationship was always strained on both sides.[20]

From the European point of view, Indian brokers held entirely too much power and, moreover, often employed it in competition with the Europeans themselves. By 1680, European merchants were already attempting to alter the indigenous system by insisting on dealing with groups of merchants operating like their own joint stock companies rather than with individuals with privileged claims on their European patrons and monopolistic power over native producers (Brennig 1977: 338–340; see also Arasaratnam 1979; Subrahmanyam 1990). But these efforts to circumvent the Indian mercantile elite were by and large unsuccessful in that even the joint stock companies continued to be dominated by a small number of highly powerful "chief merchants" (Arasaratnam 1980).

This is not to say that efforts to circumvent the power of chief merchants were totally ineffective. From the mid-eighteenth century onward, an increasingly large European private trade and a growing English bureaucracy increased the number of Englishmen desiring contact with a variety of Indian producers, traders, and local authorities. This in turn led to increased opportunities for Indian middlemen, until virtually every major officer of the East India Company and every private European trader had his own personal middleman (Arasaratnam 1980; Basu 1982). Such middlemen came to be known as *dubashes*. According to some historians, the appearance of these *dubashes* represents a significant institutional change from the seventeenth-century situation, in which "chief merchants" served these functions. Individual *dubashes* are said not to have had the power of chief merchants. But this argument fails to take account of differences in the wealth and influence of *dubashes* situated in various places in the colonial power structure. Although the number of eighteenth-century *dubashes* grew dramatically relative to the number of seventeenth-century chief merchants, there remained a small number of individuals who continued in or acquired the position of *dubash* for leaders in the European community. These "chief *dubashes*" maintained a preeminence in Indo-European trade comparable to that of chief merchants in the seventeenth century.

In other words, the overall function and position in society of important merchants and financiers did not change from the seventeenth to the nineteenth century. There was a growth in the absolute number of Indian middleman-merchants. And all such individuals, whatever their station in colonial society, were designated by the title *dubash*. But there continued to be a small circle of elite merchants who exercised a dominant role in the organization and financing of Indo-European trade.[21]

If there was no important change in the power and institutional role of preeminent Indian merchants, there was, nevertheless, a significant impact on the ethnic make-up of merchants holding positions of power and there were also important changes in the organization of ethnicity itself. As with the early position of chief merchant, competition for *dubash* positions was at least initially factionalized between groups from right-hand castes (primarily Telugu Chettis) and left-hand castes (Telugu Brahmans and Tamil Vellalars). Over the course of the eighteenth century, individuals belonging to left-hand groups gradually gained positions of power in a hierarchy of *dubashes* that corresponded to the hierarchy of European traders whom they served (Appadurai 1974; Basu 1982; Lewandowski 1976). Thus, while the position of chief merchant/*dubash* continued to play an important role, the period was witness to a change of ethnic guard in the personnel who filled these positions.

The process, however, seems to have altered the nature of ethnic identity or at least the nature of social ties that connected members belonging to the same caste. Increasingly, during the seventeenth and eighteenth centuries, individual merchants who rose to positions of chief merchants or *dubashes* were recruited either from castes that lacked a tradition of mercantile organization (e.g., Brahmans or Vellalas) or else from mercantile castes whose organizational structure failed to adjust to the lure of European commerce. In both cases, the chief merchants and *dubashes* of the Coromandel seemed to operate with increasing independence from special ties to their caste groups. Multicaste left-hand and right-hand factions gradually lost their ability to mobilize for coordinated action. Historians are unable to discern any form of caste organization in the nineteenth century—even within a single mercantile caste group such as the Telugu Komati Chettis—in which caste members coordinated their actions to promote a common commercial goal. Of the earlier forms of multifunctional caste cooperation (Krishna Rao 1964), only shared ritual observances at caste shrines and prohibitions enforcing caste endogamy remain. And the relationship between these ties of caste and the conduct of business were apparently so attenuated as to play no role of any kind.[22]

The Historiographic Rejection of Caste in Commerce

Sanjay Subrahmanyam (1990) denies any caste basis for commercial activity, not only in the eighteenth and nineteenth centuries, but in the sixteenth and seventeenth centuries as well. Writing less than a decade after Bayly, Subrahmanyam presumably finds the evidence for multicaste and intercaste commercial activity so strong, and Weber's orientalism so patent, that he sees no need even to criticize the thesis of incompatibility between Hinduism and capitalism.[23] Like Bayly, he focuses on prominent merchants, among them the chief merchants and *dubashes* of the Coromandel. Unlike Bayly, he refers to them as "portfolio capitalists" rather than "burghers," perhaps to emphasize that their commercial activity was not confined to a single city but extended up and down the Coromandel, into the Tamil and Telugu kingdoms of inland South India and outward to Southeast Asia. In other important respects, however, Subrahmanyam depicts his portfolio capitalists in the same way as Bayly depicts his North

Indian burghers. Specifically, he describes them as more or less individualistic entrepreneurs who occupied "the middle ground between mercantile capitalism and political capitalism" (1990: 298), gaining and using political positions to further commercial interests, harnessing commercial operations to gain political influence, and in general operating at a scale unimaginable according to the orientalist conception of India as the land of *jajmani* and village moneylenders. In Subrahmanyam's words, they formed

> a group of persons who, from the second half of the sixteenth century, emerge gradually into prominence, eventually assuming formidable proportions in the first half of the seventeenth century. These persons, whom we have termed "portfolio capitalists," occupied a shadowy middle ground between state and producing economy, and combined a role in the fiscal structure with participation in inland trade, currency dealing, movements of bills of exchange, and even seaborne trade on a quite considerable scale. (1990: 355)

Although Subrahmanyam does not deign to address Weberian stereotypes, he is careful to raise three questions about more recent historiographic interpretations. In the first instance, as indicated in the preceding quotation, he calls into question the assumption (and, at times, the explicit postulate) that the phenomenon of chief merchants' acting as portfolio capitalists in the seventeenth and eighteenth centuries represents an innovation in reaction to commercial demand from the newly arrived European companies. In contrast, Subrahmanyam forcefully argues a position with which the present study is entirely sympathetic: that the portfolio capitalists who mediated between Indian textile producers and European companies performed commercial roles that extend back before the arrival of the European companies to at least the intra-Asian trade of the sixteenth and seventeenth centuries. Subrahmanyam's second characterization of portfolio capitalists is also one with which I am entirely sympathetic: that there existed no sharp separation of roles between merchants and "a 'militarily oriented elite' whose culturally sanctioned activities were land activities."[24]

It is only with a third feature of Subrahmanyam's picture of portfolio capitalists that I have reservations. Citing Washbrook's (1975, 1976, 1982) study of the nineteenth-century rise of mercantile caste associations (see Chapter 2, above), Subrahmanyam argues against close identification of any functionally defined role with any ethnographic category, by which he means caste: "We cannot believe axiomatically that southern Indian society in the sixteenth and seventeenth centuries comprised of a set of well-defined and watertight compartments, in one of which it is possible to site the mercantile communities of the region" (1990: 340). Subrahmanyam thus differs from Washbrook in denying that the precolonial organization of mercantile castes may have possessed properties that were "preadaptive" for the late nineteenth-century formation of political associations. Yet, as with Washbrook's treatment of nineteenth-century Komati merchants, it is important to emphasize that Subrahmanyam provides no information about intracaste cooperation between portfolio capitalists and that this omission leaves the question of mercantile caste organization entirely open. Moreover, it is important to separate the two conceptions of caste and commerce that Subrahmanyam attacks. It is one thing to argue that merchants engaged in war and politics, while warriors and politicians engaged in commerce. It is another thing to argue that absence of an exclusive occupational calling for some individuals rules out the possibility of any occupational specialization in the kin and caste groups to which they belong.

In this context, it is worth noting that Subrahmanyam's brief treatment of a dynastic merchant family of Balija Chettis is tantalizingly suggestive that ties of kin and caste did play an important but unexplored role in South Indian commerce. It may have been the case, as Subrahmanyam suggests, that this extended family operated with no special ties to other, less prominent members of their caste. But this was surely not always the case. And, as I shall argue for the Nakarattars, equally prominent merchant-bankers maintained commercially crucial ties to castemates that are invisible in the standard historical records.

Subrahmanyam's understanding of pre-Western portfolio capitalists is important because it deprives Weberians—and, indeed, all modernization theorists—of the argument that only involvement with Western financial institutions and rational, bureaucratic forms of government can trigger the forces of capitalism. Like more Eurocentric historians, however, Subrahmanyam still finds confirmation that Indian businessmen participated in capitalism—albeit an Indian capitalism—to the exclusion of caste and kinship. Yet, as indicated earlier in this chapter, it is precisely at the point where the unfolding commercial history of South India seems to provide an irrefutable case in support of these views that historians have shifted their attention to other issues. Had they continued with the economic concerns that motivated their studies of periods before the middle of the nineteenth century, the verdict would surely be less secure. For it is just at this time that the Nakarattars emerge on the scene in a major way. And it is precisely the qualities of their caste organization that enable them to take advantage of the changing colonial economy and become the chief merchant-bankers of South India and Southeast Asia.

PART TWO

BUSINESS

4 The Colonial Expansion

Overview

The present chapter describes the range and scope of Nakarattar commerce in the nineteenth and twentieth centuries. Special attention is paid to the Nakarattar response to changes in their economic and political environment, particularly their aggressive uses of finance capital and their skillful manipulation of the emerging colonial institutions of commerce and government. The resulting model of Nakarattar colonial adaptation provides a macrocontext for the detailed structural studies of Nakarattar commercial, political, religious, and kinship institutions presented in Chapters 6 through 10. Those chapters, in turn, describe the mechanisms by which Nakarattars achieved the dramatic expansion described immediately below.

Nakarattar commercial evolution during this period can be broken down into three overlapping phases. The first begins in the precolonial and undocumented past and extends to the middle of the nineteenth century. This period marks their expansion from a localized salt-trading caste to a broad-ranging merchant-banking caste. Their commercial activities may have continued to involve the salt trade during this time (although documentation of this involvement is rather circumstantial), but they were also clearly and massively involved in the rice, cotton, and credit markets within the Madras Presidency and between Madras, Ceylon, and Bengal.

The second phase of Nakarattar expansion has its roots in the first half of the nineteenth century, but cannot truly be said to have started until the 1860s and 1870s. In the early nineteenth-century prelude to this phase, Nakarattars seem to have followed the footsteps of the British army as it conquered and pacified Burma and Malaya. Published caste histories (e.g.,

Ramanathan Chettiar 1953: 27) place Nakarattars at various ports of Southeast Asia by the following dates: Singapore and Penang, 1825; Moulmein, 1852; Rangoon, 1854; Mandalay, 1855. The Nakarattar firms established in these outposts were branches of agencies already established in Calcutta (Lakshmanan Chettiar 1954) and had probably positioned themselves so as to oversee the provisioning and financing of British military operations. Although it is unlikely that trade to these Southeast Asian outposts played any significant role in the overall scheme of Nakarattar commerce, it did set the stage for their rapid expansion from that point.

In the second half of the nineteenth century, four historical trends coincided and opened up new commercial opportunities ideally suited for Nakarattar banking operations:

1. The British completed their conquest of Burma and Malaya in the 1850s and 1860s, opening up the interiors of these countries for colonial development and exploitation.
2. The volume of trade between Asia and Europe increased with the opening of the Suez Canal in 1869, when the possibility for large-scale export of agricultural and other bulky commodities presented itself for the first time.
3. British exchange banks established themselves firmly throughout South and Southeast Asia, foreclosing old Nakarattar investments in money lending and exchange banking for European firms, but at the same time offering Nakarattars a new source of venture capital to carry out alternative investments.
4. Finally, unlike the situation in post-1850s Madras, the provincial governments of Southeast Asia adopted policies that encouraged rather than restricted Nakarattar investments in indigenous agricultural industries.

Nakarattars responded to all of these changes in their commercial environment by loaning a greater proportion of their investment capital directly to agriculturalists, plantation owners, and mine operators throughout Southeast Asia. In this capacity they made a unique and central contribution to the growth of the plantation economy in Ceylon, the emergence of the Burmese rice market, and the development of Malaya's rubber and tin industries.

The third phase of Nakarattar commercial evolution was one of contraction rather than expansion. Starting in the 1920s and increasingly through the first half of the twentieth century, the business environment of British India was altered in crucial ways by the development of nationalistic movements in Southeast Asian countries, by the general growth of legislation restricting indigenous forms of banking, and by increased industrial opportunities within India for non-British businessmen. The consequences were significant for the Nakarattars. Their caste organization began to unravel in the face of multigovernmental interference with traditional banking practice. Elite members of the Nakarattar caste began a gradual transfer and freezing of investment capital by shifting from mercantile to industrial ventures. Nonelite Nakarattars—perhaps 80 to 90 percent of the caste —were forced to scramble for new employment opportunities and often began working as employees in government and business offices, although many of these were owned or managed by Nakarattars. The present study, however, stops short of examining this third phase, focusing its attention instead on processes leading up to and culminating in the unfolding of the Nakarattar commercial system at its peak, during the colonial period from 1870 to 1930.

Seventeenth-Century South India

In the sixteenth and seventeenth centuries, the Vijayanagar empire disintegrated after four centuries of rule. In the far south, conflict over the spoils between Bijapur and the Marathas, complicated by the most southward efforts at Mughal expansion, stimulated conflict between the kingdoms of Madurai and Tanjavur. The European trading companies arrived, and governmental centralization declined in the face of widespread civil wars (Arasaratnam 1986; Ludden 1985; Rajayyan 1974; Sathyanatha Aiyar 1924; Stein 1969, 1980). Yet the fortunes of South Indian trade apparently followed an independent course.[1] For some mercantile groups and especially for the Nakarattars, trade flourished during this period. In fact, growth in key sectors of South India's commercial activities may have contributed to the Vijayanagar empire's decline. European guns and artillery made war less expensive. Local chiefs, called *palaiyakkarars* (or, in British usage, "poligars") could more easily afford relatively small but effective armies. The resulting declarations of independence created numerous "little kingdoms" ruled over by a varied assortment of chiefs, *rajas, palaiyakkarars, setupatis, tondaimans,* and others. Many of these local "warrior chiefs" demanded recognition as rulers on a par with their nominal suzerain, the Nayak of Madurai, who was the Vijayanagar deputy in charge of the entire southern region.[2]

Military escalation continued into the eighteenth century and increased the overall demand for money and credit in order to pay for armies and guns (Rajayan 1964–65; Raman Rao 1958; Sundaram 1944–45). A large part of this demand was met by revenues from an expanding export trade with Europe and the East, coupled with significant increases in New World bullion supplied by European trading companies (Habib and Raychaudhuri 1982). But cash by itself was not sufficient. Seasonal fluctuations in production and sales, variable weather, unpredictable foreign markets, and a generally complex and uncertain economic climate all conspired to generate an enormously credit-hungry society. The myriad chiefs and "little kings" as well as the European trading companies, agriculturalists, and artisans all depended on forward advances of credit from Indian merchants and moneylenders.

The Nakarattar caste adapted to their political and economic environment in a modest fashion, at least during the seventeenth century. Their own oral traditions suggest that they were primarily employed as salt traders within a small area of ninety-six villages in the northern part of present-day Ramanathapuram District (see Map 4). Unfortunately, European records do not provide a full description of South India's salt industry during this time and do not, in fact, mention Nakarattars as salt traders either in the seventeenth or the eighteenth century. In the eighteenth century, the records suggest that salt in various forms was produced in coastal regions of southern India and traded for inland consumption in exchange for items such as wheat, cotton, rice, dry grain, tamarind, cumin seeds, and long peppers.[3] They identify castes other than Nakarattars (especially Telugu Komati and Baliga Chettis) as being involved in the coastal and international trade. Typically, kings and European companies rented coastal salt "farms" under their control to important merchants and *dubashes,* who then had salt transported by Muslim traders on cattle back to inland customers.[4]

It seems reasonable to assume that a similar state of affairs existed during the seventeenth century, and that during this earlier period Muslim traders were the source of salt for small-scale Nakarattar traders.[5] It is also possible, however, that Nakarattar trading activities extended east from their home villages as far as the Palk salt swamps and that they obtained their salt directly from salt producers or salt-bed renters. Whatever the case, it is impossible to say in what commodities besides salt Nakarattar trade was carried out or to identify the full range of Nakarattar trading territory. It does seem clear that the total scope of Nakarattar trade was only a shadow of what it was to become. Certainly, their subsequent history proves that their itinerant salt-trading activities and the social organization that supported these activities had prepared the Nakarattars to take advantage of the changing commercial environment of South India.

In the eighteenth century, the primary Nakarattar occupation—inland salt trading—became dramatically less profitable. In 1792, a widespread drought and famine reduced or halted trade between inland salt-consuming and coastal salt-producing regions of the Madras Presidency. According to Krishna Rao (1964), this interruption in normal salt-trading activities marked a watershed in the history of the Madras salt industry. According to Rao's interpretation, the drought so weakened the power of major salt renters that, in 1805, the East India Company was able to eliminate them as middlemen in the salt trade and assume monopolistic control over salt production (see below). This may be something of an exaggeration, since the East India Company promptly turned around and rented out salt beds to the highest bidder. But the ultimate effect of these various events was that the price of salt to salt traders more than doubled from that before 1805.[6]

Cotton, Pearls, Rice, and Salt, 1800–1850

The Nakarattar caste responded to the hostile "push" of salt trade disruption and East India Company pricing policies as well as to the lucrative "pull" of opportunities for money lending. In a process that is still unclear, Nakarattars developed a sophisticated financial apparatus which included provisions for making forward loans to agrarian producers, for extending short-term and long-term loans to political and military leaders, and for transmitting *hundis* or *teeps* (bills of exchange) among themselves and their clients. Along the way, Nakarattars evolved from a geographically restricted community of salt traders to a powerful, long-distance merchant-banking caste. Details of this process are hard to come by. Historical records of Nakarattar business activities only really begin in the later part of the nineteenth century. But such information as is available provides a marked contrast with the picture of localized salt trading portrayed in traditional written and oral accounts of pre-European Nakarattar history (see Chapter 7).

Nakarattar oral traditions, chronicled in a caste history written by A. V. Ramanathan Chettiar (1953), provide some indication of the territory and the commodities in which Nakarattars were chiefly involved. According to Ramanathan Chettiar, Nakarattars were important actors in the grain and cotton trade in towns that, judging from their geographic distribution, were strategically located in the central productive regions of both these commodities. One set of towns formed a north-south string in Tirunelveli that still comprises major trading towns of the region today, providing markets for cotton and other cash crops produced in their hinterlands. Another set formed a double string of towns in Tanjavur—one strand located along the coast, the other roughly thirty miles inland. This double string served a similar function for rice produced in Tanjavur as the single string of cotton trading towns in Tirunelveli. Note that fifteen miles is the approximate median distance between coastal and inland Nakarattar trading towns in Tanjavur and that this distance constitutes about one day's round trip journey carrying goods by bullock.

Besides information about the location and commodities in which Nakarattars were trading, Ramanathan Chettiar (1953) also provides information suggesting that religious and other forms of gifting provided a continuing mechanism by which cooperating groups of Nakarattar traders gained entrance into local communities (see Chapter 7 for description of the role of religious gifting and entrance to the seventeenth-century temple town of Palani).

> Until 1815, all those who were engaged in cotton business left their homes and met at the house of Arjuna Perumal Ambalakarar at Narasingampatti (5 miles west of Melur and 13 miles east of Madurai) and from there they started as a group to various cotton centres. At the end of the trading season, they returned to the said Narasingampatti from where they branched off to return home. Deeds of Palmayrah leaves have been found in the said Ambalakar's residence. According to one of those deeds, the profit of 743 and ½ varahans accrued in one partnership was spent to dig a drinking water tank in Narasingampatti. From revenue records kept in Melur Taluk office, it is known that the tank is called Nagarattar Orani or Panchuppotti Orani ["the tank built out of profits in cotton bale transactions"].[7]

Nakarattar commercial activities extended even beyond the Tamil mainland. By the end of the eighteenth century, they had gained control of pearl fisheries in the Ceylon Straits and the Gulf of Mannar, usurping this position from Muslim Maryakarar merchants who had previously been granted control of the fisheries by the *Setupati* (Raja) of Ramnad in the seventeenth century (Arasaratnam 1971a; Samaraweera 1972). Various factors seem to have been in play. For one thing, the *setupati's* influence in granting fishery rights had become considerably eroded. As early as the eighteenth century, administrative rights over the fishery were being strongly contested by the Dutch, by the Raja of Tanjavur, and by the Nawab of the Carnatic. The different claims of these parties were apparently withdrawn only in return for a financial settlement from the Nakarattars (Arasaratnam 1979; Samaraweera 1972). In addition, the Nakarattar takeover may reflect a close financial relationship that Nakarattars built with the *setupati* who was, perhaps, their largest client *zamindar* (see below). That is, Nakarattar merchants may have been in a position to influence the *setupati* to exercise whatever powers he still retained over the straits. In any case, the Nakarattars were ultimately able to exercise monopoly control over the fisheries until 1836, renting them out to Maravar and Paravar boating crews from Tuticorin.[8]

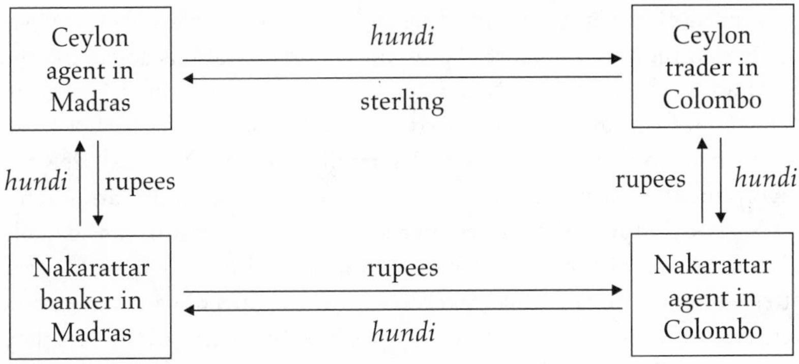

Figure 1. Simple *hundi* exchange system

From at least 1820,[9] Nakarattars also dominated the major coastal trade in arrack and other coconut products from Ceylon to Madras, in rice and cloth from Madras to Ceylon and, arguably, in salt from Madras to Calcutta and rice from Calcutta to Madras and Ceylon. It is difficult to gauge the degree of their domination, but according to contemporary observers, they had cornered the Ceylon rice market, controlling all imports not only of Tanjavur rice but of Bengal rice as well.[10]

The Nakarattars' position in the Ceylonese rice market allowed them to take advantage of a marked imbalance of trade strongly tilted in favor of rice exports from Madras to Ceylon. Ceylonese importers made up differences in the trade balance with British sterling, which was earned by trading in the European market for Ceylon cinnamon, spices, coconut products, and increasingly—until the coffee blight appeared in 1868—coffee (MacKenzie 1954: 90). But Nakarattar agents in Colombo—holding a monopoly on the import of rice—were unwilling to accept sterling as payment unless there were exceptional sterling shortages in India. Accordingly, Ceylonese rice traders appointed their own agents in Madras to whom they sent their sterling bills for sale. They then sold rupee drafts on those agents to the Nakarattar bankers in Ceylon, who discounted (i.e., cashed) the *hundi* in rupees or rupee credit at a standardized discount rate. The Nakarattar bankers, in turn, sent the *hundis* to Madras where they could be redeemed at face value (see Figure 1). British merchants and plantation owners in Ceylon met their rupee needs in a similar fashion. The Nakarattars "were thus in a position practically to hold the Colombo merchants [Ceylonese and British] to ransom, while the latter were at the same time dependent on the sterling exchange in India."[11]

Reports of Nakarattars trading Bengali rice in Ceylon are also interesting in that they lend support to present-day oral traditions describing the northward expansion of Nakarattar trade and the establishment of Nakarattar firms in Calcutta as early as 1820 (Lakshmanan Chettiar 1954: 41). They are intriguing in view of family histories that describe the involvement of early nineteenth-century Nakarattars in salt farming for trade to Ceylon and other places.[12] I also note the existence of considerable documentation of the trade in grains from Bengal for salt from Madras, attested in East India Company records for the eighteenth and nineteenth centuries.[13] All of these scattered reports bear further research. But they are consistent both with traditions of Nakarattar salt trading and with a general Nakarattar shift away from small-scale trading activities and into the large-scale financing or ownership of productive resources throughout the Madras Presidency.

There remains scope for considerable research into the precise nature of Nakarattar credit networks and of the various commodities markets with which they were involved. Whatever findings eventually result from such research, it is clear that late eighteenth- and early nineteenth-century Nakarattar commodities trading was tied to some kind of exchange banking system. That is, Nakarattars combined their trade transactions with purely financial transactions such as money lending, the remittance of funds between geographically distant locations, and even quasi-governmental treasury functions to the extent that governing authorities made use of Nakarattar financial facilities. Like any other system of credit extension and financial intermediation, the system worked ultimately because of the mutual confidence (strongly qualified by the lack of any viable alternative) between Nakarattars and their clients. During the colonial period, for reasons that will be explored in subsequent chapters, the Nakarattar system worked more successfully than did most of its competitors. Overall, the record of Nakarattar enterprise remains extremely sketchy throughout the early nineteenth century, both in Ceylon and in Madras (and even more so in Calcutta). Yet, such as it is, the evidence suggests that by 1850 the Nakarattar had already enlarged their economic niche from domestic trade to international trade and had become a major force in the commercial world of Southeast Asia.

Peshkash, Money Lending, and Repayment, 1800–1850

Nakarattar commodities trading was inextricably linked to money lending and banking. East India Company documents indicate that before the end of the eighteenth century, Indian *soukars* (moneylenders) within the

Madras Presidency—including *soukars* in Madura district, which encompassed the Nakarattar homeland—acted as brokers and renters for *palaiyakkarars* (poligars) with superior land rights, transferring funds between different *palaiyakkarars* as well as between the *palaiyakkarars* and anyone else with whom the *palaiyakkarars* transacted: army troops, merchants, agrarian producers, and European trading companies.[14] According to a British revenue officer in 1793, "Most of the Soukars of the Southern Provinces have open accounts with the Poligars and are in the habit of frequent dealings with them. For management of their concerns they have Gomastas [clerk-accountants], etc. established in the Pallams ["army camps"] to wait on the spot to receive the produce of the different crops that are assigned to liquidation of their demands."[15]

After the "Poligar Wars" of 1799–1800 and the establishment of British rule in 1801, the surviving *palaiyakkarars* were largely converted into British renters and—following the Bengali practice—were called *zamindars.* But the change of name and the cessation of violence did little to alter the revenue needs of these *palaiyakkarars*-turned-*zamindars*. On the contrary, the period from 1800 to 1850 is widely regarded as one of British overassessment and overcollection of land rents or taxes, called *peshkash* (Saruda Raju 1941; Stein 1969), and *zamindars* continued to look to local *soukars* as financial intermediaries, subrenters, and brokers for agrarian commodities produced on their lands.[16] In 1828, the Madura District subcollector reported, "It was formerly the custom to deliver over the . . . grain to a few rich merchants who of course made a considerable profit by the assistance they afforded the Zamindars in relieving them from the burden of disposing it on the market."[17] These practices did not die out, the subcollector's allusion to "former custom" notwithstanding. The Miscellaneous Correspondence volumes for Madura District during the 1850s list drafts drawn by Nakarattar grain contractors in Ramnad and Sivagangai—names that are identical with *zamindari* creditors.[18]

Faced by ever-mounting expenses and tributary obligations to the East India Company, *zamindars* relied as never before on large-scale loans from any available source of financial credit.[19] To secure these loans, they frequently leased their income-earning villages to Nakarattar creditors, assigning the revenue of villages or sometimes entire districts as security against a loan.[20] Pleading inability to pay out of their own resources, *zamindars* would then have their Nakarattar and other creditors pay their *peshkash* dues to the appropriate authority in the form of *hundis* or *teeps* (bills of exchange). Company officials often had little choice but to accept this payment and hope for the eventual cashing of these bills—

often netting as little as one-fifth of the amount listed in their books as their rightful revenue tribute (Sundaram 1944–45: 13–14).

Such procedures solved the *zamindars'* immediate cash-flow problems. But at the same time it increased their difficulties in subsequent years since, whatever original understanding had been reached with their creditors—and, needless to say, the system was rife with opportunities for fraud—the leased land never seemed to produce an income sufficient to pay off the principal plus the interest on the original loan. In addition, the *zamindar* was still faced with *peshkash* demands on his entire estate, but much of the estate's produce now went to its moneylender lessees. Perhaps the most insidious effect, however, at least from the *zamindars'* point of view, was the consequences of this technique for the East India Company's policies regarding revenue collection. Ultimately, the Company—and, after 1856, the colonial government—erected a British-based legal system as the basis for deciding and enforcing decisions on all revenue and most civil disputes. In the process, *zamindars* lost their independent jural, administrative, and military-police powers, while moneylenders, including Nakarattar moneylenders, gained considerable leverage through the exercise of legal suits in the court system.

In a study of the traditional kings and *zamindars* of South India, Pamela Price (1979) describes the banker-client relationships between some of the most prominent Nakarattars and *zamindars* in nineteenth-century Madras. She argues that, during the early decades of this period, Nakarattar loans generally were not repaid directly; rather, "payment could come in the form of lightened taxes, of trading and minting rights, and in the intimidation of robbers" (1979: 192). In other words, money lending to *zamindars* was an integral part of other commercial operations. It was the price one had to pay in order to play a successful, large-scale role in agrarian trade.

Despite this well-taken argument about the indirect benefits of *zamindar* financing, there has been only one systematic study (unavailable to me) of the financial relationships between *zamindars* and bankers during this period (actually a study of the Nawab of Arcot: Gurney 1968). Accordingly, I make the cautionary observation that the sums of money involved could be quite substantial. It seems unlikely that Nakarattars would forgo repayment—even for significant indirect benefits—if there was some way to avoid the loss, and there are good reasons to believe that they did not. One finds references, for example, to direct techniques of moneylender repayment by *zamindars* in the practice of land leasing described above. In other ways, too, Nakarattar moneylenders demonstrated their unabated appetite for direct repayment of loans. For example, a letter from the Madurai Collector, R. Peter, to the Accountant General in Fort St. George mentions the involvement of one Veerappa Chetty and another unnamed Nakarattar with the Zamindar of Sivaganga. The details of the transactions—especially the rights of the different parties in the case—are ambiguous. But the interest of the Nakarattars in recovering their money is plain.

> To: Accountant General,
> Fort St. George.
>
> Sir,
>
> In reply to your letter of the 3rd—Ultimo . . . I have the honor to state that on 28th May the late Zamindar of Shevaganga with Veerapah Chetty came in my presence. The latter stated that he would pay me 40,000 thousand [*sic*] rupees of the Sheevaganga balance, of which he said he would pay 9,000 rupees in Hoondies [*hundis*] of the Accountant General. I desired him to do so and the next day he proceeded to Ramnad. A Takeed [administrative order, memorandum] was prepared in the Cutcherry [district headquarters] dated 3rd June directing the Hoondies to be received and on the 2nd July I received a note from the cash keeper stating that the Chettiyar had not yet come to the Hoozoor to affix their signature to the bills. I therefore ordered him to carry the Bills to the account of the Shevagunga balance as they were—The Chetties came to me at Sovarencourchi on the [?] of July and signed a paper corroborating the Will in favor of the present Zamindar and then made no opposition to the Bills in the Zamindar's favor. They also advanced no claim to the Bills on the 11th September when other Chetties came forward to adjust the remaining balance, but on the 29th September when the Zamindar closed with the other Chetties they gave an arzee [petition] claiming the 9,000 rupees as they had not receipted the bills—On the 30th, this was referred to the Zamindar who on the 21st November objected to the payment of the 90,000 [*sic*] rupees which they claimed as the said Chetties were in debt to the Zemindary and he insisted first of all that their accounts should be adjusted.
>
> The payment of the Bills was entered in the names of the persons in whose favor they were drawn [the names of Veerapah and Sateeapah Chetty are noted in the margin]—and the amount has been credited to the permanent Peshcash of fusly 1230 in the accounts of July 1020 under the land revenue.
>
> *Madura 2d, June 1830.*[21]

In fairness to Price, her characterization of the rewards of *zamindar* financing is applied explicitly to the early parts of the nineteenth century, before a progressive weakening of *zamindars* and the erection of a British-based legal system made litigation an attractive course of action for Nakarattar creditors. Price is quite aware of these shifts and discusses them in her dissertation. My concern here is simply to point out that the contrast between early and late nineteenth-century relationships between moneylenders and *zamindars* lies less in the difference between indirect and direct rewards for *zamindar* financing than in the legal powers available to Nakarattars to enforce the terms of loan agreements. There remains considerable research to be done on the remedies and sanctions available to moneylenders in their pre-European and early nineteenth-century dealings with *zamindars.*

Litigation and the Emergence of Nakarattar Zamindars, *1850–1900*

As the world economy changed and Crown government replaced Company rule, Nakarattar investments typical of late eighteenth- and early nineteenth-century Madras became increasingly risky or unprofitable. The East India Company restricted and, in the end, all but abolished a system of government loans to agriculturalists (*takkavi* loans) that had secured many credit transactions during the first half of the century (Sarada Raju 1941: 142–145). Simultaneously, land also became more risky as collateral (albeit potentially more profitable; see below). It was seldom alienable in an unrestricted fashion, and "landowning" peasants generally did not own any land outright. Instead, they possessed a legally ambiguous and hence conflict-generating share in their joint-family estate. Under changes in the evolving legal system, the time required to settle legal disputes over ownership and enforce a mortgage foreclosure lengthened. Thus, only local residents, who had extralegal sanctions available to them, could safely accept land as security.[22] In Tirunelveli, the cotton trade was becoming increasingly competitive as Nadar traders developed an edge through their connection with Nadar cotton cultivators (Hardgrave 1969)—an edge not duplicable by the more highly specialized Nakarattars. Meanwhile, for reasons that are not clear, Marwaris came to dominate the credit needs of cotton traders in Coimbatore.[23] All opportunities for Indian participation in shipping were outlawed by the colonial government; at the same time, Europeans were moving to develop and monopolize new arenas of investment: notably, railroads, military supplies, and sugar (Bagchi 1972; Habib and Raychaudhuri 1982; Mahadevan 1976; Ray 1979). Finally, beginning in 1843 with the founding of the Presidency Bank of Madras, Europeans established their own exchange banks, thereby excluding Nakarattars and other indigenous moneylenders from the market in mercantile finance and currency exchange for private European firms and the market for quasi-governmental treasury functions for the East India Company.[24]

These dramatic changes in opportunities for investment had major ramifications for Nakarattar business practice. In the Madras Presidency itself, they ruled out virtually every area of investment. As a consequence, almost the only possibility for profitable investment remaining was, ironically, to invest in or convert bad debts into land ownership. The irony lies in a reversal of the agricultural commodities market in Madras. The agricultural depression that had contributed to the credit hunger of the first half of the nineteenth century at last began to relinquish its hold on the South Indian economy. Between 1823 and 1853 the value of good, wet land in Tanjavur District had risen from Rs. 12 to Rs. 39 per acre. Then between 1853 and 1868 it rose dramatically, to Rs. 151 per acre (Raghavaiyangar 1892, cited in Mahadevan 1976: 44). Between 1878 and 1903 the value of land throughout Madras rose from Rs. 245 per acre to Rs. 458 per acre (Kumar 1965: 142). Moreover, this rise in land value was fueled and surpassed by rises in the prices of grain. According to David Washbrook, for example, prices of dry grains between 1880–87 and 1918–20 rose between 50 percent and 70 percent, and went even higher during the shortages of 1918–20.[25] Meanwhile, Fort St. George raised its tax assessments on dry land only from 7 percent to 12 percent (Washbrook 1973: 158).

It is not clear that these rising prices increased the profitability of investment in land and agriculture to the extent that they compensated for investment opportunities foreclosed by British interests. Moreover, as noted above, serious legal obstacles often lay in the path of anyone seeking to wrest a clear title away from members of a landowning joint family. Nevertheless, land was sufficiently attractive so that wealthy Nakarattar families, with sufficient economic leverage over their *zamindar* clients, used this leverage, along with extensive litigation, to acquire considerable lands.

One of the most notable cases is described by Pamela Price (1979). In her account, the story begins with a transaction in which the Setupati of Ramnad leased twenty-four villages in the vicinity of Devakottai to a Devakottai Nakarattar named Al. Arunachalam. The date on which this lease occurred is not clear. But from at least the 1860s on, these villages were not to escape control of Arunachalam's family until the Zamindari Abolition Act of 1947.[26]

The loans that secured these leases for Arunachalam—or, more accurately, the loans for which these leases stood as security—were not sufficient to solve the *setupati*'s long-term financial problems. During the 1860s and 1870s, he found it necessary to mortgage additional villages, almost on a wholesale basis, to Arunachalam's family and to two other Nakarattar families as well.[27] Other, unspecified portions of Ramnad were leased to Arunachalam's son, Ramasami, and to his nephew, Pethuperumal. Two additional villages went to two brothers from a separate lineage, Chidambaram and Subramaniam. The villages from an entire two and a quarter "divisions" (*taluks?*) were leased to their father's brother Ramanadhan. And another three divisions went to two cousins from a third lineage, Me. Ar. Narayan and Me. Ct. Vairavan.[28]

In the 1870s the *setupati* was unable to meet the interest payments on loans obtained from these three families, even after the income from their leased lands was taken into account, and the entire gang of Nakarattar creditors took him to court. According to Price, only his early death saved the *zamin* from being completely divided. Instead, it was placed in the hands of a court-appointed manager until his son Baskara reached his majority in 1889. It is not clear how the Court of Wards satisfied the Nakarattars. But whatever solution was reached, it was only temporary. In the 1880s, Baskara's mother borrowed Rs. 80,000 from Ramasami to arrange a second and secret wedding for Baskara.[29] In 1889, Baskara assumed the title of *setupati*. His estate was solvent, with a revenue of Rs. 900,000 and a cash balance, at that time, of Rs. 300,000. Three days after his "rendition," Baskara gave or leased two additional "*mahanams*" (divisions of land: *mahanadus*) containing twenty-four villages to Ramasami. It is not clear what he received in return. Ten weeks later, L. Ar. Rm. Ramanadhan (by his initials, a different Ramanadhan Chettiar than the previously mentioned Nakarattar) induced Baskara's younger brother to sue for partition of the *zamin* and extended Rs. 127,000 to cover legal costs. Ultimately, the court ruled that Ramnad, as a traditional kingdom, had a special status and was not subject to division under laws concerning the Hindu joint family. However, Baskara was forced to pay his younger brother an allowance of Rs. 2,000 per month plus a lump sum payment of Rs. 250,000 to cover back allowance.

Price describes many different kinds of expenses incurred by the young *setupati*. But for our purposes, it is perhaps enough to note that by 1890 Baskara had borrowed Rs. 486,000 from Ramasami. In 1891, in return for a lease on most of Hanamanthagudy Taluk, he borrowed Rs. 800,000 from V.A.R.V. Arunachalam and S. Rm. M. Rm. Muthia (grandfather of Raja Sir Annamalai Chettiar). In the same year, he also borrowed an additional Rs. 750,000 from the British-owned Commercial and Land Bank of Madurai. By 1892, Ramasami, still Baskara's chief creditor, had permanent or term leases on 255 villages (at one time he had held title to 500, and his relatives to another 80). In 1893 Baskara's total deficits were Rs. 763,000. By 1894, he owed Ramasami alone Rs. 837,035, against which Ramasami secured a mortgage deed on the entire *zamin* of Ramnad. In that same year, Ramasami's lease to 24 villages near Devakottai was made permanent. By July of 1895, Baskara had given his various creditors 306 villages on permanent leases and 294 villages on term leases. The villages still paying revenues to Baskara's estate had diminished from 1,011 to 439. His total debt was estimated at Rs. 2 million. In 1896 Al. Ar. Ramasami was officially installed as the Zamindar of Devakottai with a domain fissioned out of Ramnad consisting of the 24 Devakottai villages and containing forty thousand acres of wet land and sixty thousand acres of dry land.[30] In 1901, Baskara was removed from the managership of Ramnad and replaced by Ramasami. In 1903, Baskara died at the age of thirty-five.

The case of the Setupati of Ramnad and the Zamindar of Devakottai illustrates events that occurred many times and with many different *zamindars* and Nakarattar creditors. It was unusual in its scale and in that only one other Nakarattar besides Al. Ar. Ramasami ever had the title *zamindar* conferred on him by the British, namely, S. Rm. M. Chidambaram, Zamindar of Andipatti.[31] But several other Nakarattars acquired permanent leases or foreclosed on mortgages secured by *zamins* and assumed the title (see Table 1). In addition, other Nakarattars acquired similar, but generally smaller, *inam* holdings. My informants estimate that perhaps two hundred Nakarattars in all were able to obtain such minor titles.

Nakarattar Commercial Expansion in Southeast Asia, 1870–1930

In spite of such elite Nakarattar land acquisition, the number of Nakarattar families attaining land titles remained a very small proportion of their total numbers. Taking an 1890s estimate of the population as approximately ten thousand people,[32] these two hundred relatively large-scale, landholding Nakarattars could have represented at most one-fifth and more likely represented one-tenth or even one-twentieth of the joint-family units (*valavus*) whose heads might have sought to receive title.[33] Moreover, many of the *zamins* were actually quite unproductive and, according to a Nakarattar caste historian, were acquired as speculative investments in the hope that the government would eventually irrigate the land or build an adjacent rail line.[34] For the majority of Nakarattars, then, and for elite Nakarattars who were not satisfied with the acquisition

Table 1. Nakarattar Acquisition of *Zamins* in Nineteenth-Century Madras

	Name of Proprietor	*District*	Taluk *(revenue zone)*	*Village(s) or* Zamindari(s)
1.	V. A. R. Arunachalam Chettiar	Madura		Okkur and Peravali
2.	Al. Ar. Rm. Arunachalam Chettiar	Madura	Tiruvadanai	Devakottai Zamindari
3.	P. Chidambaram Chettiar	Madura	Palaiyappattu	Sirupalai
4.	P. L. S. A. Annamalai Chettiar	Madura	Palaiyappattu	Kilakottai
5.	S. Rm. M. Chidambaram Chettiar	Coimbatore	Karur	Andipatti
6.	S. A. Nagappa Chettiar	Tanjore	Tanjore	Velavadipatti and Verayadipatti (portion)
7.	Rm. Ar. Rm. Arunachalam Chettiar	Tanjore	Patukkottai	Karakkottai Kambarkovil Omakkavaya Kuthankudi Kothamangalam
8.	Ramanathan Chettiar	Tanjore	Patukkottai	Padirankottai Tenpatti
	Arunachalam Chettiar			Anandagopala-puram Ten-patti
	Palaniappa Chettiar			Alivalam Palattali Vathatikottai
9.	Muttukkaruppan Chettiar	Tanjore	Patukkottai	Padirankottai
	Olagappa Chettiar			Vadapadi
	Ramaswamy Chettiar			Anandagopala-puram Vadapadi
	Lakshmana Chettiar			Kollukkadu Yenadi

Source: Mahadevan (1976: 47); based on Asylum Press Almanack and Directory of Madras and Southern India (1909: 1693, 1699, 1706); and Raghavaiynagar (1892: cxiv).

of land and titles in Madras, the constricting climate for financial investment in India must have been a considerable stimulus to search for new ways of putting their money to use.

Their opportunity came with the growth of the plantation economy in Ceylon, the emergence of the Burmese rice market, and the development of Malaya's rubber and tin industries. From the mid–nineteenth century onward, British banks largely monopolized the servicing of British credit needs in these countries, and with a few notable exceptions they remained aloof from servicing the credit needs of the non-British. Unlike in Madras, however, the provincial governments of Southeast Asia adopted policies that initially encouraged rather than restricted investment by Nakarattar moneylenders. Displaced from the credit markets of Madras, and displaced from British investment and exchange markets throughout greater British India, the Nakarattars found a new niche in servicing the credit needs of the indigenous Southeast Asians and migrant Indians who fought with each other and with the British in a race to produce agrarian commodities for the European export market. Nakarattars were not the sole source of credit. Particularly in mainland Southeast Asia, they faced competition from the Chinese, who also maintained a formidable network of moneylenders. But the Nakarattars were in a particularly advantageous position. In addition to their own financial and organizational resources, Nakarattars—especially elite Nakarattars—retained ties to British banks and firms and used these ties as a further and substantial source of investment capital. In many ways, this practice merely represented a continuation of practices established during the eighteenth and early nineteenth centuries in Madras and Ceylon. In expanding this general role of financial intermediary, however, they effectively excluded any competing group from the specific niche of intermediary between the British and indigenous Southeast Asians within the overall financial system of British India.

It is difficult to arrive at a reliable quantitative estimate for the scale of Nakarattar commerce during the late colonial period. The earliest figure offered by a knowledgeable source suggests that, in 1896, their total assets amounted to Rs. 100 million (Sundara Iyer 1906, cited in Pillai 1930: 1174), but it is not clear how this estimate was formed. The difficulties in ascertaining any accurate estimate of Nakarattar finances are reflected by the multiple and inconsistent estimates of their assets, ranging from Rs. 536 million to Rs. 1.3 billion, contained in the 1930 reports of the Provincial Banking Enquiry Committees of Madras and Burma and the 1934 report of the Ceylon Banking Enquiry Committee. In the depressed economic environment of that time and in the atmosphere of emergent nationalism and populist politics that characterized public debate in the

1930s, most of the evidence obtained in a public "enquiry" on any topic was highly biased and prejudicial. Enquiries into money lending and banking, agricultural indebtedness, and commercial or industrial finance were no exception. On one hand, the vast majority of relevant testimony was collected from Nakarattar debtors, who painted a predictably black picture of their creditors. On the other hand, testimony by Nakarattar bankers can hardly be accepted as an unbiased alternative. Such as it is, however, Nakarattar evidence provides the only picture we have of the extent of Nakarattar business operations. I present sample estimates of Nakarattar working capital and assets in Tables 2 and 3.

Of the various estimates of Chettiar capital, those provided by A. Savaranatha Pillai (1930) are particularly interesting in view of the qualifications that he attaches to them. Pillai was the Assistant Commissioner for Income Tax for Madras. His figures were prepared from tax returns compiled by tax officers for "circles" in which Nakarattars had their principal place of business.[35] As a consequence, they are unlikely to reflect any additional bias beyond the distortions built into procedures for recording Nakarattar income.

Pillai describes the kinds of distortions these figures are likely to represent. First, the information they contain is derived from faulty self-reporting of Nakarattar assets in Madras. Pillai notes that Nakarattars frequently underreported their earnings, showing accounts for selected branches of their firms rather than total earnings. Moreover, many Nakarattar firms (including all of the largest firms, according to one informant) maintained their legal headquarters in the principality of Pudukottai —a tax-exempt, "princely state"—and did not report their assets and earnings at all. Secondly, Nakarattars did not report all of their business capital, even inaccurately. By Pillai's estimate, they left out the capital of at least 1,600 Nakarattars whose principal business was located in Burma, and of 193 Nakarattars whose business lay in Madras but outside the areas reported in those tax returns on which his account was based (Pillai 1930: 1172). Consequently, Pillai's subordinates were able to provide only undocumented estimates of these assets. Finally—and this is a major point of misinterpretation that Pillai does not mention but which will concern us in Chapter 5—the division between the Nakarattars' "own capital" and "borrowed capital" refers to aggregate measures of all Nakarattar capital in each specific locale, not individual loans and deposits between the Nakarattar firms within locales. Such interfirm transactions would cancel each other out in any aggregate analysis—a point that is frequently overlooked. As a result, many analysts apparently take Pillai's characterization of the ratio of "own to borrowed capital" and similar characterizations of

Table 2. Three Estimates of Nakarattar Working Capital, 1930 (one crore equals Rs. 10 million)

A. REPORT OF THE BURMA PROVINCIAL BANKING ENQUIRY COMMITTEE

Location of Working Capital	*Amount (crores)*
Burma	75
Federated Malay States	25
Ceylon	14
Cochin China	5
Madras Presidency	1
Total	120

Source: Krishnan (1954: 36).

B. ORAL EVIDENCE OF KARAIKUDI ARUNACHALAM CHETTIAR

Type of Investment	*Amount (crores)*
Money lending employed in business (own capital)	36
Investment in houses and jewels	10
Chettiars in Pudukottah State, many of whom do business in British India (own capital)	14
Their houses and jewels	4.5
Investments in land, estates, etc. in India, Federated Malay States, etc.	15
Total	79.5

Source: Madras Provincial Banking Enquiry Committee (1930 IV: 252).

C. WRITTEN EVIDENCE OF RAJA SIR MUTHIA CHETTIAR, NAKARATTAR REPRESENTATIVE TO THE MPBEC

Type of Investment	*Amount (crores)*
Cash	80–90
Houses and other property	15–20
Jewels	5
Non-Chettiar capital (borrowed)	15
Total	115–130

Source: Madras Provincial Banking Enquiry Committee (1930 I: 186).

Table 3. Total Working Capital of Nakarattar Agencies by Principal Business Location or "Circle," 1930 (one lakh equals Rs. 100,000)

A. TOTAL CAPITAL (OWNED AND BORROWED) EMPLOYED LOCALLY AND IN OTHER PLACES BY NATTUKOTTAI CHETTIAR AGENCIES WHO DO LOCAL BANKING BUSINESS

Name of Circle	*Number of Bankers Doing Business Locally*	*Amount of Borrowed Capital Invested (lakhs)*	*Borrowed Capital (lakhs)*	*Volume of Business (lakhs)*	*Expenses (lakhs)*
Chettinad					
Karaikudi I	33	238.82	108.72	347.54	10.77
Karaikudi II	14	59.03	123.89	182.92	13.31
Karaikudi III	74	101.75	53.43	155.18	5.11
Sivaganga	15	113.78	58.90	172.68	3.85
Total	136	513.38	344.94	858.32[a]	33.01
Beyond Chettinad					
Trichinopoly I (Tiruchirapalli)	21	43.85	22.45	66.30	2.59
Trichinopoly II (Tiruchirapalli)	12	12.44	2.21	14.65	0.79
Dindigul	19	11.97	25.23	37.20	1.99
Madurai, North	4	0.65	2.30	2.95	0.22
Madurai, South	8	18.93	17.53	36.46	4.52
Virudhanagar	10	6.17	5.15	11.68	0.78
Tuticorin	22	17.82	10.76	28.58	1.52
Tinnevelly (Tirunelveli)	11	12.42	28.22	40.64	2.69
Total	107	124.25	114.21	238.46	15.10
Grand Total	243	637.63	459.15	1,096.78	48.14

Source: Pillai (1930: 1188).

[a]Distribution: Local money-lending Rs. 217.54, Burma Rs. 313.64, Federated Malay States, Rs. 265.19, Ceylon Rs. 61.95.

Table 3—*Continued*

B. TOTAL OWN AND BORROWED CAPITAL OF THE NATTUKOTTAI CHETTIS ASSESSED BY THE FOUR CHETTINAD OFFICERS EMPLOYED IN BUSINESS IN ALL PLACES: LOCALLY, BURMA AND FOREIGN PLACES.

Name of Circle	*Number of Assessees*	*Own Capital (lakhs)*	*Borrowed Capital (lakhs)*
1. Karaikudi I	934	823.47	518.26
2. Karaikudi II	885	651.43	451.75
3. Karaikudi III	648	451.75	203.43
4. Sivaganga	415	456.54	224.04
Total	2,882	2,483.19	1,481.62

Source: Pillai (1930: 1188).

their own business by Nakarattars as applying to individual firms or agencies in a locale, rather than as applying to their aggregation.

With these considerations in mind, the properties that stand out most prominently in the various estimates of Nakarattar business are the Nakarattar investments outside of India and especially in Burma. The following discussion summarizes well-documented conclusions from half a dozen studies of the processes by which the Nakarattar caste expanded its role in colonial Southeast Asia.

Ceylon, 1870–1930

Throughout the nineteenth century and into the 1920s, Nakarattars continued to dominate the rice market in Ceylon (Bastianpillai 1964; Pillai 1930: 1179; Mahadevan 1976: 103). From the mid–nineteenth century onwards, however, their commercial activities were strongly affected by two changes in the Ceylonese economy. One of these changes was the arrival of British exchange banks to fund the Ceylon coffee boom of 1840 to 1870.[36] The second change was the overall growth in Ceylon's export market, triggered by the opening of the Suez Canal in 1869 and further altered by the destruction of Ceylon's coffee industry in the 1870s and the growth of its tea and rubber industries. The Suez Canal provided the means for much swifter transit time in Asian-European trade generally and, consequently, reduced transportation costs and increased profits in the shipment of all kinds of commodities. Initially, this change provided little scope for Nakarattar investment, for the most profitable investment and the one which dominated the Ceylonese

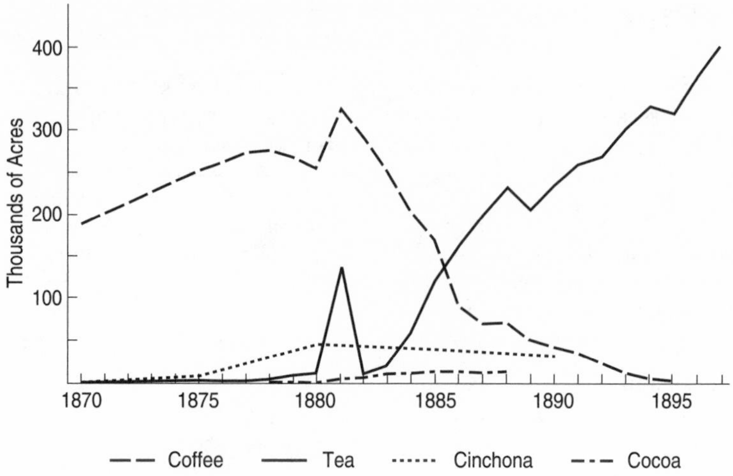

Figure 2. Areas under selected export crops, Ceylon, 1870–87. Figures for cinchona are five-yearly. *Source:* Rajaratnam (1961); based on Ceylon Blue Book Statistics, Colonial Office, Ceylon (1870–81); Ferguson's Handbook & Directory and Compendium of Useful Information (1870–81); Owen (1881).

economy between 1840 and 1880 was coffee, and most coffee plantations were in the hands of the British planters and were financed by British banks.[37] In the late 1870s, however, a coffee-leaf fungus (*hemeleia vastatrix*) destroyed the coffee industry. In the five years between 1881 and 1886, production of coffee dropped from its peak, when the area under cultivation was approximately 322,000 acres, to virtually no acreage under cultivation at all.[38]

In the aftermath of the blight, Ceylon plantation owners looked for alternatives to coffee. In the process, native Ceylonese found opportunities to increase their share as producers in the (slightly) more diversified economy of Ceylon. The new export crops included cinchona (from which quinine is produced), coconut, cocoa, and the two crops that were to become Ceylon's major exports: tea and, after 1900, rubber (Bastianpillai 1964; Rajaratnam 1961). (See Figures 2 and 3 and Table 4). By the end of British rule, the Ceylonese controlled perhaps 20 percent of the production of tea and 35 percent of the production of rubber, which together accounted for 90 percent of Ceylon's export. In addition, the Ceylonese controlled 100 percent of the production of coconut (Arasaratnam 1964: 161), which continued as the major Ceylonese export product even during the coffee boom.

Ceylonese growers and planters entering the growing plantation industries faced one serious problem, however: no British bank would

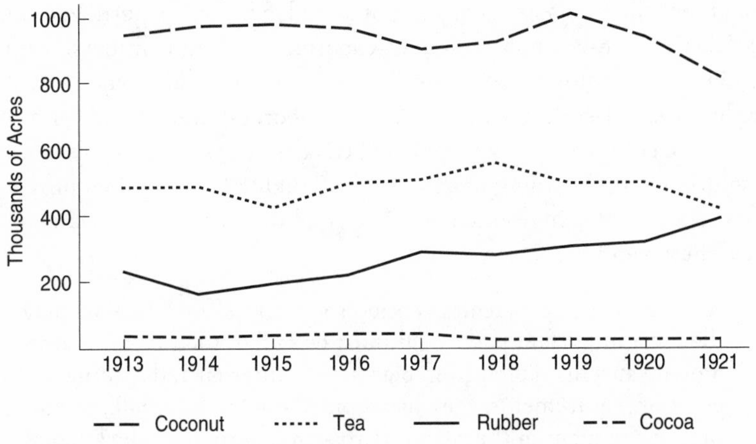

Figure 3. Areas under selected export crops, Ceylon, 1913–21. *Source:* Rajaratnam (1961); based on Ceylon Blue Book Statistics, Colonial Office, Ceylon (1913–21).

Table 4. Ceylon Export Commodities as Percentage of Total Export Trade, 1921–29

Commodity	*1921*	*1922*	*1923*	*1924*	*1925*	*1926*	*1927*	*1928*	*1929*
Areca nut	1.3	1.1	1.1	—	—	—	—	—	—
Cinnamon	—	—	—	—	—	—	1.1	1.3	—
Cocoa	—	1.1	—	—	—	—	—	—	1.0
Desiccated coconut	10.4	6.8	6.5	5.7	3.8	3.4	4.6	5.1	2.9
Coir	—	1.1	1.3	1.4	—	—	1.2	1.2	1.1
Copra	9.5	9.7	5.2	8.0	7.8	7.8	7.1	8.1	6.5
Oil	5.9	5.0	4.0	4.1	3.4	3.1	3.7	4.9	4.4
Rubber	21.0	22.4	17.9	37.6	36.6	36.6	28.9	20.6	22.9
Tea	43.9	49.0	52.9	55.8	40.5	42.3	40.6	51.3	50.4
Gold	—	—	—	—	—	—	—	—	4.0
Others	8.1	6.2	6.6	7.1	6.9	6.7	6.0	7.7	6.8

Source: Rajaratnam (1961: 17); based on Ceylon Blue Book Statistics, Colonial Office, Ceylon (1921–29).

lend them the funds necessary to purchase land, seed, or fertilizer. Similarly, Ceylonese importers and exporters, coconut millers, arrack renters, and "country boutiques" (rural moneylenders who provided credit to small-scale farmers and farm laborers) were faced with the same problem: where to get credit. The Nakarattars were happy to offer a solution and, according to the Ceylon Banking Commission, provided almost all of the investment capital employed to finance indigenous Ceylonese ventures.

> Among the private credit agencies, the Nattukottai Chettiars play the most important part. . . . It must be said to their credit that in moving surplus capital from places, both internal and external to the point of requirements, they have contributed in no small measure to the development of the island. European enterprises relied upon English funds to acquire lands and develop them into flourishing estates. The Ceylonese had no such external support or own savings to help them. They turned to the Chettiar and found a ready response. (CBC 1934 I: paras. 159–162)

It is difficult to gauge exactly how much capital Nakarattars channeled into the production of different crops in Ceylon for the same reasons it is difficult to gauge overall Nakarattar investment. But their involvement was substantial. Between 1870 and 1916, the number of Nakarattar firms in Ceylon increased from 150 to 700.[39] By 1929, at the peak of their business, the total volume of business conducted by Nakarattar businessmen was estimated at Rs. 150 million (CBC 1934 I: 42). For reasons touched on shortly below, this volume dropped to Rs. 100 million by 1934, the major difference being a decline in loans available to Nakarattars from British banks. With this decline accounted for, however, it is possible to accept figures prepared by the Colombo Nattukottai Chettiar Association in 1934 (CBC 1934 I: 42; see Table 5) as providing an indication of their business activity. These figures indicate that Nakarattar loans to Ceylonese that were secured by mortgages totaled approximately Rs. 20 million and that loans secured by their pawnbroking operations came to another Rs. 4 million. Nakarattars loaned out slightly more than the amount of these combined categories—Rs. 25 million—in unsecured loans on promissory notes. Finally Nakarattars also deposited about Rs. 5 million with British banks. Besides these assets, totaling Rs. 54 million, the caste association figures also indicate that Nakarattars invested about Rs. 46 million in their own business and properties. That is, their assets were almost evenly distributed between money lending and non–money lending business ventures, with a slight preference for money lending.

Table 5. Nakarattar Assets in Ceylon, 1934

	Value (rupees)
Business and properties	
Agricultural land and estates (about 50,000 acres): 70% coconut, 15% rubber, 15% tea, cocoa, etc.	30,000,000
Residential property in principal towns	6,000,000
Business capital in retail shops, estate suppliers, rice trade, import business, etc.	10,000,000
Total	46,000,000
Loans and deposits	
Pawnbroking advances	40,000,000
Loans against mortgages	20,000,000
Other advances: against promissory notes, etc.	25,000,000
Deposits in British banks	50,000,000
Total	54,000,000
Grand Total	100,000,000

Source: Ceylon Banking Commission (1934I: 42).

Although no confirming evidence was available to me during my research, it seems likely that the proportion of Nakarattar investment in money lending expanded relative to their investment in trade and other business ventures after the 1850s. The major difference in Nakarattar business operations after this time lay in additional sources of short-term funds available to them with the establishment of the British exchange banks. These banks were faced with the problem of investing the considerable funds deposited with them by their British clients. Although the British would not extend credit to Ceylonese, they would make short-term loans to reputable Nakarattar bankers (*adathis*) secured only by the cosignature of a second Nakarattar. Nakarattars, in turn, loaned these funds to Ceylonese at a higher rate (Weersooria 1973).

This is not to say that the British banks provided unlimited credit to every Nakarattar. On the contrary, they attempted to build safeguards into their Nakarattar loan operations by excluding small Nakarattar firms from consideration. Loans would be made only if the recipient or cosignatory was on an approved *adathi* list (see Chapter 6) prepared by the head office of the Imperial Bank of India, which was supposed to keep track of credit worthiness and indicate the maximum amount of loans for which each firm was eligible.[40] But the safeguards never really worked. As one expert witness testified before the Ceylon Banking Commission,

> As the due dates of the loans vary in the different banks, the Chettiars used to borrow from one bank to pay off their dues to others so that a Chettiar firm which is financially embarrassed can easily tide over its difficulties and if it is actually insolvent the heaviest loss is entailed upon the bank to which the loan is repayable last in order of time.
>
> . . . The system of inter-Chetty lending was the chief support of the successful working of Chettiar Banking. When in need of liquid funds they lent freely among themselves, at the usual inter-Chetty rate (6 percent or under) or at the rate charged by the banks, whichever was higher, if, in order to accommodate a brother in the trade, a Chettiar had to borrow from a bank. Thus so long as some among the Chettiars had untapped margins of credit at the banks, none of them, whose position was otherwise sound and could prove it to be such to his prospective Chetty creditor, had to fear, in all normal times, any inability to meet his short term obligation to his bank.
>
> Thus the Chettiars through the age-old practice of being their own mutual lenders of last resort, were able to use loans from banks, sometimes from the same bank, to meet the maturing bank loans. To the extent this happened, it was the banks' own money which enabled the Chettiars to keep their loan contracts with the banks with striking promptness.[41]

The implication is that Nakarattars financed not only short-term loans from their own short-term borrowings, but also risky short-term loans and even long-term loans. If their clients could not repay or if their own short-term borrowings came due before the repayment by a client, Nakarattars could simply repay the British banks, in the manner described in the testimony above, by borrowing from a fellow Nakarattar. The second Nakarattar, in turn, might have borrowed from the very bank being repaid! Since no security was required on the short-term loans that Nakarattars borrowed from British banks, and since Nakarattars found it easy to circumvent the kinds of limits that British banks placed on loans to them, virtually the only constraint on Nakarattar borrowing was their own sense of caution. In the face of a highly expansive export economy, however, there was little need to exercise caution.

The bubble burst in the "Chetty Crisis" of 1925 with the failure of the A. R. A. R. S. M. firm.[42] In the ensuing bankruptcy hearings, the High Court of Madras estimated the firm's Indian assets at Rs. 800 thousand and Indian liabilities at Rs. 3.7 million; its Ceylon assets at Rs. 150 thousand and its Ceylon liabilities at Rs. 1.7 million. According to the Ceylon Banking Commission,

> The discovery of the questionable practices of the firm of A. R. A. R. S. M. led [British] banks to look upon those practices as not particular to that individual firm but as possible types which could be and might be adopted by other firms of Chettiars in the island. Accordingly, the banks decided to revise the securities on which they had been doing business with the Chettiars until then and they found to their dismay that many of the securities offered to them by the Chettiars were not safe and others were neither sufficient or adequate. (CBC 1934 II: 253)

The disingenuous British statement of "sudden discovery" served them as a rationale for suspending further credit and calling in all outstanding loans to Nakarattar bankers. No evidence is available to me that suggests any alternative explanation for this change in British bank lending policy. But it is hardly credible that the British banks would loan out Rs. 25 million without some idea about the security of the loans. In any case, their abrupt cessation of all loans to Nakarattars required the Nakarattars, in turn, to call in their loans to Ceylonese clients. The result, as reported by the Colombo Nakarattar association, was a decline in their business volume from Rs. 150 million to Rs. 100 million between 1929 and 1934 (CBC 1934 I: 42).

This was only the start of a series of events that rendered Ceylon inhospitable for continued Nakarattar investment. In addition, and dramatically amplifying every event, the worldwide depression sent prices for agricultural commodities plummeting—including those for tea, rubber, and coconut. What had once seemed safe and profitable loans to Ceylonese made on the basis of projections about expanding markets rapidly became losses. As these loans came due, Nakarattars (faced with their own credit difficulties) refused to grant extensions. Where no other solution was possible, Nakarattars took possession of lands or moveable property securing roughly half the outstanding debts. These actions, in turn, stimulated Ceylonese resentment of the Tamil moneylenders and led to a series of legislative acts and legal proceedings that ultimately drove the Nakarattars out of Ceylon.[43]

Burma, 1870–1930

Nakarattar commercial activities in Burma followed a very similar pattern to those in Ceylon. They were different in that Burma's economic environment provided even greater incentives for money-lending activities (in contrast to investment in trade or fixed capital) than did the environment of Ceylon. They were also different in that, in place of Ceylon's plantation crops, Nakarattars directed their Burmese investments primarily toward what Furnivall (1956) has called the development of the Burmese "rice frontier."[44]

Nakarattars arrived in Burma with the British conquest of Arakan and part of Tenasserim in 1826. The rest of Lower Burma fell in 1852. Upper Burma was not taken until 1886. But by then the Nakarattar-financed development of Lower Burma was already well underway. Nakarattars began to move into Burma in greater numbers following the conquest of Lower Burma. The first major agency houses are reported in Moulmein by 1852 and in Rangoon in 1854. But it was not until the opening of the Suez Canal in 1869 that Nakarattars were really attracted to Burma in a major way.

The canal dramatically reduced the transit time of trade with Europe and, in one fell swoop, opened up the European market for Burmese rice. Lower Burma had been troubled by decades of war and was extremely underdeveloped and underpopulated. In what has become the standard interpretation, Burma was a frontier waiting to be developed. Hoping to encourage that development (and the attendant increase in revenue), colonial authorities enacted the Lower Burma Land and Revenue Act of 1876, which established important changes in Burma's land tenure laws (Adas 1974a; Furnivall 1956; Siegelman 1962). The intended purpose of the act was to provide settlers with a clear title of ownership to land that they occupied and on which they paid taxes for a period of twelve years. An additional, unintended (but, from the colonial point of view, beneficial) consequence of the act was that it provided settlers with land to mortgage as security for loans to buy seed and fertilizer, and to meet other expenses.

As in Ceylon, a major reason for the Nakarattars' success in Burma is that they incurred relatively low costs in acquiring loanable funds from each other, from the British banks, or from the Imperial Bank of India; low costs, that is, relative to the cost of credit faced by Burmese or Chinese lenders who lacked access to these institutions.[45] Consequently, Nakarattars could charge lower rates of interest than their competitors did and still make a healthy profit. No figures are available to me that allow for a precise reconstruction of the Burmese credit market between 1870 and 1930. But figures are available for the years immediately after this time. They provide a good indication of Burmese interest rates from various sources (Table 6), and, although there may have been fluctuations in rate averages over the sixty-year period, there is no reason to believe that the overall structure of the credit market would have altered.

Table 6. Interest Rates on Burmese Credit Market, 1935–42

Loan Source	*Rate (% per annum)*
Sources offering restricted or no services to agriculturalists	
Exchange banks and leading commercial banks	4–6
Coop societies and government loans	12
Dawson's Bank	9–21
West Coast Burmese bankers and moneylenders	6–18
Sources offering loans to agriculturalists	
Burmese moneylenders	12–35
Chinese and other moneylenders offering *sapabe, sekywe, sa-pe,* and similar loans	200+
Nakarattar bankers	9–34

Source: Tun Wai (1962: 136).

This is not to say that Nakarattars thereby endeared themselves to their clients. On the contrary, they were the objects of considerable resentment (Adas 1974a). Moreover, as Siegelman (1962: 240) points out, although Nakarattar interest charges were relatively low, their rates (and the concomitant profits) exceeded the profits that could be obtained by rice cultivation. This was particularly the case when, as a condition of his loan, a cultivator was required to sell his crop or repay the loan by giving the moneylender title to his crop at a predetermined, submarket price. The issue raises the interesting question of whether the Land and Revenue Act of 1876 had any consequences other than providing security for Nakarattar agricultural investment and enticing agricultural labor from Upper Burma and Madras with misleading promises of land ownership. In other words, the Act of 1876 seems to have accomplished little more than to provide new clothing for precolonial forms of agricultural tenancy and landless labor.

In any case, the situation was ideal for Nakarattar operations. The rice-frontier economy of Lower Burma was even more expansive than Ceylon's, and a broader spectrum of agriculturalists could offer good security for loans. The consequences are not surprising. Figures on Nakarattar investment provided by the Burma Provincial Banking Enquiry Committee in 1930 (BPBEC I: 211; see below) indicate a preference for money lending over other forms of investment of roughly two to one. Tun Wai believes the ratio to have been far higher than this.

	Moneylending Capital	*Trading and Fixed Capital*
Upper Burma	Rs. 30 million	Rs. 10 million
Lower Burma	450–500 million	210–260 million

The bulk of Nakarattar investment went directly to loans for agriculturalists. Reports for 1929 indicate that in Lower Burma (where Nakarattars invested the bulk of their money) about Rs. 110–120 million was advanced in short-term loans to agriculturalists. Another Rs. 32–33 million was advanced in intermediate and long-term loans (BPBEC 1930 I: 2). In addition, Nakarattar investment in rice trading was also substantial. Nakarattars provided roughly two-thirds of all agricultural credit, and in many of Burma's provinces Nakarattars provided nearly 100 percent of loans to rice cultivators (BPBEC 1930 I: 67–68). These loans frequently took the form of forward contracts which entitled the moneylender to receive the crop in repayment. It is not clear whether taking possession of such crops should be regarded as a return of interest on Nakarattar money-lending activities rather than as a profit from their investments in rice trading. But in any case, according to A. Savaranatha Pillai (1930: 1177), Nakarattars used their advantageous position as both moneylenders and rice traders to control as much as 50 percent of Burma's rice crop. From this point, their choices broadened. They could sell the rice to British traders, or they could compete with the British, either sending it directly to Madras and Ceylon or, from at least 1916 on, by first milling it in Nakarattar-owned mills in Burma (Indian Industrial Commission 1919 V: 543, cited in Mahadevan 1976: 191). Besides these investments, a few elite Nakarattars were also involved in Burma timber and oil (Krishnan 1959: 31).

Available estimates of Nakarattar sources and investments of capital share all the problems already encountered in grappling with data collected by the Madras and Ceylon banking enquiry committees. In addition, new problems creep into the task of interpreting available Burmese data. Tun Wai (1962: 42), a Burmese banking authority, presents consolidated balance sheets for Nakarattar liabilities and assets in 1929 and 1934, respectively, prepared for him by the Rangoon Nattukottai Chettiar Association (see Figures 4 and 5). Examination of the assets and liabilities for 1929 immediately indicates the highly liquid quality of Nakarattar assets prior to the depression: Tun Wai estimates that 100 percent of Nakarattar assets were in cash, *hundis,* or loans. After the depression, slightly less than 17 percent of Nakarattar assets were liquid; the balance was tied up in land and houses.

However, Tun Wai's classification is problematic on at least two counts. For one thing, he employs categories entitled "Deposits in Madras" and

ASSETS	
Cash in hand, *hundis* discounted, and advances made	Rs. 652 million
	Rs. 652 million
LIABILITIES	
Proprietors' and relatives' capital	Rs. 5.50 million
Deposits in Madras	2
Deposits in Burma	57
Advances from Madras banks (British?)	13
Advances from Burmese banks (British?)	30
	652 million

Figure 4. Consolidated balance sheet for estimated Nakarattar business operations in Burma, 1929. *Source:* Rangoon Nattukottai Chettiar Association in Tun Wai (1962: 42).

ASSETS	
Cash in hand, *hundis* discounted, and advances made	Rs. 100 million
Land and houses	650 million
	750 million
LIABILITIES	
Proprietors' and relatives' capital	Rs. 450 million
Deposits in Madras	225
Deposits in Burma	70
Advances from Madras banks	0
Advances from Burmese banks (British?)	5
	750 million

Figure 5. Consolidated balance sheet for estimated Nakarattar business operations in Burma, 1935–42. *Source:* Rangoon Nattukottai Chettiar Association in Tun Wai (1962: 42).

"Deposits in Burma" as liabilities. This is somewhat mysterious. Since the amounts under these categories appear as liabilities rather than assets, they cannot actually refer to deposits (i.e., assets) held in Madras and Burma. One wonders, therefore, whether they refer to advances from Nakarattars in Madras and Burma (probably in the form of two- or three-month term deposits, in the form of *thavanai hundi*—see Chapter 5). If so, the figures should recur under the heading "Assets" since one Nakarattar firm's deposit in another's Burmese agency was simultaneously an asset of the first and a liability of the second. They do not, in fact, recur in this fashion. Nevertheless, disregarding one or the other side of ledger entries for interfirm deposits is entirely consistent with the kinds of practices in which Nakarattars were caught out in Ceylon. So the question is left open.

A second problem arises in the category of liabilities that Tun Wai lists as "Proprietor's and Relatives' Capital." He is careful to acknowledge the difference between these two categories in his text, identifying them correctly by their Nakarattar terms as *mudal panam* and *sontha thavanai panam,* respectively. He also notes that the proprietor's capital generally made up only 5–10 percent of a Nakarattar banker's capital, while the proprietor's relatives' share made up 60–70 percent. But he never explores the implications of this Nakarattar distinction. Indeed, it never arises again in his analysis and was dismissed in the construction of his chart.

I explore the varieties of Nakarattar deposits in more detail in Chapter 5. For the present, suffice it to say that the significance of the distinction between the proprietor's capital and Nakarattar deposits of various kinds, still to be explored, cannot be overemphasized. Keeping it firmly in mind, the lesson from Tun Wai's balance sheets and his additional comments in the text is, once again, that Nakarattars provided a considerable amount of their working capital from interfirm loans, including their *sontha thavanai panam* deposits from relatives. These were further complemented by loans from British exchange banks and the Imperial bank. They used very little of their own capital in carrying out their banking business. To place the issue in comparative perspective, the Nakarattars used what is known in Western financial circles as "leverage."

Driven by the world demand for rice and financed by Nakarattar banking operations, Burmese agriculture proved itself the most lucrative Nakarattar investment in British India. By 1929, the number of Nakarattar firms operating in Burma had reached 1,498 (BPBEC 1930 I: 195–196). By 1930, they had channeled from 60 to 80 percent of their total assets into Burmese business: by some estimates, Rs. 750 million (see above). Their role was perhaps even greater than in Ceylon. As they were the primary financiers of Burma's rice industry, their impact is directly visible in statistical measures of the growth of paddy acreage, of expanding rice and paddy exports, and of the wholesale price of paddy in Rangoon markets (see Figures 6–9). The consequences of the world depression were no less remarkable. As commodities dropped and Nakarattar clients were no longer able to meet their interest payments on loans, Nakarattars foreclosed on mortgages and wound up owning over three million acres, roughly 30 percent of all Burmese rice-producing land.

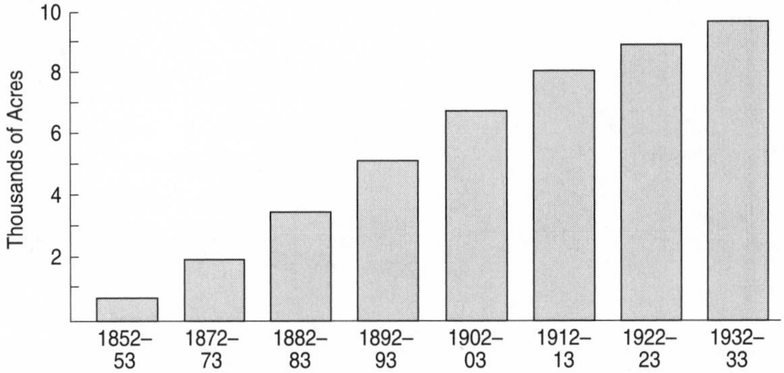

Figure 6. Acreage under paddy cultivation in Lower Burma, selected years, 1852–1933. *Source:* Furnivall (1956: 56–57).

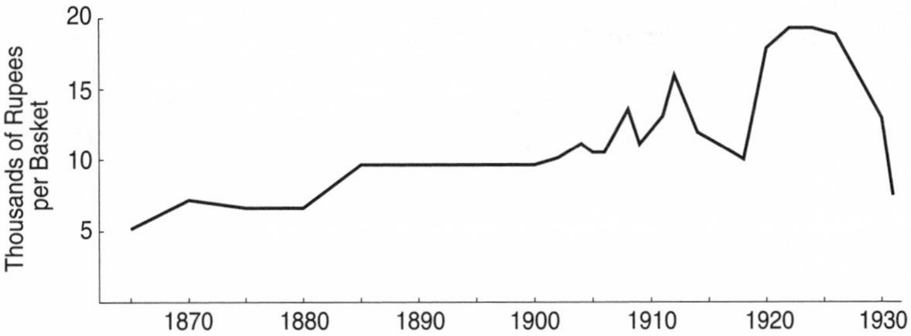

Figure 7. Wholesale price of paddy in Rangoon markets, 1865–1931. *Source:* Cheng (1968: 73); reproduced in Mahadevan (1978a: 341).

Malaya in the Late Nineteenth and Early Twentieth Centuries

A similar process of British pacification and integration into the world economy occurred in Malaya. Again, Nakarattar capital followed the British flag. Arriving at the newly opened British ports of Malacca, Penang, and Singapore in the first third of the nineteenth century, Nakarattars quickly moved to dominate the Asian opium market by extending credit to Chinese traders. By the 1870s and 1880s, they financed most of the opium trade in Singapore and Penang and monopolized a position as intermediaries between British exchange banks and Chinese traders. According to Compton Mackenzie's study of the Chartered Bank of India, Australia, and China, most of that British bank's business

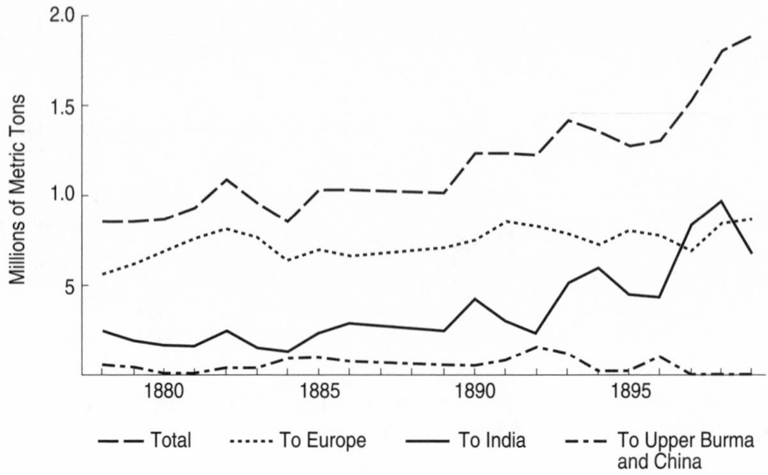

Figure 8. Exports of rice from Lower Burma, by destination, 1878–86 and 1889–99. Actual figures are available for only eleven months; one month is estimated. *Source:* Siegelman (1962: 105). Figures for 1878–86 based on Report on the Administration of Upper Burma during 1886 (1887: 27). Figures for 1889–99 based on Nisbet (1901: 431).

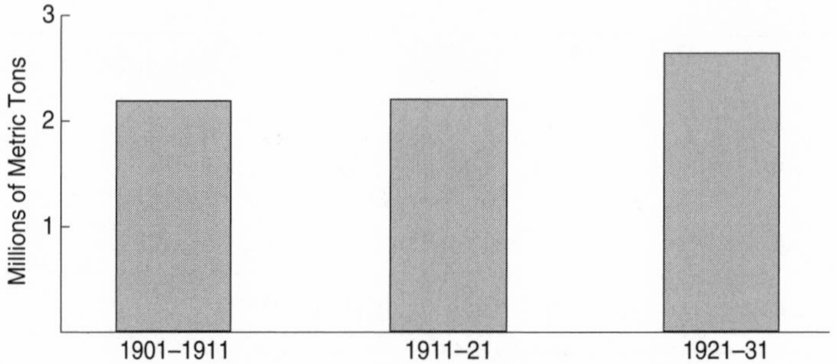

Figure 9. Decennial export of rice and paddy from Burma, 1901–31. *Source:* Cheng (1968: 201); reproduced in Mahadevan (1978a: 241).

with local non-Europeans consisted in the discount of Chinese promissory notes made over to Nakarattar bankers (MacKenzie 1954: 108–112; see also Allen and Donnithorne 1957: 204–405; Mahadevan 1978b: 147). In fact, Nakarattars obtained most of their Malayan revenue in this way: discounting (i.e., cashing) Chinese promissory notes and bills of exchange and rediscounting them at European banks (Allen and Donnithorne 1957: 205). The European banks were not willing to extend discounting services directly to Chinese traders themselves, but they were quite happy to deal with agents for the largest Nakarattar firms. Nakarattar profits were generated by the difference between their discount rate and the British discount rate.

When, beginning in 1914, the British moved in a major way to dig mines and build plantations in Malaya, the Nakarattars were positioned to provide their customary financial services. The opening up of the Malayan interior to commodity production for international trade followed the same "developing frontier" pattern as in Burma (Allen and Donnithorne 1957; MacKenzie 1954; Mahadevan 1978b; Sandhu 1969). In 1900, in Malayan territory there were perhaps 5,000 acres devoted to rubber cultivation; in 1911, there were 543,000 acres; in 1938, there were 3,272,000 acres (Mahadevan 1978b: 147). Malayan production of rubber to meet the growing world demand is also measured by her exports of rubber (see Figure 10).

The biggest beneficiaries were undoubtedly European firms such as Dunlop or Guthries (Allen and Donnithorne 1957: 112–114). But Nakarattars, who secured loans with mortgages to rubber gardens and plantations and who—at least in the case of the largest firms—invested money directly in the purchase of rubber estates, wound up in 1938 with most of the 87,795 acres owned by Indians in Malaya (Arasaratnam 1970: 96; Mahadevan 1978b: 150; Sandhu 1969: 288). Malaya's tin industry developed simultaneously with her rubber industry. As recently as 1910, the Chinese controlled more than three-quarters of the tin industry. But shortly after this, the Europeans moved in and, by 1930, controlled more than three-fifths of Malaya's tin export (Allen and Donnithorne 1957: 42; Mahadevan 1978b: 149; Sandhu 1969: 279). Meanwhile, tin exports rose from 40,000 tons in 1895 to 67,000 tons in 1929 (Mahadevan 1978b: 149; Sandhu 1969: 279). Like the owners of rubber gardens and plantations, tin mine owners (especially Chinese and Malayan owners) found difficulty in obtaining credit from European bankers and frequently turned to Nakarattars. This situation, in turn, introduced the Nakarattars to direct investment in mining, both through foreclosure on defaulted loans and through direct purchase.

The depression of the 1930s hit Malaya's export-oriented colonial economy just as it had Burma's. Prices on tin and rubber plummeted. The immediate effects were witnessed in widespread default and foreclosure on loans and the consequent transfer of property to Nakarattar banking firms. The government attempted to stop this transfer in 1931 by introducing the "Small Holding (Restriction of Sale) Bill" under which no sale of land in

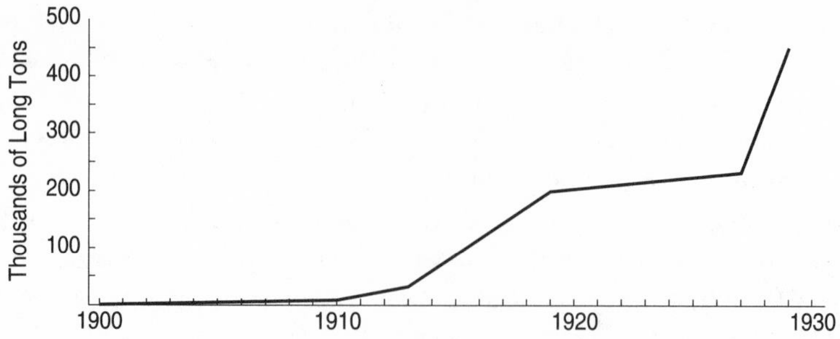

Figure 10. Exports of crude rubber from Malaya, selected years, 1900–1929. *Source:* Mahadevan (1978b: 147), based on Allen and Donnithorne (1957: 295).

excess of twenty-five acres could be sold without the consent of the State. Many small Nakarattar firms went bankrupt, as did some medium- and large-size firms. But in general the effects were not catastrophic to the degree that they were in Burma, and many Nakarattars remained and continued to invest and profit in various sectors of Malaya's economy.

A Final Comment on Nakarattar Commercial Expansion

Nakarattar businessmen boasted a remarkably successful commercial record during the colonial period. They outcompeted other groups for an important slot in the Southeast Asian credit market. They doubled their assets every ten years for the thirty-year period for which figures are available (1900–1939; Pillai 1930 I: 186). Even the brief overview of their investment activities given above reveals their impact in financing much of Burma's rice industry, much of Malaya's tin and rubber trade, the Southeast Asian opium trade, and an important part of Ceylon's plantation economy. I have not described the similar role they played in Indochina.[46] But for the period from 1870 to 1930, the pattern of their specialization as a merchant-banking caste with a uniquely important role in Southeast Asian society is beyond question.

Nakarattar success was clearly linked to their ability to master the changing institutional framework of British colonial government and to act as middlemen between the colonial government and colonial society at large. The dramatic economic expansion of the caste as a whole can only be understood as a consequence of the effectiveness of the system of Nakarattar social organization for carrying out activities of financial intermediation, capital accumulation, and investment.

5 Banker's Trust and the Culture of Banking

Banker's Trust?

The notion of "banker's trust" has a paradoxical quality, like "burning cold" or "military intelligence." Common sense (another paradoxical notion) tells us that bankers have no trust. Perhaps this feeling explains the appeal of Marxist and Weberian assumptions that capitalist economies tend to destroy precapitalist social formations based on trust. From the classic perspective, primordial social ties mandate relations of trust (or something like them) in kin groups and castes only so long as the members of these groups do not operate directly—as bankers do—within a capitalist economic system. The classic view is reinforced by recent influential studies of indigenous Indian commerce during the colonial period. According to historians such as Christopher Bayly (1981, 1983) and David Washbrook (1975, 1976), powerful merchants traded goods and credit within complex networks that transcended ties of kinship and elevated ties of class over ties of caste. The implication, again, is that caste and kinship played little or no role in the emerging capitalist economy of colonial India.

Yet ties of caste and kinship can make substantial contributions to a capitalist's enterprise. And trust is an essential ingredient for making loans or deposits, regardless of whether a banker and client maintain a primordial or a contractual relationship. The present chapter suggests that, in at least the case of the Nakarattars, even merchant-bankers whose businesses crosscut caste boundaries relied on caste and kin organization for a significant proportion of their credit needs. Nakarattars built their commercial empire out of a complex network of interdependent family business firms. Each firm was involved in commodities trading, money lending, domestic and overseas banking operations, or industrial investment. Beyond this specialization—making possible every other commercial venture in which it engaged—each family firm operated as a commercial bank: taking money on deposit and drafting bills and other financial instruments for use in the transfer of lendable capital to branch offices and to other banks. As a result, every Nakarattar firm was tied together with all of the others to form a unified banking system.

This is not to say that the banking system resembled an economist's model of Western-style banking systems. In the Nakarattar system, banking firms as well as other communal institutions were all tied together by relationships of territory, descent, marriage, and common cult membership (see Chapters 8, 9 and 10). In other words, the Nakarattar banking system was a caste-based banking system. Nevertheless, Nakarattar and Western-style banking systems shared two fundamental properties: (1) they maintained networks of individual banks which directly or indirectly invested and deposited funds in one another; and (2) these networks supported special institutions for accumulating and distributing reserves of capital that affected rates of interest and the cost and supply of credit and money. The present chapter explores Nakarattar financial transactions and the financial instruments that were transacted.

Nakarattar Interest Rates and Deposit Banking

Nakarattars took two primary considerations into account when they made a financial transaction: (a) the nature of the social relationship established by the transaction, and (b) the conditions under which the principal amount of the transaction needed to be returned to the creditor. On this dual basis Nakarattar bankers distinguished four basic kinds of deposits and many kinds of loans. My concern here is only with deposits.

Nakarattar bankers accepted two kinds of current deposits into *kadai kanakkus* ("shop" accounts). These comprised demand deposits and a uniquely Nakarattar transaction called a *nadappu* or "walking" deposit (discussed below). Nakarattars also accepted fixed-term (two-, three-, or six-month) deposits from fellow Nakarattars into *thavanai kanakkus* ("resting" accounts) and fixed-term deposits from non-Nakarattars into *vayan vatti kanakkus* (fixed-interest accounts). The interest rate for *nadappu* deposits served as a benchmark for rates paid on other deposits and in this respect was similar to the prime lending rate set by the central bank of a modern nation-state. The *nadappu* rate represented the interest that Nakarattars paid each other for deposits made into their *kadai kanakku* accounts. The rate was established on the sixteenth day of every month at meetings of Nakarattar bankers in major business centers—notably, Devakottai, Madras, Colombo, Penang, and Rangoon. *Kadai kanakku* deposits paid simple interest at the *nadappu* rate calculated for the period during which a deposit was maintained. By contrast, *thavanai* deposits paid compound interest calculated by adding the appropriate increment to the principal at intervals of two, three, or six months, depending on the terms of the deposit. *Vayan vatti* deposits paid interest at a rate calculated by the addition of a few annas per month over the *nadappu* rate (1 anna = 1/16 rupee). But, like *kadai kanakku* deposits, they paid only simple interest.[1]

These Nakarattar interest-setting practices established a staggered system of interest rates, which had two consequences. First, it allowed bankers to attract relatively cheap *nadappu* deposits from fellow Nakarattars for use in current accounts, subject to unpredictable demand. Second, it allowed them to attract more expensive, but more predictable, fixed-term *thavanai* deposits from fellow Nakarattars with no immediate cash-flow crisis. In both cases, Nakarattars assured themselves of access to deposit capital at a cost that was cheaper than the *vayan vatti* rate paid to non-Nakarattars, and far cheaper than the interest charges incurred by borrowing money in secured or unsecured loans (see Appendix A).

One aspect of Nakarattar techniques for establishing and standardizing interest rates deserves comment in the present context. The procedure is described in the Report of the Burma Provincial Banking Enquiry Committee:

> [The *nadappu* rate] is fixed in the evening of the 16th of every Tamil month at a meeting held at 9 p.m. in the Nakarattar temple at Rangoon, and it holds good for all the current Nakarattar month including the sixteen days already passed. . . . The meeting discusses the general financial situation, and fixes the current [*nadappu*] rate for the current month with this, taking into account the current pitch and tendency of the thavanai rate, the rates current amongst the Marwaris, Multanis, and Gujeratis [other Indian banking castes] and the rates for advances by the joint-stock banks to Nakarattars. As every firm has both income and expenses determined largely by this rate, great care is taken to fix the rate according to the needs of the situation. But for the first sixteen days of the month before the rate is fixed, there is a general consensus of opinion as to the rate that will be fixed, the weekly adjustment of thavanai rate and the discussions incidental to that adjustment being sufficient guide. (BPBEC 1930 I: 225)

According to this description, the relationship between *nadappu* and *thavanai* rates gave mathematical priority to the former in that the simple *nadappu* rate was taken as the basis for calculating compound interest payments on *thavanai* deposits. In practice, however, *nadappu* rates were fit to the fluctuating interest paid on *thavanai* rates; that is, they were fit to interest rates that Nakarattars were willing to pay in order to maintain a predictable reserve of capital in the form of *thavanai* deposits. Prior to the 1920s, determining the *thavanai* rate had apparently been a relatively informal affair, subject to competition among Nakarattars for deposits. But by 1920, the *thavanai* rate was "fixed in a systematic way every Sunday morning at 9 o'clock by a meeting in Rangoon temple, subject to modification during the week in case that [was] generally desired by the community. . . . It [was] not fixed according to the current [*nadappu*] rate; in fact the relationship [was] the other way about, the course of the thavanai rate being a consideration when fixing the current rate" (BPBEC 1930 I: 227).

The significance of this procedure in the present context is the light it casts on the Nakarattar understanding of banking. For Nakarattars, the primary consideration in setting interest rates was to attract fixed-term *thavanai* deposits and thereby maintain a predictable reserve of capital to underwrite the full range of their credit-extending activities. Without this ability, each individual banker would have had to depend on his own personal capital to finance money lending and commodities trading. But, by working together in a reliable and systematic way, by setting interest rates, and by ensuring each other inexpensive access to deposit capital, Nakarattars were able to draw upon the collective assets of the entire caste.

This is not to say that each Nakarattar attracted deposits from all Nakarattars. The system as a whole was divided into local segments, based on residential and kinship groupings as well as on the location of agency houses. Membership in these different segments was not exclusive, and Nakarattars maintained crosscutting ties in various differently constituted segments. But segmentation did not eliminate the flow of deposit capital. Rather, it created the channels through which capital flowed, by defining social and financial distances between bankers. Finally, the largest Nakarattar bankers, called *adathis* or parent bankers, functioned as linchpins for the entire system by acting as clearinghouses for the transfer of financial instruments from firms who might have no dealings with each other but who shared a common relationship with an *adathi.*

Hundi *Transactions and Other Transfers of Credit between Nakarattars*

The major Nakarattar financial instrument for all transactions was the *hundi,* a kind of bill of exchange or written order for payment that its drawers used much in the way that Americans use checks drawn on their checking accounts. In order to draw a *hundi,* a client had to open an account and maintain a correspondence relationship with a banker.[2]

Hundis were sometimes used just to transfer funds from one location to another (a service employed primarily by Nakarattars among themselves), but they were more typically employed in financing trade transactions by Nakarattars and non-Nakarattars alike. Tun Wai (1962: 50) estimates that, before 1930, perhaps 75 percent of Nakarattar *hundis* in Burma were trade *hundis.* In such cases, a paddy merchant, for example, bought a shipment of paddy at a local market in Burma with cash that he transferred to the seller by drawing a *hundi* on his account in a local Nakarattar banking office. The Nakarattar banker cashed the *hundi,* receiving a discounting fee of 1 to 3 percent, and took custody of the railroad receipt for the paddy shipment, even though the transaction was not a loan and did not incur rates of interest charged on loans. The banker sent the *hundi* and the receipt to his firm's main office in Rangoon along with instructions to debit the merchant's account. If the banker had no office in Rangoon, he sent the *hundi* and receipt to another banker (perhaps, but not necessarily, an *adathi*) with whom he maintained an account. The first banker could thus rediscount the *hundi* with the second banker, who normally extended the service without charging a further discounting fee. In order to regain the railway receipt and take possession of his paddy from either banker, the merchant had to maintain a deposit account with the Rangoon banker in a satisfactory manner.[3]

Nakarattars made use of four basic *hundis:*

1. *Dharsan hundis,* or demand drafts (literally, "sight" *hundis*), were payable against a *kadai kanakku* account within three days of presentation to a person and at a place specified in the *hundi.*
2. *Nadappu hundis* (literally, "walking" *hundis*) were also payable against a *kadai kanakku* account. *Nadappu hundis* were instruments unique to Nakarattars and were neither demand drafts nor fixed-period, term drafts but instead were cashed at the convenience of the banker (the drawee), whose only obligation was to pay interest at the *nadappu* rate to the person who drew the *hundi* until the *hundi* was cashed.
3. *Thavanai hundis* (literally, "resting" *hundis*) were payable against *thavanai* accounts and operated like short-term certificates of deposit. The bankers (the drawees) did not need to pay on demand until after the specified date, usually sixty to ninety days after the bill was drawn.[4] Their term to maturity was called a *thavanai,* a "period of rest."

4. *Pay order hundis* were used as receipts given in lieu of dowry payments made during a marriage ceremony. They were drawn against special compound-interest-bearing *thavanai* accounts known as *accimar panam* accounts (discussed below).[5]

Available information about *dharsan* and *nadappu hundis* is generally confusing and inconsistent. For example, although most authorities suggest that all Nakarattar demand drafts paid interest at the *nadappu* rate, examination of sample *hundis* reproduced in the Report of the Madras Provincial Banking Enquiry Committee (1930) reveals a subset of *dharsan hundis* that paid no interest (see Appendix B).

In fact, this inconsistency is less problematic than the suggestion that both *hundis* paid identical interest at the *nadappu* rate. If it was the case that no *dharsan hundi* paid interest, people would have paid the *dharsan* discount fee only if they wanted to transfer capital and guarantee cashing at their convenience rather than their banker's. They would have drawn *nadappu hundis* only if they had no expectation of any cash-flow crisis, if they viewed their *nadappu* deposits as safe interest-bearing deposits, and if they had no worries about their banker's ultimate ability and willingness to cash the *hundi.* The fact is, however, that some *dharsan hundis* did pay interest. Their availability creates a puzzle because the liquidity of *dharsan hundis* would have eliminated any incentive to draw *nadappu hundis,* which had an identical yield but uncertain conditions of cashing. One possible solution is that Nakarattar bankers may have had sufficient control over mechanisms for transferring funds to withhold *dharsan hundis* from clients and, instead, to offer *nadappu hundis* as the only available option. Another and even more likely solution is that the drawing of *hundis* was quite a flexible matter and hinged on the specific situation of drawer and drawee. This explanation would account for inconsistency on the part of analysts attempting to construct a uniform model of Nakarattar *hundis.*

The kind of flexibility that seems to be suggested by the evidence of *hundis* themselves raises another problem, however, because Nakarattar bankers also offered clients facilities for drawing sixty- to ninety-day *thavanai* deposits. It is not clear why anyone should wish to deposit his money at the lower *nadappu* rate of interest unless he was assured of definite repayment more quickly than the terms to maturity offered by *thavanai hundis.* We can only assume that the actual performance of Nakarattar bankers confirmed their financial trustworthiness and ability to meet demands for repayment without causing unacceptable cost or delay.[6]

Hundis were not regulated under colonial laws concerning negotiable instruments and were distinguished from "true" bills of exchange on the ground that their terms for encashment were not unconditionally specified. In general, the *hundis* specified two conditions of payment: (1) they indicated the particular fund which the drawer was to reimburse or a particular account which was to be debited with the amount, and (2) they included a statement of the transaction which gave rise to the bill. In addition, *nadappu hundis* specified no obligatory conditions for cashing whatsoever. Because of the former stipulations and because of the absence of stipulations about payment in the case of *nadappu hundis,* all Nakarattar *hundis* fell outside the scope of the Negotiable Instruments Act, and hence were legally unenforceable (MPBEC 1930 I: 51–52; BPBEC 1930: 150, also cited in Tun Wai 1962: 50; Krishnan 1959: 53).

Despite this lack of stipulation, it is important not to invest the legal view of *hundis* as nonnegotiable with more significance than it deserves, especially when that view coincides with an unclear understanding about the sanctions and procedures under which *hundis* were actually drawn. Although Nakarattar *hundis* had no standing in a court of law, Nakarattar bankers made collective decisions about interest rates that standardized the cost of credit. In addition, their own communal tribunals (*panchayats*) and their practice of maintaining custody of railway and shipping receipts on trade *hundis* provided a check on dishonest practices. In other words, together with careful accounting procedures (see below) and a practice of systematic correspondence between cooperating bankers, the various collective Nakarattar institutions effectively regulated transactions and minimized the risk of default to a remarkable extent. Indeed, one banking expert, whose personal knowledge of the system allowed him to keep the law in perspective, notes: "In the case of 136 firms doing business in Chettinad to the extent of 11 crores of rupees [Rs. 110,000,000] the bad debts come to only Rs. 4.3 lakhs [Rs. 430,000] which works out to 1/2 percent on the total volume of business" (Krishnan 1959: 41).

Accounting

The clearest evidence for reconstructing the Nakarattars' financial activities during the colonial period is contained in account books and ledgers maintained during the heyday of their Southeast Asian commercial empire. In many cases, these books may presently be found moldering and ant-eaten in dusty corners of the great houses of Chettinad, the Nakarattar homeland in Tamil Nadu. The detailed record that they leave us of commercial activities throughout South India and Southeast Asia represents a still untapped resource for historians. But it is one that is rapidly vanishing and merits attention before the opportunity is irrevocably lost. The following discussion is based on analysis of account books maintained by a large Burmese agency for the years 1912–1915 and 1918–1921. I refer to these books primarily to describe Nakarattar accounting categories and the sources of capital available to a Nakarattar agency. I do not use them to characterize the specific financial role of this firm (let alone of Nakarattars taken collectively) in the context of Burmese and Nakarattar commercial history.

I carried out my analysis with the assistance of a retired Nakarattar banker, who deciphered both the standard Tamil alphabetic code employed for numerals and the handwriting of the agency's bookkeepers.[7] Even more importantly, he interpreted the different categories of entries and explained to me some of the strategy that went into operating a successful business operation in Burma. With his help, it was possible to clarify many aspects of Nakarattar business practice that remain vague in descriptions supplied by the reports of the Banking Enquiry Committees of Burma, Ceylon, and Madras.

Nakarattar account books were designed to accomplish many functions. One book, called a *peredu,* recorded all payments and receipts. My informant claimed that it represented a general ledger and that it employed double-entry bookkeeping. I am not at present prepared to grant the accuracy of these English glosses of a technical Tamil accounting vocabulary, as the ledgers do not, in fact, appear to comply with the principles of double-entry bookkeeping. The *peredu* I examined seemed to consist of a number of subsidiary ledgers describing various transactions and listing the associated payments or receipts in two separate columns: one for credit entries (*adhaya*) and one for debit entries (*varavu*). Unlike the transactions in an American double-entry bookkeeping system, however, each transaction was recorded as a single entry. There was no simultaneous entry crediting or debiting the agency's cash account for the same amount. Instead, the two columns of figures describing each account seemed to provide a way of correlating the expenses incurred by the account with the income it generated. In some cases, this gave the appearance of a standard, Western-style double-entry system (i.e., where credits equal debits). But this similarity was purely accidental, or else it reflected some real-world understanding that existed between banker and client, rather than a bookkeeping procedure. Since this is a point about which there is some confusion, it is worth emphasizing that a *peredu's* debit and credit entries seemed to represent clearly separate transactions and frequently showed a net difference between credits and debits. Nevertheless, its correlation of income and expenses incurred by an account may be what my informant meant by double-entry bookkeeping. It is also the case that each column of figures recorded in the *peredu* maintained a running total and provided a final net balance for each year. But I could locate no general ledger summarizing all of the various transactions, nor any overall balance sheet. In other words, a *peredu* lacked the defining characteristics of a Western-style general ledger.[8]

In general, the function of Nakarattar books was to provide a picture of an agency's relationship with each of its clients, with separate listings of expenses and revenues. This function served the interests of both the agent and his client. Entries were carefully made on the occasion of any financial transaction, rather like in a passbook in a U.S. savings bank. In some cases, they were even initialed by the client. In any case, the information these ledgers contained could, in principle, have been pulled together into a general ledger and a balance sheet. But they were not. In Table 7, I provide a list of the different kinds of subsidiary ledgers apparently contained in the *peredu* of a Burmese agency house. Figure 11 represents my own provisional summary of these figures, utilizing a general ledger projected on the basis of information contained in the *peredu* ledgers. And Figure 12 provides a balance sheet for the agency for the period under review.[9]

Nakarattar books were not confined to the various component ledgers constituting a *peredu*. They also included a *pekki pustakam*, a subsidiary book containing figures for outstanding dues, debts, and deposits. No record of payments or receipts was maintained in the *pekki pustakam*. However, a separate book of *vatti chittis* (interest calculation sheets) did provide records of interest payments for clients who maintained deposits with the agency. A daily cash book (*kurippu*) kept track of the complicated transactions that went on every day. The amounts listed as paid or received in the *kurippu* may also have been recorded in the last component ledger of the *peredu*. But, because these final entries lack any description of the content of transactions they record, I am not entirely confident about this interpretation. Finally, copies of all correspondence were maintained in a *press copy book*. I was unable to recover any Tamil name for this book. It consisted of carbon tracings—"press copies"—of all correspondence.[10] Taken together, the information contained in these Nakarattar books of account and correspondence cast considerable light on the role of this particular agency at this specific period in history. But, as already indicated, the present paper confines itself to a structural analysis of the agency's relationships with its various depositors, especially as these are captured in the *peredu* accounting categories of the Burmese agency whose books were available to me.

Table 7. Summary of Ledgers of a *Peredu* Account Book for a Rangoon Agency, 1915–19

Subsidiary Ledger	*Credit (rupees)*	*Debit (rupees)*
(1) Auspicious credits in the name of various deities (expense: cash paid to deities' accounts)	23	23
(2) Capital remitted from overseas headquarters	21,000	21,000
(3) *Adhaya-varavu* (profit and loss account): net receipt after deducting interest payments due on deposits kept (primarily interest receipts)	74,649	74,649
(4) Salary summaries	n/a	n/a
(5) Capital remitted to overseas headquarters	20,877	20,877
(6) Interest payments and miscellaneous expenses	51,515	51,515
(7) Long-term deposits of Nakarattars (34 clients)	75,262	75,262
(8) Fixed assets purchased during year	57	57
(9) Charitable expenses	216	216
(10) Firm's business expenses in Cambodia	3,656	3,656
(11) Short-term (two-month) deposits (156 clients)	—	—
(12) Firm's business in Maniyuva branch	70,377	69,077
(13) Local Nakara Dandayuthapani Temple accounts and deposits by other Nakarattar firms on behalf of various temples	6,545	6,545
(14) Deposits kept by Nemam Temple	77,300	77,300
(15) Deposits from Burmese and Chinese VIPs and from Indian friends (many bearing no interest)	—	—
(16) Other current accounts (demand deposits)	—	—

Note: Dashes indicate that no totals were available.

CASH		ASSETS		LIABILITIES		INCOME	EXPENSES
Debit	Credit	Debit	Credit	Debit	Credit		
(1) Rs. 23	(1) Rs. 23				(1) Rs. 23		(1) Rs. 23
(2) 21,000					(2) 21,000		
(3) 74,649						(3)Rs. 74,649	
	(5) 20,877			(5) Rs. 20,877			
	(6) 51,515						(6) 51,515
(7) 75,262					(7) 75,262		
	(8) 57						
	(9) 216						(9) 216
	(10) 3,656						(10) 3,656
(12) 70,377	(12) 2,854					(12) 67,523	
(13) 6,545					(13) 6,545		
(14) 77,300					(14) 77,300		
325,156	79,198			20,877	180,130		
(Balance) 245,958					(Balance) 159,253	142,172	55,410

Figure 11. Provisional general ledger for a Rangoon agency, 1915–19. (For key to numbered accounts, see Table 7.)

ASSETS	
Cash	Rs. 245,958
Other assets	57
	246,015
LIABILITIES	
(including expenses)	159,253
RETAINED EARNINGS	142,172
	−55,410
	86,762
	246,015

Figure 12. Provisional balance sheet for a Rangoon agency, 1915–19.

Proprietor's Capital and Deposit Capital from Other Nakarattars

Before presenting my analysis, I wish to emphasize an important distinction between, on the one hand, governmental classifications of total Nakarattar assets and, on the other hand, Nakarattar accounting categories employed as part of individual business operations. This distinction is important because most analyses of Nakarattar capital are concerned with the former and base their classifications on testimony and interviews with members of the Madras, Rangoon, or Colombo Nattukottai Nakarattar Associations, presented to various Provincial Banking Enquiry Committees around 1930. In general, these documents estimate that the ratio of Nakarattar "borrowed capital" to "own capital" was between 15 percent and 35 percent. The report of the Burma Provincial Banking Enquiry Committee (1930 I: 211–219) provides the highest estimate of the proportion of borrowed capital in Nakarattar operations, noting that "out of total Nakarattar working capital of over 75 crores [Rs. 750 million], over 2/3rds, i.e., 53.5 crores [Rs. 535 million], was the capital of the proprietors or partners of the firm; 11.5 crores [Rs. 115 million] were deposits from Nakarattars, and Rs. 10 crores [Rs. 100 million] was the sum borrowed from the European banks and non-Nakarattars."

Based on this and similar kinds of testimony about the distribution of Nakarattar assets, authorities such as Pillai (1930 I: 186) and Tun Wai (1962) draw conclusions about aggregate Nakarattar liabilities. As noted in Chapter 4, for example, Tun Wai (1962: 42) makes use of figures supplied by Nakarattar expert witnesses when he classifies Nakarattar liabilities in predepression and postdepression Burma, noting that the Nakarattars' own capital represented 60 percent of all their capital in 1929 and 84 percent in 1935. Examination of the assets and liabilities for 1929 (Figure 4) confirms the highly liquid quality of Nakarattar assets prior to the depression described in Chapter 4. Tun Wai estimates that 100 percent of Nakarattar assets were in cash, *hundis,* or loans at that time. By contrast, their 1935 assets and liabilities (Figure 5) indicate the impact of the depression on the liquidity of these assets. The point I wish to emphasize here, however, is Tun Wai's primary focus on the overall role of the Nakarattars in Burma. He is not concerned with either the social or the financial implications of distinctions that Nakarattars made in accounting categories used by individual businessmen. This is because, like expert witnesses from the Rangoon or Madras Nakarattar associations, Tun Wai was not describing the capital structure of an individual agency or firm, but the aggregate capital of the entire caste's operations in Burma.

By contrast, as Tun Wai notes, Nakarattar businessmen did need to maintain accounts of individual transactions, and they were careful to distinguish between the proprietors' own capital (*mudal panam*) and deposits by close relatives (*sontha thavanai panam*). Unfortunately, not all authorities are as careful as Tun Wai and some, apparently, succumb to a temptation to generalize from the characterization of aggregate Nakarattar capital to the capital structure of individual Nakarattar firms and agencies. Such commentators simply assume that the aggregate category, made up of funds owned by all Nakarattars and their relatives, is identical to an individual Nakarattar businessman's classification of his own personal capital. Philip Siegelman (1962: 157), for example, even glosses Tun Wai's combined category of proprietor's and relatives' capital with the Nakarattar term for just the proprietor's capital, *mudal panam.* Once such assumptions are made, the conclusion is obvious: Nakarattar banking relied very little on deposits. But this conclusion is not supported by available evidence. On the contrary, it is clear from information contained in Nakarattar account books and from interviews with surviving Nakarattar bankers that there are major differences between aggregate classifications of Nakarattar assets provided to banking enquiry committees and the nonaggregated classifications of liabilities that Nakarattars employed in their own account books. One of the most significant differences reflects precisely the importance of different kinds of deposits just among Nakarattars themselves.

My informants all confirm Tun Wai's interpretation of *mudal panam* as confined in its application to proprietor's capital only. But none of them employed the single contrasting category of *sontha thavanai panam.* Instead, my Nakarattar informants offered a variety of terms segmenting the domain of relatives and kinship. It is likely that *sontha thavanai panam* was an umbrella term for deposits from any kin (*contakkarar*). Bankers whom I consulted, however, did not use this term at all, but rather the term *mempanam* ("surplus funds") as an even more-embracing umbrella category to refer to any deposit besides the proprietor's own *mudal panam*. This category included deposits by relatives such as *accimar panam* (dowry deposits from in-laws) and dowry deposits from any other Nakarattar outside the joint family (*valavu*) that owned the firm. In addition, *mempanam* also included deposits from non-kin Nakarattars and from non-Nakarattars. The different subcategories of *mempanam* funds are identified as follows:[11]

1. *mudal panam:* principal's personal funds
2. *mempanam:* all other funds
   a. *accimar panam:* literally, deposits from Nakarattar women; usually dowry monies of wife and daughters-in-law of the proprietor—his affinal relatives (*tayati*)
   b. *thanadumural panam* or *thandu morai panam:* deposits from other Nakarattars including agnatic relatives from the proprietor's lineage (*kuttikkira pankali*) and clan (*kovil*) and non-kin from his own and neighboring villages[12]
   c. *kovil panam* or *dharma panam:* deposits from Nakarattar-controlled or -influenced temples
   d. *adathi kadai panam:* loans from Nakarattar "parent banks" (*adathis*)
   e. deposits from Burmese or Chinese clients
   f. *vellaikkaran panam:* loans from European banks, available to only 3–4 percent of Nakarattar bankers—the largest *adathis* or parent banks.

If we isolate entries for the *mempanam* deposits in the *peredu* available to me (corresponding to its items 1, 7, 13, and 14 in Table 7 and Figure 11) and compare them with entries credited to the proprietor's headquarters account (item 2), the lesson is startling. In this agency, at least, *mudal panam*—the proprietor's own capital—did not constitute 65 to 85 percent of its sources of funds, as it would have if there had been a direct correspondence between, on the one hand, the proportion of aggregate Nakarattar-owned funds to all Nakarattar working capital in Burma and, on the other hand, the proportion of an individual proprietor's own capital contribution to the total working capital of his agency house. Instead, the proprietor's funds in this specific agency constituted barely 12.5 percent of the funds deposited by his relatives.

To summarize, Nakarattar proprietors generally contributed 10 to 20 percent of the working capital of their agency offices in the form of long-term *thavanai* deposits. These were frequently repaid to the proprietor in a sequence of regular remittances during the course of his agent's three-year tenure as head of the agency house. Conventions for financial transactions between a banking agency and its clients also depended on maintenance of deposit accounts with the agency. According to Krishnan (1959: 125), non-Nakarattar deposits made up, at most, another 20 percent of an individual agency's working capital. In other words, taking into account the proprietor's own deposits (*mudal panam*) and various kinds of non-Nakarattar deposits, it is possible to estimate the proportion of working capital contributed by deposits from other Nakarattar firms as being between 60 and 80 percent of all deposits. Again, this calculation is supported by books from the Burmese agency analyzed above.

One final feature of Nakarattar financial transactions should also be remarked in connection with the distinction between Nakarattar and non-Nakarattar clients. In the case of non-Nakarattar clients, transactions were always recorded on a cash basis; that is, only actual cash receipts and disbursements were entered in a firm's ledger. By contrast, transactions between Nakarattars (including between the proprietor and his own agency) were recorded on a mercantile or accrual basis; that is, they credited each other with the appropriate amount of interest due and exchanged *vatti chitti* sheets (memoranda of interest calculations). The accounts they held with each other were normally reconciled only at three-year intervals, coinciding with the termination of a Nakarattar agent's tenure as head of a banking agency.

Conclusion

It bears emphasizing that Nakarattars loaned and deposited money with one another in caste-defined social relationships based on business territory, residential location, descent, marriage, and common cult membership. Unlike the case in modern Western banking systems, it was transactions between exchange spheres defined according to these principles, rather than decisions by a government-controlled central bank, that regulated reserve levels and assured public confidence in individual Nakarattars as representatives of the entire caste. In other words, the Nakarattar banking system was a caste-based banking system. Individual Nakarattars organized their lives around the participation and management of various communal institutions adapted to the task of accumulating and distributing reserves of capital. The financial transactions in which they engaged created an ensemble of social relations that constituted the Nakarattars as a particular kind of community: a financial community that functioned as both a caste and a bank within the wider Indian society.

6 A Collectivist Spirit of Capitalism

Two Spirits of Capitalism

There are a great many similarities to be drawn between Nakarattar bankers and Weber's Protestant capitalists. The most important of these is undoubtedly the systematic and methodical pursuit of wealth by individuals. As we saw in Chapter 5, this pursuit was facilitated by elaborate accounting procedures to track income and expenses associated with every aspect of daily life: not only transactions between bankers and clients or proprietors and agents, but also transactions between the coparceners of joint families, between the two sides of a marriage alliance, and between every kind of Nakarattar social unit and the myriad deities they worshipped (cf. Chapter 9). Another outstanding similarity between Nakarattars and Weberian Protestants is a markedly ascetic lifestyle. Although the present chapter touches only briefly on this aspect of their culture, in its description of their Spartan banking offices, Nakarattar frugality would have done credit to the strictest Puritan, and has been widely remarked ever since they came to the attention of European chroniclers at the end of the nineteenth century (Capper 1877; Cave 1900; Playne 1914–15; Thurston 1909).

Such similarities, however, mask fundamental differences. According to Weber's analysis, the Calvinist doctrine of predestination and the impossibility of human influence over God's will led to the general Protestant rejection of Catholic magic. This, in turn, led to a "lonely," "individualistic" search for proof of salvation that sanctioned an ascetic pursuit of economic callings. Profit was sought not for its intrinsic value, but as proof of the individual's state of grace. Capitalists did not seek personal rewards, emotional enjoyments, or any action that could be interpreted as "idolatry of the flesh." Rather, they sought "the good of the many," or "the public good." An individual's state of grace was judged in terms of the person's impact on society as a whole, although this could be gauged by personal wealth.

For the Nakarattars also, profit making went hand in hand with moral duty. Indeed the link was, in many ways, tighter than that which Weber ascribes to his Calvinist businessmen. Not only was business a calling, a religious duty, and even a form of worship, but even apparently nonbusiness forms of ritual worship and religious endowment (*arccanai, yatra, kattalai*) were forms of business contracted with the deity. Yet, despite these similarities, the spirit of Nakarattar capitalism was radically different from the spirit of Calvinist capitalism. The Nakarattars' God had multiple forms that were easily approached and influenced in pursuit of worldly goals. Individuals did not, however, use their magical worship in pursuit of personal enjoyment any more than Weber's Protestants did. On the other hand, neither did they pursue the good of the general public. Rather, their actions were directed toward the good of specific social groups to which they belonged: their joint families, lineages, villages, clans, business associations operating out of specific localities, and the caste as a whole. All of these groups were marked by common and collective forms of worship in cults of specific deities, and these collective ritual practices were central to the way business was carried out in the wider society. Thus, the Nakarattar Hindu ethic was marked, from the Weberian viewpoint, by a paradoxical amalgam of rationality and collectivism, rather than by rational individualism.[1]

One source of difficulty in efforts to compare Nakarattar and Protestant capitalists directly is the popular assumption—due largely to Weber's treatment of all Hindu religious doctrine—that Hindu beliefs about religious merit and reincarnation hold the same central influence over behavior that Weber ascribes to Calvinist beliefs about spiritual grace and predestination. This is simply a mistake. Contrary to Weber's treatment and to subsequent popular Western notions about Hinduism, religious duty (*dharma*) as prescribed for different castes in Hindu scriptures is aimed at achieving intangible, other-worldly goals (*adrstartha*). It has very little to say about the conduct of everyday life. In particular, it has almost nothing to say about a person's livelihood (*jivika*) or the pursuit of tangible, this-worldly goals (*drstartha*) by members of different castes (cf. Rocher 1975).

An equally important difficulty encountered in comparisons between Nakarattars and Protestants was pointed out by Edward Harper (1964) more than twenty years ago: namely, that Hindus are, by and large, less concerned with orthodoxy than with orthopraxy. Thus, whatever the arguments for rooting explanations of Protestant conduct in interpretations of doctrine (and even Weber occasionally expressed misgivings about this tactic), any appeals to religious doctrines for explaining Hindu conduct should be treated with extreme caution. In this chapter, at least, I am much more concerned about the capitalist spirit expressed in ritual and business practices than the spirit expressed by religious doctrine. My essay does not attempt to survey the full range of practices influenced by the Nakarattars' capitalist spirit. Instead, it reports more narrowly on those characteristics of practices in Nakarattar "business stations" that illustrate their collectivist orientation.

Three Models of Nakarattar Banking Organization

Scholars who have studied the Nakarattar banking system point to three institutions as central to its organization: the family, the agency, and the local caste association. But the historical interpretation of these institutions is contradictory. According to the Japanese sociologist Shoji Ito (1966), familial institutions have undergone an evolution that corresponds to the post-1930s diversion of Nakarattar investment funds from mercantile and banking activities into capitalized industry. Contrary to the model formulated in my own work, Ito believes that the preindustrial Nakarattar banking system was based on autonomous decision-making powers vested in the conjugal unit of their kinship organization, the *pulli*. He supports this position by appealing to Thurston's (1909) description of the yearly allowance allotted to *pullis* by the senior male of the joint family to which the *pulli* belonged. According to Ito, the allocation of these allowances gave *pullis* complete independence from joint family control.

Ito argues that, unlike many other castes, the Nakarattars emphasized decision making by the *pulli*, rather than by joint families, which resulted in an individualistic, Western-like motivation structure for Nakarattar businessmen rather than a structure of group-oriented motivations directed toward the needs of larger kinship units or of the caste as a whole. From this conclusion, he draws two further inferences. First, he explains the great success of the Nakarattars in expanding their banking and trading operations into Southeast Asia during the period from 1870 to 1930 as a consequence of their efficient agency-banking system and its operation by individualistic entrepreneurs. Second, he argues that industrial investment emerged after 1930 because the traditional kinship units constituting the Nakarattar firm (i.e., the *pullis* or Nakarattar conjugal families) began to coordinate their actions through the operation of joint families in order to exploit novel opportunities for investment requiring the large-scale, collective pooling of capital.

Ito's model, as already noted, is contradicted by my own findings. Rather than refute it at this point, however, I simply wish to recapitulate the historical thesis of his argument: namely, that Nakarattar commercial organization evolved from a Western-style, individualistic mode of organization that was compatible with agency banking to a putatively Indian-style, joint-family–oriented mode of organization capable of controlling and managing an industrial "combine," monopoly, or conglomerate. I also note that both modes of organization are compatible with theories of Indian commercial organization that downplay *any* role for caste organization in the conduct of commerce, a position with which Ito appears comfortable. In fact, the only reference that he makes to caste organization beyond the level of the family firm is a reference to locally based caste associations that set interest rates for all Nakarattar agencies operating under their jurisdiction. But even here, the lesson Ito draws is that these associations promoted the individualism of their members. He does not reflect on the collective organization and cooperation presupposed by the operation of these associations.

One recent scholar who does consider the role of interbank organization of Nakarattar firms and agencies is Raman Mahadevan (1976). Mahadevan recognizes traditional intracaste coordination of family firms through localized communal organizations called *panchayats.* Nakarattar *panchayats* served as forums for the exchange of information, for resolving disputes, for setting collective interest rates, and for representing Nakarattar interests to local government. Beginning in the 1920s, they were superceded in some places by Nakarattar caste associations. In Mahadevan's view, this shift reflects a period of increasing economic differentiation and stratification within the caste, a pattern that is in part responsible for the emergence of these new forms of community organization. According to Mahadevan, caste associations lack the "sodality" of traditional institutions and represent a growth in the autonomy of individual firms. In other words, Mahadevan sees in the institutional evolution of Nakarattar banking a diminution of the importance of collective organization: precisely the opposite trend from that described by Ito.

The following discussion presents a model of Nakarattar organization that I propose as an alternative to both Ito's and Mahadevan's interpretations. To begin with, I agree with both scholars insofar as they see a post-1920s change in the organization of Nakarattar commercial activities. It seems to me that Ito is correct in seeing that there was a shift into industry,[2] that the capital available to Nakarattar conjugal families was insufficient for large-scale industrial investment, and that Nakarattars therefore engaged in coordinated joint-family investment in industry. I disagree with Ito about his assertion that the joint-family firm represented a novel response to industrialization. There is no evidence that conjugal units (as opposed to joint families) constituted the basis of the Nakarattar family firm prior to industrialization. Indeed, my own research suggests that financially successful families responded to incentives for staying together as a joint family and pooling their resources regardless of the nature of their investment or the period in which they did business. That is, joint-family firms are not peculiar to twentieth-century, industrial-investing families. They are also found among elite nineteenth-century families of merchant-bankers, whose early prominence in the political economy of South India paved the way for their twentieth-century investments in industry.

With regard to Mahadevan's model, I agree with his observation about a post-1920s emergence and substitution of caste associations for *panchayats.* But I disagree with his interpretation. In my view, the emergence of Nakarattar caste associations represents a political adaptation to colonial rule, not a consequence of economic differentiation between caste members. While there is certainly evidence of social stratification and economic differentiation within the caste, there is no more evidence that this is a twentieth-century development than there is that joint families are a twentieth-century phenomenon. On the contrary, evidence for elite status among an elect subset of Nakarattars extends back to the nineteenth-century Nakarattar *zamindars* and even back to seventeenth-century Nakarattar donors to South Indian temples (Chapter 7). In fact, it seems to me that a small group of elite Nakarattars, called *adathis* or parent bankers (see below), performed an extremely important role in colonial India, mediating multiple circuits of capital between discrete segments of nonelite Nakarattars, the colonial government, and the society of British India as a whole.[3]

The major part of the present chapter describes the institutional organization of the Nakarattar banking system in the period from 1870 to 1930. I divide my discussion into sections that describe the component institutions of the system. These sections focus initially on family firms and agencies that functioned like commercial banks with branch offices; on large-scale firms (*adathis*) that functioned, in addition, like reserve banks; and on communal caste organizations (*vitutis* and *panchayats*) that facilitated the flow of information and credit while providing mechanisms for avoiding or resolving conflict.[4]

Families and Firms

Nakarattar banking firms were basically "family firms" which owned and directed the operation of one or more banking offices, plantations, manufacturing companies, or other business ventures outside the South Indian Nakarattar homeland of Chettinad. In general, firms were owned by an undivided joint family (*valavu*) containing several coresident "hearthholds" or "conjugal families" (*pullis*) and extending to three or four generations under direction of the oldest active male. Whatever its tangible investments, a Nakarattar family firm's greatest intangible asset was its reputation. Without a reputation for trustworthiness (*nanayam*), no family could attract deposits or reassure clients of honesty (or, at least, predictability) and flexibility in the extension of credit. Not surprisingly, family firms were subject to careful public scrutiny. The joint family, itself, was individuated and publicly identified by a distinctive *vitu vilacam* ("house name") that was formed by stringing together the initial letters of the names of three or four generations of lineal male ancestors, the last name belonging to the senior living male member. Before the 1930s, each family traditionally employed its *vitu vilacam* as a *tolil vilacam* ("business name"). It was used as the name of the business firm and was even attached as a prefix to the names of members of other families or other castes who worked for the firm.[5] When a family divided or when a particular business was solely the property of a single branch of the joint family, the senior male of the newly formed family unit assumed the role of proprietor and added his own initials to that of the family. For example, a Nakarattar named A. K. A. Ct. Alagappa, the son of A. K. A. Ct. Chidambaram, would have taken the name A. K. A. Ct. Al. Alagappa when his father died and he inherited the firm. If Alagappa had employed a non-Nakarattar, that employee would also have been entitled to use the family's *tolil vilacam:* for example, A. K. A. Ct. Al. Adaikkappa Tevar.[6] If Alagappa had a younger brother at the time of his father's death, they might have decided to continue ownership of the firm in the joint family, with Alagappa taking over the role of their father as proprietor, or they might have decided to partition the family and the firm. In the first case, Alagappa's brother would have added Alagappa's initials to the *tolil vilacam* used to prefix his own name: for example, A. K. A. Ct. Al. Muthia. In the latter case, Alagappa's brother would have retained the *tolil vilacam* of their father's business, but would have added his own initials in order to distinguish his firm from his brother's: thus, A. K. A. Ct. M. Muthia. These naming practices gave the lists of Nakarattar firms that appear in various published contexts an appearance of alphabet soup. But to Nakarattars, they constituted a detailed road map, readily consulted and easily interpretable.

The precise relationship between the joint family designated by its *vitu vilacam* and the family firm designated by an often identical *tolil vilacam* was subject to shifting and contentious legal interpretations. By and large, colonial courts recognized Nakarattar *tolil vilacams* as designations of business corporations and as distinct from the names of families or individuals who made use of the otherwise identical initials to designate themselves. In Ceylon, the interpretation was even codified under the Business Names Ordinance of 1918, which, among other things, denied an individual's right to carry on business under his *vitu vilacam* unless it was properly registered as a *tolil vilacam* with the authorities. There remained, however, ambiguities regarding the legal status of individuals who had proprietary interests in a firm or whose purely contractual connection with the firm entitled them to use the firm's name as part of their own.

In situations in which a conflict of interest arose, the opponents in the conflict frequently sought legal judgment that the ambiguous actor in question had been acting on his own behalf or, conversely, that he had been acting as representative of the firm. It depended on whose ox had been gored and where the remedy lay. But underlying individual motivation and self-interest were fundamental questions about the cultural and legal definitions of social groups and social responsibilities. The issues concerned the financial rights and liabilities enjoyed respectively by four sets of actors: the family's coparceners, the family firm's partners (if any), the firm's proprietor or partners and its agents, and the creditors and borrowers of the firm. Each set, at different times, found itself to have either common goals or conflicting interests. The latter case frequently led to litigation.

Weersooria (1973: 76–125) has reviewed a large body of legal cases in Ceylon that focus on precisely these issues. A few examples provide a sense of the kinds of conflict that could arise. In one court case, a creditor argued that a Nakarattar firm was liable for any obligation that the firm's agent incurred while using the firm's *vilacam* as part of his name. The firm, for their part, denied blanket liability and argued that their employee's customary use of their *vilacam* as part of his name did not imply liability unless he had been given full power of attorney. Otherwise they were liable only for those obligations incurred within the restricted range of their agent's contractually specified exercise of power. They argued further that if the plaintiff had a quarrel, it was with their agent as an individual, not with them. Other cases sounded a similar note. In one instance, for example, a Nakarattar creditor argued that there was no legal distinction between a firm and its joint family owners in order to win legal recognition of the family's liability for the firm's obligations. On still another occasion, a Nakarattar argued that there was a distinction between firm and family on grounds that his investments in Ceylon represented a private business venture, exempt from claims by his brothers. In all of these cases, and numerous others as well, legal definitions of Nakarattar firms, families, and agents were ambiguous, context-sensitive, and subject to constantly shifting and competing interests.

There may be some temptation to misinterpret the significance of these kinds of ambiguity and the attendant possibilities for independent action by family members or nonfamily employees of the family firm. But there is a major difference between, on the one hand, ambiguities in status and, on the other hand, economic autonomy for individual businessmen. It was the joint family that was the focus of individual action and that constituted the primary social unit around which Nakarattars constructed their business firms. Legal ambiguities in the definition of the firm generated conflict, and Nakarattars (and their clients) frequently sought to take advantage of alternative judicial interpretations of rights and obligations. But if such ambiguities generated conflict, they also created flexibility for Nakarattar joint families in responding to the changing business and legal environment of colonial Asia.

Pulli *and* Valavu *(The Conjugal Family and the Joint Family)*

The *pulli* was the basic reproductive and daily consumptive unit of the Nakarattar caste. It normally comprised a married man, his wife, their children, and other dependents. A *pulli* was formed by registration of a marriage in a Nakarattar clan temple (see Chapter 9) and remained in existence as long as any of its members retained the potential for having children. Hence, both widowers and unmarried children were considered as representing the original *pulli* formed by the widower and his wife at the time of their marriage; both widower and children were capable of adding new members to the *pulli*. By contrast, a widow with or without married children (but having no unmarried children) was considered only a "half-*pulli*." A widow was viewed as incapable of adding any further members to her *pulli*.

The literal meaning of the term *pulli* is "dot," from a trading practice in which dots were employed for reckoning or counting a quantity of some trade good.[7] In a similar fashion, *pullis* were the units employed by Nakarattars to enumerate their own population. Nakarattars spoke of the number of *pullis* belonging to a village or to a variety of larger kin units, to be described in the present and following chapters (*valavu, kuttikkira pankali,* and *kovil*).[8]

Much has been made of the fact that *pullis* were often allotted a yearly allowance by the senior male in the joint family to which they belonged. Nakarattar *pullis* used this allowance to cover living expenses and to contribute to the cost of private investment (Krishnan 1959; Thurston 1909). Indeed, citing these allowances, Shoji Ito, (1966: 370) concludes that *pullis* constituted the basic organizational unit of Nakarattar business and that they were completely independent of higher-level units of Nakarattar kin organization until the 1930s.

All of Ito's conclusions are directly contradicted by my own findings. To begin with, the *pulli* was but the smallest unit of Nakarattar kinship organization (see Chapters 8 and 9) and, in many ways, seems to be the least implicated in the overall organization of Nakarattar business activity during the colonial period. They were not, in general, independent economic or even residential units. Most of their properties and business activities were held as part of the undivided estate of a *valavu,* the Nakarattar joint family unit to which the *pulli* belonged.[9]

Although each *pulli* had its own living quarters and cooking hearth, they traditionally shared a common family house with other *pullis* belonging to the larger *valavu.*[10] Thus it is more accurate to view the traditional *pulli* as a hearthhold rather than a household. Its characteristic activities were oriented around procreation and consumption. Even the vaunted personal allowances to individual *pullis* were not made on a cash basis, but were charged to the *pulli*'s account with its *valavu.* These accounts were not reconciled until partition of the *valavu.* At this time debits and credits in the *pulli*'s account were justified just like any business account, and the differences adjusted against the *pulli*'s share (*panku*) of the estate. Moreover, no important decision was independently made by the head of a *pulli.* At the very least, he had to ask the approval of the head of the *valavu,* who had veto power and commonly acted as an active manager and director of all business activities by members of the *valavu.*

The term *valavu* literally denotes the architectural portion of a Nakarattar house, consisting of a central courtyard and the surrounding ring of rooms housing each of the resident *pullis* (see Plates 9–10). This usage was extended to apply to the undivided, extended joint family, usually containing several *pullis* and sometimes covering three or four generations.[11] *Valavu* members were traditionally coresidential, an enormously sensible practice, especially during the period when Nakarattars carried out the bulk of their business abroad. At that time, a young man commonly left his wife and children in the care of his father and brothers and worked abroad for a period of three years as an agent, either for his own family's banking firm or for another family's firm. Later, after he had established his own business, he might occasionally go on a short tour of his branch offices.

Within a Nakarattar *valavu,* it was the oldest adult male who presided over major decisions affecting its members. Respect for his leadership was marked. Even men of forty or fifty years, with a record of successful business enterprise in their own right, deferred to the decisions of the eldest male until he voluntarily stepped down. In many families, they would neither speak nor sit in his presence. Nor would they undertake any major private undertaking without his permission.

This is not to deny the tremendous pressures operating upon married males of the family to claim their *panku* (share) of the family estate and establish their own separate family unit. In some cases, these pressures were expressed by the rapid partition of the family soon after the death of the male head. Occasionally, friction between brothers was so great that one or all of them demanded their shares when their father was still alive. In the family of a contemporary Nakarattar industrialist, tension erupted when the youngest son (a man in his late thirties) sought independence from his father and his oldest brother, who had already assumed most of the decision-making activities for the joint estate. The tension escalated to the point where the brothers engaged in public brawls, and the youngest brother was even rumored to have hit his father. Ultimately, the estate was partitioned. The brothers received ownership of separate industrial companies that had been part of the common estate. Both brothers continued to live in houses constructed in the compound of their father's residence in an urban center outside of Chettinad. But they refused to speak to each other or attend the marriages of each other's children.

Nevertheless, this extreme tension represents an exceptional case. It was far more common for a *valavu* to approach the Nakarattar ideal and remain together as a three- or four-generation unit under the leadership of its eldest male. The typical pattern is illustrated by the recent history of the family of a major Nakarattar banker, industrialist, and philanthropist. When he died, overall control of the family enterprises devolved upon his eldest son. Strains for partition were kept in check by family politics and by appeals to the Hindu ideal of the joint family. When the son himself died, however, the joint family ideal fell into conflict with equally potent preferences for direct lineal inheritance. Under the classical model, the son's younger brother—who succeeded to the position of oldest male in the extended family—could have been expected to assume overall managerial responsibility (Tambiah 1973b). However, the son's own son, named after his grandfather, had been trained in modern business management in America and had been deeply involved in family decision-making processes even before his father's death. He and his uncle differed radically in their views about appropriate investment policy, about other aspects of business management and operations, and about the management of family-directed colleges and other philanthropic activities. These disagreements led to protracted arguments, negotiations, lawsuits, and ultimately to partition of the family's assets. Until partition, however—and in contrast to the case of the exceptionally divided family described above—this more cohesive family illustrates how the joint family ideal was able to counter competitive tendencies among brothers even after the death of their father. On the other hand, this solidarity in the conjugal family was not sufficient to counter competition between collaterals in different generations—in this case, between father's brother and brother's son.

Considerations such as these make it seem likely that the Nakarattar domestic-cum-business developmental cycle was different from domestic cycles of kin groups based on reproductive conjugal units like the Nakarattar *pulli* or the American nuclear family. Unlike such typically studied cases, in which parents are replaced by children (Benedict 1968; Goody 1958), the Nakarattar *valavu* was a purely productive unit in which brothers replaced each other in order of seniority. Both kinds of developmental cycles are influenced by the biological facts of birth, maturation, old age, and death. But the Nakarattar cycle involved a larger unit of organization and a longer period for the full cycle. In addition, the cycle of partition was affected by the death of the eldest male in a way that differed markedly from developmental cycles in kin groups based on the conjugal unit. The entire issue contains considerable scope for further research. The lesson in the present context, however, is the important role of the *valavu* as the basic unit of Nakarattar business ownership: the Nakarattar family firm.[12]

Proprietors and Agents

Despite occasions when a hearthhold component of a joint family seemed to act independently—either as an expedient legal fiction or as a sociological fact due to internal friction within a family—the chief locus of Nakarattar decision making remained the joint family, with its senior male as proprietor of the family firm. In business dealings, he was normally referred to as *mudali* ("principal"). In general, proprietors left the daily operation of their overseas business firms to hired agents (*melals*) and field staff (*kattu kanakkupillai*) while they stayed in India. Nevertheless, proprietors maintained a continual correspondence with their overseas agents, and many of them made periodical tours of inspection. While in India, proprietors were engaged in a constant round of marriages, funerals, village festivals, and other social functions, during which time they compared business notes with their fellow bankers, discussed investment opportunities, sought information about changing government policies, and simply kept track of each other's success, failure, and overall creditworthiness.

Before the 1930s, most Nakarattar bankers received a specialized training for their profession from an early age. As young boys, they learned multiplication tables and memorized formulas for computing compound interest in a traditional Tamil style on the verandas of their Chettinad homes, probably from a member of their family. From about the age of ten, they learned how to make ledger entries in a business ledger/journal (*peredu*) with information received periodically from the family's business office(s) overseas. Before reaching his teens, a boy left his Chettinad home and was apprenticed for three years as an errand boy (*pettiyadi paiyan*) to his family's business agent in a business office abroad. He returned home wearing gold rings, diamond earrings, a gold chain, and a gold belt. And he carried with him all the talismans of his trade: gold coins, diamonds, gems, pearls, rubies, and topaz.

After a short period of reunion with his family and friends, a young Nakarattar man was considered ready to undertake direction of a banking agency on his own. But, on his first time out, he seldom would be put in a charge of a business office belonging to his own family's firm. Occasionally, he might find employment as agent for the branch office of a family in a segment of the patrilineal descent group (*kuttikkira pankali*), which consisted of his own joint family plus close collateral families, usually headed by the brothers of his father or paternal grandfather. Sometimes, however, animosity left over from divisive family partitions prevented this form of cooperation between collateral families. Accordingly, in much the way that Nakarattar parents sought families with which to establish a marriage alliance for their daughters, they sought families who would employ their sons and thereby establish a business alliance. In fact, the two quests were intimately related. In-laws—especially maternal in-laws (*tayatis*)—were often approached as potential employers. Their firms were well known. They could be counted on to feel some responsibility toward their daughter's husband. And they were, themselves, in a good position to evaluate the trustworthiness of their son-in-law. Often, the connection between ties of interfamilial employment and those of marriage alliance served both functions simultaneously, since successful agents were frequently approached as possible grooms for the proprietor's daughters even where no previous alliance had existed. Both quests were the topics of discussion among Nakarattars gathered together for weddings, funerals, and village ceremonies. And young men in search of their first business agency were evaluated on the basis of their potential business acumen and their potential for linking two families in a mutually beneficial marriage alliance.[13]

Agents were not always young boys. More experienced men were often hired, particularly in the case of important agencies. Such men normally had run agencies before or had owned their own businesses but, for whatever reason, during the time in question had insufficient funds to operate their own businesses. Alternatively, but rarely, such men might be acting as their own agents and in this situation found themselves in positions to act as agents for other firms as well. In some cases, especially trusted non-Nakarattars would be hired, but this was rare.

An agent was usually appointed for a three-year tour of duty called a *kanakku* (an "account"). Salaries were negotiated by the proprietor through intermediaries and, in the 1930s, ranged from 800 to 6000 *varakans* (one *varakan* = Rs. 3.5) depending upon the turnover of the firm and the experience of the agent. Fifty percent of the estimated salary for the three-year period was remitted to the agent's family immediately upon his departure for the business station. The remainder was paid to the agent in the form of living expenses during his period of employment and, at the end of the *kanakku,* as a bonus in the form of a share of the profits. My informants estimate that in Malaya, for example, the agent's share was 4 percent on plantation income, 4 percent on rental income, and 6–10 percent on income derived from banking business. In some instances, it was possible for an agent to negotiate shares of up to 12.5 percent of the business.

Just before his departure, the agent visited the proprietor at his residence in Chettinad. There, he signed a contract of appointment (basically, an indemnity bond) and received power of attorney to act as the proprietor's agent in the field. As in contemporary America, there was some flexibility in specification of the agent's powers, the precise terms varying from case to case. But in general he was given the powers to buy and sell property, to discharge mortgages, to draw loans, and to engage or discharge employees.

The agent and the proprietor then proceeded to the proprietor's family deity and together worshipped the deity and asked for blessings. Afterwards, the proprietor gave the agent oral instructions concerning the conduct of business, the handling of finances, relations with competing firms, and dealing with the Nakarattar *adathis* who acted as clearinghouses for the majority of Nakarattar transactions. Collecting expenses for travel in advance, the agent proceeded to his port of embarkation, perhaps taking with him a letter of introduction to an *adathi*—an elite Nakarattar banker with vast financial resources—who maintained among his many branch offices a local office at the agent's port of departure. Agents leaving for Burma usually left from Madras; for Malaya, from Nagapattinam or Madras; and for Ceylon, from Tuticorin or, after 1914, from Dhanuskodi.

On arrival at his destination port, the agent worshipped at the local Nakarattar temple and dispatched telegrams to his family, to the proprietor, and to the agent he was to replace at his firm's business office. He then proceeded on the next leg of his journey to reach the business office, normally located at a railway station or river port in the interior of the foreign country in which he was to spend his next three years. On arriving at his office, he was welcomed by all the resident Nakarattars, eager for news from Chettinad. His arrival was celebrated by a short commensal meal and was followed by a collective visit to the local temple for worship.

On the first day determined by horoscope to be auspicious, the new agent formally took charge of the business office from the retiring agent. He was presented with what my informants described as the firm's "general ledger" (*peredu*—but see Chapter 5) as well as the agency's other books of account, and he was introduced to the firm's clients on their business premises. The retiring agent would call in as many loans as possible to give the new agent the maximum freedom to invest at his own discretion. He then reviewed the outstanding loans with the new agent. Debts from sound clients were listed in one ledger (*pekki pustakam*) and considered as secured loans and good investments. Debts felt to be bad risks were listed in a separate ledger for collection by the new agent, but the old agent was held liable for them. Both agents checked the balances outstanding with the firm's clients and issued new receipts to the clients signed by the new agent.

When all this was accomplished—a process that could take up to six months—the retiring agent was ready to depart. The new agent certified the retiring agent's bonus calculated at the agreed-upon percentage of the firm's profits over the three-year period of his appointment. If the new agent was not prepared to accept a debt as a good risk, the matter might be settled by intervention of agents from other firms who would agree to take on the debt. If this was not possible, the matter was left for three years until the new agent himself returned to Chettinad.

On reaching India, the retiring agent went straight to the proprietor's residence with all of his baggage. The proprietor had the right to confiscate any of the agent's belongings. The agent then gave the proprietor all of the letters written to him by the proprietor while he was in the field. Afterwards, he proceeded to his own village. For the next few weeks and during the next marriage season, he would be the center of village gossip, especially about his improved financial status and the benefits of a marriage alliance with his family.

If an agent's tenure was successful, he would be called upon by the proprietor to help bring duplicate ledgers up to date, and to advise the proprietor on the best course of action to take during the upcoming three years. If a retiring agent was not in a position to start his own firm, the proprietor might make arrangements to engage him again as agent at the same business office or at another location. As a measure of trust, the agent's power was generally increased by removing any restrictions that might have been placed on the power of attorney granted him during his first appointment. In addition, his bonus would most likely be increased by agreeing that he should receive a larger share of the profits from his agency.

The Nakarattar Agency

Nakarattar agents conducted their business out of modest offices called *kitangi* or *arai* normally located in a communal building housing both the offices of other Nakarattar bankers and also a communal temple (*kovil*) or rest house (*vituti, chattiram,* or *choultry*). The offices were quite small—perhaps eight feet by four feet of floor space—and contained a wooden box or low desk which held cash, jewels, business papers, correspondence, account books, and a pair of scales. The agent's responsibilities consisted in making daily visits to the local Nakarattar temple; keeping track of cash positions and requirements by reviewing the day book (*kurippu*); corresponding with the firm's proprietor; keeping track of exchange rates, commodity prices, and local governmental laws and policies; representing the proprietor at community meetings; and upholding the reputation of the firm by entertaining guests in as lavish a manner as possible.

The bulk of work in running an agency, however, was actually carried out by a staff (*kattu kanakkupillai*) consisting of a first assistant (*mudalal*), subordinate staff (*aduthal*), a cook (*camaiyalkaran*), and an errand boy (*pettiyadi paiyan*). Large firms also frequently retained a court clerk (*kirani*) and a cashier. None of these employees needed to be Nakarattars. The first assistant was responsible for initiating choice of clientele. In many cases, he did practically everything else as well, and even checked the cash locked in wooden chests before handing over to the agent the key to the *kitangi* and closing up shop for the day. Field staff were the only employees necessarily fluent in the local language. In Burma, they visited clients in their own houses, inspected lands owned by the firm and leased to clients, maintained good relations with village officers, and saw to it that land records were kept in good order. In Malaya they visited tin mines and rubber estates owned by the firm and oversaw salary advances and loans to laborers and other employees. In urban areas, where the agency made unsecured loans to retail shopkeepers and small-scale traders on a *kandu kisti* basis,[14] the field staff made daily rounds to collect repayment on these loans. The subordinate staff were generally clerks who kept ledgers, made copies of weekly statements, kept petty cash accounts relating to staff meals, and attended to simple registration work required by notary publics, income taxes, and other bureaucratic duties. They also drafted documents, agreements, and contracts with solicitors and insurance companies. Large agencies were often massively involved in litigation and employed separate court clerks for this purpose. The court clerk was responsible for all of the paperwork transacted in the various subcourts, district courts, and high courts of the country of business. Suits were filed mostly against Burmese, Malayan, and Chinese clients. Occasionally there were suits against other Nakarattar firms, suits for the dissolution of a partnership between a proprietor and his son, and appeals against orders brought by civil or revenue authorities. Large banking houses also kept full-time cashiers. All agents employed cooks to provide meals for themselves and their staff. The cooks were normally recruited from the Mukkulatar castes of Chettinad. Finally, Nakarattar agencies also employed an errand boy, or "bearer boy," who kept cash at the counter and ran personal errands for the rest of the staff. An errand boy was entrusted with considerable financial responsibility. He might be sent to other business houses to borrow, loan, or pay back tens of thousands of rupees without any documentation. This money was called *kaimattu panam* (hand money). The errand boy held the lowest position in the agency. He received almost no salary beyond room and board and a small bonus at the end of his appointment. But he did receive an excellent training, and most Nakarattars started their banking careers as errand boys. Moreover, an appointment as errand boy provided a young man with an important opportunity to make business contacts that would serve him well during his first tour of business as an agent in his own right.

Adathis: *The Nakarattar Elite*

Nakarattar firms were distinguished by the size of the business they controlled. Thus, according to several of my informants, there was a basic distinction between the majority of Nakarattars, whose business was confined to a single geographic arena (Burma, Malaya, or Ceylon, but not more than one), and the relatively small number of *adathis,* who were spoken of as "important men" and who controlled wealthy "parent banks" and managed business enterprises throughout South and Southeast Asia. Another important distinction which cut across the distinction between *adathis* and other Nakarattars was between independent businessmen, who controlled their own enterprises, and "minor families," who left decision making in the hands of trusted independent bankers who were normally *adathis*.

It is difficult to judge the percentage of total Nakarattar firms that constituted *adathi* firms. On one hand, my informants estimated their numbers at between 5 percent and 10 percent. This seems consistent with the number of Nakarattars who obtained title to *zamindari* lands in Madras (Chapter 4). On the other hand, this estimate seems somewhat high measured against indices of the internal stratification of Nakarattars doing business in Burma (their primary place of business). One useful index is provided by figures on Nakarattar land ownership in Burma. These figures were submitted in 1953 to the chargé d'affairs of the Indian embassy in Burma as part of a Nakarattar effort to gain compensation for lands lost when they were expelled from Burma. I have broken down the figures arbitrarily into larger clusters based on the size of the landholding and have calculated the percentage of Nakarattar firms that fall into each cluster (Table 8). I emphasize that this clustering is undertaken only to highlight patterns in land ownership. Although there is a marked internal stratification by land ownership, there is—with the exception of what I take to be a segment consisting of (although not necessarily exhausting) Nakarattar *adathis*—no evidence that the clusters correspond to a hierarchy of exclusive or self-conscious social classes.

A corroborating index of stratification is provided by the numbers of branch offices or agencies held by different Nakarattar firms (Table 9). I take the twelve largest Nakarattar landowners as representing (if not exhausting) Nakarattar *adathis* in Burma.[15] If *adathis* are defined by their ability to transmit funds between regions, then it is not inappropriate to extend the set to include the twenty or so firms that maintain at least half a dozen offices in Burma. In any case, many of the firms in one or both of these groups seem to possess traits besides wealth in land that my informants indicated were also constitutive of *adathi* status. They maintained multiple branch offices throughout Burma. The twelve largest landholders all served as Nakarattar representatives on the Indian Chamber of Commerce in Burma.[16] Six with whom I am familiar from my field work had business offices and investments in India as well as Burma, and some of these were involved extensively in Ceylon as well. Most of these Nakarattar proprietors served as officers of various caste organizations (e.g., as

Table 8. Nakarattar Land-Ownership in Burma, ca. 1940

Size of Holding (in acres)	*Number of Firms*	*Percentage of Firms in Cluster*	*Total Acreage*
Small			
Below 1,000	574	54.5	217,164
Medium			
1,000–2,000	194	40.7	269,429
2,000–3,000	125		294,600
3,000–4,000	72		244,650
4,000–5,000	38		174,227
Large			
5,000–6,000	19	3.7	95,160
6,000–7,000	8		52,339
7,000–8,000	6		43,900
8,000–9,000	4		34,589
9,000–10,000	2		18,360
Very Large			
Above 10,000	12	1.1	272,158
Total	1,054	100.0	1,718,158

Source: Mahadevan (1976: 182).

Table 9. Nakarattar Agencies (Offices) per Firm in Burma, 1935–42

Number of Agencies per Firm	*Number of Firms*	*Total Agencies*
Rangoon firms		
1	75–100	88
2–3	60–80	210
7–8	15–20	144
41	1	41
Total		483
District Firms		
1	900–1,000	950
2–3	100–200	450
Total		1,400
All firms	1,401	1,883

Source: Secretary of the Rangoon Nattukottai Chettiar Association, compiled by Tun Wai (1962: 41).

administrators for Nakarattar *vitutis*—see below) and in locations where they did business. They or members of their families frequently held political office in Burma, India, or Ceylon. Finally, all members of this group of notables were likely to have been major contributors and to have served on boards of trustees for temples and for charitable or educational institutions. In other words, this small group of Nakarattar notables formed an elite group of interlocking connections and influence among the business, governmental, social, and religious institutions of Asian society.

Adathis operated with a large working capital of their own. In addition, they had access to deposits, loans, overdraft privileges, and other sources of credit from the Imperial Bank of India, from European commercial banks, from recognized banking houses owned by members of non-Nakarattar castes such as Marwaris, from religious and charitable endowments, and from other Nakarattar bankers. The importance of these resources was considerable—especially the importance of loans made available to *adathis* by the European banks. According to A. Savaranatha Pillai, Assistant Commissioner for Income Tax of Madras in 1930,

> Besides deposits that Chettis receive from members of their own community and from the public and the loans taken from the Imperial Bank, they also borrow money from other banks—the National Bank, Mercantile Bank, Hongkong and Shanghai Bank, the Chartered Bank, the P. and O. Bank, Yokohama Specie Bank, the Lloyds Bank. The total amount so borrowed is not known. The extent to which each individual Chetti borrows depends on his personal capacity, the favor he finds in the eyes of bank authorities. There are instances in which some Chettis have managed to get a borrowed capital ten times as great as their own capital. There are many cases in which borrowed capital is up to 2 1/2 times of their own capital. Taking Chettinad as a whole the borrowed capital comes to about 50% of their own capital with reference to the estimates made by the [Income Tax] officers having jurisdiction over the area. (Pillai 1930: 1180)

Pillai was apparently unaware of the correlation between *adathi* status among Nakarattars and creditworthiness of individual Nakarattars among Europeans. But my informants were emphatic that only major, *adathi* houses were favored with access to loans from European banks.[17] Thus, the huge amount of funds that Pillai describes as available to Nakarattar bankers was actually channeled through an extremely small cadre of very powerful men.

Besides these advantages, *adathis* also had access to other sources of funds denied smaller-scale Nakarattars. While all Nakarattars transacted *hundis* (bills of exchange), *adathi* firms acted as clearinghouses: if a non-

adathi or even a non-Nakarattar wished to remit money from his overseas business operations, he could draw up a *hundi,* much the way Americans write checks, and have it cashed by an *adathi* with whom he maintained an account. Nakarattar *hundis* could be used much as bills of exchange are used in commodities transactions and also—uniquely—as interest-bearing certificates of deposit. In either case, *hundis* drawn on *adathis* had special value relative to those drawn on non-*adathi* firms. They were widely negotiable and liquid at almost any time—more so than *hundis* drawn by non-*adathis.* Accordingly, they would frequently be kept uncashed as insurance against a time when cash was needed on short notice. One consequence of this was to provide still further resources to *adathis,* who could count at any time on high demand but low turnover for bills drawn on themselves. Moreover, because *hundis* drawn on *adathis* were such a good risk, they provided for quick and easy remittance of funds from Southeast Asian business operations to India. *Adathis* maintained offices all over Chettinad and in the major ports where Nakarattars did business: Madras, Nagapattinam, Tuticorin, Calcutta, Colombo, Rangoon, Penang, and Singapore. The smaller Nakarattar firms maintained accounts with *adathis* who kept offices in their primary places of business as well as offices in Madras and, perhaps, offices close to their native villages in Chettinad. According to Pillai, the efficiency of *hundi* remittance through the *adathi* system contributed to the large proportion of Nakarattar capital maintained overseas: "When funds are required for local requirements [in India] the Chettis draw upon their *adathis* in Madras. A telegram before 3 o'clock brings them money by next post." (1930: 1180). As a consequence, Nakarattars were freed from the necessity of maintaining liquid capital in India, where it was highly taxed, and could deploy their investments in the far more profitable arenas of Southeast Asia.

Finally, Nakarattar *adathis* also served as political leaders on municipal and district boards, as mayors of cities that served as provincial capitals, as members of legislative councils, and as chairmen and members of the boards of trustees for temples and other charitable institutions in local communities wherever they did business. Such forms of public and religious service made their own distinctive contributions to an *adathi*'s overall ability to control wealth, although the available data do not allow one to judge the incremental advantages to *adathi* resources beyond those extended directly or indirectly to nonelite Nakarattars.

In other words, although all Nakarattar firms acted like commercial banks—making loans, taking deposits and so forth—Nakarattar *adathis* acted like reserve banks for the Nakarattar banking system as a whole. By gaining and controlling access to financial resources outside the system, *adathis* directly affected money supply. As influential voices in regional interest-setting meetings (see below), *adathis* not only affected the cost of regional systems of credit, but also helped to standardize interest rates across the multiple regions in which they did business. *Adathis* served as clearinghouses for bills of exchange transacted across the entire sphere of Nakarattar enterprise. Finally, consciously or unconsciously, *adathis* created a major impact on local and regional credit markets by using the massive capital resources at their disposal—an impact similar to that created by a central bank's open-market operations.

Nakaravitutis

When a Nakarattar businessman entered a local business community for the first time, his fellow Nakarattars welcomed him by hosting a commensal meal for him and by joining with him to worship at the local Nakarattar-supported temple. These welcoming rituals symbolized Nakarattar conventions of friendship and business morality that carried over into extensions of financial trust and credit to one another and to non-Nakarattars for whom they accorded preferred, semi-Nakarattar status. Business associates bonded by such communal relationships were granted lenient terms with respect to overdraft privileges or loans on minimal or no security. This was especially true in the case of transactions that were between Nakarattars, which were recorded in account books on a mercantile or accrual basis rather than a cash basis. Transactions between Nakarattars were subject to justification only after many transactions, and the difference between deposits and withdrawals at any given time could be substantial. In other words, in addition to cheap loans and high interest payments on deposits, Nakarattars provided for each other relatively unlimited credit opportunities.

There were, nevertheless, several conventions built into the Nakarattar banking system that provided checks on the extent to which credit could be extended. These conventions also served to safeguard the moral obligation to extend credit from too strong a confrontation with private interests. The obligations and limits of cooperation among local communities of Nakarattar businessmen were formalized in the institutions of the *nakaravituti* and the *panchayat*. I have already commented on the function of *nakaravitutis* in providing venues for regular meetings for setting standardized interest rates or reaching other collective decisions. These institutions also performed two other important functions: the facilitation of information and credit transfers, and the resolution of conflict.

Nakaravitutis (*vitutis* belonging to Nakarattars) were ostensibly community-supported lodging houses located in the same building as or adjacent to Nakarattar-supported temples. They were frequently referred to as

Nakarattar *matams*.[18] On the first floor, they contained private rooms, dormitories, storage rooms, meeting rooms, dining halls, and (for those open to women) private kitchens. On the second floor each *vituti* contained a shrine or temple. The *vituti* was directed by a board of trustees and employed a manager and staff to provide services for traveling Nakarattars. These services included, in addition to provision of lodging and meals, provision of mailing facilities, making travel arrangements, clearing baggage at local customs houses, and arranging for absentee prayers at local temples. In short, *vitutis* were extremely useful in the mobile world of the Nakarattar.

Vitutis were normally financed primarily by large gifts or endowments (*kattalais*) from wealthy Nakarattar *adathis*, although less-prominent Nakarattars with local interests frequently contributed to the endowment fund. Operating costs were also subscribed through endowment. Thus, many of the redistributive functions performed by endowment of temples and temple festivals (Chapters 7 and 9) were also performed by endowment of the closely associated *nakaravituti*. In addition, every guest paid what amounted to a nominal rent (called *makimai*, like the Nakarattar religious tithe) fixed by the manager of each *vituti* and subject to revision according to need. Where the *vituti* was associated with a pilgrimage site, women made additional payments to cover the cost of specific offerings to the deity (e.g., *pal kattalai*, "milk endowments"). Even when visiting Nakarattars chose not to stay at a local *vituti*, and stayed instead in the home of a friend or in an expensive hotel, they paid *makimai*.

Vitutis located in the villages of Chettinad were basically extensions of the major Nakarattar village temples and were used to conduct local community meetings or hold village-wide religious ceremonies. Such ceremonial pilgrim houses were generally not used as lodging houses. There was no need. They were paid for by all the Nakarattar families in the village, although the major cost would normally have been born by the dominant, wealthy family or families.

Nakarattar clan temples (*nakarakkovil*) all had their own *vitutis* paid for by clan members; there were separate *vitutis* for men and women and, in some cases, additional *vitutis* for subclans. These *vitutis* were used as lodging houses by Nakarattars visiting the temple on business, such as to register a forthcoming marriage in the family or to pay arrears of temple dues. They were also used for general assemblies for clan meetings.

Nakarattars also built *vitutis* wherever they did business. After the opening of Madras harbor in the 1880s, one finds separate Madras *vitutis* built by Nakarattars of Devakottai and Karaikudi: the former to serve Nakarattars engaged in internal trade, the latter to house traveling women. The Nakarattar Association of Tiruchirapalli also built a community lodging house in Madras, and Nakarattars who did business in Burma constructed the Rangoon *nakaravituti* there. Nakarattars who did business in Ceylon built a *vituti* in Tuticorin. The Nakarattar Association of Malaya built a *vituti* at Nagapattinam. And the Nakarattars of Singapore built a *vituti* at Penang. The cities and countries where all of these *vitutis* were located served as major markets for the groups who built the *vitutis.* Similarly Nakarattar businessmen constructed *vitutis* in every major place of business throughout Southeast Asia: in Colombo, Rangoon, Penang, Singapore, and so on.

Nakaravitutis were more than lodging houses. They were social institutions in which Nakarattars came together, exchanged information, and made interdependent decisions. As such, *vitutis* constituted corporate bodies whose officers represented the interests of local Nakarattar communities. *Vitutis* at major pilgrimage centers received contributions from Nakarattars and oversaw temple festivals funded by these donations—both annual festivals, such as those carried out since the seventeenth century at Palani (Chapter 7), and special festivals, such as Nakarattar-funded temple renewals (*kumpapisekams*). *Vitutis* also undertook the feeding of large numbers of holy men and mendicants on such occasions, and of a fixed number of such people throughout the year. Unlike the private temples of Chettinad, however, *nakaravitutis* shared these honors with representatives from other communities who also participated in the ritual cycle of major Hindu pilgrimage centers.[19]

At *vituti*-sponsored festivals and at more mundane convocations (such as weekly or monthly meetings to set interest rates), *vitutis* maintained a constant schedule of collective events in which their members came together and exchanged notes on business. As clearinghouses for information about each other and about business opportunities generally, these collective events effected investment decisions, including decisions about the optimum allocation of investment funds and the amount of credit to extend to a fellow Nakarattar. In other words, *vitutis* provided Nakarattars with access to information about each other's business. They provided opportunities to scout out investment opportunities and arrange for loans by fellow Nakarattars looking for investments. At the same time, the information they provided served as checks against incautious business behavior and unreasonable requests for credit.[20]

Nakarattar Panchayats

Access to public information about each other's business also served to limit situations in which disputes might arise between Nakarattars due to private misunderstandings. When such disputes arose (as they inevitably did), *nakaravitutis,* along with temples and (at one time) Saivite monasteries (*matams*), provided venues for extraordinary meetings of the community to resolve disputes. These meetings were held under the jurisdiction of a respected elder or elders in the concerned community and were called *panchayats*—on the pan-Indian model—although disputes were typically mediated or arbitrated by a single person.[21]

Little has been observed of Nakarattar *panchayats* in operation. They clearly served both religious and business functions and had long been associated with temples and with sectarian religious orders housed in Saivaite *matams.*[22] But the basis for many of the disputes reportedly brought to *panchayats* seems to have remained constant. Among coparceners, for example, differences might arise over the provision for a widowed mother or unmarried sisters. Related disputes might arise regarding the payment of seasonal prestations (*murais*) to married sisters. In both of these cases, the underlying basis for the argument would be strain between two or more brothers who maintained the traditional joint family for business purposes, but who were unable to arrive at a mutually satisfactory allocation of decision-making powers. In some cases the strain might become intolerable, especially to the younger brother, who would then press for partition of the family estate. If the disputes could not be resolved within the family, the matter might be taken to the village temple *panchayat.* Disputes between in-laws about dowry payments or treatment of the daughter and wife might be appealed to a clan temple *panchayat* if the families came from different villages. Other disputes between families from the same clan might also be resolved at a clan temple *panchayat.*[23] In addition, *panchayats* were called in cases where the individual was seen as flaunting the rules of the community, for example, by refusing to pay a tithe for support of the community temple or, in principle, by marrying a woman from another caste.[24] Finally, disputes between Nakarattar businessmen over payment of interest on loans, return of deposits, or other business matters might be appealed to a *panchayat* called at a temple in the place of business, in the men's natal village if they came from the same village, or at the men's clan temple if they were members of the same clan. It is not clear whether there was a pattern in the choice of venue. But, at least until the 1920s, if there was a dispute between Nakarattars from Devakottai over the honoring of a *hundi,* the matter was raised in Devakottai rather than in those places where the transaction had been carried out (Krishnan 1959: 65).

It is this case that perhaps most clearly illustrates the business value of Nakarattar techniques for conflict resolution. Nakarattar financial transactions transcended local boundaries. There was no single local context in which Nakarattars did business and hence no single local temple to which appeal might be made for community sanction. By maintaining their own village-based and clan-based communal organizations in Chettinad, however, Nakarattars maintained a hold upon every member of their community, no matter where the person did business. Suppose that one Nakarattar refused to accept a *panchayat* decision about payment of interest owed on a *hundi* transaction. In some cases, a *panchayat* might decide to take action, such as prohibiting Nakarattar families from intermarrying with the offender's family until he complied with their decision. Whether or not such extreme measures were taken, news of his untrustworthiness would spread rapidly throughout the network of localized Nakarattar communities defined by temples and *vitutis* serving Nakarattar villages, clans, and business stations. No Nakarattar would do business with him. A major part of his working capital and an important and reliable source of liquid credit would be denied him. He would soon be out of business. Armed with these sanctions, Nakarattar communal organization remained strong and effective until the twentieth century, when changes in the apparatus of colonial government began to offer alternatives to and protection from collective caste action. But until incremental colonial governmental reforms took effect during the 1920s and 1930s, individual Nakarattars ensured themselves of access to the collective pool of Nakarattar capital by maintaining moral norms and institutional sanctions for business cooperation and caste organization.

Finally, notice that techniques of Nakarattar conflict resolution were by no means centralized under a single Nakarattar chief or an overarching Nakarattar caste *panchayat*.[25] On the contrary, they were highly segmentary and context-sensitive, responding to various combinations of local interests generated in disputes between Nakarattars from different villages, different clans, and different business stations. This segmentary quality in no way prevented the caste from responding as a whole to the decisions reached by a *panchayat* meeting. But this is hardly surprising. The contribution of segmentary organizational mechanisms for maintaining collective action has been recognized since at least Evans-Pritchard's (1940) study of the Nuer (for further discussion of the specific Nakarattar construction of segmentary organization, see Chapter 9).

Collectivism and Capitalism

The introductory sections of this chapter outlined an argument begun in Chapter 5, that, contrary to Weber, magic and collectivism are *not* impediments to capitalism. Indeed, they form the basis of a distinctive capitalist ethic in Hindu India. The body of this chapter has supported my contention by presenting information about the collective organization of Nakarattar capitalism. The following chapter addresses the capitalistic uses of magic. My purpose in all this, however, is not to add yet one more redundant criticism of Weber's analysis of Hinduism, but to reconsider the stress Weber places on the role of *individualism* in capitalist practice: a quality that anthropological and historical studies continue to install as *the* definitive element of true capitalism.[26] Thus, as we saw in Chapter 3, many corrective interpretations of Indian economic history and Hindu business practice refute Weber by showing that Hindu businessmen are entirely capable of acting as individualistic entrepreneurs. Nevertheless, there is danger of throwing the baby of caste out with the Weberian bath water. Not all Hindu business practice was individualistic. In many cases, castes did function corporately, not in the way envisioned by Weber, but in other ways that are poorly understood because almost no one considers them.[27] In other words, there is a need to consider what kinds of *collectivism* may have been at work and may continue to be at work in Indian forms of capitalism.

A Weberian rejoinder might be that the traditional, collectivist orientation of Hinduism is precisely what prevented the extension of its capitalistic variants—represented by the Nakarattars—into the wider Hindu population.[28] Such a rejoinder seems quite dubious, both in terms of documented capitalist formations throughout India and also in terms of some of the weakest links in Weber's argument. In regard to the first point, one need only look to the development of economic practice and organization among non-Nakarattar groups in India—including, in South India alone, Brahman castes (Krishnan 1959), castes specializing in craft production (Mines 1984), and agrarian castes (Hardgrave 1968). But besides this, Weber's own observation that modern capitalism is to be distinguished from other capitalisms (e.g., adventurer's capitalism or pariah capitalism) primarily by the presence of a completely organized work force (Weber 1958: 186, 271) combines with his scattered and insubstantial comments about the displacement of Protestant capitalism by modern, secular capitalism to weaken his argument (180–181). He gives no clear account of the processes of displacement, raising the possibility that non-Protestant ethics might, under appropriate conditions, also lead to a completely organized work force. Christopher Bayly (1989) makes a very similar point with respect to North Indian society. Given the Indian examples, it seems reasonable that whatever "nonreligious" forces extended the Protestant ethic to the entire society in Europe might also be at work extending the Hindu capitalist ethic in India. And this suggestion, at least, offers us a modest point of agreement with Weber on which to end this chapter. For, in his more cautious moments, Weber (1958: 91, 183) insists that he was only exploring a set of conditions sufficient for the emergence of capitalism and that he was not making the claim that Protestantism was necessary, let alone necessary and sufficient.

PART THREE

RITUAL AND KINSHIP

7 The Magic of Capitalism and the Mercantile Elite

Magical Capitalism

Most efforts to describe Nakarattar business point to Nakarattars' ascetic life style and their total commitment to business, in short, to a Hindu version of Weber's Protestant ethic (Day 1972; Mahadevan 1976; Siegelman 1962; Thurston 1909). Mention is made in passing of their massive religious endowment, of their construction of lavish houses in their homeland of Chettinad, and of their extravagant dowries. But such apparently non-business, nonprofit activities are not integrated with the otherwise totalistic Nakarattar business ethic. Indeed the question of how these activities are integrated is scarcely treated.

The most important exception to this generalization is provided indirectly by Milton Singer's (1972) effort to develop a non-Weberian interpretation of Hindu industrialists in 1960s Madras. Yet even here, despite trenchant criticism of many of Weber's arguments and a powerful analysis of the positive role of joint families in industrial organization, Singer ultimately offers a Weberian apologia for the coexistence of Hindu ritual and capitalist practice. Along with Weber, Singer apparently assumes that ritual and business are inconsistent and suggests that Hindu businessmen *compartmentalize* their religious life from their business life, conducting worship in their homes and temples in as minimal fashion as possible. Moreover, he suggests that religious endowments and other ritual gifts represent compensatory devices by which businessmen pay other people to worship for them. He labels this rather Catholic interpretation of Hindu religious gifting as *vicarious ritualization.*

To my knowledge, no one has taken issue with Singer on this interpretation. Yet it depends crucially on three problematic assumptions. They involve, respectively, a mistake about historical fact, an ethnocentric view of religion, and a failure to appreciate the radical but incomplete transformation of Hindu religious endowments under colonial and postcolonial rule.

Historical issues arise in Singer's implicit assumption that religious endowment, as a form of vicarious ritualization, is a novel ritual response to a novel business climate. Yet it is clear from published South Indian cases of religious gifting in eleventh-century Chidambaram (Hall 1980; Spencer 1968), fourteenth- and fifteenth-century Tirupati (Stein 1960), seventeenth-century Palani (Rudner 1987 and this chapter, below), and nineteenth-century Madurai and Ramnad (Breckenridge 1976; Price 1979) that this assumption is wrong. In each of these cases, various forms of religious gifting constituted mechanisms by which merchants and mercantile communities entered a new locality, created viable social identities, and gained authoritative entitlement for their commercial enterprises. It is also quite clear that temples which received merchant endowments acted as capital-accumulating institutions, that mercantile leaders were frequently able to exercise control over temple expenditure and investment, and that this control included reinvestment in the business enterprises of the merchants themselves. In other words, religious endowment has been a central component in Hindu business practice since long before the age of instant communication, rapid transportation, and capital-intensive industry.

Moreover, the problem with interpreting religious endowment as *vicarious* ritualization goes far beyond incompatibility with historical fact. At its core, such an interpretation relies on an ethnocentric assumption that religion is, by definition, *other-worldly* and that it interferes with secular, *this-worldly* business concerns. Conversely, such an interpretation implies that mundane goals such as profit making interfere with genuinely religious ends such as attaining or proving salvation. From this broadly Weberian perspective—and Singer must be included among the Weberians in this regard—just such a dichotomy between secular and transcendental realms was the stimulus to Protestant ascetic individualism, in which all this-worldly profits were directed toward the public good so as not to interfere with the other-worldly goals of the individual. But it does not follow from this argument that in religions where ritual action is *magical,* in the sense that it is directed toward this-worldly ends, it is incompatible with personal asceticism or even individualism.

This chapter examines crucial connections between this-worldly Nakarattar ritual—both religious and secular—and more "formal" Nakarattar commercial activities in two historical periods separated by three centuries. In addition, it illustrates the continuing role of the Nakarattar elite in South India's political economy. The exercise will demonstrate that in both historical periods, members of the Nakarattar elite made rational use of economically "irrational" ritual in their capacity as central links in a collectively oriented, political economy, whose participants included the Nakarattar caste as a whole, noncaste investors, religious and educational institutions, and political authorities.

Nakarattar Worship and Trade in Seventeenth-Century Palani

Palm-leaf manuscripts (*olais*) maintained at Palani Temple in Madurai District make it possible to reconstruct the way the Nakarattar caste carried out its business and participated generally in seventeenth-century South Indian society. These manuscripts, which constitute the Nakarattar *Arappattayankal* (The Six Nakarattar Deeds of Gift),[1] confirm Nakarattar oral tradition that the caste was primarily involved in the trade of salt. In addition, the records provide important information about the mechanics of trade and particularly about the crucial connections that existed between trade and religion.[2]

Manuscript	*Date*
1. List of Palani Temple Practices	1600
2. Deed of Gift by the Nakarattar of the Seven Cities	1608
3. Minutes on Coronation in the Matam	1610
4. Deed of Alagiya Desikar	1627
5. Deed of Gift by the Nakarattar of the Seven Cities	1766
6. List of Atinam Piranmalai Practices	1770
7. Deed of Gift by the Nakarattar of the Seven Cities	1788
8. Deed of the Gift to the Matam	1805

The "deeds" (*pattayams*) tell a story, beginning in 1600, of the initiation and growth of Nakarattar trade in the pilgrimage/market town of Palani and of the concomitant growth in Nakarattar ritual involvement and religious gifting to Palani Temple. The story begins with the arrival in Palani of Kumarappan, a Nakarattar salt trader from Chettinad, "The Land of the Chettis." The manuscripts describe his first contact with a Palani Temple priest, his initial worship (*puja*) of the temple deity, the growth of his commercial activities in the temple market, and his endowment of the temple and subsequent installation as a trustee (*dharma karta*) of the endowment.

According to these texts, Kumarappan was the first Nakarattar to establish trade in the salt-deficient region of Palani. He stayed in the house of the Palani Temple priest and operated his business in the street outside the priest's house. From the beginning, he marked up his margin of profit by one-eighth and gave the markup as an offering and tithe (*makimai*) to the deity of Palani Temple, Lord Velayuda (a manifestation of Murugan). Food paid for by Kumarappan's *makimai* was prepared by the priest's wife and offered to the deity by the priest. Afterwards it was distributed as sacramental food (*prasad*), first to the priest and then to Kumarappan, his employees, and local mendicants (*paradesis*). In addition, Kumarappan paid the priest and his wife each a small sum of money (two *panams*).

In other words, even at this early stage, commerce entailed much more than simply opening up a shop in the local marketplace and setting prices for goods according to local conditions of supply and demand. In particular, it involved establishing a relationship with the deity of Palani, mediated by the deity's priest. Kumarappan satisfied this condition by undertaking regular acts of individual worship (*arccanai*) on a monthly basis each time he returned to Palani to trade.

Kumarappan not only expanded his own salt trade in Palani during the next few years but also, in the fourth year, was instrumental in bringing five additional Nakarattar salt traders into the community. Kumarappan arranged for each of them to emulate his lead and mark up their profit for *makimai* given as part of individual worship of the Palani deity conducted by the temple priest. In the first deed of gift, Kumarappan attests,

> "The gift of food has been on the increase since I first came here. My profit goes on increasing from the time Parvati [the priest's wife] started cooking for us. Until now the funds that accrued by way of profit markup for the Lord were eighty-five rupees. This time I got forty-two *panams* through profit markup. Thus there is a total of rupees 96-4-0 for the Lord." So thought Kumarappan. This way the Lord made a profit and the sons of Chettis also made a profit. The Nakarattars came to know of this. Some of them started working for wages for the Lord and some for Kumarappan of Nemam. Four for the Lord and two for him. This way they came selling salt, stayed in Pandaram's house, and ate what Parvati cooked for five or six years. Through markup and straight profit the Lord gained one hundred to one hundred and twenty *varakans* [one *varakan* = Rs. 3.5].[3]

News of the successful Nakarattar business venture reached a local chief in political control of Palani (the Nayak of Vijayagiri) and the Pandyan king of Madurai (Tirumali Nayak), who was sovereign over the Tamil kingdom encompassing Chettinad and Palani. News of Nakarattar trade also reached the Saivite sectarian leader, Isaniya Sivacariya, whose monastery was located in Piranmalai at the western edge of Chettinad. The sectarian leader was guru both to the Pandyan king and to all male Nakarattars. He proposed that Kumarappan should arrange for an annual pilgrimage, sanctioned by the Pandyan king, to celebrate the deity's wedding on a date in the Tamil month of *Tai* (corresponding to January–February in the Roman calendar).

The collective worship of the pilgrimage and marriage festival was significantly different from the individual worship in which Kumarappan and the other Nakarattars initially engaged. Individual worship (*arccanai*) established a more or less private relationship between trader and deity, mediated by the priest. But the pilgrimage established a collective festival (*tiruvila*) and generated a system of ritual transactions between all the notables of the Palani community: not only traders, priests, and deity, but local chiefs, paramount kings, and sectarian leaders. By participating in the annual festival, each of these notables recognized and ritually sanctioned the social identity of all of the others.

For Kumarappan, the annual pilgrimage took on significance far beyond what it offered to his fellow Nakarattar salt traders. Kumarappan was the founder and organizer of Nakarattar trade and worship in Palani. He was the person to whom the sectarian leader went in order to establish the pilgrimage for the first time. He was the person who made preparations for lodging, transportation, food, and worship for all of the pilgrims. He even conveyed the Palani priest to the sectarian leader's monastery for the beginning of the pilgrimage. Finally, and significantly, Kumarappan was entrusted with collecting and managing all funds donated by the pilgrims as regular fees at recurring rituals of monetary gifting during the pilgrimage, and ultimately with managing an endowment (*kattalai*) initiated by Kumarappan to maintain the pilgrimage in perpetuity.

As manager of the endowment, Kumarappan was not only the master of ritual ceremonies, but also the chief executive of what amounted to a joint business venture with the deity of Palani. His managerial position carried, in addition to ritual honors, the responsibility of investing all funds endowed for worship of the deity. There was no specification or limit as to how these investments should be made. His appointment as *dharma karta*—the executor of important collective rituals—was recognized by kings, sectarian leaders, and priests, but his actions were sanctioned only by the deity himself. Kumarappan shared some honors with other notables who were similarly generous in contributing to temple endowments. But his special status reflected not only his generosity (*vallanmai*) but also, and perhaps more importantly, his fiduciary trustworthiness (*nanayam*) and his commitment and effectiveness as a businessman. The honors he received did not simply recognize his worship of the deity (in either private or collective forms). Nor were they given in recognition of his personal offerings to the deity as a part of worship (in *makimai* or *kattalai*). Rather, Kumarappan's honors recognized his special role in stimulating and managing the worship and donations of other Nakarattars. In effect, the collective worship at Palani constituted Kumarappan as a leader of the Nakarattars, and empowered him to act as trustee of all funds donated to the deity. His honors were the emblems of his office.

Temples as Political Institutions in the Seventeenth Century

The preceding interpretation of Nakarattar religious gifting at Palani fits within recent historiographic interpretations of South Indian temples as not simply architectural structures but also institutions that carried out two important social functions in South Indian society: (1) a *group formation* function, as the focus for collective acts of capital accumulation and redistribution; and (2) an *integrative* function, as political arenas for corporate groups formed by collective redistributive action. Although little attention has been paid to the role of individual gifts (*arccanai*) in this regard, the operation of collective gifts (*kattalai*) has become increasingly clear.

In a definitive paper on the ritual and political operation of South Indian temples, Appadurai and Breckenridge (1976) address the group formation function of temples. They integrate anthropological insights about the association of political chieftainship and economic redistribution with case studies of temple donors and their identity as leaders of various corporate groups, including families, castes, guilds, kingdoms, and even business corporations. Interpreting endowment to a temple as a form of collective gift, the researchers summarize their findings about endowment as follows:

> (1) an endowment represents the mobilization, organization and pooling of resources (i.e., capital, land, labor, etc.);
>
> (2) an endowment generates one or more ritual contexts in which to distribute and to receive honors;
>
> (3) an endowment permits the entry and incorporation of corporate units into the temple (i.e., families, castes, monasteries or *matam* -s, sects, kings, etc.) either as temple servants (*stanikar* -s, managers, priests, assistants, drummers, pipers, etc.) or as donors;
>
> (4) an endowment supports, however partially and however incompletely, the reigning deity. But, because the reigning deity

> is limited since it is made of stone, authority with respect to endowment resources and ritual remains in the hands of the donor or an agent appointed by him or her. (Appadurai and Breckenridge 1976: 201)

In other words, an endowment entails collective action, ritual designation of a leader, allocation to that leader of authoritative control over collective resources, and recognition of the group as a corporate entity represented by the distinctive role of its leader on various occasions of worship to the deity. Appadurai and Breckenridge, however, draw their conclusions about the group formation function of endowment primarily from research on practices in the nineteenth and twentieth centuries. My interpretation of the seventeenth-century deeds of gift from Palani builds on their interpretation and demonstrates that such processes were also in play at least two hundred years earlier.

Complementing these findings about the role of temple endowment in group formation, studies on the overall political role of temples in South Indian society during the Vijayanagar period (1300–1700) make it clear that temples served a second political function (Appadurai 1981a; Mahalingam 1967; Stein 1977, 1980). Specifically, temples played an integrative role in regional politics by providing an important interactional arena for extralocal sovereigns, leaders of local corporate groups of various kinds, and religious sectarian leaders. Appadurai's (1981) work on Vaishnavite sectarian movements offers an especially useful takeoff point for the present study. It develops a model of mutual recognition and legitimization between extralocal sovereigns and local sectarian leaders mediated by temples in the seventeenth century. According to Appadurai,

> Warrior-kings bartered the control of agrarian resources gained by military prowess for access to the redistributive processes of the temples, which were controlled by sectarian leaders. Conversely, in their own struggles with each other, and their own local and regional efforts to consolidate their control over temples, sectarian leaders found the support of these warrior-kings timely and profitable. (1981: 74)

Such political interpretations of worship have recently been subject to criticism by C. J. Fuller, who argues that they are based on an interpretation of *puja* (worship) as an asymmetric exchange between god and devotee that ultimately reduces *puja* entirely to politics (1992: 81). Fuller disagrees with this premise, arguing that devotees exchange nothing with their gods in acts of worship. Instead, they express devotion with various offertory actions (*upacharas*) which the gods find pleasing. In Fuller's view, the gods never actually either consume or alienate these offerings.

As a consequence, the gods are under no obligation to reciprocate by making any counterprestation to their devotees. Yet, out of pleasure with their devotee's devotion, they bless the offering—which the devotees, not the gods, subsequently consume.[4]

Fuller recognizes that temple rituals include a distribution of divinely transvalued offerings (*prasad*) and honors (*maryatai*). But, contrary to many standard analyses (e.g., Babb 1975), he insists that these sacralized offerings should not be confused with tangible leftover substances (*jutha*) from divine consumption (Fuller 1992: 77). Further, he insists that the ritual distribution of *prasad* and *maryatai* is completely separable from the performance of the various *upacharas,* the offertory rituals which Fuller designates exclusively as worship (*puja*). Finally, he insists that, unlike the distribution of *prasad,* the offering of an *upachara* is free from the taint of politics. For Fuller, the root Hindu metaphor for understanding *puja* reflects not the political relationship between king and subject but the domestic relationship between husband and wife, exemplified by the wife's preparation of meals and her consumption of leftovers (1992: 78–79).

Fuller, it seems to me, goes too far in separating the political aspects of ritual located in the distribution of *prasad* and *maryatai* from the domestic aspects of devotional offerings in *puja.* To begin with, his appeal to the relationship between husband and wife as a root metaphor for understanding *upachara* calls the whole issue into question since, as he recognizes himself, the wife does consume her husband's leftovers. Secondly, the redistributive model proposed by Appadurai and Breckenridge is not limited to interactions between priests and deities. On the contrary, whatever goes on between priest and deity, the Appadurai-Breckenridge model is primarily concerned with a system of indirect exchanges between devotees. (Indeed, it could be argued that the Appadurai-Breckenridge model is problematic because it leaves priests, as mediators with gods, entirely out of the picture!) According to Appadurai and Breckenridge, the system is initiated by a donative group which pools its resources and presents an offering to its leader. This leader, in turn, presents the collective offering to a priest, who (not to beg the issue) does something which sacralizes the offering in a ritual interaction with the deity. The priest then returns the sacralized offering to the leader of the donative group, who then distributes it to his followers. Fuller addresses neither the obvious questions that arise about his interpretation of husband-wife relations as lacking exchange or the irrelevance of the mechanics of sacralization for the exchange processes that concern the Appadurai-Breckenridge model. As a consequence, his rejection of a model of exchange between devotee and deity and his refusal to identify *prasad* and *maryatai* with *jutha* must remain controversial for the time being.

Fortunately, the precise status of *upachara* rituals does not affect the general arguments I have made about the entire redistributive sequence of temple rituals, of which *upacharas* form only one part. *Upacharas*, after all, represent the liminal offertory phase of a long ritual sequence, which begins with purificatory acts that remove devotees from everyday life in preparation for interaction with the gods and which ends with the asymmetric distribution of *prasad* and *maryatai* that reconstitutes society. No one would disagree that it is possible to isolate phases of separation, liminality, and incorporation in any ritual sequence (van Gennep 1909; Turner 1977 [1969]). It is not clear, however, that any such phase should be viewed as exclusively either political or domestic. Moreover, if the entire sequence of rituals is taken into account—and it is the entire sequence that concerns us in interpreting both *arccanai* and *tiruvila* forms of worship—then it is impossible not to observe the pattern of collective pooling and redistribution that lies at the heart of the Appadurai-Breckenridge model.

I agree with Fuller that this model is overly dominated by a political perspective. Appadurai's analysis, in particular, focuses precisely on the role of kings and sectarian leaders in society—an emphasis which, in its concern with kingship, reflects a resurgent theme in South Indian studies that has disinterred the work of A. M. Hocart (1950) on Indic society as a kingship-centered ritual polity (see also Breckenridge 1977; Dirks 1988; Price 1979). The correction, however, lies not in denying any role for politics in religious ritual but in seeing how politics participates in ritual. *Puja* involves a variety of actors in Indian society. By taking them into account, in their variety, it becomes possible to explore nonpolitical dimensions of *puja* without rejecting the role of politics.[5] In the present context, my analysis of events at Palani demonstrates how an actor who is neither king nor sectarian leader, but an itinerant trader, used both integrative and group formation properties of collective rituals, and also the less-encompassing rites of individual gifting and worship, to enter the local polities and market towns of South India. Given the political bias of the Appadurai-Breckenridge model and given Fuller's misgivings that it is blind to Hindu devotionalism, it is important to emphasize that neither the political perspective represented in Appadurai's work nor the economic perspective represented here denies or excludes the more soteriological concerns that have traditionally defined Western understandings of religion. On the contrary, my central argument continues to emphasize the inseparability of religion, politics, and economics.

Purity, Protection, Trust, and Mercantile Elites

Kumarappan, who led his mercantile castemates into the ritual/market center of Palani, displayed the markers of leadership worn by leaders of any group in caste society. He was the *yajaman:* the sacrifier (Hubert and Mauss 1964) who collected his group's pooled resources, offered these resources in his capacity as the group's ritual representative at the court of a godlike king or kinglike god, and then received and redistributed the resources (sanctified by contact with king or god) back to his group. The ritual process constituted Kumarappan as the group's leader and, indeed, constituted and reconstituted both the leader and the group itself on every occasion of its performance.

This Hocartian model is extremely useful, but extremely general. Caste society is portrayed as a segmentary society bound together by rituals of religious gifting in which all take an equal part. Viewed from its perspective, the leaders of any group are identically sacrifiers: replicas of one another and ultimately replicas of the king who is sacrifier for all of society. But this very generality raises a crucial question. If the ritual representatives of any group in society are equally sacrifiers for their groups and, in this respect, replicas of each other, what distinguishes their ritual roles and the ritual roles of the groups they represent?

Answers to this question that are available in the literature are partial at best. The most prominent one concerns just the ritual role of priests and no other ritual specialty. The answer, alluded to by Hocart himself (1950) and developed in some detail by Hubert and Mauss (1964), distinguishes priests from *sacrifiers* on the basis of their role as *sacrificers*—that is, as ritual specialists whose specific function is to convey the offering from sacrifier to king or deity. Ethnographic studies exploring the role of the priest in Indian society have focused most often on Brahman priests (Appadurai 1983; Babb 1975; Fuller 1979; Harper 1964), although a few have focused on non-Brahman priests (Claus 1978; Dumont 1957a; Inglis 1985; Parry 1982). In either case, the analyst's attention has been drawn to aspects of the priest's identity that qualify him for this special role: his ritual purity in the case of Brahmans, and his impurity in the case of non-Brahmans.[6]

Such studies lead in turn (it seems inevitably) to a Dumontian conception of caste society as structured by principles of hierarchy—narrowly construed as group ranking along a status dimension of relative purity (Dumont 1980 [1970]). Yet the fact of the matter is that ritual purity primarily concerns only a single ritual identity: that of the sacrificial or mediatory priest.[7] Hindu values of relative purity are largely irrelevant to other identities involved in the processes of religious gifting—including, notably, processes of endowment to Hindu temples. Purity or impurity may qualify an individual to act as a priest. It may even provide sufficient ground for denying entrance of an entire group to the donative and redistributive processes that constitute a temple community (for case studies, see Breckenridge 1977; Hardgrave 1969). But once a group is recognized as a legitimate participant in a temple's transactional network, relative purity is not necessarily relevant for assessing its ritual relationship to other groups (Appadurai 1981b). We are again left with the question of what distinguishes the ritual roles of different groups and their representatives in the court of king or deity and in society as a whole.

As we have seen, a Hocartian alternative to the focus on priests and purity focuses on the identity of the king as royal donor. In Hindu contexts, gifting—especially endowment—operates to integrate any actor into the moral community of a temple. Generosity (*vallanmai*) is the moral obligation (*dharma*) of any wealthy man. Accordingly, it is necessary to identify the particular quality that sets the king apart from other sacrifiers. Case studies of South Indian kingdoms suggest that the quality that distinguishes kings from other donors is their additional status as royal protector (*paripalakkar:* Breckenridge 1977). The Nayak of Vijayagiri embodies this role in the history of Palani.

Taken together, the Dumontian and Hocartian approaches identify and distinguish the ritual identities of two separate transactors in networks of religious gifting. But even in combination, they provide definitions only of the identities of kings and priests. In my analysis of Nakarattar entry into Palani, I have provided an analysis of the ritual identity of still one more transactor in a temple's ritual network, the elite merchant: an identity that has received remarkably little attention, given its importance for temples and for South Indian society generally. Kumarappan's identity in the network of interacting identities that made up a seventeenth-century temple was that of endowment manager. His salient status in this capacity (and, in later times, the salient status of temple managers and trustees) was evaluated along a dimension neither of relative purity nor of kingly protection, but of fiduciary trustworthiness. In his capacity as trustee, Kumarappan transacted with the deity and with other members of the temple community. In return he received a rightful and tangible share of the endowment that he managed. In the history recorded by the Palani manuscripts, this share took form of the temple's reinvestment of Kumarappan's and others' donations back into Kumarappan's business. This, in turn, led to further endowments to the temple and increased Nakarattar involvement in the Palani economy.

Worship and Commerce

In sum, the history of Nakarattar religious gifting at Palani temple exemplifies Nakarattars' involvement with temples throughout precolonial South India. Religious gifts performed not only religious and political functions but also distinctive economic functions, including the acquisition and reinvestment of funds in mercantile enterprises. Just as there was no separation of religion and politics—indeed, in many ways, worship *was* politics—so, too, there was no separation of religion and economics. The Nakarattar caste and other castes of itinerant traders engaged in worship as a way of trade, and they engaged in trade by worshiping the deities of their customers. The system as a whole constituted a profit-generating "circuit of capital" in which the circulating capital comprised a culturally defined world of religious-cum-economic goods. Nakarattars "invested" profits from their salt trade in religious gifts. Religious gifts were transformed and redistributed as honors. Honors were the currency of trust. And trustworthiness gained Nakarattars access to the market for salt. Elite Nakarattars acted as intermediaries between the various institutions that controlled production and access to salt, money, gifts, and honors.

As commerce expanded in the seventeenth and subsequent centuries, so did the demand for and supply of money. The Nakarattar caste, already specialized around activities of money accumulation and investment, was preadapted to take advantage of this commercial expansion. Its territorial isolation placed it at a temporary disadvantage relative to coastal castes that first established links with the growing international trade, especially the trade in textiles. But Nakarattars' ritual techniques for penetrating new markets, pooling capital, and transmitting money would very quickly overcome the early geographic advantages of their competitors.

The Emergence of Provincial Politics

From the Nakarattars' seventeenth-century entrance into Palani, I now want to shift attention to their twentieth-century entrance into the city of Madras. The database for the later period is naturally much richer, and the picture of Nakarattar activities much more complicated. Before attempting to sketch this picture, I provide some background information about overall trends in colonial politics. During the last few years, a number of influential historians have called attention to an evolutionary dimension in nineteenth- and twentieth-century colonial Indian politics. The evolution they describe reflects a decentralization of British power and the development of representational forms of Indian government.[8] The trend was officially initiated by passage of the Ripon reforms in 1884 and 1892. But it is generally agreed that Indian colonial government resisted the spirit of the Ripon proposals until passage of the Morley-Minto Act of 1909, the Montague-Chelmsford reforms of 1921, and the Government of India Act of 1935.

The details of these government acts need not detain us. Their cumulative effect was to provide for Indian nominations and elections to municipal, district, and provincial governing bodies, with local and district boards electing members of the provincial legislative assembly, and the legislative assembly and chief minister nominating members to local boards. These institutional changes, in turn, encouraged participation of local elites in the provincial government in order to retain and, in some cases, increase political power in their home districts and municipalities.

From the British point of view, the changes represented a decentralization and sharing of power with indigenous elites. From the Indian point of view, however, the changes are more accurately viewed as a move toward centralization. Rural elites, whose bases of power had been focused on villages, towns, small administrative units called *taluks,* or the kingdomlike (or chiefdomlike) landed estates called *zamins,* began to participate (directly or indirectly) in integrated political action in the provincial capitol of Madras City.

This is not to say that precolonial local polities were unintegrated in regional and pan-regional networks. But our understanding of precolonial political integration remains tentative at best.[9] Consequently, it is difficult to tease apart features of the evolutionary model of colonial decentralization and "Indianization" that concern genuine integration of imperial/provincial politics and local politics from features of the model that merely reflect a British style of integration. In particular, it remains remarkably difficult to compare the degree of integration maintained by colonial governments, in both their centralized and decentralized phases, with the degree of integration maintained by an enormously varied assortment of indigenous temples, religious sects, and chiefs and kings ruling over pre-British chiefdoms and empires.

The Creation of "the Public" and the Question of Privilege

In the present context, the comparative issue arises in attempting to evaluate the changing role of mercantile elites in commerce, worship, and politics. In what follows, I examine some notable ruptures and an important continuity in the political style of elite Nakarattar merchants between the seventeenth and twentieth centuries, particularly with regard to elite religious gifting and its nineteenth- and twentieth-century secular counterparts. As we have just seen, religious endowment (*kattalai*) in the seventeenth century was meaningful as an offering in a collective act of worship (*tiruvila*). It represented one component in a paradigm of religious gifting and should be understood, in part, in opposition to merchant tithes (*makimais*) offered in individual acts of worship (*arccanai*). A temple manager (*dharma karta*) who managed endowments in the interests of the deity did so by virtue of his own business acumen and wealth. As the deity prospered, so did the temple manager; as the temple manager prospered, so did the deity. There was no necessary separation in the interests of the two. On the contrary, deity and temple manager were mutually dependent.

Over the course of the nineteenth century, however, as the British consolidated and centralized their power, all institutions that played an important role in the apparatus of government underwent a transformation, including temples.[10] Initially, early nineteenth-century district collectors, the primary agents and directors of British rule, acted as kingly donors and protectors of Hindu temples, supporting and even acting as *dharma kartas.* Gradually, under a series of reform-minded government acts, the collectors acceded to missionary pressure and attempted to withdraw from governmental involvement in Hindu worship. But the more they struggled to free themselves from participating in temple politics, the more entangled they became: withdrawal entailed finding suitable native trustees to oversee endowments for which the British collectors had held responsibility; finding suitable trustees entailed setting standards for suitability; and setting standards entailed defining the role of the trustee, of the trust, and ultimately of the deity itself.

Over the course of the nineteenth and early twentieth centuries, temples became encompassed in Anglo-Indian law under the general category of religious and charitable institutions.[11] The social meaning of endowment took on British values, focused around ideals about secular philanthropy and Christian religion. Religious gifting came to be considered, by extension from British norms, as transcendental or other-worldly in orientation—a development with particularly dramatic implications for the evolving colonial conception of a deity and its chief devotee, the *dharma karta.* On the one hand, the deity itself came to be viewed as a kind of public property; access to it, as a public right; endowments to it, as public trusts. On the other hand, the *dharma karta* came to be defined, in the first instance, as the *trustee* of a public fund, with fiduciary responsibility for the deity. From this new perspective, if religious gifting had (by definition) the "nonreligious" side effect of creating an investable fund of capital, such a fund was considered a public resource, not the *karmic* property of private shareholders in a venture undertaken by deity and devotees. Under law, a trustee might receive a fee for services or expenses, but under no circumstances should he receive a share of the trust fund over which he had control, for this would have involved him in a conflict of interest with the deity and with the public good.

In sum, the colonial reinterpretation of religious endowment as a form of philanthropy separated the interests of deity and trustee and gave an entirely new meaning to religious gifting. Worship in the colonial period was interpreted by law as either *private* or *public*—a significant difference from the precolonial distinction between *individual* and *collective* worship. It does not follow from this change, however, that precolonial values no longer played a role in colonial (or postcolonial) society. In what follows, I will suggest that they simply disappeared from view. Moreover, although officially banned from large-scale, "public" temples, precolonial values continued to operate in the myriad "private" temples that fill the Indian landscape. Indeed, there are good reasons to believe that these values are still operating invisibly—albeit illegally—in institutions officially classified as public including public institutions that are secular rather than religious. This, at least, is the view that underlies my interpretation of the following account of Nakarattar gifting, religious and secular, in the twentieth-century port city of Madras.

The Case of Raja Sir Muthia and the Politics of Madras, 1928–1969

Nakarattars' commercial interests in Southeast Asia involved them in such Tamil port cities as Tuticorin and Dhanuskodi from at least the beginning of the nineteenth century. But they played no significant role in Madras City until the construction of a modern harbor in 1896. Accordingly, and justifiably, accounts of Madras City politics before their arrival make no mention of them. Less justifiably, Nakarattars are also largely absent, or underappreciated, in twentieth-century studies. The absence seems attributable to an overwhelming historiographic bias toward questions about the Indian nationalist movement. And even studies that focus on the loyalist Dravidian Renaissance and anti-Brahman movements (which I touch on, below) do not address the issue of specifically mercantile political interests.

Nevertheless, once the Nakarattars had been lured into Madras by the newly built harbor, they began to participate in city politics in a major way: for example, by forming a caste association with special representation on the legislative council and port trust, and by establishing and dominating an Indian Chamber of Commerce, which also had representation in government administration. Nakarattars are thereby distinguished from mercantile elites in preceding eras, who seem to have been eclipsed not only by Nakarattars, but also by rising administrative and professional elites (Suntharalingam 1974). Nakarattars are also distinct from the rural elites with whom they shared the Justice party in the 1920s and 1930s. In this respect, the Nakarattars represent a kind of hybrid elite, combining properties attributed to both the emerging bourgeoisie and the traditional rural magnate.

Of all the members of the Nakarattar elite,[12] the best known, most politically active individuals belonged to the S. Rm. descent line (*kuttikkira pankali*). Its most famous branch came to prominence through the business, political, and philanthropic acumen of S. Rm. A. M. Annamalai, who was ultimately recognized by the colonial government with the title "Raja Sir." The notoriety he won for his family and the hereditary title itself are often misconceived as indicating that the house of S. Rm. A. M. constituted a royal Nakarattar dynasty. In fact, the title is a relatively recent British creation. It was not granted to Annamalai until the middle of the twentieth century, and it pertains to his "rule" only over the newly formed village of Chettinad, not over the Nakarattar residential homeland as a whole. There were many other Nakarattar families with equal or greater economic wealth, if not the same political clout—both other branches of S. Rm. and families from totally different descent lines as well. Nevertheless, the history of the S. Rm. A. M. lineage, and especially the careers of Raja Sir Annamalai and his son, Raja Sir Muthia, illustrate both changes and continuities in the role of a South Indian mercantile elite.[13]

On their own behalf and as managing agents for many client Nakarattars, the S. Rm. A. M. lineage controlled businesses in Tamil Nadu, Ceylon, and Burma since at least the middle of the nineteenth century and had offices in Madras City before the advent of the twentieth century. In 1908, Annamalai—with a group of primarily Nakarattar bankers—founded (and took control of) the Indian Bank as a joint stock company in Madras, taking over the niche left after the failure of the British Arbuthnot's Bank.[14] They were involved in the grain, cotton, and salt trade of Madras during the first half of the nineteenth century,[15] and during the twentieth century they further expanded their commercial activities into new areas, including formal, Western-style banking; insurance; textile spinning and weaving; and construction. They operated a powerful agency in nineteenth-century Columbo which became a base for their later involvement in the twentieth-century Ceylonese cement and construction industries (Weersooria 1973). They were among the first Nakarattars to establish a banking agency in nineteenth-century Burma, where they became one of the largest Nakarattar firms, with many branch offices outside Rangoon, in the Burmese interior. In the twentieth century they have made enormous profits in Burmese timber and oil.

Not surprisingly, members of the S. Rm. A. M. lineage took a keen interest in the political opportunities offered by evolving colonial institutions in Madras. Frequently, these involved profound changes, not just in location (i.e., the establishment of a major agency house and palatial residence in Madras City), but also in political instrumentality. The politics of gifting continued from the seventeenth century on. So did a politics of litigation, which became a central feature of Indian life in the nineteenth century (cf. Breckenridge 1977). In the twentieth century, both of these activities were encompassed by the politics of colonial government.

S. Rm. A. M. Annamalai was among the first Nakarattars—and indeed among the first Indians—to take advantage of the new opportunities. From 1909 to 1912 he was mayor of the municipality of Karaikudi. In 1913, he was elected for the first time to the Madras Legislative Council. I do not have a full record of the total number of terms Annamalai spent as a member of the legislature. In 1920, he served in the Council of State in New Delhi as one of four representatives from Madras Presidency. And in 1923, he may be found winning reelection to the Madras Legislative Council.[16]

From 1920, Annamalai was on the board for the Imperial Bank. At some point in his career he was given the title Rao Bahadur, and later received the title Raja Sir for his political role and financial support in creating a Tamil University at Chidambaram, fittingly named Annamalai University. He was also deeply involved in the Tamil Icai movement: he founded the Raja Annamalai Music College in Chidambaram in 1929, placed it under control of Annamalai University in 1932, and endowed prizes for writing textbooks on Tamil music (Arooran 1980). All of these public and business positions indicate but do not exhaust the extent of his influence in the Madras Presidency, which grew even more powerful after the carefully orchestrated political debut of his son, Muthia.

In 1928, Muthia was appointed to the Madras Provincial Banking Enquiry Committee at the age of 23. From 1929 on, he was a council member in the corporation of Madras. In 1931, the council voted him its president and repeated its choice in 1932. During this period, I am told, Annamalai brought pressure to bear upon the Legislative Council to alter the charter of Madras from corporation to municipality and concomitantly to alter its leadership from a relatively weak council president to a powerful city mayor. This does not seem unlikely because 1933 witnessed Madras City's first mayoralty election. The elections were postponed six months, until after Muthia's twenty-fifth birthday; the minimal age required of the municipal mayor was twenty-five. Muthia was elected.[17]

Throughout his career, Muthia was active in party politics. He served as Chief Whip and Chairman of the Justice party, where he became known as an independent, pragmatic political moderate. Publicly, he was a staunch Dravidianist and provided strong support for the pro-Tamil movement, both politically and also through endowment and guidance of Annamalai University (Arooran 1980). Behind the scenes, he served his own interests and protected his power base without too much concern for party loyalty or for public canons of political ethics. During the 1934 Legislative Assembly election, Muthia withheld support from Justice party candidates R. K. Shanmugam Chetty (not a Nakarattar) and A. Ramaswami Mudalier. The Justicites lost and the Justice leader, the Raja of Bobbili (the owner of a large, multivillage estate), dismissed Muthia from his position as party Whip. Four months later, Muthia sought revenge: he filed a motion of no confidence in his own party's ministry. Lord Erskine, Governor of Madras, describes what happened next in correspondence to the Governor General of India, Lord Willingdon:

> If he were to use ordinary political methods . . . nobody could object, but he has set about getting his revenge by what can only be described as mass bribery. . . . He is reputed to have spent Rs. 30,000 up to now and to be quite prepared to spend another 30,000 as well. . . . I must say that I thought I knew something about playing funny politics but I must take off my hat to these Indians. They are past masters at the art. The last few days have been an orgy of corruption and intrigue.[18]

Muthia's no-confidence motion failed despite his efforts at "mass bribery." But the setback was only temporary. By 1936, Bobbili needed his support in the face of threats from still other Justice factions and made the redoubtable Muthia a minister in his government.

The effectiveness of the S. Rm. A. M. family's political power is also indicated by the history of protests from dissident Nakarattar factions. For example, in 1937 a Nakarattar meeting in Ramnad denounced the S. Rm. A. M.–controlled, Justicite Nakarattar Association as unrepresentative and pledged support for the increasingly powerful Congress party, the party of Mahatma Gandhi (*Hindu,* Feb. 2, 1939, cited in Baker 1976: 301). By 1938, the Justice party was out of power and the Congress party had formed its own ministry, but Muthia still had considerable influence. As leader of the Legislative Assembly, he was said to have made a deal with the Congress party government over taxes (*peshkash*) on his large landed estates and was censured by the Self Respect Conferences held in Tanjavur and Madurai in 1938.[19]

Such an apparent blow as the 1934 dismissal or the 1938 censure might have weakened the political influence of another man. But, as his political longevity suggests, public office and party position were only two features of Muthia's strength. For changes in the institutional structures of colonial government had not replaced precolonial ritual politics, but blended with them, transforming and being transformed in a complex and mutually adaptive process. In particular, Indian leaders still depended on cultural processes of legitimization to sanction their political authority.

Junctures and Disjunctures in the Culture of Elite Endowment

In keeping with the pattern of the mercantile elites that had operated three hundred years earlier in Palani, Annamalai and Muthia were massive donors to their clan and village temples and to temples serving the local community wherever they did business. But, in addition to these acts of religious gifting, they adopted British notions of public service and philanthropy, involving themselves, from the 1920s onward, in educational projects and works of municipal improvement. At the same time, they transformed the basically European values underlying these activities and harnessed them to a regionally and linguistically based movement of Tamil separatism and revitalization.

It would be a mistake to view the wedding of Tamil and British values as an effect of British policy on a totally reactive Indian population or to isolate that wedding from other processes in Madras society with which it was deeply involved. On the contrary, the roots of the movement for Tamil revitalization can be found in battles fought by early nineteenth-century elites who embraced the British cause of secular education, in part as a weapon in their religious fight against Christian missionaries (Suntharalingam 1974).

As early as 1839, the Governor of Madras, Lord Elphinstone, had promulgated a "Minute on Education," in which he stated, "The great object of the British Government ought to be the promotion of European literature and science among the natives of India. . . . All funds appropriated [for educational projects] would be best employed on English education alone" (cited in Suntharalingam 1974: 59). The Madras elite who endorsed these goals were largely composed of mercantile families who had maintained a long history of involvement with the British in Madras City. Throughout their history, they had participated in religious and philanthropic activities that combined the responsibilities of trustee described in the case of Kumarappan at Palani with the responsibilities of kingly protector represented by the Palani chief, the Nayak of Vijayagiri.[20] In performing this dual role they fought against Christian missionary efforts to influence colonial policies about Hindu religious practices, and they supported colonial aspirations to separate government policy from religious dogma and controversy. Ironically, as part of their support, they began to channel some of their endowment activity away from Hindu institutions and into secular, British-style schools and colleges (Basu 1984).

In the twentieth century, the battle against Christianity became irrelevant, and members of the mercantile elite (including Nakarattar notables) forged an alliance with members of the provincial landed elite, transforming the educational movement for use in their political war against the nationalist Congress party. The chief architect of this political strategy was Raja Sir Annamalai.[21] Like many other members of the Madras elite, Annamalai participated in new colonial forms of endowment in addition to more traditional forms of religious gifting. By 1912, Annamalai's brother Ramaswamy had founded a secondary school and had built roads and sewage facilities in the important Hindu religious center of Chidambaram. In 1920, Annamalai used the secondary school as the basis for founding Sri Minakshi College.

Annamalai never lost his admiration for British education. But it was at just this time that elite Tamil values concerning education took on a noticeably different orientation. Early British policies designed to provide an education entirely in English were overthrown by growing regional and linguistic separatism as Indian politicians began to build and move into the emerging arena of provincial politics (Arooran 1980; Baker 1976; Irschick 1969). During the 1920s and 1930s, Tamil separatism and revitalization—the Tamil Renaissance as it came to be called—formed the ideological basis for the Justice party (in which Raja Sir Muthia played a central role) by portraying the rising National Congress party as a bunch of North Indian Brahmans, who would impose their regional interests, their Sanscritic culture, and—worst of all—their Hindi language on the outnumbered Tamils of South India. The Justice party preferred British rule to the threat of Congress party rule. The British, for their part, had other priorities than English education for Tamils. But they were happy to find loyalist allies and willing to help the cause of Tamil culture, especially when their help could be channeled through institutions such as colleges and universities that embodied British values, even without the English language.

The Tamil Renaissance was strengthened by the 1921 Montague-Chelmsford Reforms, which gave the increasingly Indianized provincial governments more legislative and revenue powers (Baker 1976; Seal 1973; Washbrook 1976). In 1927, the Madras ministry, under leadership of

Annamalai's political ally, Chief Minister P. Subbarayan, formed a committee to "investigate the need" for a Tamil university (*Madras Mail,* February 1, 1927, cited in Arooran 1980: 48). One week later, the Chief Minister spoke at the anniversary of Minakshi College, asserting, "When the time comes for founding a Tamil University, Sir Annamalai Nakarattar [he had not yet received the title "Raja"] will, I hope, develop . . . a real residential unitary University. I hope that the Sri Minakshi College will develop not only as a college but also into a Sri Minakshi University at Chidambaram" (*Madras Mail,* February 8, 1927, quoted in Arooran 1980: 50). In 1928, the committee submitted a unanimous recommendation for establishing a Tamil university outside Madras City, with centers located at Madurai, Tirunelveli, Tiruchirappalli, Coimbatore, Kumbakonam, and Chidambaram (*Madras Mail,* March 31 and April 5, 1928, cited in Arooran 1980: 132–133). Simultaneously, Annamalai offered an endowment of Rs. 200,000 "in furtherance of the scheme of a unitary and residential University at Chidambaram" (*Madras Mail,* March 30, 1928, cited in Arooran 1980: 133). In August 1928, the Madras Legislative Council introduced a bill to establish a single teaching and residential university at Chidambaram (Government of Madras, G.O. 365, August 24, 1928). In the following December, the bill was passed in the Council and received assent from the Governor of Madras and the Viceroy of India (Government of Madras, G.O. 605, December 21, 1928). As passed, the bill matched Annamalai's endowment of Rs. 200,000 and promised a recurring annual grant of Rs. 15,000. The government later raised its initial grant with an additional contribution of Rs. 70,000 for the University's endowment (Government of Madras, Education Proceedings 1928–29: 39).

Annamalai's role in founding the university at Chidambaram paralleled exactly Kumarappan's role in founding the Palani pilgrimage, and he received the identical reward. The university itself was named Annamalai University in his honor. He was appointed Pro-Chancellor with overall managerial responsibilities for the university's considerable endowment. Ultimately, he received the coveted title "Raja Sir" for his role in the university's creation.

Economic Power, Elite Endowment, and Political Authority

It is difficult to uncover the complex dynamic between economic power, elite endowment, and political authority, for elite manipulations of political office—either in government or in religious and charitable institutions—are not normally part of the public record. Despite this difficulty, the private uses to which Raja Sirs Annamalai and Muthia put their power and authority are very much alive in the rumors and reminiscences of South Indians living in Madras today, in some cases sixty years after the event. The following discussion, then, is based on hearsay.[22] But the events it describes were common knowledge among the political cognoscenti when I did my fieldwork, and I am reasonably confident about the truth of the following account. At the very least, it accurately reflects a general Nakarattar perception and, more importantly, a general Nakarattar attitude toward elite members of the caste.

To begin with, the underlying basis of the S. Rm. A. M. family's power in Madras was the control of major sources for large-scale credit in the city, the Presidency, and throughout South and Southeast Asia, and Annamalai's and Muthia's influence extended to the Indian Bank, the Imperial Bank, the Reserve Bank of India, and, in short, to most of the major sources for credit and financial exchange available to Indian businessmen. In fact, the S. Rm. A. M. family's control of these banks stimulated two non–S. Rm. A. M. Nakarattar families, Sr. M. Ct. Chidambaram and Kalimuthu Thiagarajan, to found the India Overseas Bank and the Bank of Madurai, respectively. In any case, and particularly in the case of the Indian Bank, controlled by the S. Rm. A. M. family from 1908 to 1969 (when it was nationalized), every loan made by the bank is said to have cost the borrower a clandestine 2 percent fee. The fee was paid to Raja Sir Muthia, either directly, in the form of "black money," or indirectly, in the form of "white money" donated to philanthropic endeavors associated with the family name and under the influence of family members serving on their boards of trustees.

One of my informants offered the following example of the way in which Annamalai and Muthia could use philanthropy to benefit from a "white money" donation to public charity. The Maharajah of Tranvancore was one of the first persons (if not the first) to open temples to *harijans* in 1936. In 1938, Rajagopalacharia, head of Congress and Chief Minister of the Madras Presidency, unveiled a statue of the Maharajah in the High Court compound in Madras City. Raja Annamalai wanted to build an even bigger statue of himself opposite the Maharajah's statue. He built or caused to be built a music academy, Raja Annamalai Mandram, as a contribution to the renaissance of Tamil culture. After his death, according to his wishes, Muthia erected Annamalai's statue in front of the Mandram. It is twice as tall as the Maharajah of Travancore's statue, which it faces. It is built on government land, leased to the Tamil Music Association for 99 years from 1942 for one rupee per year. It was built by donations from the general public, although a large portion of these were actually from other Nakarattars. Rumor has it that the donations constituted a portion of Muthia's clandestine 2 percent fee on loans made in Madras between 1936 and 1942. The academy is rented to the public for musical events and other large functions for Rs. 1,000–2,000 per day. My impression is that the profits (gross income less maintenance costs) are controlled by Muthia.

Another example is provided by the operation of Annamalai University.[23] During the course of my fieldwork in 1981, I asked a Nakarattar, who had been employed by the institution, why Annamalai University was so frequently subject to strikes by faculty and students. He responded with what I first took to be an irrelevant story about its dental school. Apparently, government funds for all university construction projects were deposited in the Indian Bank. The dental school was no exception. Although construction funds were deposited in the Indian bank, they were not disbursed until new funds for another large project were received. Meanwhile, of course, the bank, owned by the S. Rm. A. M. family, made use of the dental school funds. In the context of my question, my informant's story implied that Raja Sir Muthia, as Pro-Chancellor of the University, had deliberately adopted policies that would anger the students and instigate the strike. The strike slowed down the process of construction and hence the process of disbursements. As with many of these stories, it is difficult to judge the truth of the allegation and impossible to prove. But it is undeniable that Muthia's positions in the university, the Indian Bank, and other governmental bodies were fraught with potential conflicts of interest.

If the exercise of philanthropy to and political authority over public institutions produced economic profits, it is also the case that economic power contributed, in return, to the exercise of political influence. In 1909, Annamalai formed the Southern India Chamber of Commerce—a lobbying organization that represented the rising interests of Indian businessmen in Madras. He and his family have controlled the chamber ever since. In this regard, it is significant to observe that it is members of the S. Rm. A. M. family who have actually headed the chamber for the longest periods of its history, and that it is Annamalai and Muthia who have headed the chamber during its celebrations of Silver and Golden Jubilee years.[24] By controlling the chamber, the S. Rm. A. M. family gained not only direct influence on the Madras Legislative Council, by control of the chamber's reserved seat, but also indirect influence, by control of other institutions that also had input on the Legislative Council and that directly affected every aspect of the economic life of Madras. Indeed, to this day, the Chamber—dominated by Raja Sir Muthia until his death in 1984—has representatives in the railroad, port trusts, Telephone Advisory Committee, universities, and various consumer advocacy bodies.

Control of the private social clubs of Madras City's elite was a further bulwark for S. Rm. A. M. family political and economic power. The institutions included the Madras Race Club, the Cricket Club of India, the Indian Hockey Federation, the Cosmopolitan Club, and the Gymkhana Club. In each of these sodalities, Annamalai and Muthia exercised control over membership. I gathered no information about the exact mechanisms of this control or about the kinds of social pressure that this control brought to bear upon the notables of Madras. But since these institutions largely constituted the interactional arena for Madras elite society, I assume the influence was considerable.

There were also direct benefits to be gained. For example, in the early 1930s, Muthia (who was then Mayor of Madras City) opened the Lady Willingdon Club, a recreational club for the one hundred elite ladies of the city (Willingdon had been Governor of Madras and was later Viceroy of India). Membership in the club was determined by a nominating committee controlled by the S. Rm. A. M. family. Annamalai and Muthia donated fifty acres of land to the club. The land, however, was half of one hundred acres of city land that Muthia, as mayor, had leased jointly to himself and his father at one rupee per year for ninety-nine years. Under the circumstances, and in the worthy cause of a social club named after his wife, Governor Willingdon naturally went along. Muthia retained control of the land until his death.

It is interesting to note that although the Lady Willingdon Club presently appears rather run-down, the other fifty acres are quite nicely kept up and contain various institutions, all ostensibly flowing from S. Rm. A. M. family largess. They include the Rani Meiyamma Club (named after Annamalai's wife), the Raja Annamalai building, housing offices for Air India and Indian Airways (since 1980), and an institute for research into Tamil, Sanskrit, and other Indian languages. As with Annamalai University and the Madras music academy, the Annamalai Mandram, one payoff of S. Rm. A. M. family philanthropy was an enhanced public image derived from naming public buildings after Raja Sir Annamalai. In addition, or so it was suggested to me, the S. Rm. A. M. family may have received other payoffs. In particular, it is questionable how much of the contributions for other developments on the leased one hundred acres came from S. Rm. A. M. family pockets, and how much came through skillful manipulation of still other public institutions. For example, in the case of the Raja Annamalai Building, two years' rent for the airline companies was taken in advance from the Government of India and deposited in the Indian Bank controlled by the S. Rm. A. M. family since the early decades of this century, on whose board Raja Sir Muthia sat until

1969, and over which he was rumored to have considerable influence until his death. The actual funds for construction came from an interest-paying loan from the Indian Bank. The advance rent given by the government was used as security. The total sum (roughly ten times the advance rent) was then paid to the raja's own contracting company, South India Corporation (one of the largest contractors in South India), which then built the Raja Annamalai Building.

The case of the Sanskrit Institute is more complicated yet. Beginning in 1966, in honor of Madras Governor K. K. Shah's interest in Sanskrit studies, Raja Sir Muthia manipulated various endowments over which he had influence to provide Rs. 500,000 as seed money to build the institute. Rumor has it that Muthia's payoff came in the form of government contracts by the grateful Shah to companies of Muthia's choice, especially his own Chettinad Cements. Muthia more than made back his philanthropic investment, which, in any case, had been carried out with ostensibly public money. As in the previous example, the essential point is the control of public resources (at local, provincial, and national levels) for private gain, and the use of social ties with political authorities over long periods of time (from Governor Lord Willingdon, who initially acquiesced in and sanctioned the leasing of city land, to Governor K. K. Shaw, who acquiesced in and sanctioned construction of the Sanskrit Institute).

The Historical Continuity of South Indian Mercantile Elites

Whatever the truth of these popular if (perhaps) apocryphal stories, they raise a number of questions about historical continuity in the commercial role of religious gifting and secular philanthropy. There is no denying the major changes that took place between the seventeenth and the twentieth centuries with respect to the social organization of political institutions and the cultural construction of political values. Yet dramatic disjunctures in South Indian politics mask an underlying continuity in South Indian commerce, particularly in the role of elite merchants, which integrates both domains of social action. Kumarappan, in the seventeenth century, and Raja Sirs Annamalai and Muthia, in the twentieth century, epitomize this continuing role of the mercantile elite over very long periods of South Indian history.

I do not mean to imply that all South Indian mercantile elites operated identically at all times and in all places. In the precolonial period, elite merchants acquired titles and offices such as "Salt Chetti." During the colonial period, they acquired titles and offices including Rao Bahadur, Zamindar, Raja, Mayor, and Minister. Other periods offered different titles and offices. In addition, different historical periods provided alternative opportunities for participating in commercial, political, and religious institutions. There were different local and extralocal political forces subject to brokerage, different extralocal financial resources available for local use, and different extralocal markets for local producers. Finally, the resources and organization of an elite merchant's caste varied considerably, depending upon his identity as Nakarattar, Komati Chetti, Brahman, Mudaliar, Nadar, or Kaikkolar. Nevertheless, although the specific mix of ingredients for elitehood varied, the underlying structure of recognized leadership within caste or kin groups, political control of business-oriented local polities, powerful economic brokerage between local polities and extralocal authorities, and large-scale religious and charitable endowment remained constant.[25] Taken together, these qualities constituted structural prerequisites for trust (*marravan nampikkai*) and trustworthiness (*nanayam*), and these in turn constituted the moral basis of credit on which all mercantile activities were based. Indeed, the relationship between mercantile trustworthiness and economic power was reciprocal and functional. Religious gifting and secular philanthropy—far from constituting irrational expenditures for other-worldly ends—were investments in the conditions that made worldly commerce possible.

Plates

The plates in this book range from images of people to images of houses and temples to images of life-cycle ceremonies. They are drawn from a variety of sources, including Nakarattar publications and other documents of the colonial period as well as photographs of contemporary architecture and rituals.

The Public Image

Nakarattars were known to colonial society as archetypal merchant-bankers. Plate 1 portrays a Nakarattar banker in Colombo, a visage known by Nakarattar clients throughout India and Southeast Asia. Plates 2 and 3 show S. Rm. A. Muthia Chettiar, the most visible representative of the Nakarattar community to the colonial government, in two of his most prominent roles: in Plate 2 as Mayor of Madras (1932) and in Plate 3 as Minister for Education, Health and Local Administration (1936–37). See Chapter 7.

Plate 1. A Nakarattar banker in Colombo (1925). Reprinted from Weerasooria (1973) by permission of Tisara Prakasakayo Ltd.

Plate 2. Raja Sir Muthia as first Mayor of Madras (1932). Reprinted from Annamalai University (1965).

Plate 3. Raja Sir Muthia as Minister for Education, Health and Local Administration (1936). Reprinted from Annamalai University (1965).

Political Constituencies of Raja Sir Muthia

As with Plates 2 and 3, Plates 4 through 8 are reproduced from the commemorative volume published for Raja Sir Muthia's sixtieth birthday celebration (*shastiaptapurti kalyanam*), and date from the period before he received his knighthood and the title "Raja Sir." The photographs illustrate many of the Raja's political connections, discussed in Chapter 7: the Banking Enquiry Committee on which he served in 1929 (Plate 4), the Justice party upon his election as Chief Whip and Chairman in 1930 (Plate 5), prominent supporters from Karaikudi on the occasion of his election as Mayor of Madras in 1932 (Plate 6), members of the South India Chamber of Commerce in Madras, likewise posing with him at a reception in celebration of his election in 1932 (Plate 7), and finally, his father, Raja Sir Annamalai Chettiar, with members of the Indo-Burma Chamber of Commerce in 1935 (Plate 8).

Plate 4. Banking Enquiry Committee (1929); Raja Sir Muthia second from right. Reprinted from Annamalai University (1965).

Plate 5. South India League Federation (Justice Party) on Muthia's election as Chief Whip and Chairman (1930). Reprinted from Annamalai University (1965).

Plate 6. Supporters from Karaikudi Municipality on Muthia's election as Mayor of Madras (1932). Reprinted from Annamalai University (1965).

Plate 7. Supporters from South India Chamber of Commerce on Muthia's election as Mayor of Madras (1932). Reprinted from Annamalai University (1965).

Plate 8. Raja Sir Annamalai Chettiar (seated, right) in England with members of the Indo-Burma Chamber of Commerce (1935). Reprinted from Annamalai University (1965).

Houses

The hybrid Anglo-Indian political style reflected in colonial dress and title are also reflected in the magnificent vernacular architecture of Chettinad. This style is illustrated in the increasingly elaborate Nakarattar versions of the Anglo-Indian bungalow, aptly described as "country forts" (*nattukottai*). Chapter 6 draws attention to the *valavu* (the central courtyard, surrounding corridor, and double rooms for *pullis* or conjugal families) from which many Nakarattars derive the name for their joint families. A floor plan for a relatively simple Nakarattar house (Plate 9) illustrates this feature along with an outside veranda for guests in the front of the house, a small courtyard in back for cooking, and a separate room for women "polluted" by various life-cycle crises.

All Nakarattar houses share this division into a front "male" section, a central ceremonial section, and a rear "female" section. From the last quarter of the nineteenth century on, however, Nakarattars elaborated on this common theme, adding on extra rooms around the central core and incorporating a variety of colonial architectural motifs, ranging from Mughal-inspired towers to niches with sculptures of Queen Victoria. Such elaborations are depicted in the floor plan of a more elaborated Nakarattar house (Plate 10) and in the following four photographs of Nakarattar houses. Plate 11 captures the facade from a relatively simple Nakarattar house in Attankudi. Plate 12 shows the daily activity of Nakarattar women drawing a *kolam* (auspicious design) in the street before the front entrance to their house. Plate 13 is reproduced from Raja Sir Muthia's sixtieth birthday celebration commemorative volume and shows his highly elaborate Chettinad "Palace." Plate 14 captures a detail from a gateway to the palace in which the demon devotees of Lakshmi, the Goddess of Wealth, have been replaced by British soldiers. Plate 15 shows the central courtyard in the Chettinad Palace's elaborate two-storied variant of the Nakarattar house. Further analysis and photographs of Nakarattar houses may be found in Palaniappan (1989) and Thiagarajan (1983, 1992).

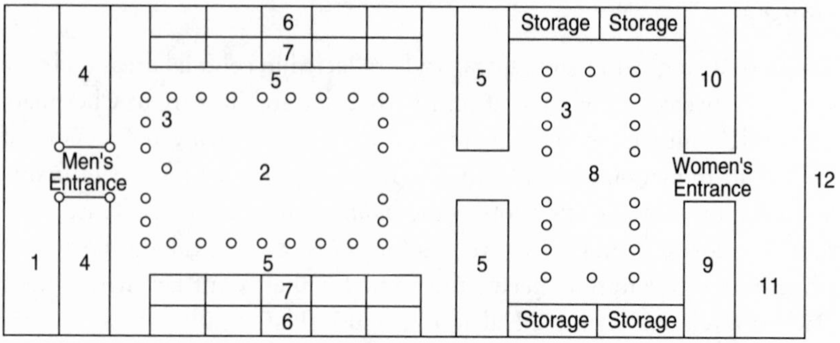

Front (Male) Section of House

1. Veranda.

Central, Ceremonial Section of House

2. *Hāl viṯu* or *viṯu:* first courtyard; literally, "hall house."
3. *Toṇṭu:* columns.
4. *Mēḷpati, tiṇṇai:* a raised platform on which people sit, usually under the veranda or on either side of the door of the house.
5. *Valavu:* aisle or corridor surrounding central courtyard; central section of house including central courtyard, aisle, and inner and outer rooms; entire house.
6. *Ull aṟai: puḷḷi's* inner room for *pūja* and storage of dowry items.
7. *Veḻi aṟai: puḷḷi's* outer, "conjugal" room.
   Kirpati: raised sitting platforms in front of each *aṟai* (not shown).

Back (Female) Section of House

8. *Kaṭṭu:* second courtyard, women's courtyard; where grains are dried, foods are prepared, and water is stored.
9. *Samayal aṟai:* kitchen.
10. *Kutchin:* a small room for women during their menses and for girls during their coming-of-age ceremony.
11. Veranda.
12. *Pin kaṭṭu:* open garden space with or without well.
    Toṭṭam: garden (not shown).
    Kēnru, kēni: well (not shown).

Plate 9. Plan of ground floor of a "simple" Nakarattar house. *Source:* Thiagarajan (1983).

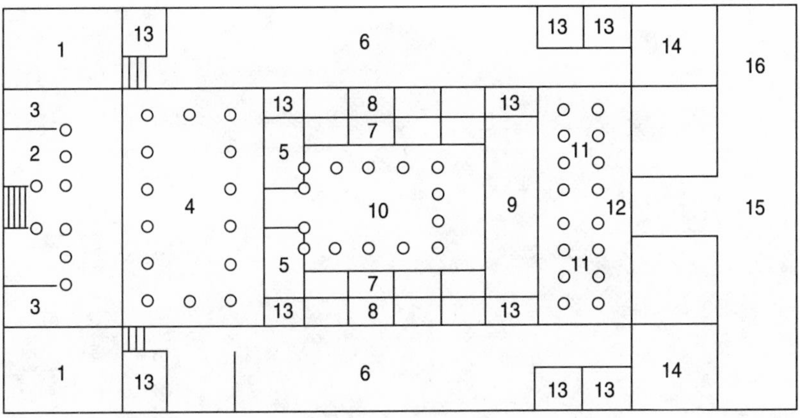

Front (Male) Section of House

1. *Munn aṟai:* front room.
2. *Muṟṟam:* courtyard.
3. *Taḻvāram:* corridor.

Central, Ceremonial Section of House

4. *Kalyāna koṭṭakai:* marriage hall.
5. *Pātakasālai, tiṇṇai:* the "public" room in a house.
6. *Bhōjana sālai:* dining hall.
7. *Veḷiaṟai:* outer room.
8. *Uḷḷaṟai:* inner room.
9. *Iraṇṭām maiya aṟai:* second central hall.
10. *Muṟṟam:* courtyard, roofed or covered with grill work.

Back (Female) Section of House

11. *Muṟṟam:* courtyard, roofed or covered with grill work.
12. *Taḻvāram:* corridor.
13. *Kalanjiyam:* store room.
14. *Samaiyal aṟai:* kitchen ("cooking room").
15. *Pin kaṭṭu:* backyard.
16. *Kēṇi:* well.

Plate 10. Plan of ground floor of an "elaborate" Nakarattar house. *Source:* Palaniappan (1989).

Plate 11. Nakarattar house, Athankudi. Photo by Peter Nabokov.

Plate 12. Women drawing *kolam* (auspicious design) in front of Nakarattar house. Photo by Peter Nabokov.

Plate 13. Raja Sir Muthia's "Palace" in Chettinad. Reprinted from Annamalai University (1965).

Plate 14. Detail of gateway to Chettinad Palace, showing Lakshmi and British "Guardians." Photo by Peter Nabokov.

Plate 15. Interior courtyard of Chettinad Palace. Photo by Peter Nabokov.

Temples and Charitable Endowments

Nakarattar house construction in Chettinad shares much in common with house construction in other parts of South India (see, e.g., Daniel 1984, Moore 1990) and indeed with other architectural forms—most notably, temples. All such forms are influenced in varying degrees by a complex set of iconic architectural principles based on Hindu religious ideas about cosmic creation, sacrifice, and regeneration (cf. Beck 1976b; Daniel 1984; Kramrisch 1946; Meister 1983, 1986; Michell 1988; Moore 1990; Varahamihira 1869–74: Chs. 53, 56). The central idea is that properly designed buildings (*kattitam:* literally, "bounded spaces") represent an image of the personified Hindu universe in microcosm: creation spreading outward toward the eight cardinal directions from a central point where formless divinity is manifest, worshiped, and celebrated in ritual. The center/periphery contrast already noted for Nakarattar houses constitutes only a specific version of this core theme, which is expressed most dramatically in the relationship between the sanctum of the temple (Sk: *garbagrihya,* Tm: *karpakkirikam:* literally, "womb room") and its outer walls (cf. Meister 1986).

The floor plan for Ilayathakudi Temple (Plate 16) illustrates the relationship between central sanctum and peripheral shrines. In addition, it also reflects an architectural concern for locational significance defined along both a front–back axis and a right–left axis. The front–back orientation, already remarked in the case of houses, is reflected in Ilayathakudi Temple by the outward and easterly gaze of the temple's principal deity, Kailasanatasvami (Siva) and the inward, westerly, devotional gaze of devotees as they enter the temple through the pillared hall (*muna mantapam*) and towered gateway (*koparam*). The right–left orientation, expressed in Nakarattar houses by the placement of the kitchen (*samayalarai*) and of the room for the seclusion of women, is expressed in temples by the location of the kitchen (*matappalli*) and of a shrine for demon devotees (*yakasalai*). In both the house and the temple, relatively pure entities and activities are positioned on the right-hand side of the divine center, and relatively impure entities and activities on the left-hand side.

The multiplicity of shrines to secondary deities in Ilayathakudi Temple is obvious (their names are given a Tamil transcription in the floor plan, Plate 16). Invisible is the division of honors (*maryatai*) in the yearly round of rituals among different "shareholders" in the temple (*kovil pankalis*). Also invisible is the rotation of rights (*murai*) to sit on the temple board of trustees and the political interplay among trustees and other prominent members of the temple clan concerning any allocation of temple resources or conduct of ritual practices. See Chapter 7 for discussion.

Their apparent architectural invisibility notwithstanding, many of these political properties of the temple influence the construction of secondary shrines and the performance of rituals at all shrines—including, for example, the allocation of separate shrines to Ganesh (Tm: *Kanapati*—the elephant-headed son of Siva) to temple members from Peramaratur, Perasantur, and Sirusettur. A local historical reading of Ilayathakudi Temple is beyond the scope of the present study, but evidence suggests that temple architecture should be seen not only as reflecting general cosmological principles, but also as reflecting and constituting locally specific political processes. Photographs of Iraniyur Temple (Plates 17 and 18) provide a glimpse of the material consequences of Chettinad ritual politics. A parallel secular manifestation is illustrated by the Raja Annamalai Mandram (music academy) in Madras (Plate 19; again, see Chapter 7 for discussion).

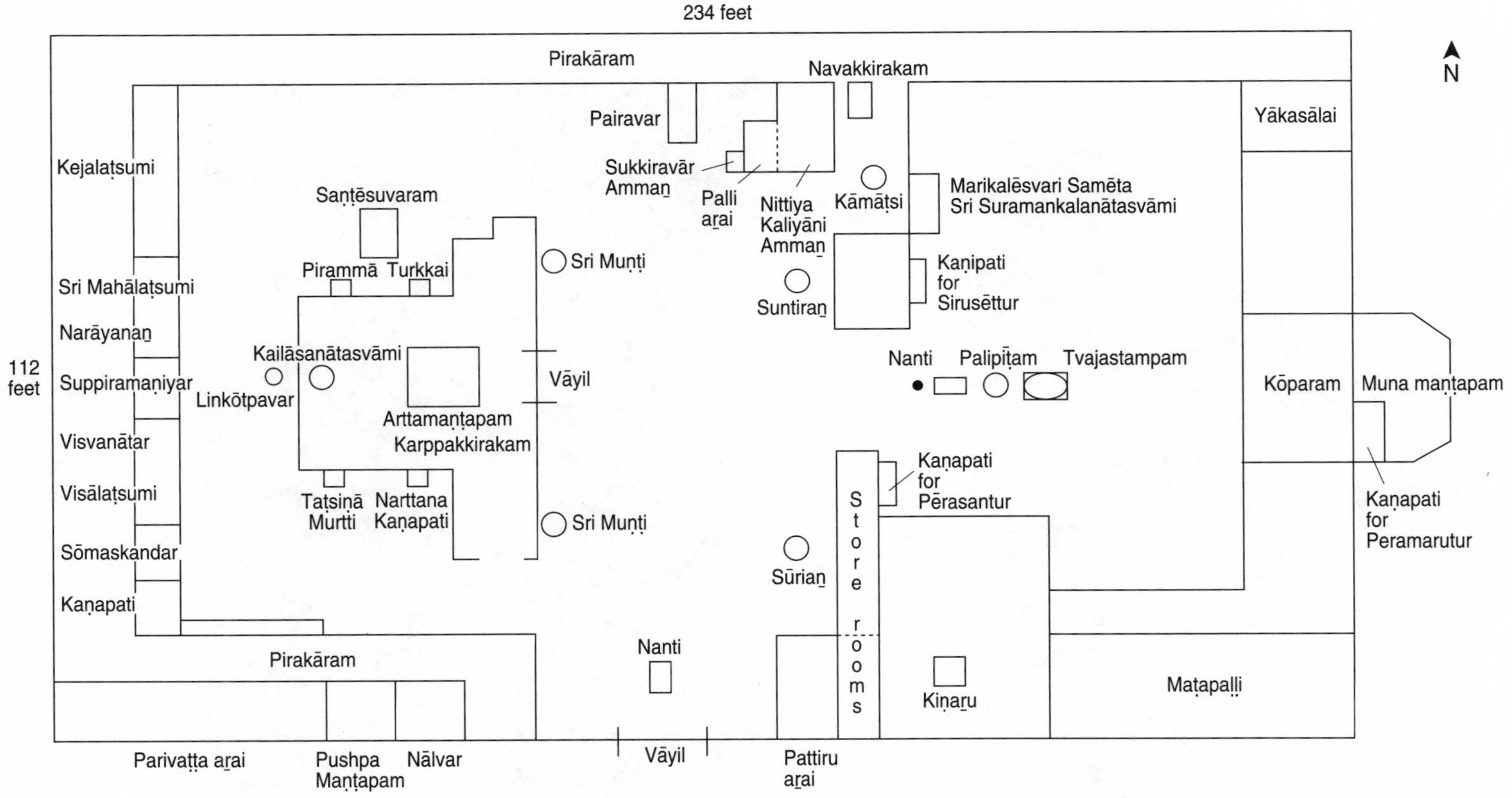

Plate 16. Floor plan of Ilayathakudi Temple. Based on a drawing by V. Thennappan, Devakottai, July 5, 1981.

Plate 17. Iraniyur Temple (exterior). Photo by Peter Nabokov.

Plate 18. Iraniyur Temple (interior of mandapam). Photo by Peter Nabokov.

Plate 19. Raja Annamalai Mandram (music academy and auditorium). Reprinted from Annamalai University (1965).

Life-Cycle Ceremonies

Ancestor worship forms part of a continuum of religious practice that mixes seamlessly with the worship of village and Sanskritic deities (see Chapter 10). Photographs of a family's founders are often displayed over the front entrance to the central courtyard of a Nakarattar house, alongside notable members of Indian society. In many houses these photographs might also be interspersed with paintings of Hindu gods and goddesses. Plate 20 shows a family priest (*purohit*) making daily *puja* offerings at the family shrine (*sami arai*). Similar devotions figure into life-cycle ceremonies that play important roles in both the reproduction and the transformation of Nakarattar culture (See Chapter 9). Plates 21 through 23 illustrate scenes from the renewal of a marriage alliance between two families at a second wedding ceremony performed for the couple on the occasion of the groom's sixtieth birthday (his *shastiaptapurti kalyanam*).

Plate 20. Priest performing *puja* in family shrine (*sami arai*). Photo by Peter Nabokov.

Plate 21. *Shastiaptapurti kalyanam* (sixtieth birthday celebration): Priests performing ceremonies in central courtyard with guests in surrounding corridor. Photo by Peter Nabokov.

Plate 22. *Shastiaptapurti kalyanam:* The second "wedding" of Raja Sir Muthia and his wife. Reprinted from Annamalai University (1965).

Plate 23. Shastiaptapurti kalyanam: Male guests at "wedding" meal. Photo by Peter Nabokov.

8 Marriage Alliance

Introduction

We return repeatedly to the role of trust in the conduct of commerce and to the commercial transaction as an index of trust. Besides building and signaling trust through elite endowments, Nakarattars also built and signaled trust through various kinds of nonelite transactions, especially nonelite transactions between relatives. The items exchanged in these transactions ranged from gifts, deposits, and loans to payments, goods, and services; every exchange was carefully entered in the appropriate ledgers of Nakarattar family firms. Some of these transactions appear, from an economic point of view, to be trusting to the point of irrationality—at least, until one looks beyond the short-term payoff. Yet it is clear that low-interest, long-term loans and deposits to relatives—like nonvicarious ritual gifting by elites—had substantial financial rewards.

There is a danger here. Such a formulation makes it sound as though successful Nakarattar business was prescribed by codes of conduct for kin, by recipes for relatives. Such thinking obscures the freedom with which Nakarattars could manipulate kinship ties to minimize risk in financial transactions, and it completely hides the way that Nakarattars used financial transactions to create the framework of kinship itself. But once we remind ourselves of the dangers of reification, what is important to realize is that in kinship, as in finance, trust was the essential ingredient. Its presence was required for transactions to take place; its absence was enough to sever a kin relationship.

The present chapter begins by providing a brief overview of trust between relatives, measured (quite literally) by Nakarattar terms for kinship. Its nine subsequent sections then focus upon and analyze various transactions between affinal kin, or "in-laws." The preliminary section of definitions describes the overall range of Nakarattar kin relations as designated by terms for different groupings of kin. The second section identifies characteristic relations of affinity and marriage alliance that hold between members of these groups. The third section explores some of the pragmatic considerations that affected marriage alliance formation and the complex alliance structures that sometimes resulted. I give special attention to the intersection of marriage alliance and territorial segmentation in Chettinad and to additional complicating factors that arose in the wake of Nakarattar business activities in different parts of Southeast Asia. The fourth section provides an illustrative case of an alliance in operation. The fifth section describes the ceremonial prestations that symbolized Nakarattar marriage alliances, contrasting them with those that symbolized non-Nakarattar castes. The sixth through ninth sections examine the implications of Nakarattar marriage alliance for standard theories about kinship terminology, marriage rules, and affinal prestations among South Indian castes generally, and especially for the theories of Louis Dumont (1983). The conclusion looks forward to Chapter 10 where I consider why Nakarattar marriage alliance differs from the pattern predicted by standard theories of Dravidian kinship, relating the Nakarattar pattern to Marriott's (1976) theory of Hindu transactions, and viewing the Nakarattar pattern as a specific adaptation to the caste's occupational niche as merchant-bankers.

My information about Nakarattar kinship was collected primarily from directed and undirected interviews carried out during my field work in Tamil Nadu in 1981. Some data were obtained by observing contemporary weddings. But many of the practices described below are no longer performed and are only dimly remembered by some of the older Nakarattars. Accordingly, my description of Nakarattar marriage alliance is offered as a reconstruction of customs before 1930. I believe these customs were in force during the primary focal period of this book, 1870–1930, and I present my description in the past tense.

Preliminary Definitions: Terms for Kin Groups

Nakarattar terms for kin groups segmented the caste into contrasting categories that provided an index to three levels of social distance: (a) structured kinship (including relations between in-laws), (b) diffuse kinship, and (c) common membership in the Nakarattar caste, but no kinship ties. These levels are depicted in Figure 13. At its most diffuse level, Nakarattar kinship terms distinguished caste members who were kin (*contakkarar*) from those who were not (*contam illai*). Kin included all of one's

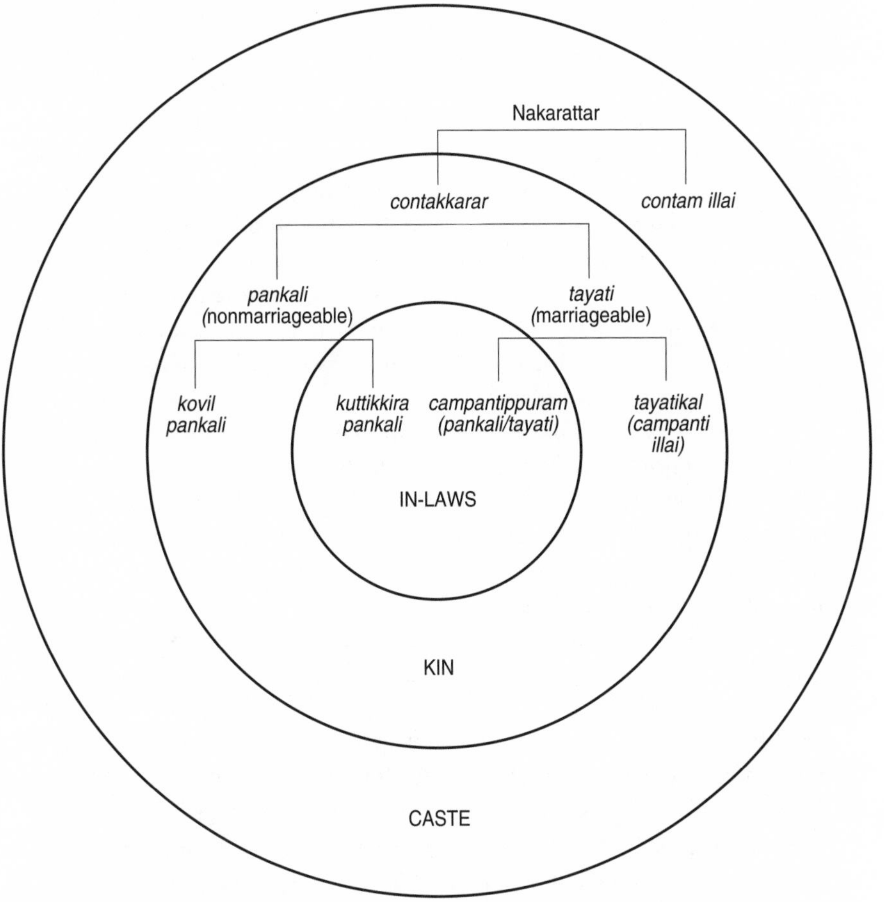

Figure 13. Levels of social distance in Nakarattar kin relations.

agnatic relations, collectively referred to as *pankali:* that is, members of a person's clan (*kovil pankali*) as well as members of one's lineage (*kuttikkira pankali*).[1] Kin also included members of a one's spouse's lineage, all of whom were referred to as *campantippuram* ("in-laws"). Once kinship relations were established between two sets of *kuttikkira pankali* through marriage, they lingered on even after the paired descent groups had terminated jural obligations contracted at the time of the marriage. Affinal relations between kin groups did not extend to members of a spouse's temple clan outside his or her lineage.

Nakarattars employed the terms *tayapillai* and *tayati* (plurals *tayappillaikal* and *tayatikal*), in both a broad and a narrow sense. In the broad sense the terms referred to members of descent groups with whom Nakarattars had once established a marriage alliance, even if they no longer maintained the alliance as such. The terms indicated that marriages had previously occurred between female *tayatis* and male *pankalis.* In this sense, *tayati* designated a more diffuse relationship of kinship than a *campantippuram* relationship, that is, a relationship between descent groups observing an ongoing marriage alliance. Relationships within this diffuse body of affines were recognized, and they might be activated by persons seeking favors, much as were the ties between otherwise unrelated members of the same temple-clan. There did not, however, exist any institutionalized set of rights and obligations for *tayatis* such as those incurred by two lineages actively allied by marriage.

Nakarattars viewed all of the husband's agnatic relatives as the basic unit of reference for the wife as well as the husband. They constituted an enormously extended family into which the wife had married and were referred to by the focal couple and its offspring simply as "our *pankali.*" Active *campantippuram* members who belonged to the wife's uterine descent groups, however, were marked by a narrow use of the term *tayati,* signaled in discussion by reference to specific moral obligations.

Marriage Alliance, Affinal Kindreds, and Tayatis

Exactly what was a Nakarattar marriage alliance? Minimally, it was a negotiated agreement between two sets of descent groups related to the husband and wife of a married couple. The primary groups involved were the joint family (*valavu*) [2] and the encompassing lineage segment (*kuttikkira pankali*) of each individual. The linked groups in a Nakarattar marriage alliance created an affinal kindred defined by consanguineal relationship to one or the other spouse of a married couple.

Membership in Nakarattar affinal kindreds was not reckoned by a criterion of genealogical distance from a specific individual,[3] and for this reason some anthropologists may be tempted to conceive of the group formed by a marriage alliance as a kind of compound descent group, comprising the husband's clan and the wife's lineage.[4] But conceiving the affinal kindred in this fashion, underestimates important differences between descent groups and kindreds that have been all too infrequently acknowledged.[5] In the first place, an affinal kindred was not defined by descent from a common ancestor and, on the basis of this substantive consideration, should not be confused with any kind of descent group.[6] Secondly, and perhaps more importantly, structural relationships between members of an affinal kindred—including relationships marked by important financial transactions—were marked by relations of reciprocity. In this, they differed notably from the redistributive relations that mark Nakarattar descent groups. As we shall see in Chapter 9, descent groups were organized around temple cults that—like the multicaste temple cults described in Chapter 7—provided a focus for the collective pooling and redistribution of resources to their members. These cults, whether constituted of a clan, a multivillage lineage, or the multicaste inhabitants of a Chettinad village, formed corporate units that reproduced themselves from generation to generation. By contrast, affinal kindreds were marked, with one exception, by a set of prestations between two sets of allied descent groups. These affinal prestations generated, in Sahlins' (1966) words, a "between-group relationship" rather than a "within-group relationship." Moreover, among the Nakarattars, the relationship between parties of an affinal kindred was not inherently reproductive.

Affinal kindreds could be initiated by a marriage between two joint families or two larger lineage segments without any previous participation in a marriage alliance. They lasted for at least two generations, during which time their members bore rights and responsibilities to each other. But, counter to most models of marriage alliance in Dravidian kinship, Nakarattar marriage alliances were not automatically renewed. At most, affinal kindreds might, under appropriate conditions, be renewed indefinitely by successive two-generation alliances.

Some researchers studying Dravidian marriage have found it useful to distinguish between, on the one hand, an *alliance relationship,* formed by the first marriage between families of extended lineages, and, on the other hand, an *alliance,* where the relationship is perpetuated (Burkhart 1978). In the former case, the alliance seems oriented primarily toward the respective joint families of the married couple. In the latter case, the couple's total affinal kindred is implicated, with ramifications that may extend to a core group of repeatedly intermarried families in a marriage circle (Burkhart 1978). On the assumption that Dravidian kinship terminology necessarily entails perpetual alliance, scholars such as Dumont (1957b) reserve the term *alliance* for the recursive, self-generating form. In the following discussion, I differ from this usage and employ *alliance* and *alliance relationship* interchangeably, for both perpetual and "one-shot" alliances. I qualify my usage with appropriate adjectives as needed to indicate whether the alliance is regenerative or terminated after a finite period.

Members of Nakarattar affinal kindreds cooperated in a variety of ways. They were tied together, in part, by a recurring sequence of ceremonies and rituals that provided opportunities to exchange information and lobby one another for assistance in various enterprises, of both a business and a nonbusiness nature. These same cyclic and singular ceremonies constituted occasions on which resources were accumulated and deposited to form a trust fund in the bride's name, over which she maintained nominal control. In effect, the deposits—referred to as *accimar panam* (married woman's money)—constituted a bequest, insofar as they were normally intended for the benefit of descendants of the newly married couple, and especially for any daughters that might be born to the couple. Since a share of the bride's natal family's estate was set aside for her and her descendants (especially her daughters) through the mechanism of the dowry, it is accurate to view the formation of these trusts as reflecting a secondary line of inheritance through the female line. If the bride died before bearing any children, all monies deposited as *accimar panam* trusts traditionally reverted to the bride's natal family.

A considerable length of time could pass before the bride's children were old enough to benefit from or control their mother's *accimar panam* in any direct way. Normally, it was not spent until they incurred educational or marriage expenses. In some cases, the fund or some portion of it even remained indefinitely as a kind of communal property under control of the husband's joint family. In the meantime, the accumulated resources provided financial reserves on which all the different joint families of the alliance kindred could make various claims (see Chapter 5).

This is not to say that affinally allied joint families and other descent groups made equal contributions or had equal claims on the accumulated resources. On the contrary, the status of a married person's respective descent groups varied according to the rights, duties, and privileges each spouse possessed with respect to his or her hearthhold (*pulli*), joint family (*valavu*), or lineage (*kuttikkira pankali*). These claims varied widely according to the individual circumstances of the family group involved. In principle, as already noted, the resources in question belonged to the bride. The major part was given by her father (*amman, mamakkarar*) or brother (*attan, maittunan*) in the form of *cir tanam* ("dowry") and in related gifts.[7] However, since she was largely subject to control by her husband, and he was normally subject to control by the senior male in his joint family (see Chapter 6), her rights were largely nominal. On the other hand, the lack of direct control over decisions allocating the use of funds in the trust did not eliminate all privilege of access for the wife's natal joint family or other joint family among the couple's *tayatis.* In some cases, the long process of negotiation leading up to the marriage could result in an agreement that some portion of the fund be deposited in the business enterprises of the *tayatis.*

In general, Nakarattar families felt some aversion to investing an affinal trust in businesses owned by either family in a marriage alliance. One of my informants went so far as to say that such funds were never invested in family business since "it was risky to put all the eggs in one basket." Accordingly, affinal gifts were frequently deposited in the business of third parties, either in interest-bearing accounts or in the form of special, interest-bearing *hundis.* Although these *hundis* were technically discountable on sight, they were used as long-term certificates of deposit and were rarely cashed without considerable advance warning (see Chapter 5). In some situations, an independent banking business might be established in the bride's name. This was especially the case in situations where a son-in-law had no financial assets of his own and could not expect to inherit any. In all of these cases, however, the effect was to open up a line of credit nominally to the bride, but in effect to the various members of the kindred according to their specific claims in the alliance.

Some of the factors contributing to the formation of a marriage alliance have already been examined from the point of view of a family's choice of grooms for its daughters (Chapter 6). A candidate was normally selected after he had already completed his first three-year term as the agent for a Nakarattar banking firm. Accordingly, his future potential as a businessman was subject to knowledgeable evaluation in the marriage-arranging season that followed his return to Chettinad. In fact, although I have no statistical data, it is my impression that a young man was often groomed for the part of son-in-law by a prospective affine, who first hired the young man as an agent for his business firm. If the young man proved himself abroad and relations remained cordial between agent and principal, the family could then propose a long-term alliance through marriage with a daughter.

Selection of the bride for a family's son proceeded along a different route. For example, more emphasis was placed on a bride's physical beauty than on a groom's. Another difference was that a bride's potential capital contributions to an alliance were not evaluated on the basis of expected inheritance or demonstrated business acumen. In fact, until 1947, Hindu women had no rights of inheritance, and there was no way to test in advance the potential contribution a wife's council might eventually make to her family's decision making. Nevertheless, a bride generally did make a substantial contribution to her husband's family business. The bride's counterpart to a groom's inheritance was her dowry along with other affinal prestations that resulted from a marriage alliance between two families.

The size of a dowry was determined by delicate negotiations between families. If the groom's family was seen as too greedy or the bride's as too stingy, a wedding could be called off, although blame would be placed elsewhere—for example, on the sudden discovery of a previously unnoticed misalignment of horoscopes or a previously unknown "parallel cousin" common to both families.[8] Other affinal prestations were not subject to explicit agreement, but a general understanding and set of expectations would be generated and generally followed.

Vattakais *and Territorial Endogamy*

Nakarattar marriage alliances reflected and influenced principles of territorial organization. The major territorial factor affecting them was a system of prohibitions that circumscribed bounded, endogamous territories called *vattakais.* In these *vattakais,* Nakarattars established *panchayats* (councils of influential elders) for making certain kinds of collective decisions and for resolving certain kinds of conflict. That is, the Nakarattar caste encompassed what amounted to incipient subcastes or microcastes governed by the external sanctions of judicial bodies. They did not, however, form marriage circles by adherence to normative obligations of reciprocal marriage exchange. Accordingly, their social organization did not reflect any strictly "elementary structure of kinship" (Lévi-Strauss 1969).

The pre-1930s system of Nakarattar *vattakai*-bound microcastes survives today only in fossilized form, as a statistical pattern among contemporary alliances and in the memory of a handful of Nakarattar historians who have taken an interest in their own past. Thus, the evidence for reconstructing colonial structures of Nakarattar marriage is meager and difficult to come by. Such as it is, I am encouraged by its fit with other components of Nakarattar caste organization during the colonial period. However, the organization and functional implications of *vattakai* endogamy did not become apparent to me until after I had left Tamil Nadu, and I did not pursue a systematic inquiry as part of my field investigation.

My first clue to the historical operation of the system came, typically, while discussing another topic with an informant. I had been trying to ascertain whether any Nakarattar employed the Tamil term *nakaram* or the English phrase "marriage circle" in reference to exogamous Nakarattar clans (Chapter 9)—a usage reported by various non-Nakarattar writers on the topic.[9] (Chandrasekhar 1980; Price 1979). My informant at the time—a knowledgeable man in his seventies with a long history as an industrialist, a regional politician, and a man active in the internal politics of the Nakarattars—agreed with other informants that the usage was unheard of. But he wondered whether the writers in question were referring to a territorial division of Chettinad into "West Circle," "East Circle," and "South Circle." On further questioning he referred to these circles as *vattakais,*[10] and offered the information that these *vattakais* were traditionally endogamous, although *vattakai* endogamy was now breaking down. According to this man, the cultural principle underlying endogamy was simply a preference for geographical proximity: "No family wanted to send its daughter too far away."

Although I am confident that this rationalization accurately reports Nakarattars' sentiment about their daughters, it cannot account for *vattakai* endogamy. In a relatively uniform topographic terrain such as Chettinad, such a preference would result in an evenly distributed network of marriage alliances, not the tripartite system of bounded endogamous segments that existed. I continued to enquire about Nakarattar *vattakais* with all of my informants. But during the course of my field work I found only three or four other Nakarattars who had heard the term *vattakai,* and none of them were able to describe the whereabouts of *vattakai* boundaries or identify the sets of Chettinad villages that were members of the different *vattakais.*

I received no further clues until I returned to America and began to go closely over some of the Tamil documents I had collected during my stay in Tamil Nadu. At this time, I noticed a significant reference in the book *Chettinadum Tamilum* (Chettinad and Tamil) written by my principal informant, Lakshmanan Chettiar, known as Somalay (1953: 12): "In Chettinad, Chettiars still hold their community meetings on the pattern of Chola village assemblies. The sub-divisions, *vattakai* and *karai* are still mentioned." An appendix to Somalay's book contains a table of seven territorial divisions including three *vattakais* (for a version of this table, reordered according to the Latin alphabet, see the key to Map 4; see also Maps 3 and 4).

A tabulation of 91 sample marriages that occurred in 1980–1981, taken from the marriage register of Neman clan temple, indicated that 64 of the marriages (70%) were endogamous within these clusters even today. Moreover, 10 of the 27 mixed *vattakai* marriages (37%) occurred within Melappattur and Mela Vattakais, and another 12 within Pathinattur Vattakai, Kila Vattakai, and Kilappattur (44%). My speculation is that the seven-way territorial division represents a post–seventeenth-century fission of an earlier three-way division, and that these two large clusters of interterritory marriage actually maintain an underlying *vattakai* endogamy. But even if this theory is incorrect, there remains a considerable nonrandom clustering of territorially bounded marriage zones (see Table 10).

Table 10. Cluster Analysis of Endogamous and Exogamous Nakarattar Marriages, by *Vattakai*

Vattakai	*A*	*B*	*C*	*D*	*E*	*F*	*G*
A. Pathinattur	33		1	4	3	5	
B. Melappattur		16	6				
C. Mela Vattakai		4	7				
D. Kila Vattakai			1	5	1		
E. Terku Vattakai					1		
F. Kilappattur						1	
G. Nindarkarai Pirivu							

I wrote Lakshmanan Chettiar asking about the function and organization of *vattakais.* He returned the following reply:

> A cluster of villages, in Chettiar terminology, is called *vattakai.* There are three major *vattakais* and three minor ones. Till fifty years ago, there used to be held *vattakai* conferences of Nagarathars [Nakarattars]. No such meet has since met. Representatives from the village temples (of the Nakarathars) in each *vattakai* still meet on rare occasion to decide austerity measures in marriages, etc.
>
> Till say 1939, there were not many roads in Chettinad. Transport was few and far between. For marriage and *vevu* ceremonies, death rituals, etc., the *Pangalis* [*pankalis:* members of local lineage segments] used to march on foot. Therefore, it was the custom to contract matrimonial alliances within a ten-mile radius. In those days, it was possible to have first-hand knowledge of the families only within such short distance. If a boy (groom) could not get a suitable match within the *vattakai* or if a girl could not be given away within this territorial jurisdiction, it was considered as a stigma to that family.
>
> Adoption was not confined to the *vattakai.*
>
> Since 1939, things have changed vastly. Even now 2/3 of all Chettiar marriages take place within the *vattakai.* But marriage within the *vattakai* is no longer the rule. All villages are connected by road, by public transport and by telephone. To check up anyone's credentials or verify family background is very easy. During World War II, families which stayed on in Malaysia and Singapore contracted marriages among themselves without reference to *vattakai* and this has caught on. In [one of the Chettinad villages] for instance, people have contracted marriages with almost every village in Chettinad. [A textile industrialist residing in the village] set the ball rolling by

> effecting marriage alliances with all textile mill-owner families in Chettinad. In Devakottai, it was the tradition to finalize marriages with families within the town. There are 2,000 families and so it was not a problem to find a suitable match. But, in Devakottai too, people are slowly and in increasing numbers effecting marriages elsewhere. If two families are in business in Salem or say in Coimbatore and are sufficiently acquainted with each other over the years, the *vattakai* ceases to be a bar. I can speak of at least a thousand instances where the *vattakai* system has been given the go-by. (Lakshmanan Chettiar, personal communication, March 1981)

In this letter, Lakshmanan Chettiar subscribes to the notion that preferences for affinal proximity explain the formation of *vattakai*. The explanation is no more satisfactory coming from him than from my previous informant. But his further amplification, along with the comments in his book, suggest some of the reasons for the preference and some of the reasons why it should now be breaking down. Apparently, *vattakais* at one point constituted regional assemblies built upon ancient political assemblies operating in the Chettinad region of Pandyanadu.[11] As such, they must have provided a crosscutting organizational framework that complemented those of lineage, clan, and business station described in Chapters 6 and 9. As we shall see more clearly in Chapter 9, the village temple provided a framework for political coordination within a single village. The clan temples provided an institution capable of sanctioning the behavior of dispersed clan members from multiple villages. The *vattakai panchayat* apparently provided a coordinating institution for Nakarattars belonging both to different villages and to different clans. Thus, it must have operated in Chettinad like *vitutis* or caste associations operated in Nakarattar business stations (see Chapter 6). Significantly, the most prominent feature in my informants' descriptions of *vattakai* deterioration concerned the substitution of principles of business association for residential proximity in determining suitability for marriage alliance. This substitution most likely took place because, both in the case of Nakarattars sharing common business stations and in the case of Nakarattars sharing a common industry, business-related sodalities provided alternatives to *vattakais* as institutions for distributing information and resolving disputes among segments of dispersed clans and localized lineages. The *vattakai* system declined with the creation of the new colonial political framework —especially with the creation of the system of electoral district boards in 1936. By the end of this period, *vattakais* retained (significantly in this context) only some coordinative functions in setting limits on the cost of a dowry.

Affinal Gifts as Interest-Earning Trusts: An Illustration

In 1980–81, most of my informants complained about the high cost of a dowry which, they felt, had grown out of control during the last fifty years (see Table 11). It is difficult to judge the accuracy of this nostalgic vision of times gone by. Memories of low-cost dowry do not fit well with the prominent role given to dowry deposits (*accimar panam*) in turn-of-the-century banking practice (Chapter 5). Unfortunately, in the absence of pre-1930s documentation for dowry expenses, it is necessary to consider a modern example. Given my contemporary informants' nostalgia, one must be cautious in taking the magnitude of money involved as a basis for historical projection. I am more confident about continuity in the structure of affinal prestations and in the social and financial ties they created.

I illustrate the kinds of financial claims that affinal allies may place on each other—especially the claims that a married couple (*pulli*) may place on members of the wife's natal family (*tayatis,* in the narrow sense)—by presenting a brief account of a relatively extended case. The story begins with a marriage that occurred in the late 1930s. It continues with the marriages of this initial couple's children. As an analysis of a single case, it should not be regarded as typical. It will be apparent that I collected more information about the marriages of my informant's daughters than about his own marriage forty years before. Nevertheless, similarities between the two generations of marriages suggest that no significant change had taken place.

My informant described both families in the 1930s as upper middle-class. The groom's family business was located primarily in Burma. Its income was estimated at about Rs. 40,000; its assets at about Rs. 500,000–600,000. The business interests of the bride's family were located in Ceylon and Malaysia. The income of her family was about Rs. 50,000–60,000, with assets of about Rs. 300,000–400,000. Their natal villages were located within six kilometers of each other. There had been no previous mar-

Table 11. Estimates of Appropriate Dowries, 1930–80 (in thousands of rupees)

Class	*1930*	*1940*	*1950*	*1960*	*1970*	*1980*
Rich	25	60	75	150	200	300
Middle-class	10	16	20	25	25	35
Poor	2	3	4	5	6	10

riage alliance between their respective families. My informant summarized the arrangements for the marriage ceremony in the following words.

> Wedding expenses (*kalyanaccelavu*) were shared by both families. The bride's family contributed about Rs. 5,000; the groom's, Rs. 4,000. Normally, the groom's family would only have spent about Rs. 2,000. But my father spent an extra Rs. 1,500 for special musical performances.
>
> My wife's dowry (*cir tanam*) was Rs. 5,000, a high figure at that time.
>
> We received wedding gifts (*cir varicai*) worth about Rs. 25,000.
>
> Some gifts (*mamiyar caman*—i.e., from the bride's mother's brother) were also given to the groom's mother including saris, jewelry, utensils, etc. Their value was less than Rs. 2,000. No money gifts were given to the groom's mother before 1941. (Interview with Lakshmanan Chettiar, May 1981)

The marriage produced four daughters, born between 1940 and 1960. They were married at ages that ranged from sixteen to twenty-three (the later they were born, the older they were married).[12] Table 12 itemizes the various expenses incurred on the occasion of their weddings, along with my informant's explanatory comments.

Based on this information, it is possible to make a few observations about the financial investment that marriages represented to this Nakarattar family. It is also possible to indicate something of the kinds of financial cooperation that occurred within the affinal kindred established at the time of the initial marriage alliance. To begin with, there is a discrepancy in the kind of information collected for the father's and the children's weddings. In the former case, we have information both about the expenses of marrying one's daughter, and also about the income and assets of the intermarrying families (notice, it is my informant's wife's natal family who bore the brunt of the expenses). But we do not know what other kinds of expenses these families faced—especially what expenses other than my informant's wedding were borne by his wife's natal family. Nevertheless, it is possible to observe that the total cost of the wedding to her natal family of Rs. 37,000 represented about 10 percent of its assets and about 60 percent of one year's income.

In the case of the children's generation, we do not know the assets and income of the allied families. But we do know that my informant's family acted as in-laws under similar obligations for the weddings of at least his four daughters. We are also able to estimate the relationship that each wedding bore to the others as a proportion of the expenses incurred by all the weddings. I note, further, that my informant had only one son, his

Table 12. Marriage Expenses Incurred in Marriages of a Nakarattar Banking Family

	Prestations (rupees)	Comments
Informant (m. 1939)		
Dowry (*cir tanam*)	5,000	[See text]
Gifts to couple (*cir varicai*)	25,000	
Gifts to husband's mother, in kind (*mamiyar caman*)	2,000	
Wedding expenses (*kalyana-c-celavu*)	9,000	
Total	41,500	
First Daughter (m. 1957)		
Dowry	11,000	"Here, groom's family had business in Malaysia and I invited many guests. Wedding expenses are due to huge number of guests."
Gifts to couple	45,000	
Gifts to husband's mother	3,500	
Wedding expenses	15,000	
Total	74,500	
Second Daughter (m. 1965)		
Dowry	7,000	"Less expensive because married to my sister's son. . . . They accepted whatever I wanted to give."
Gifts to couple	40,000	
Gifts to husband's mother, in kind	2,000	
Wedding expenses	6,000	
Total	55,000	
Third Daughter (m. 1971)		
Dowry	6,500	"Groom's family was poor. . . . But there was a scarcity of good grooms."
Gifts to couple	35,000	
Gifts to husband's mother (in cash)	3,000	
Wedding expenses	4,000	
Total	48,500	
Fourth Daughter (m. 1981)		
Dowry	20,000	"[High figure for gifts to couple] due to high price of gold and gift articles. In fact, real value is one-fourth that of first daughter's wedding."
Gifts to couple	50,000	
Gifts to husband's mother	10,000	
Wedding expenses	6,000	
Total	86,000	

Source: Interview with S. M. Lakshmanan Chettiar, May 1981.

youngest child. This proportion of daughters to sons and especially the absolute number of daughters represents a piece of financial misfortune for Nakarattars and for Tamil families generally, as indicated by the common blessing "May you have a hundred sons," and also by the Tamil proverb "Five daughters will ruin the wealthiest man." Accordingly, this potential source of bias should be kept in mind if generalizations are drawn from my illustrative case.

Finally, my informant indicated that his family had lost most of their money when the majority of Nakarattars left Burma in 1941, never to receive compensation for their substantial landholdings and other Burmese assets. This is confirmed by information he provided me about the amount of dowry appropriate for Nakarattars falling into different economic classes. I present his estimates in Table 11. They demonstrate clearly that he views his family's fortunes as having declined from upper middle-class to lower middle-class and perhaps even to "poor" status. They also give some indication of trends in dowry payments during the last fifty years.

All of these considerations indicate that my informant could be regarded as something of a hardship case. Nevertheless, my impression is that the means he employed for financing the enormous expenditures required by the marriages of his daughters are typical of Nakarattars generally and cast considerable light on economic transactions between Nakarattar kin groups within affinal kindreds. The sources of marriage funds are presented below.

Sale of ancestral properties	25%
Use of father's savings in gold and silver (informant's share of his family's estate)	10%
Share from sale of land in Burma (informant's share of his family's estate)	5%
Own earnings	10%
Borrowing from friends	5%
Gifts from wife's parents	30%
Income from wife's share of a banking business founded by wife's father	15%

The important lesson here is that 45 percent of the considerable expenses incurred by my informant in marrying off his daughters were borne in turn by his wife's uterine family. The process by which these funds were accumulated reflects even more deeply the ongoing operation of a Nakarattar marriage alliance. My informant's second daughter was named after her maternal grandmother. In recognition of their special relationship, this grandmother gave her granddaughter Rs. 1,001 one week after she was born. The amount was kept in deposit as *accimar panam* in a firm of tanners in Dindigul. Every year, the principal plus interest was redeposited. Occasionally, the grandmother took the opportunity to round off the amount when the deposit reached an "odd" figure.[13] Periodic festivals such as Deepavali also marked occasions for new contributions to the fund. Assuming that these gifts made up the bulk of the funds donated by the family comprising my informant's in-laws for the marriage of his second daughter, and accepting the figure of 30 percent as accurately reflecting their contribution to the cost of her wedding, the trust established in her name must finally have reached perhaps Rs. 16,500. It is a sum that reflects a substantial credit line directly linking the recipient firm of tanners and my informant's joint family and indirectly available to other joint families among my informant's affinal kindred.

The Ritual Construction of Nakarattar Marriage Alliances

The ritual construction of a Nakarattar marriage alliance provided a detailed picture of many normative relationships between members of affinal kindreds.[14] In the following analysis, I focus on Nakarattar ceremonial transactions commencing with prenuptial rituals and continuing long after the wedding celebration, for the life of a marriage alliance.[15] Such transactions were carefully recorded by Nakarattars in special notebooks that, as we shall see, formed a thoroughgoing bookkeeping system for tracking relations of trust and cooperation between kin. My point of departure is Dumont's (1957b) analysis of a similar chain of the prestations and counterprestations that symbolize marriage alliances among non-Nakarattar castes—specifically, in a Vellalar ("farmer") caste of Tirunelveli and some Kallar and Maravar ("warrior") castes of Chettinad and neighboring regions.

If I correctly understand Dumont, these affinal prestations fall into essentially two categories. Dumont describes the first category of prestations as *external prestations*—called *cir* or *curul*—which are presented back and forth between families allied by the marriage of their son and daughter.

> [W]ith the ceremony proper [the couple] begins the series of visits to and stays with F [the wife's family], the couple being every time accompanied by a number of baskets [*cir*] containing foodstuffs and other articles for consumption, from M [the husband's family] to F, increased back from F to M. Prestations from F dominate more and

> more as time goes on until finally—it may be two or three years after the marriage ceremony—the young couple establish a separate household near M, and receive the necessary pots and pans from F without any return gift. This is the "*cir* of going apart." (1957b: 30)

Dumont describes the second category of prestations as "internal prestations" — called moi:

> During the marriage ceremony, in both houses, money is collected among the bridegroom's relatives on the one hand and the bride's relatives on the other. This is called *moi;* its effect is to make the relatives contribute to the expenses of the family. (1957b: 30)

Dumont notes that *moi* takes various forms among the different groups he studied: among the Mudukkulattur Maravar, *moi* is absent at weddings but present at funerals and female puberty rites; among the Nangudi Vellalar, *moi* is replaced by collections where the two groups of *pankali* pool their gifts in a common fund rather than contributing to two separate funds; similarly, among the Paganeri Kallar, all who attend the feast contribute *moi,* which consists of a small contribution of rice and also a collection of money, called *revei,* which is accompanied by a gift of thanks in return.

These variations in the composition of *moi*-giving groups cast doubt on the generality of Dumont's contrast of *cir* and *moi* as a difference between external and internal gifts—that is, between gifts given between the bride's and groom's *pankalis* and gifts given within each *pankali.* But Dumont never elaborates on the significance of this distinction, even among those castes where it does seem to hold. I will offer some speculative thoughts on the issue after examining the kinds of prestations found among the Nakarattar.

Cir

Nakarattar affinal prestations took a variety of forms, some of which overlap with those described by Dumont. To begin with, Nakarattars applied the term *cir* in compound terms referring to two kinds of gifts: *cir tanam* (dowry) and *cir varicai* (gifts to the couple on the occasion of the wedding). As is partially the case in the groups studied by Dumont, both of these varieties of *cir* can be viewed as forms of prestation by the bride's family to the groom's family, or to the new *pulli* formed on the occasion of the marriage and assimilated into the groom's family. Nevertheless, there are some important aspects of Nakarattar varieties of *cir* that deserve special notice. Most importantly, unlike the prestations of *cir* described by Dumont, neither *cir tanam* nor *cir varicai* was reciprocated by the groom's family. Nor was there any continuing cycle of *cir* exchange through the years, although the dowry was sometimes paid in installments. This is not to say that there were no continuing prestations between the families. But these were referred to by different terms, described below.

Cir tanam consisted of a large sum of money which technically remained the property of the bride. In practice, it was deposited in the business belonging to the groom's *valavu* or was used to open up a long-term, interest-paying deposit account (*accimar panam*) in another Nakarattar family's business. In either case, the groom's *valavu* exercised considerable control over its use. However, if the bride died without giving birth to any children, the sum was returned to her family.

A similar arrangement was made concerning *cir varicai*. In this context, the bride's and the groom's families both maintained lists of the bridal gifts, called *kalyanattukku caman vaitta vivaram*. If the bride died without any issue, the gifts were returned to the bride's family. Prestations of *cir varicai* (*varicai* = "row on row") were quite similar to prestations of *cir* among the groups described by Dumont. They constituted a variety of items, including those for use by the bride, items for use by future children (including items reserved for the *cir varicai* of any daughters that might be born), and items for use by the groom (which would not be returned to the bride's family in the event of the childless death of the bride). The difference was that among the Nakarattar, *cir varicai* was given all at once on the occasion of the wedding itself.

Moi

Nakarattar applied the term *moi* to gifts given by any person attending a wedding. As with the Nangudi Vellalar, but unlike among the Kallar, Nakarattar *moi* were not confined to internal prestations, within the bride's and groom's respective *pankalis*. It was the case that these groups were ritually marked in the presentation of *moi*. But the marking was a complicated affair involving a variety of groups both inside and outside the couple's affinal kindred. Nakarattar *moi* did not represent any complementary gifting to the married couple, let alone a reciprocal exchange between the two separate sets of *pankalis* comprising affinal kindred. Nor was *moi* directed primarily toward providing the young couple with a substantial sum of money for use in establishing their *pulli*. Instead, *moi* generally took the form of symbolic tokens: a single rupee or the gift of a small amount of copper. These gifts were recorded in an account book (*moippana etu*).

The order in which gifts of *moi* were entered reflected an internal segmentation of Nakarattar affinal kindred into five categories. The first entry was that of the deceased father of the groom's oldest living patrilineal relative in direct line of descent (e.g., the groom's deceased FFF if his FF was still living). In this way the groom's *valavu*—the joint family or minimal lineage segment, which was midway between his *kuttikkira pankali* and his *pulli*—was given special recognition. The gift, however, was normally only one rupee and thus was symbolic rather than substantial.

After this entry, the names of all members of the groom's *kuttikkira pankali* were listed in genealogical order, whether or not they attended. Each attending *pankali* gave a small amount of copper—another symbolic gift—and a mark was placed by his name. By marking off the names of the attending *pankalis* from a comprehensive list in the *moippana etu,* Nakarattars maintained a record of the current state of solidarity and cooperation among different segments of their lineage.

The bride's uterine *pankalis* were listed after the groom's attending *pankalis,* as were relatives of the bride through her mother's line. In short, the couple's *tayatis* comprised the next group listed in the *moippana etu.* Nakarattars recognized lineal distinctions between the couple's *tayatis* by the order in which each was listed. The wife's father (*amman* or *mamakkarar*), who was first on the list of *tayatis,* gave a substantial amount (I did not collect information about standards for judging its substantiality). Other *tayatis* of the couple gave symbolic tokens.

The fourth group in the *moippana etu* were termed *catunkukkarar* (ceremony doers). They consisted of the groom's sisters (*nattanars*), who were entitled to certain rights, duties, and ceremonies during the wedding ceremony and for whom the groom and his sons acted (or would eventually act) as *tayatis,* observing *cir*-giving and *murai*-giving obligations for the *nattanars' pulli.*

Finally, there was a residual category of *moi*-givers that consisted of anybody else who attended the wedding. This group could even include friends or employees who did not belong to the Nakarattar caste.

Murai

Murai constituted customary and continuing external gifts from the wife's family to the husband's family. They partially corresponded to Dumont's description of *cir* among non-Nakarattar groups, and complemented Nakarattar *cir tanam* and *cir varicai.* However, they continued beyond the immediate occasion of the wedding. Like the two Nakarattar *cir* prestations, *murai* constituted asymmetrical prestations from the wife's family to the husband's. The primary kin groups involved were her *murai*-giving uterine *valavu* and her *murai*-receiving affinal *pulli* (i.e., the wife's father's *pulli* and the *pulli* formed by her marriage to her husband). The groups of *kuttikkira pankalis* and *tayatis* to which these smaller kin groups belonged were indirectly allied through the alliance of their children. Their token *moi* prestations and their optional presence on the occasion of *murai* prestations ritually distinguished their status from the directly allied *valavus* and *pullis.*

Occasions for giving *murai* included seasonal festivals such as those occurring on the Hindu holidays of Pongal or Deepavali. Nakarattars also gave *murai* on the occasion of the wife's father's sixtieth birthday (*shasti-aptapurti santi kalyanam*), by which time he should have determined the eventual division of his properties (if he had not already divided them) and should have satisfied all dowry obligations for any other daughters. Finally, Nakarattars presented *murai* to the husband's family on the occasion of any other marriage occurring in their families.

The obligation to give *murai* on these occasions was taken seriously. Even if there was a quarrel, say, between a woman and her brother, such that he refused to attend her husband's sixtieth birthday celebration, he was still obligated to send *murai* through an intermediary and to cover the cost of a new gold marriage pendant (*tali*) and sari for his sister, a *veshti* for her husband, and garlands and other auspicious articles for the ceremony.

The limits of *murai* obligations were especially significant for indicating the duration of a marriage alliance. *Murai* obligations between a woman's uterine *valavu* and her affinal *pulli* held force for the life of the married couple and of their unmarried children. Initially, *murais* were given by a married woman's father (her husband's *amman* or *mamakkarar*). But even after her father's death, *murai* continued to be given by her brothers (her husband's *attan* or *maittunan*). If she died before her husband and children, her father or her brothers continued to present *murai* on appropriate occasions. Finally, even if both husband and wife died, surviving members of the wife's uterine *pulli* continued to present *murai* to her surviving children until they married and formed a new *pulli.*

When a woman's sons married, her father and sons performed a modest ceremonial role at the wedding. But the major *cir*-giving and *murai*-giving responsibilities were assumed by the new bride's father's *pulli.* In principle, it was possible for a woman's son to marry her brother's daughter. In this case, the original marriage alliance between her uterine family and her husband's family was renewed, and the flow of prestations continued unaltered. But there was no requirement to renew an alliance in this way, and it happened infrequently. My informants felt that perhaps 90 to 95 percent of the time, marriages took place with families who were not already in-laws (*campantippuram*). When a woman's daughters married, her husband and sons assumed *murai* obligations for their in-laws. But a major portion of their obligations was absorbed by the mother's own *cir tanam* and *murai,* deposited for the purpose in an *accimar panam* trust. She and her husband and sons made use of the bulk of this money to cover the cost of her daughters' *cir* and *murai.*

A marriage alliance between descent groups—at least in the sense in which it was symbolized by *murai* prestations—thus had a kind of developmental cycle of its own, which lasted about two generations. Longer-term alliances between Nakarattar descent groups were possible, in principle, and were effected by arranging for marriage between first cross-cousins (i.e., FZD=MBS or MBD=FZS). But the incidence of such renewals was quite scarce. I consider the implications of the infrequent exercise of this option to renew marriage alliances between *valavus* (i.e., marriage of first cross-cousins) in subsequent sections of this chapter.

Vevu

Vevu constituted prestations of special ceremonial *murai* given by all *pankalis* on important life-cycle ceremonies for family members including the initial wedding, the birth of a first child (wealthy families gave *vevu* for the first boy and the first girl), the first menses of the first daughter, and the sixtieth birthday of the father. The difference between *vevu* and *murai* was that occasions for giving *vevu* required the physical presence of *pankalis* and *tayatis* (not just a representative or messenger of the wife's father or brother). In addition, *vevu* was given on exceptional ceremonial occasions. In contrast, *murai* were given on a periodic and continuous basis and could be sent by an intermediary.

Finally, Nakarattar *tayatis* were also responsible for a special form of funerary *vevu* called *pirantu itattukkoti* "bringing unbleached (ceremonial) cloth from the house of birth (of the wife)." When a man or woman died, the wife's father or brothers, accompanied by their *pankalis,* brought appropriate funeral garb for the deceased, along with sandalwood and other items required for the funeral pyre. They also supplied baskets of rice and vegetables to feed the mourners.

Summary of Affinal Prestations

The preceding observations highlight significant differences between Nakarattar and non-Nakarattar expressions of marriage alliance, especially with regard to the Pramalai Kallar described by Dumont. In the case of the Kallar, external prestations (all termed *cir*) were initially symmetrical between husband's and wife's *pankalis.* Over the course of time, they became increasingly asymmetric until, in the end, the bride's family bore an enormously disproportionate share of the burden (1957b: 32). Yet Kallar marriage alliances made a symbolic show of reciprocity through the initial exchange of *cir.* Thus, even though subsequent prestations tilted in favor of the husband's family, members of a Kallar marriage alliance could still point out that *cir* had been exchanged on both sides.

Among the Nakarattar, *cir tanam, cir varicai, murai, vevu,* and the funerary prestations of *pirantu ituttukkoti* together corresponded to the single category of Kallar external prestations. Two differences stand out. Firstly, Nakarattar external prestations exhibited greater qualitative variety, marked by an elaborated terminological system. Secondly, this variety was associated with a pronounced asymmetry in the direction of prestations. The uniform matrilateral asymmetry of Nakarattar prestations and the nonuniformity and variety of their classification combined to produce a mirror image of the Kallar pattern. Nakarattar alliances were not balanced by even initial reciprocal prestations of *cir.* All of their different external prestations flowed asymmetrically from the wife's family to the groom's.[16]

Nakarattar and Kallar castes also differed with respect to what Dumont called "internal prestations," or at least with respect to prestations termed *moi.* In the case of the Kallar, *moi* defined two separate groups. Prestations were made within ("internal" to) lineage segments, each of which made substantial contributions to the member family whose son or daughter was married. In the case of the Nakarattar, individuals from different descent groups of the entire affinal kindred all gave token *moi* directly to the newly married couple. The different subgroupings of donors were distinguished by the order and classification of names on the *moippanu etu.* But all of them coalesced as a single group, allied by the common focus of its members on the married couple. The symbolic differentiation of status between categories of *moi*-givers reflected degrees of social distance between the couple's kin (see Figure 13) and corresponded to differences in access to credit generated by a woman's *accimar panam* deposits. But this single graded structure was markedly different from the bifurcated structure generated by *moi*-giving practices among the Kallar segments, each of which made substantial contributions to the member family whose son or daughter was married.

Positive Marriage Rules and Virtual Affinity

According to Dumont (*passim*), all intermarrying descent groups in South Indian castes classify one another as either marriageable (*affines*) or as nonmarriageable (kin). In addition, affines are themselves classified into two subcategories: (a) *perfect affines,* whose affinity is expressed by an existing bond of marriage between their respective descent groups, and (2) *virtual affines,* whose affinity is expressed only by their terminological classification (1957b: 25, 27). Perfect affinity exists only when there is an ongoing alliance between two descent groups. Virtual affinity exists when there is no such alliance. Virtual affinity may even exist when there has never been an alliance. In such cases, Dravidians employ (and when queried, agree that they employ) a recursive algorithm: "Kin of my kin are kin; affines of my kin are affines; affines of my affines are kin." Dumont's distinction corresponds to the Nakarattar classification of, on one hand, *campantippuram* (in-laws) and, on the other hand, both *tayatis* (in the broad sense, meaning members of previously allied descent groups) and also all marriageable non-kin (see Figure 13).

The distinction between perfect and virtual affines is parallel to Leach's (1961) distinction between *local descent groups* and *descent lines.* Both distinctions follow from careful analyses of the social organization of specific kinship systems and contain a lesson worth reviewing in the context of any subsequent analysis: namely, that it is important to distinguish between a system of classification and a set of social groups. In Leach's words,

> The notion of a local line is to be distinguished from the parallel concept of a descent line (line of descent) which has frequently been used by Radcliffe-Brown and his pupils. Descent lines have nothing whatever to do with local grouping, they are merely a diagrammatic device for displaying the categories of the kinship system in relation to a central individual called Ego. The number of basic descent lines in such a diagram depends merely upon how many different kinds of relative are recognized in the grandfather's generation. It has nothing to do with the number of local descent groups existing in the society. (1961: 57).

After forty years, anthropologists continue to have difficulty maintaining these distinctions.[17] And it has proven especially difficult to maintain them in the context of analyses of affinal relationships.[18] The biggest difficulty arises due to a misconception about the operation of prescriptive marriage rules, such as the putative Dravidian marriage rule "Thy children must marry affines." According to Dumont, for example,

> The regulation causes marriage to be transmitted much as membership in the descent group is transmitted. With it, marriage acquires a diachronic dimension, it becomes an institution enduring from generation to generation, which I therefore call "marriage alliance" or simply "alliance."

> . . . [In South India], sons of affines are ipso facto affines, at least in a virtual or rather a general sense, before or without becoming so individually.
>
> I submit that, in societies where there are (positive) marriage regulations: (1) marriage should be considered as part of a marriage alliance institution running through generations; (2) the concept of affinity should be extended so as to include not only immediate, individual relationships (affines in the ordinary sense) but also the people who inherit such a relationship from their parents, those who share it as siblings of the individual affines, etc.; (3) there is likely to be an affinal content in terms which are generally considered to connote consanguinity or "genealogical" relationships (such as mother's brother, etc.). (1957b: 25)

In this passage, Dumont talks first of the transmission of marriage, not affinity. He then asserts that relationships of affinity apply to ("should be extended to") not only perfect affines, who have actually established a marriage alliance, but also virtual affines, who are not married, who may never marry, and who are, in fact, only marriageable. In so doing, Dumont sacrifices the distinction between perfect and virtual affines in order to argue the central theme of his essay, that affinity is an important principle of Dravidian kinship. Yet, granting that affinity is an independent principle, in what does it consist? Apparently, all that is truly common to perfect and virtual affines is the marriageability of their children. They share none of the other relationships or obligations that hold between families allied together by marriage as affinal kindred.

If this is the case, it raises a serious problem for Dumont's thesis, since marriageability—even terminologically marked marriageability—is not a consequence of any positive marriage rule. To see this, consider the case of Dumont's Pramalai Kallar, who, unlike the Nakarattar, do seem to subscribe (at least partially) to a rule prescribing marriage of the eldest son with the mother's brother's daughter (MBD), and not just with any woman also designated by the same term (Dumont 1957b: 14). When the rule is followed, marriage alliances are established between distinct Kallar descent groups that persist from generation to generation. Are similar alliance relationships established between the descent groups of virtual affines? No. The defining feature of virtual affinity is precisely its lack of a real alliance. Virtual affinity establishes no relationship between specific groups, but only the potential for a relationship.

Positive marriage rules only make sense in the case of perfect affines—that is, between bounded descent groups which maintain a perpetual relationship of alliance between them. What would it mean to say that there is a positive marriage rule requiring marriage with a marriageable category whose "virtually married" members number hundreds or even thousands of different descent groups? Virtually nothing. No enduring relationship need be generated between any two groups of virtual affines from marriage to marriage because there is no marriage.

There is only one common feature besides marriageability that is shared by Dravidian kin whom Dumont classifies as perfect or virtual affines. This additional feature is nothing less than the misinterpreted formal aspect of marriageability: that is, its terminological marking by identical kinship terms. But it is a non sequitur to argue that applicability of a common term, signifying marriageability, eliminates any distinction between the two otherwise separate categories.

Marriage alliance between perfect affines may follow from adherence to a positive marriage rule. But it may also result from a variety of pragmatic considerations. The Pramalai Kallars illustrate the former case. Nakarattars illustrate the latter: they do not maintain any positive marriage rule for allied perfect affines. In neither caste is there either rule or alliance between virtual affines.

I suspect that the temptation to conflate perfect and virtual affines actually arises from a conflation of semantic and jural rules. The former classify kin categories in a semantic domain defined by descent and marriage. The latter stipulate rules for behavior between members of actively allied kin groups. The two sets of rules are quite distinct and independent. Thus, Nakarattars share the terminological marking of affines (both perfect and virtual) with Kallars. But they do not stipulate rules for perpetuating marriage alliance, even among perfect affines.

Ironically, it should be easier to recognize the distinction between semantic and jural rules among the Kallar than among the Nakarattar. Kallars maintain two sets of jural rules that apply differentially to the terminologically unmarked categories of perfect and virtual affines. The composite category of Kallar affines is subject to rules stipulating jural marriageability. But only (apparently unmarked) perfect affines are subject to normative rights and duties—termed *uravin murai*—that perpetuate marriage alliance between pairs of descent groups.

In-Laws, Murai, *and Terminological Marking*

In fact, among many South Indian castes, including the Nakarattar, perfect affines were distinguished from virtual affines in discussing ceremonial occasions where the affine was a male in-law with obligations to give gifts of *cir* or *murai* to the married couple (see above). In these cases, the normal kin term designating the kinsperson's relation to the groom as a virtual affine was modified or replaced by an alternative term that indicated his change of status from a virtual affine to a perfect affine. The Nakarattar, for example, exhibited the following usages: *amman* versus *mamakkarar* (for MB vs. WF) and *attan* versus *maittunan* (for MBS vs. ZH). I address aspects of the precise import of this status marking immediately below. In the present context, however, all that matters is that a terminological marker for perfect affines with *cir*-giving or *murai*-giving obligations designated a discrete social identity subject to positive jural rules.[19]

Among the Nakarattar, the marked status of a *cir*- or *murai*-giving, perfect affine did not carry any additional obligation to renew the marriage alliance as stipulated by a positive marriage rule. That is, although perfect and virtual affines were distinguished by the presence of *murai* obligations among the former, they were similar in the absence of any positive marriage rule. This property of the Nakarattar variant of Dravidian kinship raises two further questions in regard to Dumont's theories. In the first place, did the restriction of terminological markers in these contexts just to perfect affines with *murai*-giving obligations indicate that virtual affines who did not give *murai* were therefore not affines in any sense? The question is implied by Dumont himself, whose argument that affinity and marriage alliance are synonymous is designed to combat any doubts, either about the "affinity" of virtual affines or about the "independence" of affinity from consanguinity. But this argument is both dubious and unwarranted. Not only were relationships of marriageability between kin independent of consanguineal and alliance ties, but the only times when there was no incidental overlapping of consanguineal and affinal categories were precisely those cases where no real marriage had occurred—that is, precisely in cases of virtual affinity between consanguineously unrelated members of the same endogamous caste. Conversely, marriage ceremonies performed precisely the functions of conferring consanguineal status on otherwise nonconsanguineal affines and conferring perfect affinal status on otherwise merely virtual affines, regardless of their prior status as kin.

The Maternal Uncle, the Wife's Father, and Murai

A second question arises in consideration of an obscure component of the elaborate ceremonies performed at a Nakarattar wedding.[20] According to one of my informants, the wife's father (*amman, mamakkarar*) enacted a distinctive role in these ceremonies that seems to have expressed the right of his family (the couple's *tayatis*) to renew the alliance by marrying future children in their family to any subsequent children born in the groom's *pulli*. That is, according to this informant, *murai* obligations were morally linked to the *murai*-giver's right to enforce an alliance-renewing marriage rule.

> During a wedding, the *mamakkarar* stands in attendance throughout the marriage and is within early reach. He wears a ceremonial uniform with a gold-laced shawl in reddish color around his waist or belly. From the moment the bride groom leaves his home for the marriage celebrations to the bride's place and until the bridal couple's ceremonial setting foot at their new home, the *mamakkarar* leads the bride or the bridegroom at every step. He has to lead the way, to guide the bride or groom, to help the groom to mount up and dismount from the horse, to direct him to the prayers of the temple and to assist the Brahman priest in the rituals. If the *mamakkarar* family has a child of the opposite sex and suitable in age, to match the sister's child, marriage is contracted amongst them. If for any reason such a marriage is not consummated, the parties may agree to disagree. It is only as proof of this "no objection certificate" that the presence of the *mamakkarar* is insisted on throughout. In other words, a *mamakkarar* has the right of first refusal.

Here, apparently, is concrete evidence of a positive marriage rule operating in association with a rule about *murai* prestations. Both rules apply to two specific kin categories, WF and HF. The marriage rule, in particular, apparently generates the WF's right to renew a marriage alliance between two families in a way that is similar to marriage rules called *uravin murai* among Kallars, Nadars, and other South Indian castes. In the face of such a cogent and forceful opinion, it is important to note that this was the only expression even resembling *uravin murai* rules that I discovered among the Nakarattar. I heard no reports, for example, of sanction-free rights to "kidnap" a bride by *tayati* groups, as was reported about some Kallar groups. Nor did Nakarattars refer to their MBD as *urimai pen* (rightful woman) as was the case among representatives of Nadar and Kallar groups from whom I gathered information. It is the case that my informant successfully established a claim on the son of his in-laws' family as a groom for his second daughter (see comments in Table 12). But I have no indication that this alliance might be renewed in any subsequent generation. Moreover, as already noted, the incidence of multigenerational alliances was extremely low among all Nakarattars, and it may be that my informant (who could be an extremely persuasive negotiator) had managed to create a nonstandard "right" in the process of arranging the marriage (see Linda May, 1985). This lone exception aside, it had not occurred to any of my other Nakarattar informants that their caste maintained *uravin murai.* On the contrary, even those familiar with its operation denied that it operated among the Nakarattar.

This is significant. Positive rules enjoining asymmetrical, matrilateral cross-cousin marriage seem to have played a role in the social organization of nonmercantile castes such as the Kallars. The implication of my informant's claims is that his exercise of *uravin murai* rights represented an expression of a positive marriage rule among Nakarattars, although one that compelled symmetrical, bilateral cross-cousin marriage. If my informant was accurate about present-day Nakarattars, then it would not be unreasonable to assume that their ancestors also subscribed to such a rule. But in this case my informant's opinion is suspect. Whatever may be the case among non-Nakarattar castes, the Nakarattar expression of the rule —if expressed at all—is so feeble as to have no discernible effect, either manifest or latent.

The issue of possible linkage between *murai* obligations and marriage rules lies at the core of Dumont's argument about the self-renewing or perpetual character of Dravidian marriage alliance. According to Dumont, obligations to give external gifts such as *cir* or *murai* between allied descent groups symbolize the operation of a positive marriage rule. He provides no explicit rationale for this assertion. But he does offer several examples in which a mother's brother is replaced in his role as gift-giver by his sons or other agnates (1957b: 89–90). The implication is that *uravin murai* rights to renew the alliance are associated with obligations to give gifts; since the latter, at least, seem to be inherited by subsequent generations, so must be the former.

As with Dumont's non-Nakarattar groups, Nakarattars also engaged in a continuing series of external prestations from *tayatis* representatives to their daughter's (or sister's) *pulli*. Moreover, as with Dumont's non-Nakarattar groups, Nakarattar *murai*-givers replaced one another as representatives of the obligated *tayatis*. In the Nakarattar case, however, gifts and personnel replacements did not extend beyond the second generation. They had a distinct termination point, marked by the wedding of the final child born to the *pulli* that initiated the alliance. Either party had an option to renew the alliance. But they were not obligated to do so. Indeed, perhaps 95 percent of the time, the alliance was relinquished, and a different group established *tayati* obligations. In other words, although Nakarattar marriage alliance had what Dumont calls a *diachronic* quality, it was not therefore perpetual and self-renewing.[21]

A Note on Ethnographic Reports of Nakarattar Marriage Rules

If (contrary to my informant) Nakarattars did not subscribe to a positive marriage rule enjoining symmetrical cross-cousin marriage, did they subscribe to any other positive marriage rule? According to Thurston (1909 V: 265), Nakarattars did follow a positive rule for asymmetrical, patrilateral cross-cousin marriage. In the ideal exemplification, a man married his father's sister's daughter (FZD), a perfect affine in the Dravidian system. That is, an initial alliance in one generation stimulated a second alliance in the succeeding generation. Compliance with this rule would have precluded both bilateral cross-cousin marriage and matrilateral cross-cousin marriage.

Thurston's report seems to be confirmed by similar observations that contrast matrilateral cross-cousin marriage among landholding castes and patrilateral cross-cousin marriages among mercantile castes in the Kongu region of Coimbatore, located northwest of Chettinad. According to Brenda Beck (1972), who provided this report, the contrast is associated with the presence of status hierarchy among descent groups within landholding castes and the absence of descent groups (and hence, the absence of hierarchical relations between descent groups) within mercantile castes. The issue is somewhat complicated by an additional, associated contrast between the kinship term systems of these groups. But, in the end, Beck interprets the various differences with reference to Lévi-Straussian theories about the elementary structures of kinship.

> The [landholding] sub-castes make no distinction between the terms for mother's brother and father's sister's husband, nor between terms for matrilateral and patrilateral cousins. The [mercantile] sub-castes, by contrast, use slightly inferior terms for matrilateral uncles and cousins, while they reserve slightly superior terms for their patrilateral equivalents. This tendency to distinguish between wife-givers and wife-takers is associated with their special emphasis on dowry and their determination that the receiver of the bride be superior. This does not contradict their patrilateral cross-cousin marriage preference when it exists, however; for the superior-inferior distinction is easily reversed in succeeding generations. This is so because among the mercantile sub-castes, clan lines are weak. The hierarchy of individual givers and takers rather than that of whole descent groups is considered of prime importance. (Beck 1972: 13)

Having read Thurston and Beck before arriving in India, I was looking forward to analyzing the functional consequences of Nakarattar patrilateral marriage rules, a kin term system that marked wife-givers and wife-receivers, and an absence of clanlike descent groups. Surely, I thought, Beck is correct. This is a mercantile transformation of Dravidian kinship, which must have some practical consequences for Nakarattar commercial organization.

As we shall see in the following chapter, there is evidence in Nakarattar descent and territorial organization of an absence of hierarchy. But I am now quite convinced that, whatever situation obtains in Kongu, the Nakarattar differed from Beck's description of mercantile castes. Nakarattars maintained a nested organization of descent groups including clans (although these were territorially dispersed, and this dispersal, I suspect, is what Beck was really talking about). I am also convinced that Thurston was misinformed about the presence of a marriage rule prescribing patrilateral cross-cousin marriage. There was some kind of status marking going on in their kinship term system. But it was a marking that designated *murai* obligations, not a lateral preference for marriage.[22] Finally, there is no evidence that Nakarattars were constrained by any marriage rule, not even a rule applicable just to perfect affines and requiring marriage only to a "real" FZD. Although active marriage alliances between Nakarattar descent groups (*campatippuram* relations) were occasionally renewed by the marriage of first cross-cousins, my impression is that there was a slight preference for MBD marriage over FZD marriage. Moreover, when gently queried, when asked overtly leading questions, when chivied, harassed, and pursued beyond the bounds of civility (for I was determined to prove the existence of a FZD marriage rule), my Nakarattar informants insisted that the whole idea was silly.

Final Comment

In this chapter, we have examined the operation of Nakarattar affinity and marriage alliance. I noted that the inclusive or nested relationships of Nakarattar descent groups (ranging from hearthhold to joint family to local lineage segment to clan) generated a correspondingly multiplex set of affinal ties. But these affinal ties exemplified characteristic structural properties unlike those exemplified by non-Nakarattar castes. In particular, they contributed functionally to the organization of Nakarattar commerce by providing mechanisms for accumulating liquid resources, for undertaking cooperative ventures with limited liability, and for participating in numerous occasions for the exchange of commercial information. In the following chapter, we shall see that Nakarattar descent organization, like Nakarattar affinal organization, exemplified a characteristic mercantile adaptation. In particular, we shall see that the Nakarattars lacked the trappings of hierarchy associated with kinship organization in nonmercantile castes: namely, relations of blood purity, territorial precedence, or royal honors. We shall also see that the Nakarattar descent organization differed from that of non-Nakarattar castes with respect to a pattern of crosscutting agnatic relationships that tied together Nakarattar residential villages throughout Chettinad.

9 Temple Control and Cross-Cut Segmentation in Chettinad

Introduction

The importance of Nakarattar kinship, residence, and temple affiliation for Nakarattar banking organization has already been suggested by our analysis of the account books and ledgers from a Nakarattar agency in Burma (Chapter 5). Those books and ledgers revealed substantial deposit accounts invested by the proprietor's kin groups and temples located in Chettinad. Similar practices extend back in time to twelfth-century merchant guilds, who also staged wide-ranging commercial activities from narrowly circumscribed residential bases (Abraham 1988; Hall 1980). Itinerant Nakarattar salt traders had adopted the practice by the seventeenth century (Chapter 7). Nakarattar banking in the nineteenth and twentieth centuries only continued this pattern.

By the twentieth century—the earliest period for which we can form estimates of Nakarattar business volume—Nakarattars' investments in Chettinad made up only a small percentage of their total assets: less than 1 percent. But these investments served as a kind of monetary reserve, complementing the loans available to elite Nakarattar *adathis* through the Imperial Bank and European banks. When the Asian economy was inflationary, Nakarattars remitted huge amounts of money back to their homeland and invested it in relatively nonliquid assets: temples, houses, jewelry, and the like. When money was tight overseas, a portion of these assets was used to maintain the liquid capital required to continue with business as usual. By the 1930s, however, the world economy had become so bad that the reserve ratio of liquid Nakarattar investments in Chettinad to overseas investments was simply inadequate to meet the demand for cash.

In country after country, Nakarattar bankers found it necessary to stop lending money, to refuse further loan extensions, and to foreclose on mortgages and other securities. Even the relatively few Nakarattars whose assets remained liquid and ample in the wake of the depression cut back substantially on their money-lending activities and invested their money in industries, mines, and plantations. Yet, prior to this time and (largely as a reflex) afterwards, the Chettinad deposits—however small relative to total Nakarattar assets—were jealously guarded and carefully controlled by a tightly knit form of caste organization specifically adapted to the needs of accumulating capital and controlling the supply of investment funds to its members. Not surprisingly, Chettinad holds a special importance for Nakarattars that far transcends its status as a residential territory. This chapter looks at two key institutions in the control of economic and political resources in Chettinad: (1) the Hindu temple, whose role in commerce and politics outside of Chettinad we have already explored (Chapter 7), and (2) the Nakarattar caste itself, considered as a network of kinship relationships that tied control of temples in Chettinad by individual kin groups into a single, segmentary system.

Nakarattar Settlement and Dominance in Chettinad: The Historical Charter

Traditional caste histories published from 1895 up to the present portray the Nakarattar as useful and valued (if sometimes victimized) citizens of their society and as possessing a special political status in the traditional, medieval kingdoms of Tamil Nadu.[1] Nakarattars employed these histories to justify what, for them, was a continuation of their special role during the colonial period, not just as bankers and merchants, but as essential supporters of legitimate government and even as a branch of the government itself. In one special context, however—namely, in their Chettinad homeland—Nakarattars used their histories to define themselves as legitimate governmental authority.

The story of Nakarattar settlement in Chettinad has it that a Pandyan king invited 502 Nakarattars, belonging to seven families, to migrate to his own kingdom in order to carry out trading activities vital to the health of his realm. As an inducement and, it is implied in the histories, as their right, he gave them collectively the land of Chettinad, and he gave each of nine subgroups derived from the seven families a centrally located temple.[2] The descendants of these nine groups are said to form the exogamous dispersed clans of the Nakarattar *jati* that can be documented from the seventeenth century to the present.

By asserting that the Pandyan king gave them the temples and lands of Chettinad, the Nakarattars claim that they should be regarded as the king's surrogate protectors and rulers in Chettinad—or, simply, as local kings of Chettinad. Paraphrasing Neale's (1969) formulation, "To be given ownership is to rule." And indeed Nakarattars wielded authority and justified political action in Chettinad by reference to their historical charter. They acted as kings by seeking and attaining political authority as trustees for the kingdomlike territories that colonial authorities designated as *zamins,* by obtaining title to *zamins* in their own right, and, as the colonial system evolved, by gaining seats on governmental bodies such as municipal and district boards. In these capacities, they conducted themselves as kings by overseeing the majority of endowment and managerial tasks for temples, roads, markets, and other public facilities.

Religious Endowment

Motifs in the Nakarattar *varalaru* that depict superior Nakarattar status support their claims that they are legitimate surrogate kings of Chettinad as a whole. Nakarattars appealed to these motifs to argue that their position in colonial Chettinad society was a legitimate continuation of traditional precedent. The most dramatic Nakarattar expression of this role was large-scale religious endowment of Chettinad temples. Indeed, they were prodigious temple endowers wherever they did business. But their involvement with the temples of Chettinad has many qualities that are of special concern.

At least four kinds of temples were recipients of Nakarattar largess. There were major Saivite temples throughout South India and in important places of pilgrimage in North India as well (e.g., Kasi). Nakarattars not only gave generously to such temples, but also frequently served on their boards of trustees. There were temples in foreign (business station) lands for which, in addition to the just-mentioned activities, Nakarattar bankers met to discuss community matters, set interest rates, and so on (see Chapter 6). There were the nine clan temples of Chettinad, which, in addition to satisfying the above conditions, also housed the administration for *gotra*-like, exogamous clans (called *kovils* or "temples" themselves) that legitimized marriages and adoptions and that traditionally settled all kinds of intraclan disputes. Finally, there were temples for village goddesses and guardian gods of Chettinad which were funded largely by Nakarattar funds even though they might have been administered by and served non-Nakarattar communities, collectively called the Nattar, "people of the country."

A. V. Ramanathan Chettiar (1953), a Nakarattar caste historian, provides a cumulative estimate of the locations and amounts of Nakarattar religious endowment throughout India as of the year 1930 (see below).[3] His calculations indicate that between 1850 and 1930, Nakarattars donated Rs. 106,441,000 in temple endowments, not including their extensive endowments outside of India—a sum roughly equal to their commercial investments in India.

Nakarakkovils (9)	Rs. 10,542,500
Village temples (78)	38,314,700
Temples from neighboring villages (34)	6,492,500
Temples from Chola Nadu	29,643,500
Temples from Pandya Nadu	9,544,500
Temples from Kongu Nadu	1,241,000
Temples from Nadu Nadu	6,735,000
Temples from Thondai Nadu	3,927,000
Total	Rs. 106,440,700

Apart from the information about the size of Nakarattar endowments, one interesting artifact of Ramanathan Chettiar's tabulations stands out. In preparing his tables, Ramanathan classified Nakarattar endowments according to their location in medieval Chola territorial zones. The implication—especially in a publication that represents the Nakarattar traditional history as accurate—is that Nakarattar involvement in Tamil temples reflects a continuation of ancient practice. A further noteworthy feature of Ramanathan's table is that more than half of the reported Nakarattar endowments (the first three categories of the table) are concentrated in their Chettinad homeland: about 10 percent (Rs. 10,500,000) went to their clan temples, 36 percent (Rs. 38,315,000) went to their village temples, and 6 percent (Rs. 6,493,000) went to non-Chettiar temples in Chettinad. In addition, the endowments recorded by Ramanathan include only exceptional donations by relatively elite and wealthy Chettiars. They do not take into account periodic tithes levied by the Chettinad clan and village temples, both on a per capita basis (*pulli vari*) and also on the most wealthy members of a clan or village temple's congregation (*asti vari*).

The coincidence of reference to medieval territorial boundaries in classifying different temples and the concentration of Chettiar endowment in the temples of Chettinad is no accident. As we have already seen (Chapter 7), religious endowment could be translated into control of specific religious trusts or even into control of the entire financial resources of a temple. The translation operated through processes of redistributive exchange extending back to medieval times in South India and unaltered by otherwise significant changes in temple organization from 1817 on.[4]

In general, leaders of donative groups ranging in size from individual families to business corporations, caste associations, and finally chambers of commerce gave endowments (*kattalai*) to the deity of a temple in return for ritual honors (*maryatai*). Honors, in turn, publically defined various forms of power held both by leaders of local donative groups and by kings or representatives of the state. The nature of honors received depended upon the generosity (*vallanmai*) of the donor. Important honors consisted, for example, of the right to receive *prasad* and holy ash before anybody else in the donative group. Higher honors consisted of control (trusteeship) over all donations designated for a specific ritual trust fund. The highest honor consisted not only of control of the specific endowment in question, but of a position as trustee or *karyakkarar* ("doer") on the temple's board of trustees.[5]

This ultimate honor was really a relatively recent development. It is not clear that it was possible for anyone to control an entire temple prior to the nineteenth-century introduction of legal distinctions between public and private interests (see Chapter 7) and the legal definition of large Hindu temples that were the focus of collective pilgrimage and festivals (*tiruvila* temples) as public temples, subject to control by a board of trustees. Authors of the growing body of temple studies have focused attention on the causes and consequences of colonial redefinition of these temples as public institutions (Appadurai 1981; Breckenridge 1976; Mudaliar 1973).

Less attention has been paid to an accompanying side effect: namely, institutionalization of and legal status for the privately owned temple. In Chettinad, at least, Nakarattars made use of this development to reinforce their claims to traditional kingly status, effectively excluding other castes from trusteeship (and lesser forms of worship) in the largest temples associated with their clans and residential villages. They were so effective in this game of ritual political power that, by 1926 (immediately after the enabling legislation of 1925), they had won legal recognition of private status for clan and village temples and hereditary rights as trustees to these temples for Nakarattar families. In this position, they have continued, in many cases, to direct temple-based ritual, political, and commercial processes up to the present day.

Nakarattars won their legal battles by appealing to their traditional caste history and to other, less prejudicial evidence as proof that specific Nakarattar subdivisions were historically legitimate collective owners of their respective temples.[6] An illustration is provided by an administrative report prepared for the Board of Trustees of the Ilayathakudi clan temple in 1939 (Ilayathakudi Devasthanam 1939). In its account of the history of the temple, the report pointed to 1801 articles in the newspaper *Hindubhi* describing Nakarattar management of the temple and its *inam* (tax-free, income-earning) villages. The report noted that Nakarattar rights to management were recognized by the Madras Inams Register of 1864. It cited a "poll tax" (*pulli vari,* see below) in 1877 of all Nakarattar hearthholds (conjugal families, *pullis*) in the clan. All of these "proofs" of continuous Nakarattar involvement in the temple were used to validate a 1926 ruling by the Madras High Court in which Nakarattar trustees were confirmed as hereditary officers of the temple.[7]

Temple trusteeship was an office worth fighting for. Although trustees did not take part in decisions about day-to-day temple operations, they did make all significant policy decisions about uses of temple funds for worship, charity, salaries for temple functionaries, the sale of temple property, the rent of temple lands, and the management of temple funds for investment (often as monetary loans to individuals and business firms).

I have no good estimate for the total assets owned by Nakarattar-controlled temples between 1870 and 1930. But we can begin to speculate about the magnitude of capital involved by considering the cumulative financial power of temples across South India. According to David Washbrook (1976: 183–184),

> In 1879, the capital of the temples [in the Madras Presidency] was estimated officially at [Rs. 297,500,000], which yielded an annual income of [Rs. 17,500,000]. But these figures excluded the capital value and income of land which was held on tenures other than inam and whose worth may have been as high as half as much again. . . . Besides possessing land, major temples drew pilgrims from across the whole of India, whose purchasing power supported entire local economies; they controlled legal monopolies over the sale of many sacred commodities; they organized huge markets and fairs to coincide with their principle festivals. They represented important sources of wealth and political power in themselves.

Washbrook's figures, moreover, apply to the early part of the period under review in this paper, before a major rise in land values and other opportunities for investment that lasted up until the 1920s (Washbrook 1973).

A partial breakdown of the assets and expenditures of a single Nakarattar clan temple illustrates more precisely what was at stake for specifically Nakarattar-owned temples. My information is obtained from an administrative report by the trustees of Ilayathakudi Temple Devastanam in 1939.

It concerned property in the immediate vicinity of the temple, which, besides the temple itself, included *devastanam* estates totaling 1,249 acres in Viramatti and Kilasivalpatti villages producing approximately four thousand *kalams* of paddy (rice) as rent per annum (at 54 measures per *kalam*). It also included a coconut *tope* (grove) containing three hundred coconut trees, whose fruit was used in worship; approximately six acres of fruit trees (mangoes, limes, oranges, etc.); two acres of flower gardens (*nandavanam* gardens) for flowers used in temple worship; twenty-two major and twenty-two minor irrigation tanks; and five drinking water tanks. Finally, the temple also owned a variety of office buildings and provided living quarters for its staff consisting of eighteen houses for Brahmans in the temple *agraharam*, four separate houses for "Saivites" (non-Brahman priests?), and eighteen houses for "coolies."

The report apparently covers the last eight months of temple operations in 1939, during which time the temple employed over 16,700 workers in various maintenance and construction jobs. Table 13 lists expenditures totaling approximately Rs. 115,500 that were incurred on these different jobs and are described in the report.

The administrative report by no means represents a complete account of all temple assets, investments, or expenditures. In particular—as with the government report cited by Washbrook—the report contains no mention of non-*inam* landholdings, including probable ownership of urban property within cities in Madras or of deposits kept with Nakarattar firms in Southeast Asia.[8] Such investments were, nevertheless, an important part of temple income, and their history and future prospects were subject to considerable discussion by temple members, especially the pros and cons of investment strategies pursued by trustees from different temples. Moreover, while the overwhelming concern of a temple congregation was surely the welfare of its temple and temple deity, individual members of the congregation also benefited from temple investment policies. A set of account books for a Nakarattar agency house in Burma, for example, recorded a deposit of Rs. 70,000 from the clan temple of the agency's proprietor (see Chapter 5). In other words, whatever else they were, the temples of Chettinad were capital accumulators and distributors. In the following discussion, I describe how Nakarattar politico-territorial organization, cult membership, and descent group structure provided a framework for understanding and controlling the ritual and financial resources of Chettinad temples.

Descent and the Temple Cults of Chettinad

From the Nakarattar point of view, superior political authorities granted and confirmed their rights of ownership over Chettinad lands and temples,

Table 13. Selected Expenditures of Ilayathakudi Temple, 1939

Renovation of temple	Rs. 55,848
Construction of Mandhayamman Temple in front of Ilayattakudi Temple	300
Renovation of temples of village deities	600
Construction of *pasumadam* (cow shed)	3,067
Construction of a storage shed	3,587
Expansion and improvements to *Nakara vituti* (pilgrim rest house)	10,000
Construction of a general rest house	—
Survey of estate lands	2,708
Repairs to 22 major tanks and 22 minor tanks	7,289
Construction of a 2,000-*kalam* capacity granary to receive paddy rent from estate lands	7,973
Construction of a 50-foot road, 3.5 miles long, leading to the *taluk* headquarters at the south border of Viramathi village up to Avinipatti, and connecting Viramathi, Kilasivalpatti, Acharampatti, Kallapatti, Ilayathakudi and Avanipatti	3,651
Four tanks for domestic water supply	
Construction and maintenance of a metaled road within Ilayathakudi	3,750
Electrification of Ilayathakudi	3,750
Construction of a school and playground for 145 students	6,500
Construction of a post office	1,500
Construction of *devastanam* offices	4,972
Total	115,487

Source: Ilayattakudi Devasthanam (1939).

both in their legendary past and in the recent colonial period. Nakarattars renewed these ritual and political rights over the centuries by their faithful discharge of kingly responsibilities for temple endowment, maintenance, management, and protection. Beyond this, however, Nakarattars believed that recruitment into temple-centered cults, collective (but segmented) ownership of temples, and succession to the office of temple trustee were all based primarily on rules of agnatic transmission across generations. They drew on their beliefs about agnatic descent, inheritance, and succession when using their traditional history as a charter to guide and justify behavior.[9]

Few Nakarattar businessmen had studied systematic Hindu theories of descent and heritability. Moreover, Nakarattars employed a non-

Brahmanic, nontextual vocabulary for naming their descent groups. But, in spite of terminological differences from Vedic texts and Brahmanical teachings, Nakarattar beliefs generally coincided with classical textual doctrine about substantive and moral inheritance. In particular, Nakarattars employed ideas about descent through the male line to assign membership in four distinct kin groups, and membership in each group carried with it a set of moral rights and obligations. These groups—referred to as *pullis, valavus, pirivus, kuttikkira pankalis,* and *kovils* (see Chapter 8)—formed a nested taxonomy corresponding roughly to Brahmanic groups identified in the Dharmasastras as *parivara, kula,* and *gotra.* They also corresponded to anthropological analytic concepts of conjugal family, joint family or minimal lineage segment, localized lineage segment, maximal lineage segment, and nonlocalized clan (see Figure 14).[10]

The important property that all of these kin groups shared was that characteristic rights and duties at each level of Nakarattar kinship structure were transmitted through the male line, even if the group in question was not defined solely in terms of a descent group (e.g., the *pulli* or the village-based lineage segment). To be a Nakarattar, then, was to inherit the substantive and moral qualities of the kin groups to which one belonged. In the context of these beliefs, the initial Pandyan grant of the rights and obligations of Chettinad rulership to immigrant Nakarattar ancestors constituted a heritable moral code that devolved upon subsequent generations of Nakarattars.[11]

The issue is not straightforward. There exist apparent discrepancies between Nakarattar social organization as depicted in traditional caste histories and Nakarattar social organization as seen during the colonial period. It is true that both legendary and colonial Nakarattars were segmented into nine descent groups that were indexed by membership in an identical set of temple cults. But temple cult membership among ancestral descent groups was determined by village residence. By contrast, few colonial Nakarattars resided in the villages of their nine clan temples. In fact, the majority dwelt in ninety-six (now seventy-eight) Nakarattar residential villages throughout Chettinad.[12] More fundamentally, settlement in a residential village during the colonial past and membership in the cult of that village's temple did not require Nakarattars to relinquish membership in the clan temple from which they ultimately were descended. On the contrary, Nakarattars during the colonial period exhibited what can be idealized as a two-tier organization, in which every individual was simultaneously a member in the temple cults of both his clan and his village.

The two kinds of temples shared many similarities and a few notable differences beyond those already indicated. Both generated income by

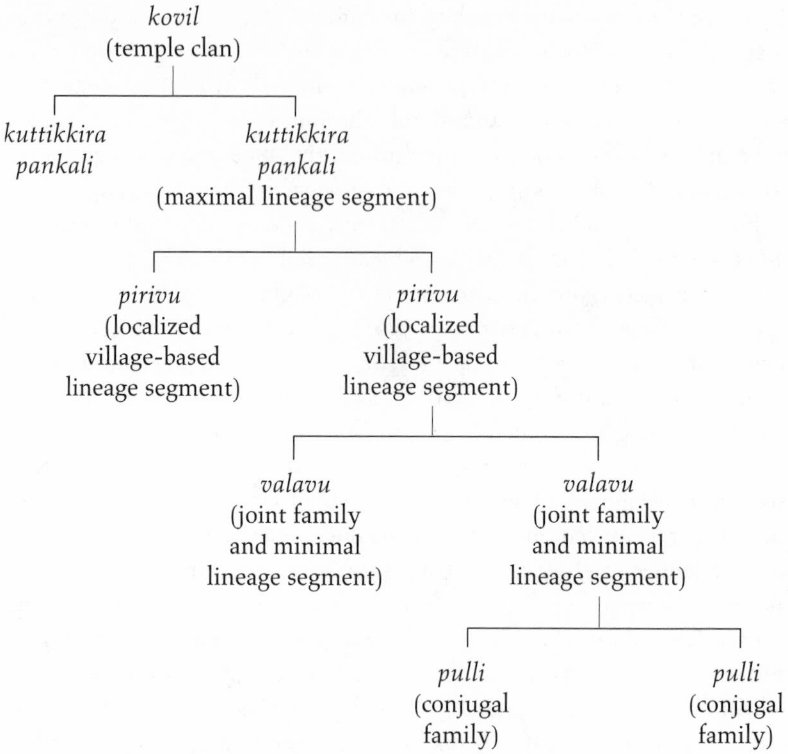

Figure 14. Nakarattar descent-based cults.

attracting endowments from their members, by tithing their members annually with a nominal head tax per family (*pulli vari*), and by tithing their richest members with occasional taxes called *asti vari.* Both kinds of temples received additional income from productive *devastanam* property such as the tax-free agricultural estates called *inams.* The largest clan temples had huge memberships that extended throughout the villages of Chettinad. All but one of the clan temples spread its congregation among from fifteen to fifty-four villages (see Figure 15). Conversely, village temple memberships were confined, by definition, to a single village. In the larger towns such as Devakottai or Karaikudi, there might be more than one residential temple; the congregation of each temple corresponded to a section or neighborhood of the town.

There were qualitative and quantitative differences in the kinds of worship that occurred in clan and village temples. Clan temples celebrated one or two collective festivals each year and played a ceremonial role in the marriages of their members. But they were not the primary focus of wor-

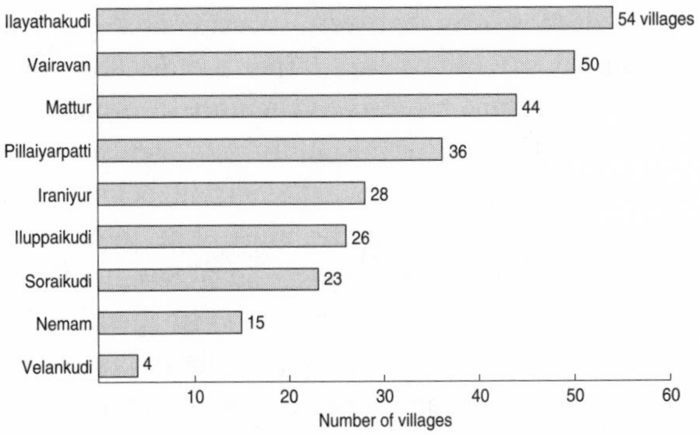

Figure 15. Representation of Nakarattar temple clans in Chettinad villages, ca. 1930. *Source:* Temple census in Ramanathan Chettiar (1953).

ship for rites concerning the welfare of the village, as was the village Siva temple. Consequently, they were not a frequent focus of worship for their members. In contrast, village temples staged six or seven seasonal festivals that also served as occasions for celebrating their members' life-cycle ceremonies.[13] In other words, village temples were more intimately bound up in the lives of their members than were clan temples.

Despite these differences, and despite my characterization of clan temples and village temples as two distinct institutions, they are best viewed as distinct only on an idealized or structural level. From a processual or diachronic point of view, they emerge as extreme ends on a continuum of descent-based cults that reflect an inverse relationship between the genealogical depth of a descent group and the presence or absence of common residence as criteria for participation. These processes can be observed in examples of the evolution of such cults from their beginnings as family rites of ghost propitiation and ancestor worship.

Among the Nakarattar, women seem particularly prone to processes of deification. If they die before their husbands, and especially if they die before giving birth to children, their ghosts (*peys*) are regarded as potential sources of both supernatural danger and supernatural blessings. In the case of one family whom I came to know, my informant's father's sister had died thirty days after her wedding at the age of twelve. The family now refer to her as their *kula teyvam* (family deity) and address her as *teyvata* (goddess), not *pey* (ghost). Following her death, she appeared nightly to her natal family in their dreams and asked for homage in return for protection. As part of the cult of their *kula teyvam*, the family maintains a special box containing saris, jewels, or other articles that once belonged to the dead girl or that were subsequently given to her spirit (*avi*).[14] For example, my informant's father promised his sister's spirit a diamond necklace in return for a son. When my informant was born, his father kept his word. The box for the family's *kula teyvam* is kept in a special room called a *sami arai* ("god room" or shrine) belonging to my informant's father's hearthhold (*pulli*) in the house of his joint family (*valavu*). The family worships their *kula teyvam* in a ceremonial rite called a *pataippu* at least once a year and sometimes as frequently as four times a year. *Pataippus* are not performed on any regularly marked occasion, but are carried out as part of important life-cycle ceremonies undergone by members of the family (e.g., on the birth of a son or the marriage of a daughter). *Paitaippus* may also be performed before any family member undertakes a major business venture or travels abroad. When a *pataippu* is performed, the *kula teyvam's* possessions are cleaned and displayed before her portrait in the *sami arai.* New gifts are offered and foods including *kanji* (a ground rice porridge), fruit, and betel are given. Afterwards, *prasad* (the sacramental food and betel) is distributed to the assembled family and invited relatives, who consume it.

In another case, four dead women of previous generations are worshipped collectively in a *pataippu* ceremony by the lineage segment into which the women had married. This lineage segment included several *valavus* comprising all of the lineage members in a single village (*pirivu*). It did not include members from *valavus* residing in other villages, who nevertheless shared membership in their maximal lineage segment, the *kuttikkira pankali.* The separate identities of the deceased women are largely fused in the minds of their descendants, whose offerings are made simply to a single *kula teyvam* referred to, again, as *teyvata.* In still other cases, family *kula teyvams* have entirely lost their identities as ancestors and are worshipped in discrete shrines or at their own temples as local village goddesses. Finally, in another case (described below), a large *kuttikkira pankali* had segmented into several subdivisions (*pirivus*) distributed among three different villages. Each subdivision worships the deity of its residential village. But members of all the subdivisions celebrate their common descent once a year by returning to their ancestral village for collective worship of their *kula teyvam.*

Taken together, these cases illustrate a general process by which rites of ancestor worship have evolved into regional cults of major deities. *Pulli*-based ancestor cults grew organically with their *pulli* as the husband claimed his inheritance, partitioned the *valavu* into which he had been born, and formed an independent *valavu* with himself as senior male. Where such *valavus* were influential and wealthy members of their residential village, they often endowed a shrine in a local temple or endowed a completely new temple to house the cult of their ancestor and to serve as a place for its worship. In some cases, other villagers (both Nakarattar and non-Nakarattar) took an increasingly large part in rites of worship, especially if the deity gained a reputation for granting boons and causing or averting suffering. If *valavus* from the village moved to a new residential village, they retained ties with their ancestral village by continued participation in major rites at the temple of their *kula teyvam.* Meanwhile, as descendants of the founding family, they retained a special position in the management of the temple's endowment (*kattalai*) and in the offering of continuing gifts to the deity and receipt of honors from the deity. Eventually, the ancestral ghost of many families assumed the trappings of a non-Brahmanic village deity: a guardian god or goddess.[15] Ultimately, what was once a private deity might become "sanskritized" (Srinivas 1952), assuming more and more of the traits associated with Brahmanical deities.

As cults underwent this gradual evolutionary process, their membership also changed, from the single *pulli* that began the cult as a rite of ancestor worship, to all the *valavu* of a single village who propitiated the ancestor of one of their members as a village deity, to, finally, a multivillage cult whose members saw the efficacy of their worship as confirmation that their *kula teyvam* was a high Hindu deity to which they had particular claim as an hereditary right. The difference between the cult's early stages and its later stages lies in the number of families that recognized the deity as their *kula teyvam,* and in the multiplication of residential villages to which these families had migrated.

This scenario represents an admittedly speculative account. But it is based on processes that have been observed in Chettinad during the last hundred years. I offer it as a plausible theory for the formation of clan and village cults observable throughout Nakarattar history and as a link between Nakarattar social organization during the colonial period and Nakarattar social organization as depicted in the story of their migration to Chettinad. If I am correct, it should be possible to identify transitional cults between the clan and village cults that characterize Nakarattar two-tier social structure.[16]

This is precisely what we do find in Chettinad. On one hand, the cults of widely dispersed Nakarattar clans are constituted of very old descent groups, whose constituent lineage groups live in multiple villages, who no longer maintain memories of consanguineal connections, and who do not collectively observe the rituals that would therefore apply. On the other hand, members of cults for Nakarattar village deities are constituted of younger descent groups, whose members reside in the same village and who maintain consanguineal relationships through the observance of ritual obligations tied to village residence and to mutual observance of each other's life-cycle ceremonies. In addition, however, it is possible to find descent-based cults that fall structurally midway between clan and village temples. Their members reside in multiple villages, but their subdivisions retain consanguineal relationships and some common ritual observances in the village of their apical ancestor. In other words, the two-tier idealization of Nakarattar social structure marks the polar ends of a culturally recognized continuum of descent-based cults of worship that vary along the inverted axes of genealogical depth and residential requirements for membership. The following two sections of this chapter explore in more detail differences in the membership, organization, and management of each of these two types of cults and their intermediate variants.

Clan Temples and Temple-Clans

Nakarattars referred both to their clan temples and to the clans themselves as "*nakarakkovils.*" For the sake of clarity, I shall diverge slightly from this usage and distinguish between temple-clans and clan temples. During the colonial period, the temple-clan was a set of otherwise unrelated lineage segments (*kuttikkira pankali,* see below) who shared hereditary cult membership in a common clan temple. Membership of individual Nakarattars in a temple-clan was determined agnatically but indirectly by membership in a lineage segment that belonged to the clan. Although every lineage segment of a Nakarattar temple-clan claimed descent from the founders of the clan's temple, and although consanguinity was presumed and intermarriage prohibited, different lineage segments from the same temple-clan did not, in general, exhibit demonstrable consanguineal ties. In other words, colonial Nakarattar clans were quite similar to the better-known clan groups represented by Brahmanic *gotras* (Khare 1970; Madan 1962). The substantive difference is that, whereas Nakarattar temple-clans trace their descent from ancestral members of specific temple cults, Brahman *gotras* trace their membership from ancestral disciples of mythical gurus called *rishis.*

The temple-clans varied in size (see Figure 16 for 1930 estimates), and some were divided into subclans (see Table 14). These two traits—their uneven population distribution and their differential segmentation—suggest a long-term historical process of sequential fission and migration, thereby lending support to the sequence described in their caste history (if not its telescoped time frame, cf. Rudner 1985). But this is a topic that requires further investigation.

Nakarattar clan temples were owned jointly by their clan members,

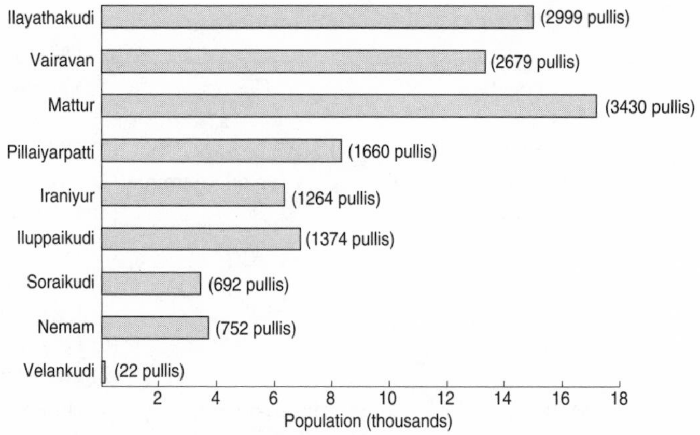

Figure 16. Nakarattar temple clans by population, ca. 1930. *Source:* Temple census in Ramanathan Chettiar (1953). Population figures were calculated as five times the number of *pullis* in a clan.

who were called *kovil pankalis* "temple shareholders". Representatives from each clan made up the executive officers and boards of trustees (*karyakkarars*) for their respective clan temple. They directed the construction and operation of the temple. They also allocated expenditures and investment of considerable sums of money. In the colonial period, the businesses of *kovil pankalis* were the primary beneficiaries of temple investments. For example, *kovil panam* deposits from a clan temple made up almost half the liabilities of a major banking agency in Burma during the colonial period from 1912 to 1915 (see Chapter 5). In addition, as illustrated earlier in this chapter by the case of Ilayathakudi Temple, temple funds were frequently spent on *devastanam* properties or on local civic improvements, such as roads or tanks for the villages of Chettinad.

Nakarattar clans supported their temples by a variety of means. Every Nakarattar household or *pulli* was tithed a nominal amount each year in a tax called a *pulli vari.* In addition, a wealth tax or *asti vari* was charged on exceptional occasions, as temple needs demanded. These contributions were taken seriously (though less so today), and individuals and their kin could be excommunicated from the community for failing to meet their contributions. This was an important sanction, for clan temples legitimized Nakarattar marriages, and without clan temple sanction no marriage could occur. Finally, clan temples received a major portion of their funding through endowments of land or money or both. Only Nakarattars belonging to the temple clan were permitted to endow the clan temple.[17]

Table 14. Nakarattar Clan and Subclan Temples

Temple	*Location*	*Deities*	*Subdivisions*
Ilayathakudi	Ilayathakudi (alias Kulasekarapuram) in Kalvasal Nadu	Kailasanattar; Nityakalaniammai	(1) Okkur (2) Arumburkolar (alias Pattanasamy) (3) Perumarudur (4) Kinkanikkur (5) Kalanivasal (6) Perasandur (7) Sirusettur
Mattur	Mattur (alias Verapandyapuram) in Keralasinga Valanadu (alias Perambur Nadu)	Ainetriswarar; Periyanayaki	(1) Uraiyur (2) Arumbakkur (3) Manalur (4) Mannur (5) Kannur (6) Karuppur (7) Kulattur
Vairavan	Verapandyapuram in Keralasinga Valanadu (alias Elakaperunteru)	Valarolinattar; Vadivudaiammai	(1) Sirukulattur: (a) Periya Vakuppu (b) Teyanar, Tevana-yakkar (c) Pillaiyar Vakuppu (2) Kalanivasal (3) Maruttendra-puram
Iraniyur (Tiruvet-pur) [a]	Iraniyur Maruttankudi (alias Rajanarayana-puram) in Ilayathakudi (alias Kulasekarapuram) in Kalvasal Nadu	Atkondanattar; Sivapuramdevi	

Table 14—*Continued*

Temple	*Location*	*Deities*	*Subdivisions*
Pillaiyarpatti (Tiruvetpur) [a]	Same as Iraniyur	1. Karpaka Pillaiyar 2. Tiruvesar and Sivakamalli (presiding deities, parents of #1) 3. Maruttesar and Vadamalarmankai (additional deities)	
Nemam	Nemam (alias Kulasekarapuram) in Keralasinga Valanadu	Jayankondacholesar; Sowndaranayaki	(All members of this temple are known as Ilanalamudaiyar)
Iluppaikkudi	Iluppaikudi (alias Pukalidam Kodutta Pattinam) in Keralasinga Valanadu (alias Perambur Nadu)	Tantondrivesar; Sounranayaki	(All members of this temple are known as Sodamanipuram-udaiyar)
Soraikudi	Soraikkudi (alias Desikanarayanapuram) in Keralasinga Valanadu	Desikanattar; Avudaiyanayaki	(All members of this temple are known as Pukalvendiya pakkamudayar)
Velankudi	Velankudi (alias Desikanarayanapuram) in Keralasinga Valanadu (alias Palaiyur Nadu)	Kandesar; Kamatchiammi	

[a]Iraniyur and Pillaiyarpatti temple clans together form a single exogamous unit called Tiruvetpur.

Clan temples served local political functions by integrating the Nakarattar community with other individuals and groups who participated in temple rites of worship, including members from non-Nakarattar *jatis* residing in Chettinad. Like any village temple, inhabitants from the surrounding villages might worship there as part of the regular round of daily worship (*naivettiyam*) maintained at any Siva temple; they might worship on an occasional basis (*arccanai*) to satisfy a vow (*nerttikkatan*) or to ask a boon and make a promise in return (*ventutal*), or they might take part in one of the few yearly rituals (*utsavam*) staged by a Nakarattar clan temple. In the last case, Nakarattars received first honors before any other caste, even Brahmans.

Members from non-Nakarattar castes also served special roles in temple rituals, including rituals peculiar to Nakarattar clan temples. In particular, clan temple *vairavis*, or "temple messengers," were traditionally drawn from the Pandaram caste. Their special role concerned rites of Nakarattar marriages and funerals pertaining to the clan temple. At marriages, *vairavis* brought a garland to the bride's house, signifying her official transfer to her husband's clan. At funerals they brought a large torch to the top of the temple tower (*kopuram*) to guide the dead person's spirit (*avi*). *Vairavis* also invited Nakarattar and non-Nakarattar notables to important temple functions. Besides these official duties, however, *vairavis* also acted in an unofficial capacity as a kind of middleman employment service between Nakarattars and non-Nakarattar employees. If labor (skilled or unskilled) was needed for constructing a house, if cooks or gardeners were required, if a new maidservant had to be found, very often it was the temple *vairavi* who learned of the need while carrying out his official duties and who brought together the potential employees and employers. In this way, activities oriented around the rituals of Nakarattar clan temples extended to and tied together people from all over Chettinad, not just those who dwelled in the immediate temple neighborhood.

For all of these reasons, Nakarattar clan temples were—with village temples—one of the primary instruments of political integration for the people of Chettinad generally, and for the Nakarattar caste in particular. This is less true today than it was before the colonial creation of novel institutions of government following the Morley-Minto and Chelmsford reforms of 1909 and 1919 and the District Board elections of 1937. During the colonial and precolonial periods, the Nakarattar village and clan temples must have played a very important role, indeed, and the Nakarattar system of decision making within clan temples tells us a good deal about their political organization.

As already noted, trustees were recruited on a hereditary basis. But, over the course of time, many Nakarattar families made substantial endowments to their clan temples, and the descendants of these families all had claims to the honors and obligations of trusteeship. In principle, Nakarattars dealt with the plethora of candidates having claims to trusteeship by rotating the office in a regular fashion between selected small groups of prominent families from throughout Chettinad (Periakarrapan 1976).

Village Temples and Dominant Lineage Segments

Almost every village of Chettinad housed a variety of temples, including a major Siva temple, a goddess temple, a village guardian temple, and a secondary goddess temple for an associated hamlet of untouchables. Members of non-Nakarattar castes such as Kallars or Konars managed the guardian god's temple (normally a temple for Ayyanar). Nakarattars referred to members of all such castes as the *Nattar,* the "people of the country." Only they had the right to open up the *hundial* (a special strongbox) into which devotees put contributions for festivals held to worship the deity of the temple. Management of the goddess temple varied. In some cases she was considered a manifestation of Parvati (the wife of Siva), and her temple was managed by Nakarattars. In other cases, she was considered as one or another *amman* (a goddess such as Mariamman). In this case, her temple was more likely managed by important members of the local Nattar community. The untouchable castes managed their own temples. Nakarattars contributed heavily to the financial costs of all of the temples in their village, but normally exercised managerial control only over the main Siva temple, which they considered their own property. In the following discussion, the phrase *village temple* refers just to these Nakarattar-controlled Siva temples.

Nakarattar village temples contrasted with clan temples in that membership in their cults was determined by the intersection of principles of descent and residence, not by descent alone. A Nakarattar was a temple cult member of the village, where a localized lineage segment—into which he had been born or adopted—maintained a common house and participated in a local temple cult. As a consequence, village temple membership was not confined to a single lineage or even a single clan, but extended to members from different lineages of different clans who shared common residence in their natal village.

Traditionally, Nakarattars lived in the same village as other members of a common lineage segment. Both male and female members of these village-bounded descent groups visited other villages in Chettinad for ceremonial purposes or made an occasional pilgrimage to a major temple outside of Chettinad. Only Nakarattar men ventured forth widely on business trips. In more recent times, Nakarattars have held their residence outside their lineage village and even outside Chettinad. But they maintained their membership in the village temple cult so long as they continued to participate in the ceremonial life of their ancestral house and the village temple.

An important variation on this theme is exemplified by the relatively large lineage segments of some of the Nakarattars whom I came to know during my field work. In one case, a Nakarattar joint family (*valavu*) had moved their residence from their ancestral village of Kattupattu to Athekkur before the turn of the century. Nevertheless, they maintained their participation in the cult of the deity in Kattupattu. They also participated in the cult of the village deity in Athekkur, along with other branches of their lineage who had moved with them. But the entire set of lineage members—those in Kattupattu, those in Athekkur, and those in still other villages and towns—retained the solidarity of the lineage by participation in the cult at Kattupattu. In another case, a set of thirty-five different families maintained records of descent from a common ancestor who lived over two hundred years ago. The thirty-five families were split into five branches, with four residing in one town, and one residing in another town. No descendants of the original ancestor lived in the tiny hamlet of his birth (which, I understand, had been abandoned).

The Nakarattar term for all of these essentially cult-based, sometimes coresidential lineage segments was *kuttikkira pankali*, "shareholders who come together" (i.e., to perform ritual ceremonies). They were constituted by members of a lineage segment whose ancestors had partitioned the common estate once held by their deceased (fore)fathers, but who retained responsibility for attending and conducting all important life-cycle rituals of their members. Their size was variable and depended on how long ago the first partition had taken place. The largest such groups that I came across resided in Devakottai. They numbered their families in the hundreds and subdivided them into segments termed *vattakais* (circles) and *pirivus* (divisions).

Tension between different subdivisions of *kuttikkira pankali* could arise after difficult and bitter partitions or in the event of political competition between previously partitioned lines.[18] In such cases, the feuding *pankalis* might express the tension between them by refusing to attend certain ceremonies, especially marriages that established affinal alliances at the expense of collateral cooperation. However, all *pankalis* tried to attend the funerals of respected elders, thus signifying their common line of descent. Many *kuttikkira pankali* maintained a common share in an ancestral house in their respective residential villages (*urs*) in Chettinad. There they retreated to perform their own life-cycle rituals. Alternatively, component joint families (*valavus*) maintained their own houses, but these houses remained in the native village, often side by side on the same street. Despite occasional strains, *kuttikkira pankalis* normally combined to assert their solidarity, especially in establishing dominance within their residential village.

For example, in one (not atypical) Chettinad village, six families were regarded as wealthy and important inhabitants. Individually, each family had assets of between one and two million rupees. But three families together formed a *kuttikkira pankali* worth about four million rupees and exercised their influence by heavily endowing the village temple and serving as its hereditary trustees. The wealthiest of these families had paid for a *kumpapisekam* (temple renewal festival) as recently as the early 1960s.

Up until 1948 and the Zamindari Abolition Act, the temple had been entitled to 50 percent of the *melvaram* of the village (literally, the "upper share"—that is, the king's or government's share—roughly 30 to 45 percent of the gross produce of the village). During the time of my field work it was almost totally dependent on Nakarattars, who contributed perhaps 75 percent to the cost of new construction, renovations, and special events. My principal informant, Lakshmanan Chettiar, provided me with a remarkably clear general description of the contemporary system of contributions to village temples:

> The contribution is a fixed amount of rice plus cash in each village. It varies according to the requirements of the temple and the size of the Nakarattar population in the village. After 1945, many villages have revised the rates. In Devakottai and some other places, no contribution is collected. The expenses of the temple are met just from the donation [*asti vari*] of the well-to-do. In some other villages, the levy [*pulli vari*] is a nominal one of 25 paise [¼ rupee] or so and is paid by all Nakarattar. In about a third of the villages, the levy varies from five to 10 rupees of cash contributions and one to seven measures [*kalams*] of rice. If any family is unable to pay either rice or cash, the entire amount may be paid either in cash or kind at rates fixed by the temple trustees each year [i.e., the amount is debited to the *pulli's* account with the temple, and interest is charged]. The rice is used to cook offering of food to the Deities. Later the cooked food is distributed to temple staff.
>
> Many young Nakarattars have no idea of the amount of the levy. Either they do not pay regularly or they confuse it with the levy they must pay to their clan temple. . . . In case the earning member of the family is dead, the widow, together with her unmarried sons

> constitute a half-*pulli* and are entitled to a 50% concession. As and when each son gets married, a new *pulli* comes into being and the temple gains a new assessee. After all the sons are married, the widow is not assessable.
>
> For some reason or other, some families pay the dues irregularly. They may pay the arrears too. During the twenty or thirty years, regular collections have not been possible in many villages. The arrears are debited to each family in the books of the temple on the last day of the Tamil year and the outstandings are liable for payment or such interest as the general body may decide. Also, it happens that some rich person offers to deposit their moneys with the temple or to advance loans to the temple when it is in distress. Thus in each village, a few families have considerable moneys to their credit in local temples. Such families can, if they so desire, offset their annual cash dues by book adjustment. But, the rice must be delivered or paid for in cash.
>
> You ask what happens to poor or indigent people who owe money to the temple. A marriage takes place in that family. Or, unfortunately, someone in the family is dead. At once, the general body or its committee meet and decide the amount to be collected from the family on that day. All factors are taken into sympathetic consideration and a liberal decision is made. Only after such clearance by the Temple Authority, the other Nakarattars of the village can attend the marriage or funeral. This system is still in vogue. (Personal communication, March 1981)

In addition to the *pulli vari* levies described above, village temples also collected an *asti vari,* or wealth tax, from the wealthiest members of the village. According to Lakshmanan Chettiar, the traditional method for arriving at *asti vari* assessments was as follows:

> First the temple board of trustees would determine that funds from other sources were not adequate for planned expenses. Then the *vairavi* [temple messenger] would send out notices to every *pulli* in the village to attend a *nakarakkutomb* [a Nakarattar meeting, *nakarakkutam*]. The people would nominate about 15 representatives from a cross-section of *pankalis* [here, local lineage groups] and *kovils* [temple clans] to form an *asti vari kutomb* [wealth tax meeting, *asti vari kuttam*]. This group would then meet and decide the general principles for assessment, the specific individuals who would be taxed, the wealth of these individuals and the amount of *asti vari* each would be charged.

The sanctions operating on wealthy villagers to pay their *asti vari* were similar to those operating on temple clan members. In one case from the

1930s, the richest man in a village refused to pay his *asti vari* assessment, claiming that everyone else had conspired against him. The rest of his *kuttikkira pankali* supported him and also refused to pay. The entire group was boycotted by the village temple committee. The act of withholding their tithe from the village temple did not affect the group's status in their clan temple. They were still entitled to receive a garland to sanctify any marriage that might take place within their families. But they were prevented from performing those parts of the marriage ceremony that required blessings from the deity of the village temple. Nor were they permitted to enjoy the services of *nakaswaram* musicians, who were temple servants and who had personal *inams* carved out of the village temple's *inam* property. In the end, the rich man and his *pankali* paid their *asti vari,* after several years had passed, along with a charge for the accumulated interest.

As far as I could determine, the practice of assessing an *asti vari* has diminished or died out during the last forty years. As Lakshmanan Chettiar noted, the *asti vari kuttams* had made their assessments on the basis of community knowledge of individual wealth. As Nakarattars increasingly shifted their residences outside of Chettinad and their occupations to nonbanking jobs that did not require public knowledge of their personal wealth, it became extremely difficult to arrive at fair assessments. Moreover, Nakarattars are no longer so committed to orthodox ritual observances, and consequently they are less open to communal sanction. Thus, with *asti vari* gone as a source of income, with income from a general *pulli vari* similarly in decline, and with income from temple *inam* lands largely abolished by law, temples must rely more than ever on endowments from the wealthiest members of their villages. It is not clear if this change has brought any alteration to the politics of temple control. But Nakarattars have so far resisted every effort by non-Nakarattars to endow the major Siva temples in their residential villages, and in some cases the temple has been closed down as a result of litigation between Nakarattar and non-Nakarattar factions.

In the village with six wealthy families described above, temple control has been vested in the dominant family of the dominant lineage of the village, who have jealously guarded their trusteeship as an hereditary right since at least the turn of the century. However, as the incident concerning disputed *asti vari* assessments indicated, not all Chettinad villages were unambiguously controlled by a single dominant lineage or a family within that lineage. Where power was divided, so was temple control. In some cases, both factions were harmoniously represented on the temple's board of trustees. In other cases, conflict erupted, leading to a stoppage of temple functions. In still other cases—and this was especially likely in the largest towns, such as Devakottai or Karaikudi—the different factions constructed and maintained separate temples, effectively splitting the village into subvillages, each with its own descent-based cult. But in no case were any of these simultaneously descent-cum-residential-cum-cult groups in any way ranked above any other such group. Individuals within each group—particularly those who served as hereditary trustees—might be ritually recognized by the receipt of special honors. But in principle any group of persons had the option in harmonious situations to endow the village temple and obtain rights to their own special honors in return, or even, perhaps, to obtain a hereditary trusteeship for their representative. In nonharmonious situations, they could effectively close the temple so that nobody had any special status, they could build their own temples, or they could move and try their luck elsewhere.

As we have seen, this structural equality was also evident in the organization of the nine Nakarattar clan temples. There, as with the village temples, trustees were recruited on a hereditary basis. Among clan temples (especially the largest), however, the possibilities for conflict between major Nakarattar families were multiplied. The Nakarattars minimized the potential for conflict and maintained equality among structurally equivalent groups by rotating the trusteeship in a regular fashion between selected prominent families from throughout Chettinad. In the concluding chapter, I will compare the two-tier political organization manifest in Nakarattar control of both village and clan temples with forms of political organization exhibited by dominant nonmercantile castes in South India.

10 Conclusion: Social Structure as Social Investment

Reflecting on various approaches to the study of Indian society, Chapter 2 of this book suggested that India must be recognized as a caste society. It also suggested, however, that *caste* must be reconceived, not as a unitary phenomenon, but as an umbrella concept, covering categories of people who are potential candidates for different kinds of practical and moral linkage. The suggestion derived from historiographic interpretations for the rise of Western-style, politically oriented caste associations in early twentieth-century India. But it need not and, I argued, should not be limited just to this context. On the contrary, the notion that people invest in caste identities of different sorts in order to accomplish different ends can be usefully employed for understanding various caste formations, ranging from dominant agrarian castes mobilized for non-Western forms of political organization such as the Pudukottai Kallar, to castes specialized around artisanal production and marketing such as the Kaikkolar, to castes organized around both banking and territorial dominance such as the Nakarattar. Caste, in short, represents a differentiated form of "symbolic capital" (Bourdieu 1977), available for different uses by members of different castes. In a less euphonious Bourdieuvian phrase, castes constitute "structured structuring structures," shaped by the activities of their members, constraining those activities, and offering distinct possibilities and payoffs for different actions.

The present chapter summarizes my findings about the symbolic capital of Nakarattar caste identity, defined by component investments in elite status, marriage alliance, descent group, and temple cult. I argue that all these "social investments" contrast in interesting ways with social investments by nonmercantile castes. In particular, I argue that the respective "social portfolios" of different castes reflect a differential specialization and diversification in liquid or fixed forms of symbolic capital. The lesson I draw is twofold: First, the Nakarattars and, arguably, other mercantile castes exhibit forms of social organization that fall outside most standard views of caste social organization. They require, as a consequence, that these standard views be modified and enlarged. Second, I argue that a fiduciary perspective on variation in caste structure suggests that castes be treated not so much as legal corporations, enduring timelessly through history, but rather as social investments, structured by and structuring human action over time.

Competing for the Past, Investing in the Future

A key institutional feature of Nakarattar caste organization is embodied in the role of the Nakarattar parent banker or *adathi,* a figure standing in the center of clearinghouse operations for financial and commodity flows and a figure of considerable economic and ritual influence throughout the Nakarattar community. Chapter 5 has already indicated the way that all Nakarattars used wealth in the form of deposits in temple trust funds *(kovil panam* or *dharma panam)* for maintaining capital reserves in their family businesses. Chapter 7 explored some of the ways that elite Nakarattars, typified in the colonial period by *adathis,* attracted such deposits (subsequently marked by the special term *adathi kadai panam*) and otherwise influenced these and other collective funds by making "charitable" endowments to temples and educational institutions. All of these gifts and endowments represented investments in elite identity and status for individuals within their caste and for Nakarattar identity and status, generally, within South Indian and Southeast Asian society.

Investments in elite status, however, did not simply reproduce a static social order. They also generated social conflict and social change. Temple endowment (*kattalai*) and various kinds of more "secular" philanthropy provide a dramatic illustration of the dynamic quality of investment in the symbolic capital of elitehood, the social relationships it creates, and the social changes it effects. I have specifically flagged religious gifting because some authorities, especially Arjun Appadurai (1981a, 1981b), have suggested that the social dynamism to which I refer springs from cultural properties of Tamil deities themselves, rather than from more general processes of conflict and change. This suggestion seems unduly restrictive, and I propose to extend Appadurai's insights about the political dynamic of worship to a wider range of elite activities than temple endowment.

Appadurai's argument is that although they were the explicit beneficiaries of temple endowments, temple gods remained silent as the stones from which their images were carved. They left the interpretation of their wishes about the disposition of temple trust funds and ritual honors to devotees who were apt to disagree with one another, especially when it came to defining and determining control of scarce ritual and material resources. As a consequence, elite devotees battled one another within the political arena of a god's temple for ritual honors and financial perquisites. They sought to establish historical charters that justified their political goals for contemporary and future control of the temple.

For example, although Chapter 7 did not explore the history of Palani Temple subsequent to Kumarappan's seventeenth-century founding of the Tai Pucam pilgrimage, oral traditions recovered by Manuel Moreno (1981, 1984) suggest that Kumarappan's family eventually lost their exclusive role as *dharma karta* in the control of Nakarattar ritual at the temple. Arguably, they even lost control of their own identity when a family of Nakarattars from a totally unrelated lineage succeeded in claiming Kumarappan as their ancestor. This new group of "descendants" were not able to claim his position as trustee—an office won by still another family through other battles—but they do, at present, claim a variety of ritual rights as Kumarappan's descendants.[1] The lesson I draw from this incident is that the history of Palani is no straightforward account of objective facts, but a contested history of history making and manipulation. The enduring battles to create and authenticate a hegemonic history of Palani reveal that temple endowment represents an investment in a specific, culturally constructed past that constitutes a form of symbolic capital, indeed a scarce resource (Appadurai 1981b) over which political factions fight for exclusive rights of definition and access.

Such an Appaduraian interpretation is entirely persuasive. But, as I suggested above, it can be expanded beyond the realm of religious gifting. In particular, as we observed in Chapter 7, secular charitable institutions that emerged in the colonial period performed a role that was equally effective in generating conflict and defining reality. They lacked the devotional focus on a deity that characterized temples. But the purpose of a secular endowment in serving the public interest (particularly the causes of the Tamil Renaissance) was as open to multiple interpretation as were the wishes of any deity. Contenders for titles, honors, and positions of power in secular endowments—like contenders for similar scarce resources in religious endowments—frequently disputed one another's credentials and performance of duties in the political and jural arenas of Madras. Even the twentieth-century case of Annamalai University, described in Chapter 7, was not as clear-cut and conflict-free as my account may have indicated. In fact, at the very time when (then) Rao Bahadur Annamalai Chettiar offered a matching donation of Rs. 200,000 to the Madras government for the Tamil University at Chidambaram, Kalimuthu Thiagarajan, another elite Nakarattar, offered Rs. 350,000 to establish a University in Madurai. On the face of it, Thiagarajan's offer was superior to Annamalai's on economic grounds. But Annamalai was better positioned politically and won the contest. The outcome resulted in his control of public resources far in excess of the amount of the endowment.

Unlike the battles for ritual honors at Palani Temple, the contest to found the first Tamil university was not about authenticating the past but about defining the present. Annamalai's victory helped define the Justice party as a leader of the movement for Tamil revitalization. It contributed to the party's credibility in labeling the National Congress party as the party of imperialist, North Indian, Brahman "carpetbaggers." But it is interesting to speculate what would have happened if Thiagarajan had won the battle for a Tamil university at Madurai. For, unlike Annamalai and Muthia, Thiagarajan was an early supporter of Congress. Nor was he alone. Other prominent Chettiars such as Sa. Ganesan and Annamalai's own son-in-law, S. Rm. Ct. Chidambaram, also played an active role in the Congress party and, like Thiagarajan, combined a strong commitment to Tamil culture with a strong commitment to Indian nationalism. In the end, they lost. And our historical view of Madras' past was established in the 1920s and 1930s, when Raja Sirs Annamalai and Muthia won their ethnohistorical battle to define Madras' present.

Such "just-so" stories from pasts that might have been illustrate the social potentiality of capitalism, even in its explicitly ritual forms. They remind us that Hindu notions of moral action, in whose service Nakarattars conducted their sacred and secular gifting, do not entail fatalism, but rather provide a framework for seeking this-worldly success as well as a framework for expressing transcendent devotion or service. For the Nakarattars, as for other Hindus, such seeking often took standardized forms, consisting of competitive investments in elite status and position. I will return to issues of Nakarattar elitehood and its implications for Nakarattar values and social structure after considering other issues in the construction of Nakarattar status relationships.

Marriage and Minimization

Elitehood was generated, in part, by investments in temples and universities. It was indexed by ritual prerogative and denoted by title. The trust and respect in which Nakarattars held elites was further reflected in special long-term deposits (*adathi kadai panam*) that helped to maintain cash reserves for Nakarattar firms and which were, themselves, indexes to long-term relations between two families. But, as important as they were, relations between *adathis* and their clients constituted only one component of Nakarattar capitalist organization. Another component was marriage alliance.

Just as relationships between an *adathi* and another Nakarattar family firm were indexed by special deposits listed in the client firm's account books, so relations of marriage alliance were specially marked in accounts called *accimar panam,* or "women's deposits." Chapter 8 illustrated the way such long-term deposits were established as trusts for women by families into which they had married. They came with a woman as part of her dowry, as *cir:* that which brings fame or glory. But, although they belonged to the woman in name, they were actually controlled by the woman's in-laws until her daughters required dowry.

Aside from the amounts given as dowry, Nakarattars were not unusual in these respects. In other regards, however, they were quite remarkable. As we saw in Chapter 8, they maintained no positive marriage rule, nor did they exhibit any of the elementary structures of kinship that anthropologists claim is entailed for people who employ a Dravidian kinship terminology. Nakarattar marriage alliances did embody normative rules that distinguished them from relations of mere marriageability between terminological affines. But the normative content of these rules applied to various *murai* (gift-giving obligations) within the alliance, not to obligations to renew an alliance between allies.[2]

When I first began to investigate marriage practices among the Nakarattars, I thought to confirm the received view that contrasted marriage rules among mercantile castes with those among nonmercantile castes. I expected to demonstrate that this contrast could be explained as a functional adaptation to, respectively, mercantile and agrarian lifestyles. The following argument summarizes the theory I had formulated to account for variability in patterns of marriage alliance among different castes. First, I adopted a standard anthropological view of marriage as a transaction of women between male-controlled descent groups. Second, I accepted Brenda Beck's (1972) suggestion that the contrasting strategies of affinal transactions affected the size of affinally allied clusters of descent groups (marriage circles) tied to each other by marriage. Third, I related this variable of marriage-circle size to Marriott's (1976) theories about Hindu transactions by speculating (contra Marriott) that "minimizing" groups do not avoid transactions of gross substances (ritual food, wives, etc.) so much as they restrict the size of the group with which they engage in such transactions. Fourth, and as a lemma to the preceding argument, I also speculated that "minimizers"—at least in the case of the Nakarattar—try to maximize the size of the group with which they engage in transactions of subtle, nonpolluting substances (money, credit, market commodities, etc.). Finally, I explained the restrictive scope of transactions in gross substances and the expansive policy of transactions in subtle substances by interpreting these transactions as expressions of a moral commitment to, respectively, long-term and short-term maintenance of the relationships. That is, I viewed transactions in different media of exchange as both symbols of and symbols for a difference in the duration of commitment to a social relationship. I anticipated that, by following marriage rules restricting the size of their marriage circles (and of other groups with whom they engaged in transactions of gross substances), Nakarattars effectively limited their liability for the welfare of a large number of kin (and other clients). They thereby freed up capital resources for "subtle" financial investments in trade, finance, and industry. By contrast, agrarian "maximizers" committed capital reserves to a large group of people in return for mutual cooperation and liability in coordinated agrarian ventures. Maximizers "capitalized" a relatively large proportion of their resources for investment in such fixed assets as military manpower, farm labor, and irrigation works. Minimizers maintained a pool of relatively liquid assets backed by a small reserve of long-term deposits such as *accimar panam,* established by gifts of *cir.*

In other words, I viewed transactional strategies of minimizers—including institutionalized rules for patrilateral marriage alliance—not as efforts to avoid every kind of transaction, but as efforts to minimize the number of long-term moral relationships and maximize the number of short-term moral relationships. I viewed maximizers in the opposite way. I interpreted the difference between the two as functional, not merely formal. And I explained the specialization of different groups in different strategies as adaptive specializations to specific economic niches.

It still seems to me that Nakarattars followed a mercantile, minimizing strategy, but not by practicing the minimizing strategy of patrilateral cross-cousin marriage. Rather, they accomplished their strategy by rejecting *any* rule that would perpetuate ties of marriage alliance: not only maximizing rules that generate large marriage circles, but even minimizing rules that generate small circles.

Nakarattar marriage strategy did, in fact, produce small marriage circles, but these circles were temporary and adjustable in the face of changing economic opportunity. They represented a form of liquid wealth, just like the financial instruments that were invested in their production and maintenance and that they, in turn, produced and maintained. Indeed, the symbolic capital of Nakarattar marriage alliance was explicitly indexed by deposits of real capital in the form of *accimar panam,* the dowry trust fund that Nakarattars established on behalf of their daughters at the time of marriage (generally in the groom's family's bank) and enlarged over the two-generation life of the marriage alliance. Finally, both of these kinds of capital were further indexed and augmented by the entire set of ceremonial prestations that marked the life of the marriage alliance.

As I observed above, Nakarattars controlled many forms of capital differing from each other along a scale of relative liquidity. Thus, Nakarattar marriage alliances were liquid relative to the kinds of capital Nakarattars invested when they sought control of a temple endowment, but fixed relative to the kinds of capital they invested in an agricultural loan. When I speak of Nakarattar marriage alliance as liquid capital, however, I am not merely making a comparison between the various forms of capital invested by Nakarattars; I am also contrasting the specific capital of Nakarattar marriage alliance with the kinds of capital represented by marriage alliances established by non-Nakarattars. The difference emerges not only with respect to the contrast between the presence and absence of marriage rules but also with respect to the twofold contrast in ceremonial prestations between Nakarattar and non-Nakarattar castes, described in Chapter 8. On the one hand, Nakarattar prestations of *cir* and *moi* failed to coincide neatly with the distinction between external and internal gifts in the manner Dumont ascribes to the Kallar, Maravar, and Vellalar castes. On the other hand, Nakarattars did not make even a token symbolic expression of reciprocity in *cir* exchanges on the occasion of a wedding (let alone on the subsequent occasions for external gifting, which are asymmetric among all groups studied). Both of these ceremonial distinctions coincided with the absence of a deferred normative obligation to return a daughter in marriage to a group from which one had taken a wife. In sum, the asymmetry and lack of marriage rules signaled both the lack of reciprocity and the determinate, one-time-only nature of the alliance (regardless of subsequent pragmatic considerations that might lead to renewal). The absence of any clear demarcation of two distinct *moi*-giving groups did not even provide an opportunity for renewal because it failed to define self-perpetuating, corporate kin groups that could renew an alliance at all![3]

Merchant and Peasant: Nakarattar and Goundar Political Structure

As in the case of marriage, so in the case of political style in the control of temples and land in Chettinad. In both instances Nakarattar practice differs from current anthropological views of dominant agrarian castes in South India, and it differs in the direction of flexibility and liquidity. The following three sections undertake two tasks: (1) to contrast Nakarattar and non-Nakarattar forms of political organization as alternative ways to invest in the symbolic capital of descent-based cults of territorial dominance, and (2) to consider implications of Nakarattar political strategy for the cultural principles by which the Nakarattars conceive social relations between different political segments.

According to Brenda Beck (1972), Nakarattars and merchant castes, in general, diverge dramatically from dominant agrarian castes. I do not refer here to the effective use of "formal" political structures institutionalized by Indian governments since the turn of the century.[4] Rather, I mean the operation of a distinctively organized "informal" political system, such as that described in Chapter 9, which predated the colonial system and which continues to underpin Nakarattar political dominance up to the present day. As we have seen, this informal system is defined by principles of descent, territory, and cult membership. The importance of such variables for understanding the organization of caste groups was pointed to by Dumont (1964) thirty years ago.[5] My analysis of Nakarattar data, however, suggests that Nakarattars constructed their social organization with respect to these variables in ways that were significantly different from investments in social organization by noncommercial castes such as the Kallar, analyzed by Dumont, or the Goundar, analyzed by Beck.

As we saw in Chapter 9, Nakarattar social organization comprised a two-tier social structure that allocated and legitimized control over specific temples by specific clans and lineages. This two-tier organization played one additional, highly important political function: it tied together what were otherwise territorially discrete temple cults in a pattern of crosscutting segmentation. Every Nakarattar was simultaneously a member of the cults of both his clan and his village. These cults crosscut Chettinad in such a way that members of the same clan belonged to different villages, and members of the same village belonged to different clans. Moreover, although lineage groups from particular clans dominated particular villages, they did not dominate adjacent villages, nor did clans dominate clusters of villages.[6] Thus, the Chettinad territory was not divided up into microregions over which different clans exercised control.

This situation contrasts dramatically with the pattern of control in agrarian castes. In the case of the Goundar Vellalar, the dominant peasant caste of Kongunadu in Coimbatore, described by Beck (1972), it can be argued that lineage groups who controlled territorial clusters of Goundar settlements all belonged to the same clan.[7] Unlike the Nakarattar, among the Goundar both tiers of descent-group organization controlled corresponding tiers of Goundar territorial organization. In other words, there was an isomorphic relationship between descent groups and territorial divisions in Goundar social organization: a relationship that was replicated again by a system of religious cults in which members of Goundar descent-cum-local groups participated.

According to Beck, the caste as a whole dominated the region of Kongunadu as a whole. Goundars asserted their common identity through collective worship at Sivan and Murugan temples inside and outside Kongunadu. The Kongunadu region was divided into discrete subregions, each of which was dominated by a different Goundar subcaste that worshiped at a Mariamman temple in the major revenue village of the subregion. Revenue villages were in turn divided into hamlets dominated by separate clans, each with its own clan goddess temple. Hamlets were divided into settlements, each with its own Vinayakar temple dominated by a specific lineage. Settlements were divided into neighborhoods with common *(nattukkal)* shrines, whose inhabitants attended each other's funerals. Neighborhoods were divided into streets, whose inhabitants attended each other's weddings. Streets were divided into houses, each with a shrine for the household's ancestors and family deities. All of these simultaneously descent-cum-territorial-cum-ritual groups formed a single nested system.

Anthropologists will already have recognized in this description of Goundar social structure the characteristic pattern of segmentary political organization familiar from African studies of the Nuer and the Tiv. Presumably, one could explain Goundar dominance in Kongunadu by appeal to their segmentary organization, and explain the subordinate status of other caste groups by the absence of any organization with equal political impact (Sahlins 1961). This seems to be what Beck has in mind when she compares the way that different non-Goundar castes of Kongunad integrate (or fail to integrate) descent and territory. From Beck's point of view, however, deviation from the Goundar pattern of isomorphism between units of descent and territory is tantamount to an absence of any organization. For example, in her analysis of "left-hand," mercantile groups, she is moved to say that they lack any descent organization (1972: 106). Since this is demonstrably not the case, I take it she means that their descent organization does not fit isomophically with a nested territorial organization. In any case, Table 15 presents an idealized table showing the nested segmentary structure among Goundar social groups (including groups at higher and lower levels of organization than just clans and lineages). It also indicates the isomorphism among organizing principles of descent, territory, and ritual cult membership.

This is all straightforward stuff. But how are we to understand the operation of the differently organized forms of Nakarattar dominance? Among the Nakarattars, descent groups and territorial groups formed two crosscutting systems. There was no isomorphic correspondence between a

Table 15. Goundar Spatial, Social, and Religious Organization

Spatial	*Social*	*Religious*
Natu (political region)		
Natu (administrative/ ceremonial unit)	*Jati*	
Gramam (revenue village)	Sub-*jati*	Subcaste temple (primarily Mariamman)
Ur (hamlet)	Clan	Clan temple (e.g., Makalyamman)
Ur (settlement)	Lineage	Lineage temple (e.g., Vinayakar)
Neighborhood	Local group that attends funerals irrespective of kin or caste	*Nattukkal*
Teru (street)	Local group that attends marriages irrespective of kin or caste	*Torunam*
Household	*Kutumpam*	Household shrine

Source: Beck (1972).

nested system of descent groups and a nested system of territorial groups. There were macro-territorial units that encompassed endogamous clusters of villages called *vattakais* (see Chapter 8). But these differed from Goundar subcaste regions, revenue villages, and hamlets in that clan membership in Nakarattar multivillage *vattakais* was mixed, and no clan emerged as a dominant political force.

Lacking an isomorphic system of descent and territorial groups, did Nakarattars therefore lack a political organization enabling them to dominate Chettinad? Obviously not. There are many ways to construct a political system besides resorting to the anthropologically classic forms of segmentary organization. The Nakarattar crosscutting segmentary organization was simply different from the nested segmentary organization of the Goundar.

Hierarchy, Territorial Precedence, and Royal Honors: The Pudukottai Kallars

Nakarattar investment in crosscutting social organization has important implications for the cultural (as opposed to formal or functional) principles by which the Nakarattars conceive social relations between different political segments. In particular, it is difficult to see how Nakarattars could combine a system of status hierarchy—which is, according to Dumont (1957b), the alleged standard hallmark of politico-ritual relations within caste groups as well as between them—with a formally crosscutting, non-hierarchical structure. And indeed, notwithstanding the presence of titled, elite members of their caste, Nakarattars have adhered to an *egalitarian* ideology that fails to fit Dumont's model of status hierarchy, a model which, as we have already noted, is overgeneralized from studies of agrarian castes. Before considering Nakarattar egalitarian political culture, however, it is useful to review ways that a nonmercantile dominant caste has overlaid a ranking system rooted in Tamil beliefs about kingship on top of a nested segmentary kinship system. Once this is accomplished, we will then be in a position to contrast the hierarchical values that have shaped a Tamil "little kingdom" with the egalitarian values of mercantile Nakarattars.

According to Dumont (1957b), nonmercantile castes such as Kallars, Maravars, and Vellalars conceive and order their internal kinship groups according to the same basic principle by which entire caste groups are ordered in relation to each other: namely, status hierarchy. Moreover, it is clear in his (1957a) monographic treatment of Pramalai Kallars and in his (1957b) comparative essay on a variety of caste groups that this hierarchy is associated with a system of territorial control. Finally, it is also clear from Dumont's data that many dominant castes exemplify a nested segmentary system of ranked descent groups and territorial units (although this system differs in some respects from Beck's descriptions of Goundar social organization).[8]

The pattern of nested and hierarchically ranked segmentary social organization that Dumont finds among many landed and military castes also emerges with particular clarity and elaboration in Nicholas Dirks' (1988) analysis of the Pudukottai Kallar.[9] Unlike Goundars, Pudukottai Kallars inflected their segmentary system with an incipient state organization under the control of a king, a political form that Aidan Southall (1956) christened "the segmentary state" and that has entered the South Indian research literature through the work of Burton Stein (1969, 1980). In the Pudukottai kingdom, structural distance between political segments was a function not only of descent, territory, and cult membership, but also of a differentiated and ranked system in which military service was exchanged for land control *(inam)* and honors *(maryatai* and *piratu).*[10]

Pudukottai Kallar relations of royal service and honor formed a superstructure for every other relationship and occasionally altered the strict isomorphism between descent and territory that was characteristic of the purely segmentary Goundar. In some cases, clusters of lineage segments *(karai, pattappeyar)* combined together to form larger, territorially bounded lineage clusters *(kuppam, teru)* on the basis of coresidence within a territorial region (sub-*natu*).[11] Among these groups, structural closeness to the king sometimes reflected the order of lineage entrance into the (in part) residentially defined lineage cluster (*kuppam*) instead of the genealogical closeness or "blood purity" of descent-group relations. In other words, residential priority could play an alternative and not just a complementary role to descent.

Pudukottai Kallar lineage clusters *(kuppams)*, in turn, were clustered together into discrete sub-*jatis*, once again through operation of the descent principle—in this case, expressed by a rule of endogamy. Sub-*jatis*, however, were grouped together into the Pudukottai Kallar *jati* not by any principle pertaining to kinship, but solely by principles of honor and service. This final integration of all Pudukottai Kallar social groups (comprising the *jati*) and all territorial segments (comprising the "little kingdom") was accomplished by the king's appointment of chiefs or commanders *(cervaikkarars)*, typically from the royal subcaste, to territories *(natus)* outside his own (Dirks: 1976: 30, 1983: 28).[12] Like the lineage clusters *(kuppams)*, Pudukottai sub-*jatis* were ranked in consideration of their order of entrance into the relevant territorial unit: here, the "little kingdom" rather than the sub-*natu*.

Despite these differences from purely segmentary systems, the segmentary state of the Pudukottai also exemplified a nested or inclusive taxonomy of social groups, including (from top to bottom) the *jati*, sub-*jati*, lineage cluster *(kuppam, teru)*, and lineage *(karai, pattappeyar)*. Again, each group was marked by participation in a common cult; the group's participation provided the context for the exchange of honors for service that tied together the different segments in the Pudukottai segmentary state and that ranked the different segments belonging to various cults in the Pudukottai status hierarchy (see Table 16).[13]

A Mythic Charter for Nakarattar Values

At this juncture, we are ready to return to the question: is the principle of hierarchy a universal principle in Indian conceptions about political relations between the constituent segments of castes? Some elements of my previous discussion about Nakarattar elites suggests that it may be. Nevertheless, the Nakarattar *varalaru*, already alluded to in Chapter 9, suggests otherwise.

The story in question concerns the consequences and implications of royal abductions of Nakarattar women. According to their traditional

Table 16. Pudukottai Kallar Spatial, Social, and Religious Organization

Spatial	*Social*	*Religious*
"Little kingdom"	*Jati*	
Natu (territorial unit) comprising a variable number of villages	*Natu* (sub-*jati* in Dirks 1983)	*Nattu teyvam*
Sub-*natu* (a smaller group of lineage-indexed [parallel] villages)	*Kuppam* (a territorially bounded lineage cluster in which intermarriage is permitted) OR *Teru* (a kind of *kuppam* containing or colaterally related to the royal lineage, and exhibiting a system of marriage prohibitions)	
Gramam (village)	*Pattappeyar, karai* lineage	*Kula teyvam, grama teyvam*

Source: Dirks (1983).

caste history, the Nakarattar accepted a Pandyan invitation to immigrate to and take possession of the land of Chettinad.[14] One day, the Pandyan king went riding in the countryside and came upon a beautiful maiden. Unaware that the girl was a Nakarattar, he carried her off to his palace. As soon as he discovered his error, however, he returned the girl to her people, without molesting her sexually or harming her in any other way.

The Nakarattar history records that he implored them not to harm the girl since he would not have carried her off if he had known who she was and since he had returned her untouched once he had discovered her identity. Furthermore, not content with this plea, he warned them that if they killed her he would collect eight heads and eight thousand gold pieces from them in retribution. Despite his warning, the Nakarattar determined that their caste regulations had been infringed upon and that, as a consequence, they were required to put the girl to death. They recognized, however, the justice of the king's demand and decided that a representative from each of seven families who had initially immigrated to Chettinad should offer himself for execution. This posed a further dilemma. The Nakarattar were still responsible for selecting an eighth person for execution, but they had no moral basis for choosing who it should be. The following translation of a passage from an early published version of the caste history describes the way in which the dilemma was solved:

> At that time one of the seven families, viz, the people of the three temples of Ilayattakudi, Iraniyur, and Pillaiyarpatti said, "Even though our family is the same our temples are three. Therefore it is us that should give the extra head." Okkurutaiyar [the leader from a subdivision of the Nakarattar of Ilayattakudi] arose and said, "We will give that extra head. We esteem honor more than our life. It is enough if all Nakarattar agree to let us receive first honors such as receiving holy ashes, etc. from temples and the gurus." The Nakarattar agreed to this. Then all of them approached the king and said, "We have brought eight heads and eight thousand gold pieces according to your orders." Hearing this, the king was deeply worried. He said to them, "I don't want to commit any additional sin other than the one I already have done [i.e., abduction of the girl]. You need not give me anything. Please return to your city." And so the Nakarattar did return to their city. (Paramasivam 1981b: 7)

One moral of this story is that the abduction of a Nakarattar maiden by the Pandyan king represented a form of hypogamous union, recognized and prohibited by Hindu doctrine as *pratiloma* marriage. In the view of the Nakarattar, compliance with *dharmic* law took precedence over any obligation to obey the king's law and justified the execution of their own daughter. At the same time, the Nakarattar also recognized that the Pandyan king acted out of justice, in compliance with his own *dharma,* and accordingly they were willing to submit themselves to his judgment. In doing so, they indicated that each of the seven Nakarattar families making up the caste was the status equal of every other family. No family commanded the others, and no family had any special obligation or honors before the others. A single subbranch of one family voluntarily offered itself as a special sacrifice on behalf of the entire caste. But its doing so constituted an exception that proved the general Nakarattar rule that every caste member belonged to the same family. In other words, the same motif that represents Nakarattar superiority over non-Nakarattars also represents Nakarattar equality among themselves.

Ambidexterity in the Nakarattar Varalaru

There have been very few systematic studies of South Indian caste histories. In fact, their discussion is most typically confined to ethnographic paraphrases of the relevant versions collected eighty years ago by Edmund Thurston (1909). Brenda Beck (1972) offers an important exception to this generalization in the same book to which I have already referred. It is her view of Indian society and its extension to the analysis of merchant caste *varalarus* that I now address.[15]

As in the case of variation in South Indian social organization, Beck interprets most South Indian caste histories as corresponding not only to the *varnic* classification scheme of the *sastras* but also to a mercantile/agrarian or "left-hand/right-hand" division of society. It seems to me that the current unqualified acceptance of this specific model of South Indian society is ill-considered. It is true, as Beck asserts, that high-ranking, left-hand *varalarus* in Kongu share some common motifs with South Indian mercantile *varalarus* from other regions. But the overlap is by no means so extensive as Beck makes out. In the case of the Nakarattar, for example, the shared motifs number only three out of the seven that Beck proposes as core motifs for all 'left-hand' *varalaru*, namely:

1. An angry king who tries to destroy the caste
2. The caste's escape from the king
3. Intermarriage with another caste and the start of a new descent line

Moreover, in other notable respects, South India's merchant *varalarus* frequently *diverge* from one another. In the case of the Nakarattar *varalaru*, the differences suggest that Beck's economically based, binary classifications of left- and right-hand castes should not be generalized beyond the Kongu region. The following list identifies distinctive contrasts between the motifs that Beck suggests characterize all merchant *varalaru* and the motifs that actually figure in the Nakarattar *varalaru:*

1. There is reference to Kaveripumpattinam, but not, as Beck suggests, exclusive reference, and greater emphasis is placed on the Nakarattar homeland of Chettinad.
2. There is no reference to alliance with any other block of castes in Chettinad, either left-hand or right-hand; indeed, there is no reference to a left-hand or right-hand classification at all.
3. The caste is almost destroyed by a king in Kaveripumpattinam, and it does reestablish its status, but it does so on the basis of its ritual functions in the royal coronation, not on the basis of its members' skill in business.
4. There is no reference to classical mythology.
5. Finally, the Nakarattar story of the caste's settlement in Chettinad exhibits a pattern of legitimization by historical (or putatively historical) kings: a trait that not only fails to appear among Beck's distinctive features for left-hand *varalarus,* but which, in fact, is among the features that she says characterize right-hand *varalarus.*

In sum, the difficulty with Beck's "economic" theory[16] of a left/right division associated with occupational specialization is that it fails to predict the right-hand stylistic features of Nakarattar histories—stylistic features which root their mercantile origins and migrations in the actions of men and kings rather than gods. In other words, Nakarattars seem to give more weight to political considerations connected with their position as a dominant caste in Chettinad than to any ritually unblemished origin. This is not to say that Nakarattars thereby adopt an unambiguously right-hand style. On the contrary, Nakarattar myths almost go out of their way to avoid ranking Nakarattar clans and lineages: an avoidance characteristic of Beck's left-hand castes. There is, at most, a single event in the Nakarattar myth of arrival and domination in Chettinad that singles out a Nakarattar subclan for preeminence over any other clan, and even this event highlights the relative equality of all clans.

In other words, just as in the case of their kinship organization, Nakarattars represent an *ambidextrous* anomaly in terms of Beck's principal diagnostic features for distinguishing between left-hand and right-hand *varalarus.* We should not be surprised. The anomaly is striking only as a consequence of the present widespread acceptance of Beck's model of South Indian society. But she presents no persuasive evidence to support her generalizations from the specific region of Kongunadu to all of South India. Moreover, a careful review of the distribution of indigenous historical uses of the left/right metaphor for social relations shows (a) that it occurs sporadically in time and space, (b) that it is employed most frequently in urban, not rural, centers, (c) that within these centers, it is employed as a political idiom, often marking a difference between establishment and *arriviste* contenders for various ritual privileges, and finally, (d) that on those occasions when political combatants are classified by the left/right metaphor, they do not invariably break down into mercantile and agrarian communities (Appadurai 1974).[17]

Cross-Cut Segmentation and Equality

The mythical motif of status equality among Nakarattar kin groups faithfully replicates life. Unlike the Kallar groups analyzed above, there were no Nakarattar kings with whom other Nakarattars could undertake an asymmetrical exchange, even though Nakarattars did receive honors in temples. Nakarattars simply did not engage among themselves in *asymmetrical* exchanges of military service for royal honor. Instead they engaged each other in *symmetrical* exchanges of credit. In other words, Nakarattar kin group relations were marked by an absence of structural hierarchy even in the presence of individual receipt of temple honors.

In general, for the Nakarattar, the symbolic expression of descent group hierarchy was negligible or relativized to contexts that cancelled each other out. As we saw in Chapter 9, at each taxonomic level in Nakarattar descent-group organization, specific kin groups maintained a shrine or temple for cult worship. At these temples, elite cult members might have been ranked according to their generosity *(vallanmai)* or trustworthiness *(nanayam)*, as measured by active participation and donorship in supporting the cult. Such minimal ranking was marked by rights to the receipt of honors from the cult deity. But the majority of cult members were ritually undifferentiated and unranked.

Moreover, unlike the invariant ranking of elites among the royal Kallar of Pudukottai, the minimal ranking exhibited by Nakarattars was relativized to specific contexts, so that cult members who were honored on one occasion did not receive special honors on another occasion, when they were replaced by some previously unhonored cult member. The effect of this "replaceability" was to offset and equalize the ritual rank acquired by cult members on different occasions. Every lineage segment had its own village temple in which it received first honors. But the segment did not by receipt of this honor obtain a higher ritual rank than any other joint family or lineage segment, which likewise had an associated village temple. Where lineage segments shared a village temple, they maintained separate shrines. Alternatively, in the same shrine of the same temple, different groups controlled different rites of worship, either on the occasions of different religious festivals or in the same festival during the performance of different ceremonies.

In the context of membership in Nakarattar temple-clan cults, the same principles of differentiated membership and performance operated to give members from different clans more or less equal access to temple honors. In addition, the nonhierarchical ordering of clan members was maintained through the system of rotating trustees. The reason for this difference from both Goundar and Kallar groups—insofar as a functional explanation provides us with a reason—was telegraphed at the beginning of our comparison of mercantile and agrarian strategies for territorial dominance. Unlike their agrarian brethren, Nakarattars dominated their own little kingdom not by force of arms but by the force of money remitted from their trading empire back to villages, temples, and descent groups in Chettinad. Conversely, the shifting tides of change in Asian and world economic systems in which they participated required an ability to mobilize money from multiple sources. Relationships of opposition and cohesion in a purely segmentary organization might suffice for dealing with the local conflicts encountered by Goundar agriculturalists. But they were limiting to a businessman interested in attracting venture capital from beyond his immediate locale. Institutionalized chains of command established in a segmentary state were useful to the Pudukottai king and his commanders in mobilizing military forces. But such hierarchical relationships could get in the way of mutually depositing and loaning bankers who were creditors on one occasion and debtors on the next and who, again, needed to maximize the possibilities for attracting capital beyond the narrow avenues defined by chains of command. The great efficiency of the Nakarattar banking system depended in large part on the freedom to draw on kinship ties that were independent of and crosscut territorial ties and, conversely, to draw on territorial ties that were independent of and crosscut ties of kinship.

Equality and Elitehood

Did Nakarattar values of equality conflict with the reputations of elite members of their caste, of their temple trustees *(dharma kartas),* and of *adathis?* Does the existence of a Nakarattar elite imply that Nakarattars subscribed to a principle of hierarchy in business matters compartmentalized from the arenas of myth, ritual, and kinship that we have just reviewed? In other words, is there not a Dumontian case to be made that Nakarattars maintained a principle of hierarchy in ordering their internal social relations, just like any other caste group?

A poetically just answer might be to argue that Nakarattar equality "encompassed" differences of economic stratification signaled by elite Nakarattar status. Indeed, I have offered evidence for precisely such encompassment in the preceding analyses of egalitarian values in the Nakarattar *jati varalaru* and of ritual mechanisms for relativising and distributing temporary elitehood in Chettinad temples, such the rotation of temple trustees. Yet this argument is only part of the answer. For the rest of the solution, it is important to recognize that, regardless of the symmetry and lack of rank among Nakarattar relationships with each other—in fact, as part of this symmetry and lack of hierarchy—Nakarattars competed with each other for non-Nakarattar clients. It was precisely in contexts external to the caste community that terms such as *adathi* had a currency. The only Nakarattars today who remember the term *adathi* are retired bankers. The only published reference to *adathis* is the Imperial Bank's "*adathi* list" of approved bankers. Those few Nakarattars that are familiar with the term *adathi* gloss it as "parent banker" without any literal Tamil translation. In other words, just like titles such as "Salt Chetti," *Zamindar, Rao Bahadur,* or even, in the most extreme case, "Raja Sir," the elite status of the *adathi* gained meaning *outside* the caste. From the *inside*, it was recognized as an asset or an investment; something to be achieved, not something ascribed; and something equally achievable by any Nakarattar businessman. Elite status among Nakarattars was a valuable tool, but it had no intrinsic value in ordering Nakarattar relationships with each other. It could be sought, obtained, and employed in relationships with non-Nakarattars without coming into conflict with Nakarattar egalitarianism.

The Symbolism of Finance

Whether advancing a loan, making a deposit, encashing a hundi, negotiating a dowry, or endowing a temple, Nakarattars exchanged goods or services in self-perpetuating and generative social relationships.[18] In every case, the exchange not only reproduced and transformed the social relationships existing among transactors, but also served as a sign or index of those relationships. In each case, transactors fetishized the objects they exchanged by objectifying them as alienable commodities or by transforming them into charismatic gifts of transcendental value. In making this argument, I do not mean to deny important differences among the various objects, services, and persons exchanged by Nakarattars, but rather to underscore two qualities that they shared in common: their use as *capital* for social investment and their significance as *symbols* of social relationships. These two qualities are inseparable.

In contrast to other items of exchange—food, land, or women, for example—Nakarattar financial instruments (including those employed for the inter-Nakarattar deposits that indexed Nakarattar social organization) were remarkable for their context-free liquidity and negotiability. They were, in McKim Marriott's (1976) terms, things which had a "subtle substance-code" among the universe of things exchanged by actors in Hindu society.[19] This subtlety—in Marriott's sense—was clearly reflected in their negotiability. Nakarattar financial instruments did not conduct pollution. Actors of different ritual status who exchanged financial instruments were not at risk as they would have been if they had exchanged such things as cooked food, garbage, or bodily waste (hair clippings, menstrual blood, etc.). Financial instruments, therefore, had a negotiability throughout society that permitted their exchange between people whose ritual status was known to be unequal and (in long-distance, indirect, or multiple-party transactions) between people whose ritual status was unknown. Beyond this negotiability, Nakarattar financial instruments were often saleable, with the larger Nakarattar firms acting as clearinghouses for instruments drawn up by smaller firms. Finally, although in many cases loans were refinanced or deposits maintained indefinitely, transactions of specific Nakarattar instruments either were automatically terminated after a fixed period of time or were terminable on demand. A transaction involving Nakarattar financial instruments was therefore, in principle, free from any of those enduring obligations that mark gift-giving relationships of generalized reciprocity (Sahlins 1966). The social relationship symbolized by a financial transaction was, to adapt Marriott's (1976) terminology, "minimized." In fact, Nakarattar financial instruments constituted a type of commodity, circulating freely in Indian and Southeast Asian society; their transaction was constrained only by considerations of price (Kopytoff 1986).

In one crucial respect, however, Nakarattar financial instruments were distinct from commodities in the idealized, market-oriented sense of the word. Although exhibiting a discrete value that left their transactors free from the obligations of generalized reciprocity, they did establish temporary bonds of trust and mutual expectation between transactors. Moreover, different kinds of instruments symbolized different bonds, for different periods, and secured by different sanctions. In other words, although financial instruments as a class of objects were, in Marriott's terms, all constituted of subtle substances in the Hindu universe of exchange, within this subtle class there existed various subtly distinguished subclasses.

This is particularly apparent in the different kinds of deposits established by interbank transactions between Nakarattars. In "purely" business contexts, these deposits included short-term *kadai kanakku* ("shop account") deposits that functioned like checking accounts and that could be drawn on by *dharsan* or *nadappu hundis* ("sight" or "walking" *hundis*). Other "purely" business transactions included long-term *thavanai* ("resting") deposits on which Nakarattars could draw *thavanai hundis,* payable after a short period of rest. But business was seldom "pure," especially among the Nakarattars themselves. So, in addition to their *kadai kanakku* deposits, Nakarattars established various long-term, ritually generated deposits *(mempanam),* including deposits for affinal relatives *(accimar panam);* deposits for lineage mates and clanmates, particularly through the medium of deposits from temples controlled by various descent-based cults or worship *(tanatu murai panam);* and deposits made to parent bankers *(adathi panam).* In other words, transactions of Nakarattar financial instruments that established different kinds of deposits with different terms to maturity also established distinct spheres of exchange between Nakarattar firms related by a variety of caste-based principles for social cooperation.[20]

The capital structure of individual firms reveals the extent of caste-based mutual risk taking through the number and size of long-term deposits. And the disposition to take risks over the long term, it seems to me, corresponds very closely to our notion of "trust": what Nakarattars refer to in Tamil as *nanayam*. It emerges in Nakarattar account books as a continuous cultural variable that distinguishes a range of long-term and short-term social relationships, exploding the overly-simple dichotomy between gifts of open-ended, generalized exchange and market commodities restricted to a momentary, one-time-only transaction.

The spheres of exchange that entailed the most trust and that were defined by ritually based, long-term deposits are especially interesting in the present context because they included transactions that were functionally equivalent to investments in long-term certificates of deposit issued by Western banks. And, like these long-term certificates of deposit, the funds they represented were not left sitting idly in the recipient firm's coffers. They were lent out. The firm then received interest. The borrower had capital he could invest or otherwise spend. At the same time, the original deposit still stood to the credit of the original long-term depositor, earning him interest and providing him security against which he could obtain loans for further investment and expenditure.

By conducting financial transactions within different spheres of exchange, individual firms were able to control their cash flow and to insure that original depositors and subsequent borrowers did not claim the funds at the same time. In this way, every deposit to a Nakarattar bank could and did serve as the basis for expanding the supply of money and credit for the system as a whole. That is, Nakarattar financial transactions generated what Western economists refer to as a "multiplier effect." The capital thereby created (along with profits and interest generated by other banking and trading operations) was expended on a wealth of items for consumption, exchange, and further investment. To put it simply, financial transactions between different Nakarattar spheres of exchange created wealth. In Marriott's terms, multisphere transactions were made possible by the subtle medium of Nakarattar financial instruments and generated an increase both in the supply of money and in the production of things with substance-codes of grosser quality, such as land, minerals, or agrarian commodities. Nakarattar financial instruments were, indeed, not only highly liquid, negotiable, and transformable, but also richly productive and generative.

The extent of Nakarattar money creation is not clear. I have not ascertained the normal reserve ratio maintained by Nakarattar bankers. The ease and reliability of interfirm loans reported by retired bankers suggest —and the practices brought to light by court records (see Chapter 4) confirm—that the ratio was remarkably high. In any case, it seems clear that the tremendous growth of Nakarattar assets in Southeast Asia cannot be entirely attributed (as it is sometimes suggested) to either a transfer of funds from India or a diversion of profits from the agricultural and mining industries of Southeast Asia.

This is not to say that the Nakarattar banking system resembled an economist's model of Western-style banking systems. It bears repeating that Nakarattars loaned and deposited money with one another in caste-defined social relationships based on business territory, residential location, descent, marriage, and common cult membership. Unlike in modern Western banking systems, it was the reputation, decisions, and reserve deposits shared among exchange spheres defined according to these principles, and not a government-controlled central bank, that played a dominant role in the regulation of reserve levels and assured public confidence in individual Nakarattars as representatives of the caste as a whole. In other words, the Nakarattar banking system was a caste-based banking system. Individual Nakarattars organized their lives around participation in and management of various communal institutions adapted to the task of accumulating and distributing reserves of capital.

Macro-, Micro-, and Mediate Analysis

I suggested in Chapter 1 of this book that anthropological studies of culture and society have moved in two increasingly divergent directions. One entails a macroperspective on the causes and consequences of people's actions within their environment, both social and natural. The other takes a microperspective on the concepts and values that motivate people's everyday lives and give them meaning. The present study has tried to mediate between these two perspectives: on one hand, describing the cultural world in which Nakarattars created, reproduced, and transformed their distinctive social institutions, and on the other hand, describing the interaction between these institutions and the world of colonial India. The result is similar, in some respects, to an old-fashioned anthropology focused on institutions of Nakarattar kinship organization: its families, lineages, clans, and kindreds.

Yet, despite certain surface similarities, I do not subscribe to assumptions about social equilibrium that mar so many classic structural-functionalist accounts written in the 1950s and 1960s. On the contrary, I have taken my task to be describing how, for a moment in India's long history, a group of people, calling themselves the Nakarattar of Chettinad, organized themselves as a particular kind of "trading diaspora" (Cohen 1969; Curtin 1984; Timberg 1978) and in so doing provided much of the financial basis for agriculture and commerce in South and Southeast Asia. The core of my analysis lies in an expanded view of the nature and functioning of capital: a view that encompasses investments of symbolic capital (Bourdieu 1977) as ways of achieving different kinds of transcendental goals (Bloch and Parry 1989), as part of elite tournaments for prestige (Appadurai 1985; Tambiah 1984), and as tactics for obtaining different kinds of more calculable, tangible rewards (Bourdieu 1977). Nakarattar symbolic capital, I have argued, consisted not only in their financial instruments but in the social relationships and institutions they symbolized. Moreover, the capital and investment goals of individual Nakarattars coincided with the capital and investment goals of collective institutions of caste and kinship. For a specific moment in Indian history, these goals reinforced and reproduced each other.[21]

It was, however, but a moment in a dynamic historical process of individual and collective investment. Nakarattar investments created a specific institutional structure. This institutional structure, in turn, provided an efficient system for transferring knowledge and money throughout the world of British South and Southeast Asia. But it was not long before that world changed, and individual Nakarattars responded to these changes by altering their investments and their institutions. It is important not to adopt the classic structural-functionalist stance and hypostatize the colonial pattern of social organization as necessarily or purposely self-reproductive. But it is also important not to ignore that pattern. One cannot understand the actions of individual Nakarattars without understanding the historical contexts, institutional and global, in which they lived their lives and which made their actions possible. Similarly, one cannot understand the mechanisms of colonial credit markets for agrarian and industrial development without understanding the institutions of informal banking constituted by Nakarattar collective practice. All three levels of analysis—the macro political economy of colonial India, the micro world of individual Nakarattar business practice, and the mediating world of Nakarattar caste and kinship—affected each other. The most general conclusion drawn by the present study, then, concerns neither caste nor capital but the necessity for integrating micro and macro studies with a mediating focus on social institutions.

Conclusion

This completes my reflections on the Nakarattars of South India, at least for the present. There remains much left undone. As I write these comments, an anthropology student at the London School of Economics is completing her Ph.D. dissertation on women and the domestic economy of the Nakarattar, another anthropologist in Japan is exploring their relationship to the goddess cults of Chettinad, and Nakarattars themselves continue to chronicle their past history, exploring the propects for creating a Chettinad museum and seeking insights into modern business tactics by exploring old business successes. My study stops in 1930, just when Nakarattars began their return from Southeast Asia. I did not explore the impoverishment of the majority of Nakarattars since that time, nor the massive investment of their elite in the full range of South Indian industry, from leather to films, and from textiles to engineering. What I have tried to do is to examine aspects of their business practice and social organization in colonial India in order to carry out a critical revision of standard Western conceptions of caste and capitalism. For the Nakarattar do not fit well with these conceptions.

Many students of India will argue that the case of the Nakarattar requires no modification to the standard view since they represent a unique exception to general patterns that the standard view accurately captures. This, it seems to me, is an unfortunate perspective. Every caste in India forms a unique case. The Nakarattar divergence from the Western concept falls well within the range of variation that exists in Indian society. Indeed, the Western conception generally has more to say about Western essentialism and orientalism than it has to say about India. In particular, it is imbued with a normative vision of Western political and economic destiny so powerful that it renders non-Western forms of capitalism invisible and inconceivable, even while depending on those forms for the pursuit of its political and economic dreams.

The last few decades have witnessed what may be the beginning of a serious internal deconstruction of Western normative visions. But the outcome of this deconstruction is far from clear. It is still largely restricted to a few small intellectual circles, and it may well prove a passing fashion. Moreover, it is still in its infancy. Most of the critical efforts directed at the standard view are precisely that: critical. No new way of conceiving India has yet emerged. And, as this study demonstrates for study after study, the old ways still prevent an appreciation of even such major players as the Nakarattar of South India. The research on which the present book is based has been possible only because of the Nakarattar themselves, who remain the people most responsible for remembering and transforming both their past and their future.

Appendix A Interest Rate Tables

Determining the prevailing interest rates for *nadappu* and *thavanai* deposits should be quite straightforward, as they were published on a regular basis by various Nakarattar journals throughout Madras and Southeast Asia, and also in the reports of the Burma, Madras, and Ceylon Banking Enquiry Committees of 1930 and 1934. In the latter, however, *thavanai* rates—which should have paid the higher rate of interest—are listed at lower levels than are *nadappu* rates. I am unable to explain this anomaly. I note that it is not only at odds with what surviving Nakarattars report about their practices (not to mention common sense), but it is even at odds with the descriptions given by banking authorities in the discursive parts of the report for which the tables were prepared. I reproduce some of these questionable figures in Tables 17, 18, and 19.

Table 17. Imperial Bank and Nakarattar Interest Rates on *Nadappu* Deposits, 1928–30

	Imperial Bank Rate		*Nakarattar Rate*			
Month	*To Nakarattars*	*To Others*	*Madras*	*Rangoon*	*Penang*	*Colombo*
1928–29						
Chittrai	7	9	10.69	9.75	8.25	9.19
Vaikasi	7	9	9.94	9.00	8.25	9.56
Ani	6	8	9.00	8.25	8.25	9.00
Adi	5	7	9.00	6.75	8.25	8.06
Avani	5	7	6.75	6.00	8.25	8.25
Purattasi	5	7	7.50	6.75	8.06	7.88
Arpisi	5	7	7.88	7.13	8.06	7.88
Karttikai	6	8	8.25	7.88	8.06	8.06
Markali	7	9	9.00	8.68	8.06	8.81
Tai	7	9	9.75	9.75	8.25	9.00
Masi	8	10	10.50	9.75	8.25	9.56
Pankuni	7	9	10.69	9.75	8.25	8.81
Average	6.25	8.25	8.92	8.27	8.19	8.67
1929–30						
Chittrai	6	7	10.13	9.00	8.25	9.00
Vaikasi	5	7	9.30	8.25	8.25	8.06
Ani	5	7	8.63	7.50	8.25	8.06
Adi	5	7	7.13	6.75	8.25	7.69
Avani	5	7	6.75	6.75	8.25	7.69
Purattasi	7	8	7.13	7.13	8.25	7.69
Arpisi	7	9	8.25	7.50	8.25	7.88
Karttikai	7	9	9.00	7.13	8.25	8.06
Average	5.88	7.63	8.29	7.55	8.25	8.02

Source: Pillai (1930: 1189).

Table 18. Nakarattar Interest Rates on *Thavanai* Deposits in Rangoon, 1928–30 (*Thavanai* period of rest: 60 days)

Month	*1928–29 (%)*	*1929–30 (%)*
Chittrai	13, 12	12, 10.5
Vaikasi	11.5, 11	11.5, 10.5
Ani	10.5	10, 9.5
Adi	10, 9, 8	9.5, 9, 8.5
Avani	8, 7.5	8.5, 9
Puratasi	8.5, 8	9, 8.5, 8.5
Arpisi	9	9.5
Kartikai	9.5, 10	9, 11, 11.5
Markali	10.5, 11	11.5, 12
Tai	12, 12.5	—
Masi	12.5	—
Panguni	12.5, 13	—

Source: Pillai (1930: 1188).

Table 19. Nakarattar Interest Rates on Loans and Deposits in Burma, 1935–42

Deposits	*Interest Rate (%)*	*Loans*	*Interest Rate (%)*
Thavanai vatti	2.83–3.5	Land and immovable property	9–15
Nadappu vatti	3.0–3.75	Valuables (gold ornaments)	12–15
Advances (British banks)	4.0–5.0	Promissory notes plus collateral	12–15
Vayan vatti	4.5–5.34	On-demand promissory notes	18–24

Source: Tun Wai (1962: 53).

Note: Like the figures prepared by Pillai for the MPBECr, Tun Wai's figures, above, are mysterious.

Appendix B *Sample* Hundis

Figures 17–21 reproduce sample *hundis* from the Madras Provincial Banking Enquiry Committee Report (1930).

At sight of this sole of exchange, please pay ____________________ or
order at ____________________ (place) the sum of Rs. __________
(words) __________________________ for value received in cash.

(Signature) ____________________

To
M. R. Ry. ______________________________

Figure 17. Form of a *dharsan hundi* without interest. *Source:* Madras Provincial Banking Enquiry Committee (1930, vol. 1:259).

2

Sivamayam

Muthumariamman Thunai

No. 30

Rs. 1,000

P. R. S. Rm.

21st January 1930—Kilasivalpatti S. A. S. (Creditor)
P. R. S. Rm. (Debtor)

Please pay to Messrs. S. A. S. or order on demand, Rs. 1,000 (Rupees one thousand only) with interest at current rate of interest and debit our account after making due entries herein.

(Signed) *P. R. S. Rm.*

Sukla, Thai, 8th

To P. R. S. Rm., Rangoon.

Figure 18. Form of a *dharsan hundi* with interest. *Source:* Madras Provincial Banking Enquiry Committee (1930, vol. 1:261).

Sivamayam

Rakthakshi Arpisi 10th—Kanadukathan—ABC Avarkal (Creditor)
Kilasivalpatti XYZ (Debtor)

I owe ABC above Rs. 3,000 on account of cash taken for the purchase of samans [things]. This sum of Rs. 3,000, please pay to ABC or order with current rates of interest and debit my account after payment is made.

To R. S. T., Rangoon	One anna	1 anna X	1 anna Y	1 anna Z

(Signed) *XYZ*

Akshaya Adi 1st—Principal of this hundi—Rs. 3,000
Interest—Rs. 451-8-0
Total—Rs. 3,451-8-0

Rangoon R. S. T. firm.

No. Madras hundi 1—Rupees 2,883-8-0—cash Rs. 568 received.

All accounts settled.

(Signed) *ABC*

Figure 19. Form of *hundi* bearing *nadappu* interest from date of issue. *Source:* Madras Provincial Banking Enquiry Committee (1930, vol. 1:268).

Rs. ________

Due ______________________________ 19 __
Place ______________________________
Date ______________________________

At ____________ days after sight please pay to ______________________ or order the sum of rupees ________ only for value received against R/R ________.

(Signature) ______________________
Drawer ______________________

To

______________________________(Drawee)
____
____
____

Figure 20. Form of a *thavanai hundi* for goods sent. *Source:* Madras Provincial Banking Enquiry Committee (1930, vol. 1:262).

Due ______________________________19__
Place ______________________________
Date ______________________________

At ________ days after date we jointly and severally promise to pay ____________ ____________ or order at the Imperial Bank of India, Madura, the sum of rupees ________ only for value ______________________ received in cash.

(Signature) ______________________

Figure 21. Form of a *thavanai hundi* for a loan. *Source:* Madras Provincial Banking Enquiry Committee (1930, vol. 1:262).

Appendix C Career of Raja Sir Muthia Chettiar

1928–32	Director of Indian Bank
1928–63	Member, Board of Pachiappa's Trust
1929	Member, Madras Provincial Banking Enquiry Committee
1929	Member (the youngest), Corporation of Madras
1930	Member, Madras Legislative Council
1931	President, Corporation of Madras
1931	Member, Provincial Finance Committee
1932–56	Member and President, Board of Imperial Bank
1933–35	Mayor (the first), City of Madras
1933–37	Member, Syndicate of Madras University
1936	Minister for Health and Education
1936	Pro-Chancellor, Madras University
1937	Minister for Hindu Religious and Charitable Endowments
1940	President, South India Chamber of Commerce
1941	Knighthood (Raja Sir)
1943	Member, Federation of Indian Chambers of Commerce
1948–82	Pro-Chancellor, Annamalai University
1952–57	Independent Member, Legislative Assembly (Tiruppatur)
1957–62	Congress (party) Member, Legislative Assembly (Karaikudi)
1962–82	Member, Madras Legislative Council

Appendix D Nakarattar Kinship Terms

The following abbreviations are used for analytic terms:

F	father
M	mother
B	brother
Z	sister
H	husband
W	wife
S	son
D	daughter
o	older
y	younger
*	Term combines with *periya* to indicate kin type older than linking term in question.
#	Term combines with *cinna* to indicate kin type younger than linking term in question.

Second Ascending Generation and Above

1.	kiḻavaṉ	HFFFF, HFFF, or eldest living male in a lineage
2.	kiḻavi	HFFFM, HFFM, or eldest living female in a lineage
3.	muppāṭṭaṉ	FFFF, MFFF, etc.
4.	muppāṭṭi	FFFM, MFFM, etc.
5.	pāṭṭaṉ	FFF, MFF, etc.
6.	pāṭṭi	FFF, MFF, etc.
7.	aiyāh	FF, MF, WFF, etc.
8.	appātwāḷ	FM
9.	āyāḷ	MM

First Ascending Generation

10.	appacci (*#)	F, FB
11.	āttāl (*#)	M, MZ

12.	ammāṉ, (*#)	MB (classificatory)
12a.	māmākkārar	MB, WF, HF
12b.	māmaṉ, māmanar	WF, HF
12c.	tāymāmaṉ,	simultaneously MB and WF; reported non-Nakarattar usage (see Burkhart 1978; Tambiah 1973a)
13.	aittai (*#)	FZ, HM, WM
13a.	ammāmuṇṭi	MBW

Ego's Generation

14.	aṇṇaṉ	oB
15.	tampi	yB
16.	ācci	oZ
17.	tankacci	yZ
18.	attāṉ	MBS, FZS, oZH (if older than ego)
19.	maittunaṉ	MBS, FZS, yZH, WB
20.	aitiyāṇṭi	MBD, FZS (whether older or younger than ego)
21.	peṇṭir, peṇṭāṭṭi	W
22.	kaṇavaṉ	H
23.	koḻuntaṉār (*#)	HB
24.	nāttaṉār (*#)	HZ
25.	koḻuntiyāḷ (*#)	WZ
26.	cakalai	WZH (co-brothers-in-law)
27.	koḻuntar peṇṭir, koḻuntaṉavaṇṭi	HBW (co-sisters-in-law)
28.	cakalattiyāḷ	co-wives (of one husband)
29.	campantiyār (campantiyaṉ m) (campantiyāḷ f)	SWF, SWM, DHF, DHM (co-parents-in-law)

First Descending Generation

30.	makaṉ	S
31.	makaḷ	D
32.	marumakaṉ	WBS, oZS, yZs
32a.	māppiḷḷai	DH
33.	marumakaḷ	WBD

Second Descending Generation

34.	pēraṉ	SS, DS
35.	pētti	SD, DD

Sample Compound ("Descriptive") Terms

21a.	aṇṇa peṇṭir, (aṇṇa miṇṭi)	oBW
21b.	tampi peṇṭir	yBW
23a.	ācci koḻuntaṉār	ZHB
24a.	ācci nātaṉār	ZHZ
19a.	aṇṇaṉ maittuṉaṉ	BWB
25a.	aṇṇaṉ koḻuntiyāḷ	BWZ
30a.	aṇṇaṉ makaṉ	oBS
30b.	tampi makaṉ	yBS

30e.	koḻuntaṉār makaṉ	HBS
30f.	nāttaṉār makaṉ	HZS
30h.	koḻuntiyāḷ makaṉ	WZS
31a.	aṇṇaṉ makaḷ	oBD
31b.	tampi makaḷ	yBD
31c.	ācci makaḷ	oZD
31d.	tankacci makaḷ	yZD
31e.	koḻuntaṉār makaḷ	HBD
31f.	nāttaṉar makaḷ	HZD
31h.	koḻuntiyāḷ makaḷ	WZD
35a.	ācci pētti	FZDD (if older than ego)
35b.	tankacci pētti	FZDD (if younger than ego)

Notes

1. INTRODUCTION

1. These population estimates come from three different sources. The 1896 figure is from an article by P. R. Sundara Iyer published in 1906 in the *Indian Review* and cited by Krishnan (1959: 31). Pillai's (1930) estimate of the Nakarattar population in 1920 is based on a caste census published in the Nakarattar journal *Oolian* in 1921–22. The 1980 population figure is based on a 1980 caste census kindly supplied to me by the Madurai Nakarattar Sangam (the Madurai Nakarattar Association).

2. The absence of the caste from the historical record before 1600 is a rather controversial point, though one beyond the scope of the present study. Many scholars point to medieval inscriptional uses of the term *nakarattar* and its variants, asserting that such uses refer to a specific caste who formed the ancestors of the contemporary Nattukottai Chettiars. I find it much more likely that medieval use of the term *nakarattar* refers variously to merchant guilds, to municipal organizations in market towns (*nakaram*), or even simply to the residents of market towns (see Rudner 1985, 1987).

3. In addition to the literature on Nakarattar history and customs cited in the text, I have consulted Chandrasekhar (1980), Cooper (1959), Evers (1972), Manickam (1978), Masters (1957), Nadarajan (1966), Naidu (1941), Ito (1966), and Thomas (1941). Various Nakarattar writers have also been very helpful, especially writers mentioned in the discussion of traditional caste histories (*jati varalaru*) in this chapter.

4. See Baker 1984: Chapter 4, especially pp. 281–290, on Nakarattar commercial practices within Madras.

5. Dumont (1977, 1980 [1970], 1986) characterizes Hindu ideology as a hierarchical system for evaluating ("valorizing") persons in terms of rela-

tive purity. In this characterization, he trades on an ambiguous use of *hierarchy* as denoting at least two concurrent relationships between members of a social group: ritual rank and segmentary inclusion. That is, Dumont asserts that, according to Hindu ideology, every person is related to every other person in a group in two ways. In the first case, every person has the property of being more or less pure than every other person, and no person is knowable independent of his place within a system of ranked relationships. In the second case, every person has the property of being a member of several social groups, each one of which is related to every other group within a single, logically inclusive taxonomic system. The first component in Dumont's definition of hierarchy—the attribution of relative purity to all members of any social group—defines a serial ordering of every person in any social group; that is, it defines a relationship between any two persons that is irreflexive, asymmetrical, transitive, and connected (R. Rudner 1966: 36). The second component in Dumont's definition of hierarchy—the attribution of segmentary membership in an inclusive taxonomy of social groups—defines a complex, connected, but nonserial ordering for every person in any social group, one that defines relationships for which it would be possible to measure the degree of similarity of persons in terms of kinship distance defined by ideas about descent (see, e.g., Evans-Pritchard 1940).

Dumont claims that societies whose members act in conformance with this kind of dual ideological ordering are "holistic"; he implies that any society whose members act in conformance with a different ideology is individualistic. Dumont seems to mean by this that holistic characterizations of persons exemplified by Hindu ideological expressions refer *only* to relational properties. For example, every Hindu characterization of a person will relate at least two or more persons in statements containing two place predicates such as "*A* is more pure than *B*" and "*A* is a member of *B*, where *B* is a group of persons, including or included by another group of which *A* is also a member." By contrast, Dumont seems to claim that societies whose members conform to nonholistic, individualistic ideologies exemplified by Western democratic capitalism characterize each other *only* with nonrelational, single-place predicates, as in the statement "*A* owns 20 acres of land."

Such generalizations about civilizational ideologies are highly oversimplified and, I would argue, are shaped by and contribute to the essentialism, exoticism, and totalism that mark much of Dumont's comparative sociology (see Appadurai 1986a).

6. Marriott has greatly elaborated his ethnosociological approach to Indian culture during the sixteen years since publication of his 1976 essay, but until recently has published few of his results. Nevertheless, gleanings about the direction of his own continuing inquiry may be found in the work of his students, such as E. V. Daniel, A. Gold, M. Moreno, D. Mines,

M. Moore, and G. Raheja. See the special ethnosociology issue of *Contributions to Indian Sociology* (1989, reprinted as Marriott 1990). See also further commentary in *Contributions to Indian Sociology* (1990).

7. Dirks (1988), in a forceful indictment of the orientalist image of India, perhaps overstates the hegemony of orientalism in Western social science. Anthropologists have long been concerned with the exercise and organization of political power, whether examining the dynamics of dominant castes (Mayer 1958; Srinivas 1959) or analyzing the structure of "little kingdoms" (a phrase that Dirks himself borrows from Cohn 1962). Even Dumont, whom Dirks holds out as the champion of kingless India, does not deny the existence of kings or other holders of power so much as he argues that they legitimized their authority by subordinating it to Brahmanical ideology (1958: 45–63, 1962: 48–77, 1980 [1970]: 152–184). Such arguments can be and have been criticized for ignoring the kingly ideologies of *raja dharma* (Derret 1976; Spellman 1964). But they cannot accurately be said to deny India *any* indigenous institutions of governance or ideologies of power and authority. Nor is it the case, as Dirks asserts, that Dumont's study of the Pramalai Kallar portrays them "as examples of a ritually marginal group that exemplified the Dravidian *isolation* of kinship from the influence of caste hierarchy" (1988: 5–6, my emphasis). On the contrary, it is precisely Dumont's point that not even kinship is immune to the pervasive force of a Hindu hierarchicizing ideology. Dumont is clear about this in his original ethnography (1957a) and in his theoretical masterpiece (1980 [1970]). But the reader is also referred to his essay (1957b, reprinted in Dumont 1983) "Hierarchy and marriage alliance in South Indian kinship." Neither in this essay nor in *Un Sous-Caste de l'Inde du Sud* (1957a) does Dumont articulate his theory of the Brahmanical underpinnings of hierarchy. Indeed, in a move quite close to Dirks' own argument, he actually locates its cultural basis in ideas about kingship. But his emphasis on the pervasive intrusion of hierarchy into the domains of caste and kinship remains constant throughout the corpus of his work (see Chapter 9 of this book). The interpretation of Dumont, however, is somewhat at a tangent to my immediate concerns. My argument with Dirks in this footnote concerns his reading of anthropological history, not his interpretation of Pudukottai Kallars and the institutions of South India's ancien régime.

2. CONCEIVING CASTE

1. In recent years, the standard model of caste has been complicated by the findings of a structural study of a mercantile/agrarian division of castes in South India (Beck 1972) and by ethnosociological studies (Marriott 1976, 1990) that, although focused on variations in Hindu strategic interaction, produced findings that implied corresponding variation

among castes whose members follow divergent strategies. Such studies have influenced some of my own revisionary efforts in the present book. See my comparison of Kaikkolars and Nakarattars in the present chapter and also in Chapter 10.

2. Baker's (1976) treatment of late nineteenth- and early twentieth-century caste politics diverges from his (1984) treatment of precolonial castes. To my knowledge, he has not drawn any connection between caste organization in precolonial and colonial South India.

3. Complications of terminology combined with questions of fact render issues related to the nature of caste even more complex than is indicated in the text. This complexity is particularly clear in the case of the Nadar Mahajana Sangam (the Nadar Association) studied by Robert Hardgrave (1969). Hardgrave treats what in my terminology is actually a caste cluster as a single caste. On one hand, as Baker and Washbrook (1975) point out—and their view is supported by my own field inquiries—it is questionable to what extent all of the Nadar castes constituting the Nadar caste cluster ever organized themselves even in a purely modern political fashion, let alone whether they interacted with respect to occupational, affinal, and martial considerations. On the other hand, discrete Nadar subcastes do seem to have operated as corporate groups, with respect to a variety of considerations, over a wide regional territory. The whole issue requires a new investigation—one, moreover, that should be speedily undertaken, as many contemporary Nadar informants (especially the educated youth) take Hardgrave's book as an authoritative source for knowledge of their own caste!

4. I elaborate my use of the term *symbolic capital* in Chapter 10.

5. In his more recent work, Washbrook (1984) seems to have modified his position on precolonial caste identity. If I follow him correctly, he has come to equate "substantialization" with endogamy, and to claim that castes have always been "substantialized" on the level of the localized endogamous *jati*. What is new, in Washbrook's view, is the "brahmanization" of *jatis*: a pan-regional evaluation not simply of local *jatis* but of *jati* cluster status, based on applications of *varnashrama* doctrine that are novel in the South Indian context. According to Washbrook, these doctrines came to be regarded as legal precedent by colonial jurists and were enforced by colonial administrators. This "invention of tradition" kind of argument (cf. Hobsbawm and Ranger 1983) is far more radical than the earlier versions of Washbrook's position described in my text, above. While there is considerable merit to such an argument—particularly with regard to his insights about the impact of the colonial legal system—it is important to note that Washbrook has altered the use of the term "substantialization" from its original application by Dumont (1970) and Barnett (1973). It is also important to note that such a radical view has difficulty accounting for the position of Brahmans in South Indian society and

also for ideological appeals to the *varna* system, both of which extend back to at least the twelfth century (for examples of such appeals, see Subrahmanya Aiyer 1954–56). Accordingly, it still seems preferable to speak of the colonially stimulated substantialization of Brahmanic doctrine.

6. Political support for an elite caste member can be expressed in a variety of ways, such as civil disobedience, migration, religious conversion, voting, and so on.

7. Srinivas uses the metaphor of the djinn of caste in several places (see, e.g., Srinivas 1962: 16).

8. It is also worth noting that Nakarattars, who share many aspects of the commercial adaptation that Washbrook claims are preadaptive for ethnicization, have proven more resistent to assimilation into ethnicized clusters of Chetti castes than have other, more localized Chetti subcastes (e.g., those belonging to the Ariya Vaisya and Aiyera Vaishya Chetti clusters).

9. Indeed, many possible objections to my interpretation of caste as symbolic capital may follow less from disagreement over empirical facts than from disagreement over which elements in the definition of a *corporation* are to be stressed. For my purposes, Maine's (1931: 154) notion of an enduring jural person with rights over property and Weber's (1947: 145) concept of a *verband,* with its reference to jural closure of membership and a definite authority structure, serve as the most useful points of departure. I would, however, qualify this synthetic view with the further, anthropologically conditioned thought that corporate authority need not be vested in a chief or *panchayat,* but may be allocated by the acephalous operation of other forms of political organization, such as a segmentary lineage (Fortes 1954). I employ such a maximally general definition in order to facilitate comparison both between differently organized castes and between castes and other kinds of corporate and noncorporate groups. Also relevant are Wolf's (1955) and Fried's (1957) interest in village communities as corporate groups, possessing joint ownership over land, and Mayer's (1966) and Boissevain's (1968) distinction between quasi groups, or coalitions, and corporate groups, on the basis of temporal continuity. For further discussion of definitional problems in uses of the term *corporation* see Appell (1983, 1984), Brown (1976, 1984), Cochrane (1971), Goodenough (1971), and Smith (1974).

10. For an analysis of the social organization and commercial activity of "petty" Chetti castes (involved only in small-scale trading), see Fanselow (1986). For North Indian examples, see Fox (1969) and Hazelhurst (1966).

11. In commercial territory, Nakarattars resemble most closely and compete in scale with such North Indian *jatis* as Marwaris, who by contrast tended to confine their business ventures to India itself (Timberg 1978). They also resemble the smaller-scale Kalladaikurichi Brahman of Tirunelveli, who conducted business primarily in Tranvancore and the region comprising present-day Kerala (Krishnan 1959; Madras Provincial

Banking Enquiry Committee 1930). The chief contrast that seems to emerge between these three groups of merchant-bankers is their geographic share of the Asian market.

12. In his contrast of the organization of Kaikkolars and of agrarian castes, Mines (1984) is building on the work of Beck (1972) and Stein (1980).

13. Kaikkolars once again reveal a similarity with Nadars, who also utilize local residence-cum-business sites like *natus,* which in their case are called *pettais,* from the term for a fortified market in which itinerant traders protected their goods and cattle and in which they engaged in trade (Vaidyalingam and Sundaramurthi interviews 1980–81). In contrast to that of Kaikkolars, however, Nadars' pan-regional commercial integration is a relatively recent phenomenon. Coordination of their *pettais* and other local business-cum-residence concentrations is accomplished only through branches of their own recently developed caste association. There is no Nadar organization comparable to the 72-*natu* system.

14. For discussion of various medieval merchant guilds, see Abraham (1988) and Hall (1980). Interestingly, the localized guildlike groups were called *nakarattars!* It was only after the eleventh century that *nakarattar* came to be applied to guild groups involved in extensive long-distance trade (see Rudner 1985).

3. THE STUDY OF COMMERCE IN INDIAN SOCIETY

1. Parts of this chapter were previously published in Rudner (1989).

2. For the classic statement of the nationalist argument, see Dutt (1950). For more modern versions and also for historians favoring one or another version of Western modernization theory, see Morris (1969).

3. Other noteworthy studies that do address Indian commercial institutions include Habib (1960, 1969, 1982), Leonard (1979), and Das Gupta and Pearson (1987).

4. For contemporary ethnographic accounts of capitalist exploitation of peasant farmers by moneylenders, see Breman (1974), Gough (1981), J. Harriss (1982), and Mencher (1978).

5. I derived the ratio of British to Indian credit by comparing Vakil and Muranjan's (1927: 532) figures for loans and investments made by Madras Presidency and British exchange banks with those made by Indian joint stock banks. If a comparison of total deposits is made, the ratio is even higher: eight to one.

	Presidency Banks (crores)	*Exchange Banks(crores)*	*Indian Joint Stock Banks (crores)*
Private Deposits	45.6 million	37.1 million	22.6 million
Bills Loaned	26.1 million	10.0 million	15.7 million
Investments	11.0 million	1.6 million	3.5 million

6. "Statement Exhibiting the Moral and Material Progress and Condition of India during the Year 1901–02, and the Nine Preceding Years" (Great Britain, Parliamentary Papers 1903 XLVI: 146–148, quoted in Bagchi 1972: 62).

7. Evidence of the Nattukottai Nagarathars' Association and of C. A. C. Kasinathan Chettiar (MPBEC 1930 I: 101–118, quoted in Bagchi 1972: 207).

8. In fact, Bagchi's (1972) argument stresses the collusive cooperation between British economic interests and colonial political authorities. But within this argument he accepts the colonial vision of India's financial underdevelopment. The actual availability of credit to Indian entrepreneurs would in fact underscore his primary argument about British monopolization of opportunities for industrial investment (see also Ray 1979).

9. There are wide extremes of scholarly opinion regarding the exploitative nature of postulated *jajmani* systems. Some authors see them as ensuring a more or less egalitarian distribution of communal goods and services (Wiser 1936; Wiser and Wiser 1969). Others see *jajmani* as an overtly exploitative institution, operating with particular rigor against the interests of landless laboring castes (Breman 1974; Gould 1964; Orenstein 1962). For more recent "cultural" accounts, see Commander (1983), Fuller (1989), Good (1982), and Raheja (1988).

10. By excess profits I here mean those above and beyond the amount required for subsistence and interest payments on back loans.

11. As many as 90 percent of all loans to peasant farmers in Madras were made by a small number of wealthy peasants (see Nicholson 1895: 230; MPBEC 1930: 79). Washbrook (1981: 73) estimates that this rural elite made up no more than 2–4 percent of the landowning population. See also Baker (1984), Bayly (1981), Murton (1973), Musgrave (1978), and Washbrook (1973).

12. For analyses of Indian bazaars see, for example, Fanselow (1986); Fox (1969), Hazelhurst (1966), Mines (1972), and Ostor (1984). See also Geertz (1963, 1979) for two influential essays on bazaar economy outside the Indian context.

13. In other regards, the difference in focus between moneylenders in village settings and in market towns is significant. Barbara Harriss (1981), for example, sees village moneylenders as potential entrepreneurs, or at least as stimulating studies which portray them as entrepreneurs to the extent that they shift their investments away from villages and into towns. At the same time, Harriss finds that studies of money lending in market towns—that is, studies of bazaar economy—portray moneylenders not as entrepreneurs but as "powerless agents of stagnation" (B. Harriss 1981: 5–12).

14. For studies of Saurastra, see Spodek (1976). For Gujarat, see Das Gupta (1979), Dobbin (1972), Gopal (1976), Haynes (1991), Morris

(1965), Pearson (1976). For the Malabar Coast, see Das Gupta (1967). For the southern Coromandal, see Appadurai (1974), Arasaratnam (1986), Basu (1982), Brennig (1977), Furber (1951), Raychaudhuri (1962), Suntharalingam (1974). For Golconda, see Siddiqui (1956). For all of southern India, see Subrahmanyam (1990). For India in general, see Chaudhuri (1978, 1985).

15. I exclude recent work on commercial activity in the medieval period (ca. 900–1500), including Hall's (1980) work on marketing towns in Chola, South India, 900–1200; Abraham's (1988) work on medieval merchant guilds in the same period; and Mines' (1984) and Ramaswamy's (1985) work on medieval weaving communities. This important body of Indian historiography has obvious relevance for the arguments in the present book, but an adequate evaluation of its significance for the colonial period must await another opportunity.

16. Baker's (1984) study of colonial and independent Tamil economy would also seem to call for comment, since it focuses explicitly on economic issues. But the overall orientation of his work bears more on issues in microeconomics than on the sociocultural issues that inform Bayly's (1983), Subrahmanyam's (1990), and my own work. To the extent that he does address such issues, Baker (1984: 282) explicitly mentions collective Nakarattar institutions that facilitated their emergence as a major commercial group in Tamil Nadu. He speculates that such institutions evolved in response to nineteenth-century economic conditions. But he does not describe them in detail, and he does not describe the pre–nineteenth-century institutions from which they evolved.

17. In the text leading up to his conclusion, Bayly (1978) discusses two forms of caste organization: *chaudhries* of endogamous ritual units—"castes" or "*jatis*"—which, "though they might consist of tradesmen were not chaudhries of trades," and *chaudhries,* which "exercised authority over both the economic and ritual life of trades where the 'guild' and 'caste' (*jati* level) were coterminous" (181). Both of these organizations were integrated within a commercial system that also included organizations structured independently of caste.

18. Arasaratnam's (1971) paper on three Tamil kingdoms represents a partial exception to historiographic blindness beyond the coastal margins. But even here, the focus on interior regions of South India emphasizes political rather than commercial organization. More recently, Subrahmanyam (1990) has attempted to remedy the omission, giving special attention precisely to inland commerce. This exceptional work represents the most comprehensive study to date and goes a long way toward remedying the kinds of omissions I have been describing. It also provides evidence of the difficulty in obtaining data about inland commerce relative to the availability of data for the coastal areas—a difficulty that no doubt contributes to the historiographic bias for coastal studies. Thus, even when

Subrahmanyam focuses on inland commerce, the inland merchants he highlights figure prominently in Indo-European commerce and are characterized by important political ties to Indian kings and European trading companies. See, for example, his treatment of a powerful family of Balija Chettis (1990: 300–314).

19. On commercial actors before 1900, see, for example, Arasaratnam (1966, 1967, 1968, 1971, 1978, 1979, 1980, 1986), Brennig (1977), and Subrahmanyam (1990).

20. Note, however, that strain between political authorities and merchant groups was equally inevitable in purely Indian contexts, so much so that it plays a role in the origin myths of virtually every South Indian merchant caste. The Nakarattar are unexceptional in this regard.

21. My interpretation that there was little change in the dominant role of elite merchants since the seventeenth century differs from that of Arasaratnam (1979) and Brennig (1977), both of whom see the eighteenth-century *dubash* system as distinctly different from the preceding organization of merchants headed by "chief merchants."

22. See discussion of Washbrook (1975, 1984) on caste in the preceding chapter.

23. Moreover, Subrahmanyam's (1990) focus extends to Muslim merchants as well as Hindu merchants.

24. Subrahmanyam (1990: 298–300) aligns himself on this issue with Arasaratnam (1986) and a Dutch author, H. W. van Santen, against Pearson (1976, 1987) and Chaudhuri (1985). He does, however, qualify this position geographically, leaving open the possibility that the situation in Southeastern India differed from that in Southwestern India, as described by Pearson (1976).

4. THE COLONIAL EXPANSION

1. For an overview of Indian political economy during this period, see Bayly (1988). For descriptions of South India's integration with the international market, see Arasaratnam (1966, 1967, 1979, 1986), Chaudhuri (1965, 1978, 1985), Das Gupta (1967), Furber (1951), Habib and Raychauduri (1982), Raychaudhuri (1962), Subrahmanyam (1990).

2. By 1565, Vijayanagar had lost all influence in the area. In 1607, Sadaika Deva Udayan won political recognition of his de facto independence from Madurai and was appointed (or "restored") as Setupati of Maravar country (present-day Ramnad District). One hundred years later, Sadaika Deva Udayan's descendant, Kilavan Setupati, had to contend with internal factions threatening to splinter his own realm. In 1708, Rangunatha, a vassal of Kilavan Setupati, attempted to detach Pudukottai from Maravar country and merge it with the territory of the Nayak of Tanjavur. Kilavan patched up this threat by marrying Rangunatha's sister

and giving him the title of Tondaiman (chief) of Pudukottai. But this move brought only a temporary peace to the territory of Ramnad. In 1733, the Nayak of Tanjavur took advantage of a turbulent dynastic succession to invade Maravar country, and he successfully engineered its partition. Tanjore acquired for itself considerable territory and divided the rest between one of the dynastic pretenders and another *palaiyakkarrar* who would later be established as the Raja of Sivaganga. In 1767, the continuing incursions of the Nayak of Tanjavur brought the Nawab of Arcot, who was ruler of Madurai and nominal overlord of Maravar country, into the fray. The Nawab allied himself first with the Dutch and then with the English. Ultimately, of course, the English emerged as the rulers of the entire region, at the turn of the nineteenth century, and proceeded to reorganize Madras and India under the most powerful centralized government they had ever known. For general overview see Stein (1969); see also Rajayyan (1974); Sathyanatha Aiyar (1924).

3. "There were four varieties of salt. The first was natural salt manufactured in the Salt Pans and the second was Swamp Salt or Spontaneous Salt which was manufactured during periods of high tides. Sea water was allowed to flow over the level earth, and return flow of water was prevented by quickly throwing up small banks, and the enclosed water was then allowed to evaporate. The third was earth salt produced by lixivation, while the fourth was edible salt which was a by-product, in the manufacture of salt-petre. Natural salt, salt-petre and salt fish were manufactured throughout the east coast. Earth salt was made in the districts of Bellary, Cuddappa and Kurnool. Earth salt was made in a few villages on the sea coast of Narsapur, Bhimavaram, Amalapuram and Vizag. Manufacture of salt was associated with two other industries (1) Salt Petre (2) Salt Fish" (Krishna Rao 1964: 63).

Krishna Rao cites the *Report of Godavari Collector 1844* as the source of this information. I assume similar practices were prevalent during the seventeenth century in the area south of the Northern Circars, but that the salt traded by Nakarattars derived from the Palk Bay salt beds, which extend out to present-day Point Calimere.

4. Madras Board of Revenue (1783); see also Appadorai (1936), Krishna Rao (1964: 65–66), and Saruda Raju (1941).

5. The Palani manuscripts (see Chapter 7) describe Nakarattars as transporting salt on their heads or on shoulder poles (*kavatis*) carried by themselves or by servants, but not at such a scale that they required cattle.

6. Although I have not investigated the matter, it seems clear that the East India Company did not succeed in eliminating indigenous middleman renters. Nor did the Company, despite claims to the contrary (Strachey and Strachey 1985 [1882]: 218), eliminate leveraged profits for middlemen. The Nakarattar provide a counterexample. Although they may have been driven or lured away from occupations as salt traders, present-day

Nakarattars remember their forefathers as participating in the nineteenth-century salt trade, precisely in the substantial role of salt renters (see further discussion in text).

7. Ramathan Chettiar (1953: 24–25). I was able to confirm some of the details of Ramanathan's report after returning from the field. Inquiries conducted through an intermediary revealed the existence of the tank in the village, and some memory of now-defunct relations between village inhabitants and Nakarattars. I am indebted to Linda May and Muthu Chidambaram for visiting Narasingampatti on my behalf. Narasingampatti lies inside Chettinad and thus does not appear in Ramanathan's list of trading towns.

8. The monopoly on the fisheries was ended by British Governor Horton, who abolished the grant of monopoly in favor of a license fee for the right of fishing. Nakarattar control of the pearl fisheries is discussed in Samaraweera (1972: 8–9). His discussion is based on Brohier (1964).

9. Chettiar Chamber of Commerce (1963: 140), cited in Mahadevan (1976: 93). Another caste historian, Seshadri Sharma, places Nakarattars in Ceylon as early as 1730 (1970: 100).

10. Copper (1877), cited in Weersoria (1973: 16). The full extent of the Nakarattars' economic power cannot be estimated. But the impact of their domination may be gauged by articles appearing in 1832 issues of the *Colombo Journal,* which singled them out for criticism from Lubbai (Tamil Muslim), Jaffna (Ceylon) Tamil, and Sinhalese traders as speculators, hoarders, and profiteers. See *Colombo Journal,* February 16, 19, and 27, 1832 (cited in Samaraweera 1972: 10). See also Samaraweera's (1972) article, which discusses their dominance and control of trade in all of the commodities mentioned above. Finally, for richly textured eyewitness accounts (not without an element of humor), see Capper (1877), Cave (1900), and Skeen (1906), all quoted at length in Weersooria (1973: 12–19).

11. MacKenzie (1954: 90). Ceylonese merchants had two even less happy alternatives. They could have sent their sterling bills to India, exchanged them for rupees, and then imported the rupees back to Ceylon. But this process took almost a month. Alternatively, Ceylonese merchants could have waited for their sterling bills to be discounted in London, bought silver, shipped it to India, and then had it minted into rupees for shipment to Ceylon. But this would have taken more than a year.

12. During my field work, one family specifically described to me their ancestor's acquisition of title as a major salt-bed renter in Tuticorin at the beginning of the nineteenth century. Another family claimed to have cornered a monopoly in the Madras-Ceylon salt trade during the latter part of the century.

13. See, for example, the Report of the Select Committee of the House of Commons of Great Britain (1832: Appendix No. 109), cited in Natara-

jan's (1941) description of trade between Madras and Bengal between 1796 and 1829.

14. In many cases, specific documentation linking such banking activities to specific Nakarattar businessmen is not available, but the location of many of these transactions in the Madurai/Ramnad region of the Madras Presidency, as well as clear references that do exist in documents, such as a letter from the Madurai Collector (see later in this chapter), suggest Nakarattar involvement. Such documents make suggestive references to elite European and Indian transmission of funds and the purchase of material resources through use of *hundis* paid to unnamed native *soukars*. See, for example, Grant (1784) and volumes of the Madras Country Correspondence (1752–1757). For further discussion, see Ludden (1978: 148–155), Saruda Raju (1941: 133–142), and Sundaram (1944–45).

15. Madras Board of Revenue (September 23, 1793: 5518–5519), quoted in Ludden (1978: 151). See also Madras Board of Revenue (August 8, 1793: 4887–4889) for a longer account, along with an invective against *soukars* in general.

16. Simultaneously with the increase in land taxation, prices for agrarian commodities from 1800 to 1850 underwent something of a depression. According to Saruda Raju (1941: 224–243), this was due, in part, to a reversal in British-Indian relationships vis-à-vis the textile trade: the British assumed the role of exporter and Madras the role of importer. Saruda Raju suggests that the resulting trade imbalance produced deficiencies in the Madras money supply which raised the price of credit and lowered the cost of commodities.

17. Board's Consultation, Madras Board of Revenue (April 14, 1828: back no. 47). On the Settlement of the Ramnad Zemindary for Fasli 1235 and 1236, p. 4 (Tamil Nadu Archives). Quoted in Price (1979: 194).

18. Price (1979: 194). It is not so clear whether Nakarattars and other *soukars* were significantly involved with smaller-scale landholders and agriculturalists, particularly if we assume that late nineteenth- and early twentieth-century patterns of money lending reflect an exaggeration of earlier practices, rather than a radical change. In the later colonial period, professional moneylenders such as Nakarattars made loans directly only to a small number of landowners, focusing the bulk of their moneylending activities on urban centers of the cotton and rice trade. The majority of agriculturalists—especially in nonirrigated farming zones—met their credit needs by borrowing from these wealthy peasants or even somewhat less wealthy peasants (normally, the headmen in their own villages), who made up yet another link in the circuit of credit (Nicholson 1895: 232; Saruda Raju 1941: 143; *Statement Exhibiting* . . . 1903 XLIV: 354; Washbrook 1973). For a qualification to this view, see Robert (1983).

19. On *Zamindars'* increasing reliance on large-scale loans, see Price (1979), Rajayan (1964–65), and Sundaram (1944–45). Price also illumi-

nates the massive, escalating, and politically necessary ceremonial costs faced by *zamindars.*

20. See description of contemporary discussion of the relationship between the Nayak of Tanjavur and native *soukars* at the end of the eighteenth century (Rajayan 1964–65: 151).

21. Madura District Records 1830, Tamil Nadu Archives. Two observations are worth noting about this letter. First, the Rs. 9,000 payment in *hundis* is said to be Rs. 90,000, which I believe to be a clerical error. Second, a handwritten marginal note identifies the unnamed Nakarattar seeking repayment as Sathappan Chetty, who may have been the ancestor by the same name of Raja Sir Annamalai and his son Raja Sir Muthia Chettiar in the twentieth century.

22. Pillai (1930: 1178). As a consequence of the length of time required to settle legal disputes, rural credit was supplied primarily by residents with lendable capital, who had sanctions available to them other than the courts. Not surprisingly, Nakarattars were important sources of credit for non-Nakarattar landed and landless laboring inhabitants of Chettinad, who were, in effect, their dependents.

23. Conceivably, Marwaris were better positioned than Nakarattars to take advantage of the Bombay market for cotton: see Baker (1984: 267–274).

24. In other words, during the second half of the nineteenth century, Nakarattars and other Indian financiers were excluded from the lucrative European credit market that had previously had no choice but to deal with them. The formation of the Presidency Bank (which merged with the Imperial Bank of India in 1927) was followed by the arrival of the Chartered Bank of India, Australia and China in 1853, The National Bank of India in 1877 (previously represented by the British firm of Binny's and Co.), and the Mercantile Bank of India in 1892 (Mahadevan 1976: 31–37). The arrival of the European banks in India is the subject of two studies (Natarajan 1934, Sadasivan 1939) that provide the basis for Mahadevan's discussion.

25. Calculated from "Statements Showing the Prices of Food Grains" in Government of Madras Land Revenue Reports for Fasli 1290 (1880–81) and for Fasli 1335 (1925–26) cited in Washbrook (1973: 157).

26. Price (1979) presents other histories of Nakarattar exploitation of *zamindar* mismanagement that begin as early as the 1820s. See, for example, her account of the Zamin of Sivaganga.

27. The events are described in Price (1979). But it is difficult for me to identify exactly who these other families are from the data she presents. The case is clear for Al. Arunachalam, whom Price correctly identifies as the father of Al. Ar. Ramasami, who became Zamindar of Devakottai.

28. Details of the three lawsuits described by Price (1979: 198) may be found in the Madras High Court's Documents in Regular Appeal No. 80

(1876), which contain the judgments for Original Suit No. 1 of 1872 (Chithambaram Chetty v. Raja Vijia Regunada Muthuramalinga Saithupathy, Zemindar of Ramnad), p. 12; Original Suit No. 3 of 1872 (Narainen Chetty and Vyravan Chetty v. Vijia Regunada Mootooramalinga Saithoopathy, Zemindar of Ramnad), p. 17; and Original Suit No. 5 of 1874 (The Collector of Madura and Agent to the Court of Wards on behalf of Baskarasami Setupati, Zemindar of Ramnad v. Ramasami Chetti son of Arunachellam Chetti), p. 3. Also cited in Price 1979: 198.

29. The Court of Wards—a "proper" British institution—would approve and pay for only one marriage for the young prince.

30. Information on the acreage of Ramasami's domain was provided in an interview with Al. Ar. Somanathan Chettiar by Raman Mahadevan in 1973 (Mahadevan 1976: 45).

31. S. Rm. M Chidambaram Chettiar was the elder brother of Raja Sir Annamalai Chettiar and grandson of S. Rm. M. Rm. Muthia in the story of the Settupatti of Ramnad. He was also father of Sir M. Ct. Muthia Chettiar. All members of the S. Rm. family hail from the village of Kanadukathan.

32. Sundara Iyer (1906, cited by Krishnan 1959: 31). Useful population figures for castes are notoriously difficult to obtain. For example, the 1901 census (Francis 1906: 149) provides a virtually meaningless number of 289,457 for the population of Chettis in India. There is no way of knowing what groups were counted as Chettis, let alone of determining the population of a subgroup such as the Nakarattars. The only other figure available for this period comes from Sundara Iyer's (1906) article in the *Indian Review* (cited by Krishnan 1959). I do not know the basis for his estimate, but he is reported to have had close personal knowledge of the Nakarattar community (Krishnan 1959: 31), and his figures may have been based on a caste census undertaken by one or another Nakarattar caste association. Census figures would most likely have been obtained by consulting with the *karyakkarars* (trustees) of Nakarattar clan temples, who maintained lists of all Nakarattar marriages.

33. It is impossible to be more precise about the number of large-scale landholding Nakarattars in the absence of other data. The range of variation in my estimate reflects uncertainty regarding the number of people constituting an average large-landholding family. For discussion of the organization of Nakarattar families and family firms, see Chapter 6.

34. Correspondence with Lakshman Chettiar, March 1982.

35. The nature of these principal business location "circles" (Pillai 1930) is somewhat mysterious. They fall within Tamil-speaking districts, but they do not exhaust the Tamil parts of Madras in which Nakarattars carried out their business. Interestingly, they seem confined within the geographic boundaries established by the medieval Pandyan kingdom, leaving out, for example, Nakarattar business locations in Madras or Tan-

javur (i.e., within the medieval Chola kingdom). Moreover, the criteria for distinguishing between the different circles of Chettinad is obscure to me, as are the implications of making such distinctions for segmenting the Nakarattar caste.

36. The British banks in Ceylon included the Bank of Ceylon (established in 1841), the Oriental Banking Corporation (1848), the Chartered Mercantile Bank (1854), and the Bank of Madras (1867): see Kannangara (1960), Mahadevan (1976: 100–101).

37. Capper (1877), quoted in Weersooria (1973: 16), notes that Nakarattar bankers were loaning substantial sums to indigenous coffee growers. But Ceylonese holdings were quite small relative to those of the British.

38. The coffee blight actually began to make inroads in production some years earlier. Coffee reached its maximum production figure in 1870. In that year, 1,054,000 pounds were grown on only 185,000 acres. This proportion contrasts with 437,000 pounds grown on 322,000 acres in 1881. Only the increasing price for coffee (from Rs. 54 to Rs. 100 per hundred pounds) and the uncertainties involved in switching to a new crop kept the acreage under coffee cultivation expanding. The sources for these figures are the *Ceylon Blue Book Statistics* (Ceylon Colonial Office 1870–81) and *Ferguson's Handbook and Directory* (1870–81). For detailed statistical analysis of the growth of Ceylon's plantation economy, see Rajaratnam (1961).

39. *Vysiamitran* (a Nakarattar caste journal published out of Colombo), December 25, 1916, cited in Mahadevan (1976: 112).

40. Ceylon Banking Commission (1934 II: 253, 316, 354–355). See Chapters 5, 6, and 10 in this book for discussion of the structural role of *adathis* in the Nakarattar banking system.

41. Evidence of J. Tyagarajah (head *shroff* for the Hongkong and Shanghai Banking Corporation), Ceylon Banking Commission (1934 II: 353–354). In Ceylon, the British banks engaged *shroffs* (normally from one of the non-Nakarattar Chetti castes of Colombo) to recommend and guarantee loans made to local bank clients. Their business depended on their knowledge of potential borrowers (Wright 1907: 317, cited in Weersooria 1973: 25). The term *shroff* has broad currency all over India. It is, in fact, a cognate form of *chetti* and is used in North India in much the same way that *chetti* is used in South India.

42. I am not confident that this is the correct *tolil vilacam* ("business name") formed from the initials of ancestors in the proprietor's patriline (see Chapter 6). For example, it might have been Ar. Ar. S. M.

43. Although a detailed analysis of Nakarattars and Ceylon's legal system is beyond the scope of the present investigation, I note that comparison of Ceylonese legal interpretations of Nakarattar practice (described by Weersooria 1973) with Nakarattars' own interpretations of these practices (described in Chapter 6) indicates significant and, for Nakarattars, serious

discrepancies. Among the relevant legislative actions were the Moneylenders Ordinance Number 2 and the Business Names Registration Ordinance, both of 1918; the establishment of an income tax in 1932 and an estate tax in 1938; and the enactment of the Pawnbrokers Ordinance of 1942. Weersooria (1973) gives excellent, brief descriptions of these acts and of their implications for the Nakarattar. In addition, he reviews the considerable body of legal decisions concerning Nakarattar banking practice in Ceylon. See especially his discussion of decisions regarding the usage of Nakarattar firm names (*tolil vilacams*) and the legal interpretation of such usage with respect to the financial liabilities of proprietors and agents. See also his discussion of legal precedent regarding the application of income taxes and estate taxes to Nakarattars, only part of whose business was in Ceylon (Weersooria 1973: 76–126).

44. On the Burmese rice market, see also Adas (1974), Andrus (1948), Cooper (1959), Mahadevan (1976, 1978a, 1978b), Siegelman (1962). My summary of this body of work (in the text) provides an adequate background for the primary focus of the present investigation: namely, internal Nakarattar social organization. Readers interested in more detailed accounts of relationships between Nakarattars and their clients are referred to the publications just cited.

45. See Chapter 5 for analysis of the interest rate structure of the Burmese credit market.

46. Nor have I described what I interpret as a third phase of Nakarattar commercial evolution, manifested in elite Nakarattar investment in industry in Madras, Burma, and Malaya. See Mahadevan (1976) for an account of Nakarattar industrialization in Indochina and Madras.

5. BANKER'S TRUST AND THE CULTURE OF BANKING

1. Descriptions of Chettiar interest rates were published in the Madras and Burma Provincial Banking Enquiry Committee Reports (MPBEC 1930; BPBEC 1930) and the Ceylon Banking Enquiry Committee Report (CBEC 1934) and reproduced in various publications thereafter. I discuss difficulties involved in interpreting these descriptions in the Appendix A.

2. Deposit accounts were separate from loan accounts, which were secured against various kinds of promissory notes or mortgages. A loan, moreover, was paid out in one lump sum and could not be recalled by issuing a *hundi.* In some cases (typically for petty shopkeepers in towns and cities), a particular kind of loan called a *kandu kisti* loan might be advanced. These loans (normally for small amounts, with interest deducted in advance and payments of the principal scheduled over a short period) yielded a high return to the moneylender (25 percent per annum or more: see MPBEC 1930 I: 227). However, *kandu kisti* accounts, like other loan accounts, were not subject to the drawing of *hundis.*

3. Many merchants extended their business relationship with Nakarattar bankers beyond purely financial transactions. For example, most Burmese and many small-scale Nakarattar merchants had no storage "go-downs" (warehouses) of their own. In such cases, merchants frequently stored and insured their paddy in a go-down conveniently owned by the bankers. Ultimately they might even sell the paddy to the bankers.

4. In practice, I am told, Nakarattar bankers were normally liberal in converting *thavanai hundis* into *dharsan hundis* if their clients were faced with unexpected cash flow problems. At the same time, the Burmese banking analyst Tun Wai observes that *thavanai* deposits, technically cashable by *hundis* after as short a term as two months, often remained with the bank of deposit "for decades" (1962: 45).

5. Pay order *hundis* are not mentioned in any published description of Nakarattar banking practices, but a retired banker informed me that they used this English phrase in reference to *hundis* drawn as dowry payments.

6. For discussion of the institutional sanctions operating to minimize conflict and resolve disputes, see Chapter 6.

7. I found no evidence for any use of "secret" codes, as described by Thurston (1909 V: 270–271), based on the alphabetic characters used to spell the names of Tamil deities and temples.

8. Without a general ledger, Nakarattar account books do not seem to provide a picture of the overall profitability of an agency. This seems peculiar. And it is possible that the books which I examined did not represent a complete set. In this regard, I note that Somalay (S. M. Lakshmanan Chettiar), a Nakarattar writer and a retired banker, makes ambiguous references to a ledger called an *ainthugai* in a rough manuscript for an unpublished book. In one instance, he uses the term to describe the duplicate ledger sheets sent by an agent to his proprietor and copied by the proprietor's son. This reference is similar to Krishnan's (1959: 34) mention of periodically mailed balance sheets by the same name. In another instance, Somalay presents an explicit definition, translating *ainthugai* as "balance sheet" and stipulating that "this contained five items—capital, borrowings, investments, other outstandings, and profits." I note that this statement contains no evidence for the use of a double-entry system. Nor does Krishnan's description of indigenous accounting methods alter my belief that double-entry systems were not used.

9. I am deeply indebted to Rachel Winslow, CPA, who helped me to prepare the general ledger and balance sheet from figures translated from the agency's *peredu*.

10. Weersooria (1973: 109) provides a similar list of the types of Nakarattar account books.

11. Interview with Lakshmanan Chettiar, March 25, 1981. Although the *mempanam* subcategories identified were gleaned from analyzing the Burmese agency's account books described in the text, only minor and

obvious modifications are required to adjust for differences in the funding sources available to Nakarattars in Malaya, Ceylon, or Singapore—or Madras, for that matter.

12. Written evidence about *thanadumaral* or *thandu morai* deposits (alternative transliterations for *tanatu murai panam*) submitted to the Madras Provincial Banking Enquiry Committee suggest that the term may also have been used as an umbrella term for all deposits from relatives, including *accimar panam* deposits from in-laws. (see evidence given by M. R. Ry. C. A. C. Kasinathan Chettiar, MPBEC 1930 II: 1116) and by the Nattukottai Nakarattars Association (MPBEC 1930 II: 1103–1109).

6. A COLLECTIVIST SPIRIT OF CAPITALISM

1. Weber, of course, nowhere considers such a paradox and proposes instead a contrast between what he terms rational individualism and traditional egocentricism as an apparently exhaustive dichotomy. Thus, in at least one place, he contrasts wealth accumulated unselfishly by a Protestant's pursuit of his calling with wealth accumulated by a pre-Protestant merchant for the sake of his family. The former he attributes to an individualistic effort to avoid worldly contamination of actions undertaken solely for the glory of God. The latter he attributes to an egocentric extension of the family founder's personality (1958: 276). Whatever may have been the case for the pre-Protestant Europeans that Weber had in mind, for the Nakarattars, just the opposite seems to have been the case. That is, familial goals were internalized and projected onto individuals, rather than the other way around.

2. Mahadevan (1976) provides the best documentation of the shift of Nakarattar investment into capitalized industry.

3. The functional equivalents of these parent bankers performed similar roles in the seventeenth century, although they did so under a different title: *ettis.*

4. I make use of three primary sources of information in my analysis. These consist of notes for an unpublished book on the Nakarattars written by a retired Nakarattar banker and caste historian, Somalay (a nom de plume derived from S. M. Lakshmanan Chettiar), interviews with Somalay and other Nakarattars conducted as part of my field research in Tamil Nadu in 1981, and a sample of a Nakarattar firm's account books from its agency house in Burma for the period from 1912 to 1915. These various primary oral and written sources are used to flesh out, verify, and refine more general accounts of the system available in already published work by Krishnan (1959), Mahadevan (1976), Naidu (1941), Pillai (1930), Siegelman (1962), Tun Wai (1962), and Weersooria (1973). The triangulation of several different sources permits one to be reasonably confident of the reconstruction of the Nakarattar banking system at its chronological

and spatial peak, before the community shifted massively from mercantile and financial to industrial ventures.

5. This practice has not been followed consistently since the 1930s. In the postwar period, many men have simply indicated their father's name and their village name when establishing their own firm; for example, P. Ct. Allagappa signifies "Palattur village, Chidambaram Allagappa." Occasionally one also finds the occupational title "Chettiar," but no indication of natal village, as with Ct. C. Allagappa for Chidambaram Chettiar Allagappa. But this last practice has lost popularity since the 1960s (this illustration as well as those provided in the text are taken from Lakshmanan Chettiar 1953).

6. In this case, "Tevar" designates the employee's caste affiliation.

7. "*Pulli parkka* = to conjecture how much a sum may be; to estimate" (Fabricius 1972: 727).

8. As an example of their use of *pullis* as units, I obtained figures from the Madurai Nakarattar Sangam for the total number of *pullis* presently registered in all nine Nakarattar clan temples (about 20,000) and hence, even in the absence of government census figures indexed by caste, feel relatively confident in accepting their estimate for the contemporary Nakarattar population at about 100,000. This coincides with Chandrasekhar's (1980) estimate, which was probably derived in the same fashion. It differs from recent estimates by Moreno (1981) and Timberg (1978).

9. A considerable body of case law has been generated specifically in reference to estate and income taxes levied against Nakarattar individuals outside of India. In these cases, there was no question of refusing to grant jural status to the Nakarattar *valavu*. These and other Hindu joint families were legally recognized as juristic individuals similar to corporations and subject to the application of Hindu Mitakshara law (cf. Kane 1946 III; Tambiah 1973a). Litigation arose only in determining whether some body of assessed property belonged to an individual or to the joint family of which he or she was a member. See Weersooria (1973: 110–116) for a review of the issues and the relevant cases in Ceylon.

10. The large family houses shared by a *valavu* may be responsible for the popular name of the Nakarattars: the Nattukottai Chettiar ("Country Fort Chettiar"). Alternatively, it is sometimes speculated that the name represents an abbreviation of Nattarasankottai, a town within Chettinad thought to be one of the Nakarattars' earliest residences.

11. Nakarattars also employ the common Tamil term *kutumpam*, marked by an emphatic article: *ore kutumpam* "one (same) family."

12. A passing comment by Evers (1972: 637) apparently supports my interpretation. There, he mentions that Nakarattar "spheres of accumulation," in contrast to "spheres of consumption," were administered by the heads of Nakarattar joint families. But he does not elaborate on the issue.

13. For further discussion of Nakarattar marriage alliances, see Chapter 8.

14. See Chapter 5, note 2 on *kandu kisti* loans.

15. I am not able to confirm at the present time that the twelve largest landowners represent all the *adathis* in Burma. Nor am I able to speculate about the presence or absence of *adathi* status among other Nakarattars outside this group. Further investigation could be carried out by querying surviving Nakarattar bankers from the period or by locating copies of the *adathi* lists maintained by the Imperial Bank of India.

16. A list of the Nakarattar firms represented on the Burma Indian Chamber of Commerce in 1925–26 gives the following firms: A. K. A. Ct. V., A. A. Krm. M. Ct., A. K. Rm. M. K., P. K. N., Rm. P., S. A. A., S. A. Rm., S. K. R. S. K. R., S. M. A. Ra., S. Rm. M. A., S. Rm. M. Ct. Sir., S. Rm. M. Rm., and T. S. N. From the Burma Indian Chamber of Commerce (1929: v), cited in Mahadevan (1976: 187).

17. See also the evidence of a Ceylon bank *shroff*—a semi-independent loan guarantee officer—presented to the Ceylon Banking Enquiry Committee in 1934 (quoted in Chapter 6).

18. *Nakaravitutis* should not be confused with the headquarters for Hindu sectarian orders, also called *matams* or *atinams.*

19. For a cultural account of the differing ritual roles of Nakarattars and Kongu Goundar Vellalars in Palani, see Marriott and Moreno (1990).

20. The "information transfer" function of these ritual events continued even when the rituals were augmented in this respect by the publication of caste journals sponsored by local caste associations. Such journals included *Dhanavanikan* (a monthly journal published from Kottaiyur in Chettinad and Rangoon, ed. A. K. Chettiar), *Dhana Vysia Ooliyan* (a weekly journal published from Karaikudi in Chettinad, ed. S. Mooragappa Chettiar), *Kumari Malar* (a monthly journal published from Madras, ed. A. K. Chettiar), *Ooliyan* (a weekly journal published from Karaikudi in Chettinad, ed. Rai Chokalingam), *Vysiamitran* (published from Devakottai in Chettinad, ed. S. T. Ramanathan Chettiar), and *Nakarattar Malar* (published from Madurai).

21. The elder mediators or arbitrators of a *panchayat* were conventionally five in number (*panch* means "five"), although reality often deviated from this ideal. The difference between a *panchayat* that resolved a dispute through mediation and one that resolved a dispute through arbitration is formal. In the latter case, both parties agreed in advance to abide by the decision by signing a legal document called a *muchalika,* which could be used as evidence in a civil suit if either party found it necessary to go to court. *Muchalikas* (from a Persian term) were broadly used in similar contexts throughout colonial India. However, it is not clear when this practice was adopted by the Nakarattars. According to Thurston (1909 V: 263),

agreements were not made in writing as recently as 1909. The presumption, then, is that *muchalikas* were a recent response to the colonial legal system.

22. As discussed in note 18, Saivite *matams* or *atinams* should not be confused with *Nakaravitutis,* which were sometimes called Nakarattar *matams. Matam panchayats* were apparently receding into the background by the end of the nineteenth century (Thurston 1909). None of my informants remember them in operation, although the palm-leaf manuscripts from Palani temple (Chapter 7) offer a glimpse of conditions in which they would have played an important role during the seventeenth century. *Kovil* (temple) *panchayats* (see Chapter 9), however, continued until at least the 1940s, although much of their role was taken over by caste associations and by the court system of colonial India during the course of the twentieth century.

23. Thurston (1909: 263) mentions a *panchayat* held for a dispute between two families from the same clan that arose over adoption.

24. I am aware of a 1940s example of a temple clan *panchayat* meeting in which a wealthy member was denied permission to marry his daughter to any family within the community until he had paid his temple dues. I am also aware of several outcaste marriages (albeit among extremely wealthy, Westernized, and modern Nakarattars) that brought no sanction from any community institution.

25. Outsiders sometimes mistake a line of the S. Rm. family for a royal Nakarattar lineage because it was represented by Raja Sir Annamalai Chettiar and his son, Raja Sir Muthia Chettiar. But Nakarattars have no royal lineages. The title "Raja Sir" was conferred by the British on Raja Sir Annamalai in the twentieth century and gives him superior, *zamindar*-like land rights over a village also created at that time. It was Annamalai's idea to name his village by the same name as the entire territory comprising the Nakarattar homeland of Chettinad—no doubt precisely in order to play on uninformed British sentiments about royalty.

26. Among works that continue to view individualism as essential to capitalism I include not only historical studies such as Shoji Ito's (1966) essay about the Nakarattar, discussed at the beginning of this chapter, but also general theoretical works, from the classic sociological theories of Marx, Durkheim, Weber, Simmel, and Mauss, through the modernization theorists of the 1960s, to recent studies in the culture of capitalism such as those by Dumont (1977, 1986) and Macfarlane (1987). For recent critical evaluations of these tendencies see Carrithers, Collins, and Lukes (1986).

27. Caste studies by Conlon (1977), Dirks (1987), Leonard (1978), and Mines (1984) do consider some of the corporate functions of caste.

28. This would be consistent with application of Weber's Jewish "double ethic" (1958: 271) to Hinduism.

7. THE MAGIC OF CAPITALISM AND THE MERCANTILE ELITE

1. The Six Deeds of Gift contain two lists of ritual practices as well as six "deeds." All the manuscripts are presently stored in Palani Temple, but transcripts have been compiled and published by the Tamil professor and Nakarattar authority V. Sp. Manickam (1963). I have not seen the original manuscripts (which are likely to have been recopied in any case). But Manickam vouches for their authenticity on the basis of internal linguistic evidence as well as personal knowledge about the conditions of their storage and preservation. The texts are written in an archaic mixture of classical Tamil and the colloquial Tamil of the seventeenth and eighteenth centuries, presenting difficult translational problems to the nonexpert. My analysis would not have been possible except for the translation provided for me by Professor K. Paramasivam (1981a), parts of which I reproduce with his kind permission.

2. I have analyzed the origins of the Nakarattar Palani pilgrimage in greater detail elsewhere (Rudner 1987).

3. Paramasivam (1981a: 3). The figure "96-4-0" makes reference to units of currency smaller than a rupee: either *chakrums* and *pannams* or *pannams* and *kasus.*

4. "The deity is not given food, which it has to reciprocate with a 'counterprestation' [referring to Babb 1975: 57] of *prasada.* Instead, the deity is served a meal, which the worshiper later consumes. The food *prasada* is not a return gift, but the same food transmuted—like all other substances that become *prasada*—by its contact with the deity in its image form. There are no food transactions and prestations in *puja,* because they are not what the food offering together with the receipt of *prasada* amount to" (Fuller 1992: 78). Nonanthropologists may be unfamiliar with the standard but technical term *prestation* introduced by Mauss (1954) to denote a gift-giving action that incurs a recursive obligation for the recipient to return a prestation.

5. Appadurai has explored the political dimensions of ostensibly purely domestic relationships between husband and wife in his (1981c) essay "Gastro-politics in South Asia."

6. My suggestion that anthropologists overemphasize the importance of status purity or impurity in Hindu ritual specialists deserves elaboration. For discussion of some of the relevant issues see Claus (1978), Das (1976), and Parry (1982).

7. For discussion of Dumont's Brahman-centered model of caste hierarchy, see papers in the *Journal of Asian Studies* (1976).

8. A distinctive "Cambridge School" represented by Baker (1976; Baker and Washbrook 1975), Seal (1973), and Washbrook (1976) views the trend as a consequence of the cost of empire, "the perennial dilemma of the Raj: If the administrative cost of intervening was not to overtake the

returns and the security of the state to be put at risk, Indian collaboration would have to be much extended. . . . Systems of nomination, representation and election were all means of enlisting Indians to work for imperial ends" (Seal 1973: 10). Other schools of thought view the shift in British policy as a response to popular British outcry for democratic reform rather than as a calculated decision to maximize profits. Still another view (Frykenberg 1965; Suntharalingam 1974) differs from both of these schools and places more weight on indigenous Indian efforts to "eat away" the system by political, legal, and illegal action, like white ants eating away a wooden edifice (Frykenburg 1965: 231–44). All of these explanations seem plausible, and certainly none is inconsistent with the others.

9. In general, the postulated pre–twentieth-century stage of centralized colonial rule is not clearly distinguished from precolonial regimes with respect to the question of local influence on regional politics. In fact, in both cases the issue is rather vague and undefined. Most discussions take a "top-down" orientation and focus on the revenue powers of the state. Some others pay attention to the intrusion of the state into villages by its appointment of village officers. Still others pay attention to the intrusion of the state into local temples. But little or no consideration is given to small-scale political regimes that extended beyond individual villages or temples. For South Indian examples of such regimes, see Beck (1976), Dirks (1988), and Price (1979).

10. As with my comments on recent interpretations of the nineteenth-century evolution of government in India, I only summarize here a well-developed historiography chronicling and analyzing the evolution of Anglo-Indian law and attitudes towards religious gifting and temples. The standard reference is Mudaliar (1974, 1976). Major monographic treatments may be found by Appadurai (1981), Fuller (1984), and Presler (1987). My view of the subject has been particularly influenced by Appadurai (1981) and Breckenridge (1976, 1977, 1983).

11. See Mudaliar (1974) on the HRCE Acts of 1817, 1863, 1925, and see Breckenridge (1977, 1983) for particularly perceptive interpretations of the social context and consequences of these acts.

12. The Nakarattar elite comprised perhaps 5 to 10 percent of the 10,000-member caste in 1900 (see Rudner 1985).

13. Other branches of the S. Rm. family and families supported by S. Rm. were also prominent participants in Madras politics. Annamalai's brother, Ramaswamy, had started a secondary school in Chidambaram sometime during the end of the nineteenth century or the beginning of the twentieth century and was praised as the first Chettiar to "have boldly deviated from the medieval ways of debasing charity and diverted it along more modern and useful channels" (*Madras Mail,* June 26, 1920, cited in Arooran 1980: 124). Annamalai built on his brother's philanthropy by founding Sri Minakshi College in Chidambaram in 1920. In

1928, Annamalai's political ally, Chief Minister P. Subbaroyan, formed a committee to decide whether there was a need to establish a Tamil university. The committee recommended a federal affiliating type of University with six principal centers at Madurai, Tirunelveli, Tiruchirapalli, Coimbatore, Kumbakonam and Chidambaram. At the same time Annamalai offered an endowment of Rs. twenty lakhs to form a unitary, residential university just at Chidambaram. Another Chettiar offered Rs. 35 lakhs to establish a unitary university at Madurai (*Madras Mail,* May 5, 1928, cited in Arooran 1980: 62). Present-day informants say the other Chettiar was Karimuthu Thiagarajan, on the advice of Annamalai's son-in-law, Venkatalchalam (C. V. Ct.) Chettiar. But the government accepted Annamalai's offer, and the Annamalai University bill, with its stipulation of a matching 20-lakh grant and an annual 1.5-lakh grant was passed by the Legislative Council, the governor, and the viceroy by the end of 1928 (for further details, see Arooran 1980).

14. I am told that Annamalai and his son Muthia exercised complete control of the Indian Bank from the time of its founding until its nationalization in 1969, and that Muthia continued to exercise considerable behind-the-scenes influence until his death in 1984.

15. Speech in Rangoon by Raja Sir Muthia Chettiar, sometime in the 1930s (S. M. Lakshmanan Chettiar, personal communication, March 1981).

16. See Baker (1976: 153–154) for a rather scandalous account of Annamalai's 1923 election.

17. From his election as mayor in 1933 until his death in 1984, Muthia held continuous formal political office. Upon completing his term as Mayor of Madras he became the Chettiar representative to the Legislative Assembly, in which capacity he served until 1952. In between he held various ministerial posts in Justice party governments (see Appendix C). From 1952 until 1957, he was elected (with Congress party support) as the independent Tirupattur representative of the Assembly. From 1957 to 1962, he served another term as the Congress party representative from Karaikudi. Following this and up until his recent death he was a nominated member of the Legislative Council (the upper house of the Madras bicameral legislature).

18. Erskine to Willingdon, March 11, 1935, Erskine Papers, vol. 5, India Office Library; cited in Baker 1976: 243.

19. Not that Muthia had a monopoly on such actions: other *zamindar* Justice leaders, including the Raja of Bobbili, the Raja of Venkatagiri, and the leader of the Legislative Council, Sir Mahomed Usman, were all said to have made or to have attempted to make similar deals with the government (cf. Baker 1976).

20. The collapse of the roles of temple trustee and kingly protector into a single category was due less to any victory of merchants over kings than

to the colonial transformation of kings into litigants on par with any other elite member of society (cf. Breckenridge 1977).

21. My information about the process of Annamalai's involvement in the educational movement comes from discussions with informants during my field work in Tamil Nadu. Thus, the events were important enough to be remembered sixty years later. I was subsequently able to confirm my informant's memories with documents cited in Arooran (1980).

22. Complaints from dissident Chettiar political factions provide the best documentation in support of this hearsay about Annamalai's and Muthia's use of power for their own purposes. See, for example, a variety of Government Orders from the Madras Department of Local Self Government in the 1920s; reports in the *Hindu* (a prominent newspaper published in Madras), April 8–9, 1921; and editorials in *Ooliyan* (a Chettiar journal published by a non–S. Rm. A. M. faction between 1935 and 1937). Most of these allege S. Rm. A. M. manipulation of the ministry and local boards to influence Chettiar-controlled temples and markets (see also Baker 1976: 269).

23. For an account of Annamalai University's history, see Arooran (1980).

24. See Kochanek (1964: 151–155) on S. Rm. A. M. influence on the Chamber of Commerce.

25. This definition of *mercantile elite* is similar to the use of the term *dominant caste* as refined by Beck (1976a). (The original formulation is from Mayer 1958 and Srinivas 1959). Like agrarian power, mercantile dominance is a function of rule and not necessarily of ownership of resources (see Neale 1969).

8. MARRIAGE ALLIANCE

1. By *lineage,* I mean here the maximal lineage segment active in Nakarattar kinship organization, not the patrilineal line of descent extending without limit from a focal individual. Nakarattar clans and lineages are described in relation to Nakarattar control of Chettinad in Chapter 9.

2. The Nakarattar joint family (*valavu*) is best considered as the minimal lineage segment of Nakarattar kinship organization. Even an inmarrying woman undergoes a ceremony at marriage in which she is placed under protection of the lineage segment's tutelary deity (*kula teyvam*), becoming, in effect, a member of her husband's lineage.

3. See Freeman (1961), for example, for a definition of *kindred* based on a criterion of genealogical distance.

4. The differential linkage to the husband's and wife's descent groups is signaled by the couple's obligation to pay a religious tithe (*pulli vari,* see Chapter 9) to the husband's clan temple, but not to the temple of the wife's father's clan.

5. For an unusual differentiation between *descent group* and *kindred,* see Carter (1973).

6. A general definitional discussion of the term *kindred* is not relevant in the present context. Suffice it to say that in dealing with this definitional problem, as in dealing with many others, I follow Goodenough (1970). See also Dumont's (1957b: 21–22) critique of Emeneau's (1941) theory of Dravidian double-unilineal descent.

7. The Tamil phrase *cir tanam* is easily confused with the Sanskrit *stri dhanam* (see, for example, Dumont 1957b: 31–32). The latter, also interpreted as a term for dowry, is generally translated as "woman's property." But the Tamil phrase here employs the word *cir* for "glory," "fame," or "beauty," not the Sanskrit word *stri.* Accordingly, I translate *cir tanam* as "property which brings fame or glory." Although Sanskrit terms are often incorporated in Tamil ritual vocabularies, the Nakarattar (and also Dumont's Kallar) clearly adopt a Tamil frame of reference for describing affinal gifts between two families allied by marriage.

8. Nakarattars practiced Dravidian cross-cousin marriage. Accordingly, the presence of common parallel cousins between two families rendered the families parallel to each other and union between them incestuous. The definitions of Dravidian "cross" and "parallel" relationships (also termed "affinal" and "kin" relationships, cf. Dumont 1957a, 1957b), and the distinction between them, have preoccupied anthropologists since Lewis Henry Morgan (1870). There is still no generally accepted interpretation. For more recent efforts to arrive at a solution see Carter (1973), David (1973), Dumont (1953, 1957a, 1957b, 1961, 1975), Kay (1965, 1967), Scheffler (1971, 1972a, 1972b, 1984), Trautmann (1981), Tyler (1966), and Yalman (1971). For a discussion of aspects of the history of these efforts, see Rudner (1990).

9. In contemporary South Indian society, *nakaram* refers to a city. Historically, *nakaram* refers to a medieval guild or municipal council. *Kovil* refers to a temple or palace. The compound term, *nakarakkovil,* is a contraction of *nakaram kovil* ("temple of the *nakaram*"), but refers to both the Nakarattar clan (literally, "temple-clan") and the Nakarattar clan temple. The derivation is not clear. See Rudner (1985).

10. *Vattakai* is an archaic form of *vattam* (literally, "circle"). Both terms have been used to denote a territorial division since the Chola period (900–1200).

11. Similarly, *karais* may once have constituted medieval regional assemblies. The terminological distinction between *vattakais* and *karais* may indicate a jurisdictional difference between Colamandalam and Pandyamadalam.

12. This shift to a later age for marriage is common throughout India.

13. The basis for judging a figure to be "odd" (hence to be "rounded off") is not clear to me. My informant gave examples of Rs. 1,420 and Rs. 1,900.

14. In describing the ritual construction of Nakarattar marriage alliance, I adopt the standard anthropological convention for abbreviating genealogical relationships, e.g., *F* for father, *M* for mother, etc. For complete list of abbreviations, see Appendix D.

15. For a description of Nakarattar nuptial ceremonies, see Thurston (1909 V: 265–268).

16. Patrilateral prestations were not institutionalized and not very much in evidence during the course of my field study. My data for them fall into three categories.

The first type of data consisted of personal observations of patrilateral gifts to first children in a small number of families. I did not collect a Tamil term for these gifts. The few examples in my data may represent examples of *murais* or *vevus.* They may exemplify a separate cultural category in their own right. Or they may simply reflect the custom of one or two families and not the Nakarattar caste as a whole.

The second type of data were reports of patrilateral prestations of gold coins to a goldsmith prior to matrilateral prestations of *sireduththal* (*cir tanam*) (Thurston 1909 V: 265). According to one informant, the coins were traditionally beaten into a thin sheet and then melted into the gold used for the *kalutturu,* a massive ceremonial necklace presented to a Nakarattar bride in addition to her *tali.* My informants, however, said that the gold was not called *paricam* or "bride price" (cf. Dumont 1957b: 83). Moreover, the practice of presenting a *kalutturu* is becoming prohibitively expensive. In fact, most contemporary marriages rent a *kalutturu* for ceremonial purposes. It may be the case that the groom's family covers the rental cost. But I have no further information on the topic.

The third type of data collected were reports of patrilateral prestations occurring at the *uppu eduththal* ("salt carrying") ceremony during a wedding (Thurston 1909 V: 266). I did not witness any such prestation in connection with the salt ceremony during weddings in which the salt ceremony was included. Among my informants who knew anything about the salt ceremony, nothing was known about any patrilateral prestations.

17. In fact, the implications of the distinction between systems of classification and systems of social groups have never been a subject of common understanding. See, for example, the differences in opinion between Leach (1961 [1951]), Lèvi-Strauss (1969), and Needham (1962) with regard to the minimal number of local groups necessary for maintaining various elementary kinship structures.

18. For a more elaborate discussion of some of the difficulties in maintaining the distinctions between perfect and virtual affines, see Rudner (1990).

19. Burkhart (1978) and Tambiah (1973a) both point to uses of the term *taymaman* in cases where WF is identical with MB. But the only lessons they draw from this usage are that "the tie with the mother's agnatic

group is stressed" (Burkhart 1978: 172) and, even more weakly, that "distinctions such as these represent a mapping of notions of genealogical distance on the kin categorical distinctions (Tambiah 1973a: 124–125).

20. A systematic analysis of Nakarattar rites of marriage would be digressive in the present context. I note briefly that not only do WF and MB receive titles that are specially marked versions of purely consanguineal kinship terms, but also the bride is ritually transferred to the protection of her husband's family deity (*kula teyvam*).

21. Questions can be raised about the applicability of Dumont's (1957b) "personnel replacement" argument even to his non-Nakarattar castes. None of the replacements he describes for *cir*-givers ever extend beyond the second generation. Thus, he fails to demonstrate that the successive replaceability of *cir*-givers within a two-generation span generates a replaceability for descent groups that succeed each other in the formation of affinal kindred. As we have seen, alliances are not automatically renewed among the Nakarattar. The question is open in the case of non-Nakarattar groups.

22. *Amman* is used for both the MB and the FZH. If two families contract a marriage alliance, both the HF and the WF are designated by *maman* or *mamanar,* indicating their "in-law," *murai*-obligated status (regardless of their identity as a real MB or FZD). For both an unmarried MBS and an unmarried FZS, *attan* is used if older than ego, and *maittunan* if younger than ego. Again, the inferior term, *maittunan,* is used for the WB even if older than ego, thereby marking his *murai* obligations, but not a lateral preference for marriage. *Attiyandi* is used for the MBD and the FZD (regardless of age in relation to ego). For a complete list of Nakarattar kin terms, see Appendix D.

9. TEMPLE CONTROL AND CROSS-CUT SEGMENTATION IN CHETTINAD

1. For traditional caste histories, see Chinnaiya Chettiar (1941–42), Chockalinga Ayyah (1919), Lakshmanan Chettiar (1953), Ramanathan Chettiar (1953), Sharma (1970), and Subramaniyan Ayyar (1895). In the absence of independent documentary evidence, these histories are best understood as ideological tracts or Malinowskian charters for behavior. For review of available documentation, see Rudner (1985). For further discussion of the Nakarattar *varalaru,* see Chapter 10.

2. According to the *varalaru,* the original seven families first arrived in Chettinad in the town of Nattarasankottai along with two other groups of non-Nakarattar Chettis. The three Chetti groups then moved to the town of Ilayathakudi. The non-Nakarattars left Chettinad entirely. Six of the seven families established themselves in their own village, separate from Ilayathakudi, and the remaining Ilayathakudi family split into three

groups, of which one remained in Ilayathakudi and the other two settled in Iraniyur and Pillaiyarpatti, respectively.

3. Ramanathan Chettiar (1953) also provides more detailed information on the individual religious gifts.

4. On religious endowment and control of religious trusts, see Appadurai (1981), Breckenridge (1976), and Mudaliar (1974). For description of a specific Nakarattar endowment in the context of a detailed analysis of nineteenth-century religious endowment generally, see Breckenridge's (1976) account of the Nagappa Chettiar *kattalai* in Meenakshi Temple in Madurai.

5. For village temples, trusteeship was frequently vested in the dominant family of the dominant lineage of the village. For the nine Nakarattar clan temples (*nakarakkovils*), *karyakkarars* were recruited on a hereditary basis, rotating in a regular fashion between selected small groups of prominent families in the clan from throughout Chettinad. In both cases, the ancestors of these families had demonstrated their generosity (*vallanmai*) and trustworthiness (*nanayam*) by contributing to the founding or renovation of the temple. For major public temples, the Hindu Religious and Charitable Endowments Board appointed individuals to nonhereditary positions on the boards of trustees. In general, however, one qualification for appointment was an act of endowment by oneself or one's ancestors.

6. Ownership of a temple depended, among other things, on the legal definition of its congregation, another complex legal problem (see Appadurai 1981). Depending on the temple under litigation, Nakarattar plaintiffs or defendants might be joint families, local lineage segments, clans, or the caste as a whole. For an account of litigation between two Nakarattar factions for control of a temple in Colombo, as well as accounts of other Nakarattar litigation in colonial Ceylon, see Weersooria (1973).

7. According to the administrative report to the Board of Trustees of Ilayathakudi Temple (Ilayathakudi Devasthanam 1939), the temple *karyakkarars* (trustees) had originally presented their argument to the Madras High Court in 1912 as part of a suit to confirm their position as hereditary trustees (Madras High Court, Appeal No. 72 of 1923, "Scheme for administration of Ilayathakudi Temple"). The 1939 report indicates that the proposed scheme was accepted in 1926 (i.e., following the Religious Endowments Act of 1925; see Mudaliar 1974). Under provisions of the accepted scheme, the temple's board of trustees was to consist of five members: two from the four traditional *karyakkarar* families, and three to be appointed by the court.

8. The Ilayathakudi Temple Report (Ilayathakudi Devasthanam 1939) may even omit reference to *inam* holdings outside the temple's immediate vicinity. My impression is that temple *devastanam* lands included *zamindari* or *inam* lands in Tanjavur; however, this impression requires confir-

mation. If I am correct about these omissions as well as omissions of non-*inam* investments, the selectivity of information contained in the report is somewhat puzzling and raises questions about the purpose of the report. I note, however, that, unlike the temple's account books, the administrative report was prepared in both Tamil and English and was still freely distributed to temple visitors forty years after its publication. In addition, before the report presents its description of selective temple expenditures, it describes the history of Nakarattar involvement with the temple and the court decisions that recognized the temple as privately owned by the Nakarattar community. For these reasons, it seems likely that the report was designed primarily for an external audience, to demonstrate how responsibly Nakarattars were meeting their obligations as owners.

9. This is not to say that Nakarattars understood or subscribed to Western, biological theories of genetic heritability. Rather, they followed their own version of Hindu beliefs about membership in different kinds of descent groups. This Nakarattar understanding of descent was similar to relevant tenets of Hindu textual traditions exemplified in the Dharmasutras, the early Dharmasastras, and Kautilya's Arthasastra. The texts maintain that every person is born into a particular caste (*jati*), clan (*kula*), and family (*parivara*). Membership in these groups is determined in part by genetic transmission of the male "seed" from the Vedic ancestor of an individual's lineage (*gotra*) and in part by the pure or impure combination of this seed with the female "field" in which it quickens and grows. Specific combinations of these parental contributions produce offspring with a characteristic blend of elemental substances (*gunas*) and concomitant moral codes for behavior (*dharma*). Shared parentage produces shared substances, shared moral codes, and comembership in common descent groups. The consequences of mixed marriages (i.e., marriages between members of descent groups possessing different blends of *gunas*) for generating a multitude of descent groups are the topic of considerable speculation. For Indological and ethnographic interpretations of the relevant texts, see Davis (1976), Inden and Nicholas (1977), Kane (1941 v. I, II), Marriott (1976), Marriott and Inden (1974), Rocher (1981), and Tambiah (1973a). For a detailed cultural account of a folk Tamil version of these beliefs, see Daniel (1984).

10. The Nakarattar conjugal family, the *pulli*, employed principles of marriage as well as descent in recruiting its members. That is, husbands and wives became members of a *pulli* at the time of their marriage, in contrast to legitimate children, who were born or adopted into the *pulli*. I distinguish the Nakarattar joint family, the *valavu*, from various forms of joint households for which it sometimes formed a basis. *Valavus* are accurately regarded as minimal lineage segments subject to the application of Mitakshara laws regarding inheritance. For more detailed discussion of the relationship between Hindu concepts of joint family and sociological considerations in the definition of joint households, see Tambiah (1973a: 75).

11. The extent to which ideas about inherited moral codes were fostered or even created in some novel fashion by interaction with the colonial government is difficult to gauge. Recent studies (Carroll 1978; Cohn 1960, 1983) seem almost to suggest they were a product of the colonial period. Against such a possibility, it must be remembered that the Nakarattar *jati* and its descent groups were in place by the seventeenth century (see Chapter 7).

12. The processes that generated growth in the number of Nakarattar residential villages have apparently been reversed in recent times as the number of villages that Nakarattars acknowledge as under their control has diminished. Nakarattars attribute this reversal to a Nakarattar migration to larger towns that depleted the population of the smaller villages.

13. The seasonal festivals of village temples included *tirttan kutittal* or *marantu kutattal* (drinking sanctified water in the seventh month of pregnancy), *putumai* (child's first birthday), *suppiti* (boy's coming-of-age ceremony), *tiruvatirai* (girl's coming-of-age ceremony), *kalyanam* (marriage), *shastiaptapurti kalyanam* (man's sixtieth birthday and marriage renewal ceremony). For a description of these ceremonies, see Thurston (1909).

14. See Harper (1959) for a discussion of similar beliefs about ghosts (*peys*), spirits (*avis*), family deities (*kula teyvams*), and village deities (*grama teyvams*).

15. See Dumont (1959) and Whitehead (1921) for, respectively, structural and descriptive accounts of the standard non-Brahmanic village pantheon of South India.

16. Mines (1984) describes processes of deification and cult formation among Kaikkolars that are quite similar to those exhibited by Nakarattars. In addition, he describes what might be considered a two-tier system of temples: one set concerned with matters of kinship, the other concerned with matters beyond the realm of kinship (e.g., trade and the state). Like Kaikkolars, Nakarattars also participated in supra-kinship temples. But these did not correspond to either the village or the clan temples described in the text. Nor, for that matter, did they correspond to any intermediate form of quasi-kinship temple. Rather, they formed a third tier of temple organization. Notice that it is not clear from Mines' account whether Kaikkolar temple-based cults of descent were segmented into two tiers.

17. Most *devastanam inam* lands had been given to the Nakarattar clan temples in past centuries. The gifts are often recorded in stone inscriptions carved on the temple walls. They are also recorded in the Inam Register of the colonial government. For a large but incomplete listing of Nakarattar money endowments during the late colonial period, see Ramanathan Chettiar (1953).

18. In general, care should be taken not to overemphasize the solidarity of *kuttikkira pankalis.* One of the fiercest political fights for control of the

North Ramnad District Board in 1937 occurred between the son-in-law (an affinal relation) and a member of a collateral *pankali* of the powerful Nakarattar leader Raja Sir Annamalai Chettiar. In this instance, the son-in-law, C. V. Ct. (Venkatachalam) Chettiar ran on the ticket of the Justice party as an ally of Annamalai. But the Raja's *pankali,* Nakappa Chettiar, ran on the Congress party ticket. One should not conclude from this alliance, however, that the converse relationship is therefore all-important. Both are open-ended relationships with options to renew or terminate. In this case, the S. Rm C. V. Ct. alliance was not permanent. A few years later, C. V. Ct. attempted to thwart Annamalai's plans to initiate Annamalai University by advising Kalimuthu Thiagarajan on tactics for gaining governmental support of a Thiagarajan University in Madurai. Ultimately, Annamalai won. Thiagarajan University was never founded (Lakshman Chettiar interview, June 22, 1981; see also Arooran 1980). For more about this story, see Chapters 7 and 10.

10. CONCLUSION

1. Specifically, the new group of "descendants" claims hereditary rights for one of its members to act as *sami ati* (literally, "god dancer"), a medium possessed by Murugan in the Tai Pucam pilgrimage festival. Some aspects of the post–seventeenth-century history of Nakarattar involvement in the Palani festival are described in Moreno (1981).

2. Following Lévi-Strauss, many anthropologists confuse semantic distinctions with jural norms, arguing that some kind of positive marriage obligation is created by a Dravidian kin classification. I have dealt with the disciplinary history of confusion surrounding this issue, elsewhere (Rudner 1990; see also Needham 1986). I mention it in this context to underscore the radical departure from most standard models of Dravidian kinship represented by Nakarattar resistance to self-perpetuating alliances.

3. In order to avoid any risk of being misunderstood, I wish to note that I am *not* saying that Nakarattars lacked corporate descent groups, but only that Nakarattars did not generally establish and perpetuate these groups through marriage alliance.

4. See Baker (1976) and Washbrook (1973, 1975, 1976) for pertinent descriptions of elite South Indian colonial politics. Baker's book, in particular, contains relevant accounts of the Ramnad elections of 1937 and of the role of Raja Sir Muthia Chettiar in Madras. For additional details, see Chapter 7, above.

5. For more recent analyses of the organization of caste groups see Beck (1972) and Dirks (1979, 1983, 1988).

6. This generalization about clan and lineage control of Chettinad villages does not apply to clusters of *devastanam* villages owned by both clan and village temples. But such clusterings do not affect my claim. *Devas-*

tanam properties were owned directly by the temple deity and managed by the temple's board of trustees. Such properties were distinct from properties and lands owned by temple cult members. Moreover, like the latter properties, they were not necessarily consolidated around a single, close, and bounded territory. While some *devastanam* properties might be located in the immediate neighborhood of the temple, others might be spread throughout Chettinad, and indeed throughout India and Southeast Asia. Even where a temple's *devastanam* properties included a cluster of contiguous villages, the cluster might be separated from other temple properties by the intervening property of a different temple.

7. Readers unfamiliar with the variety of standard schemes available for transliterating Tamil should note that Beck (1972) renders the caste name Goundar as "KavuNTar."

8. It is noteworthy that other analysts dispute Dumont's (1957b) claim that hierarchy informs every social relationship in Hindu society. Anthony Carter (1973), for example, argues that intracaste relations differ from intercaste relations precisely in virtue of their absence of hierarchy. I suspect that both Dumont and Carter have overgeneralized from their data: the military castes with which Dumont was most familiar were internally ranked (see also Dirks 1987), and the castes with which Carter was most familiar resembled the Goundar of Coimbatore and mercantile castes such as the Nakarattar and Kaikkolar (see Chapter 2, above). For a general discussion of the history and present status of cross-cultural studies of such organizational differences outside of India, see Service (1985: Chapter 9).

9. The Pudukottai Kallar differed from Dumont's Pramalai Kallar primarily in the degree to which they emphasized kingship as a concept for defining and ordering ritual and political relationships. For this reason, they are especially useful for delineating a contrast with a group such as the Nakarattar.

10. Other forms of service were also exchanged for land control and honors, especially by non-Kallar subjects. Typically, all such transactions were mediated by a redistributional ritual in the context of cult worship, within the system of temples described above. For example, a king might grant an *inam* to a retainer who would act more or less as a trustee. Produce from the land would be donated to the deity of a temple, consecrated by the appropriate act of worship, and redistributed to cult members in such a way that it symbolized and even created the status approved by the king. In this way, the king had considerable powers to influence the hierarchy of Kallar social groups.

11. Pudukottai Kallars refer to these regions also as *natus,* but to keep them distinct from the encompassing *natus* associated with caste groups I will refer to them as sub-*natus.*

12. *Cervaikkarars* are not invariably selected from the royal *natu* because considerations of service and honor override considerations of

descent at this level of organization.

13. Dirks (1983: 30) describes the system in the following way: "There are lineage deities, village deities (sometimes the deity of the highest lineage but often separate), and subcaste deities. . . . Temples both served to establish a unity—to represent a whole—and to gradate and rank the parts of that whole. Membership in a village, a lineage, and a subcaste was ultimately talked about in terms of whether one had *kaniyacci* (a right to worship and receive temple honors) in the relevant temples; while all *kaniyaccikkarars* were equal in that they all held equal right (*urimai*) or share (*panku*) to participate in the affairs of the temple, the nature of participation was ranked. The *ampalams* (headmen of subcastes) were honored first, followed in order either by a ranked list of villages (represented by their respective *ampalams*) or of lineages (likewise represented)."

14. The episode referred to in the text (the Pandyan king's abduction of a Nakarattar maiden) takes place after various catastrophic adventures in the Chola port city of Kaveripumpattinam, prior to the Nakarattar migration to Chettinad. The most easily available English version of the Nakarattar *varalaru* remains Thurston (1909), which, however, leaves out many details of the *varalaru* published by the Nakarattars themselves in Tamil (e.g., Sharma 1970) and familiar to present-day Nakarattars as part of their oral tradition. In particular, although Thurston's account presents an incident of a royal Chola kidnapping of a Nakarattar girl and its consequences, it does not offer the story of the Pandyan kidnapping described in the text.

15. Narayana Rao (1986) provides one major exception to the general lack of systematic attention to caste histories. Although the Telugu castes—the subjects of his analysis—do not employ the left-hand/right-hand metaphor to distinguish themselves, and although Rao identifies structural features in their histories that are different from those which emerge in Beck's analysis, Rao nevertheless finds a mercantile/agrarian division of castes similar to Beck's finding in Kongu. Kenneth David (1977) provides the only other systematic analysis of caste histories of which I am aware. But his discussion of *jati varalaru* in a Sri Lankan context inexplicably fails to address the Nattukottai Chettiar, even though they figure in other parts of his essay.

16. For further discussion of the "economic" model of variation between right- and left-hand castes, see, in addition to Beck (1972), Mines (1984). For a political interpretation of the variable occurrence of right-hand and left-hand factions in South Indian social structure, see Appadurai (1974). Stein (1980) provides a view of the matter that seems to share elements of both positions.

17. I am not suggesting that Beck (1972) has mischaracterized Kongunadu, but that Kongunadu should not be taken as paradigmatic for all South India. There is no need to belabor the ethnographer's perennial

temptation to overgeneralize from the localized discourse of his or her "own" people. The larger lesson I wish to draw concerns not merely the *scope* of the left-hand/right-hand model, but its status as a particular image of society presented by specific people, in specific contexts, for specific purposes. The Nakarattar *jati varalaru* presents an alternative image presented by other people, in other contexts, and for other purposes. This image and the purposes it serves both overlap with and differ from the images and purposes that Beck generalizes on an all-Tamil scale from her Kongu data.

18. An early version of this section was originally published in Rudner (1989).

19. "The media of Hindu transactions are substance-codes that may be scaled from the relatively 'gross' (*sthula*) to the relatively 'subtle' (*suksma*). 'Gross'—that is, lower, less refined, more tangible, and less widely transformable substance-codes—are contrasted with higher, less tangible substance-codes that are "subtler," more capable of transformation, and therefore imbued with greater power and value. For example, knowledge may be considered subtler than money, and money subtler than grain or land, but grain or land not so gross as cooked food or garbage, which have less power of generation. Such a scale may be understood as resembling the distinctions among communications codes capable of generating more and fewer messages; but Indian thought understands subtler substance-codes as emerging through processes of maturation or (what is considered to be the same thing) cooking. Thus subtler essences may sometimes be ripened, extracted, or distilled out of grosser ones (as fruit comes from plants, nectar from flowers, butter from milk); and grosser substance-codes may be generated or precipitated out of subtler ones (as plants come from seed, feces from food)" (Marriott 1976: 110).

20. See Chapter 5 for a full description of the various types of Nakarattar deposits.

21. Some readers will be unable to free themselves from suspicions that talk about the social functions of Nakarattar institutions necessarily implies analogy with physical or biological systems in equilibrium. Yet alternative metaphors for nonequilibrium systems are readily available. One obvious physical analogy that suggests itself is the chaos of fluid turbulence—a concept that has developed increasing fascination for both anthropologists and "harder" scientists during the last decade. Anthropologists, for diverse reasons, have become increasingly resistant to considering any contribution from the nonsocial sciences. But affinities remain: affinities that, in some cases, make explicit appeals to metaphors of fluid dynamics (e.g., Daniel 1984; Marriott 1990). All that is lacking in such anthropological interpretations is a historical perspective that looks beyond the forces at work in a single moment to the dynamics of those forces over a time series of sociocultural transformations.

Here lies the real attraction of new theories about fluid turbulence as analogies or even models for nonequilibrium, complex behavior, generally. We may never be able to describe all the individual interactions that constitute a dynamic social system. But, like very complex nonsocial systems, the behavior these interactions exhibit is hardly random. Nor are the transformations they undergo. Both social and nonsocial systems manifest collective modes of behavior, describable in terms of restrictions on possible transformations. A turbulent fluid, for example, has a potentially infinite number of degrees of freedom. Yet only a very small number of possibilities are ever realized, and these possibilities can be related to the external environment of the fluid, regardless of its initial conditions and complexity. Moreover, under certain conditions, there can exist large-scale, dissipative structures in fluid turbulence that have predictable dynamics in the short term, that persist in the long term, and that alter in predictable ways under changed environmental conditions. We do not know whether such systems can serve as models for social systems. But the possibility is intriguing and suggests interesting questions about the patterning of social life, even if these are not answerable at present. For an excellent, nontechnical introduction to the multidisciplinary work in this area see James Glieck (1987). For a recent effort to apply theories of complex systems to modeling social systems, see Lansing (1993).

Glossary

AI = Anglo-Indian
Ar = Arabic
Hn = Hindi
Sk = Sanskrit
Tel = Telugu
Tm = Tamil
Ur = Urdu

ācci (Tm): Nakarattar married woman.

āccimar paṇam (Tm): accounting category for funds invested or deposited in a Nakarattar firm by a proprietor's in-laws in conformity with a dowry agreement at the time of his marriage. The funds are usually held in trust for educational or dowry expenses of the proprietor's daughter.

aḍathi (Tm): elite "parent" banker.

aḍathi kaḍai paṇam (Tm): accounting category for deposits from Nakarattar *aḍathis;* also simply *aḍathi paṇam.*

adhaya (Sk): credit or income entry in an account (cf. *varavu*).

adṛṣṭārtha (Sk): invisible, extramundane goal of action.

aḍuthāl (Tm): subordinate staff in a large Nakarattar banking agency; literally, "next people" (i.e., next after the first assistant [*mudalal*] to a Nakarattar agent [*mēlāl*]).

agrahāram (Sk): Brahman village, neighborhood, or street.

ainthugai (reportedly): a Nakarattar general ledger.

Aippaci (Tm): October–November.

ammaṉ (Tm): goddess.

ampalakkārar (Tm): 1. one who holds an *ampalam;* thus, a village headman. 2. a Kaḷḷar subcaste living near Melur, east of Madurai.

ampalam (Tm): a share in village resources held by a dominant family in a village.

An̲i (Tm): June–July.

anna (Ur): one-sixteenth of a rupee.

an̲pu (Tm): love, devotion.

anuloma (Sk): in an unnatural order; as applied to marriage, an intercaste marriage in which the husband is member of a higher-ranking caste than the wife (cf. *pratiloma*).

ar̲ai (Tm): 1. room. 2. Nakarattar bank office (cf. *kitangi*).

Ar̲apattayankal (Tm): name of Nakarattar six deeds of gift and two additional documents, ca. 1600–1800, stored at Palani Temple; literally, "six deeds."

arccan̲ai (Sk): offering of flowers, betel, and saffron, accompanied by recitation of the sacred names of the deity, on behalf of the donor.

arrack (Ar): palm wine.

arze (Ur): petition.

asti vari (Tm): temple tithe on wealthy people.

aṭati (Tm). See *aḍathi*.

aṭati kaṭai paṇam (Tm). See *aḍathi kaḍai paṇam*.

Āṭi (Tm): July–August.

āṭīn̲am (Sk): Saivite seminary or monastery (synonym: *maṭam*).

aṭuttāl (Tm). See *aḍuthāl*.

Avaṇi (Tm): August–September.

āvi (Tm): spirit of the dead.

Ayyanar (Tm): village guardian god.

Brahman (Sk): highest ranking *varna* category, traditionally comprising priests and scholars.

camaiyalkāran (Tm): cook.

cāmān̲ (Tm): thing, object, item.

campantippuram (Tm): in-law.

cankam (Tm). See *sangam*.

catunkukkārar (Tm): groom's sisters in ceremonial roles at a wedding; literally, "ceremony-doers".

cervaikkārar (Tm): 1. Pudukottai Kaḷḷar noble or army commander. 2. Telugu caste in Tamil Nadu.

Chetti (Tm): 1. occupational title for merchant. 2. name of South Indian caste cluster.

Chettiar (Tm): honorific form of *Chetti*.

Chettinad (Tm): homeland of the Nakarattars (Nattukottai Chettiars).

Chittirai (Tm): April–May.

Chōla (Tm): 1. medieval Tamil dynasty, ca. 900–1300 A.D. 2. classical Tamil dynasty, ca. 250 B.C.–700 A.D.

choultry, chattiram (Tm): 1. a place for reception and public business. 2. a pilgrim rest house (synonym: *viṭuti*).

ciṉṉa (Tm): small, unimportant, younger (cf. *periya*).

cīr (Tm): dowry gifts or prestations from bride's family to groom's family; literally, "fame, glory, beauty" (synonym: *curul*).

cīr tāṉam (Tm): affinal prestation of money as part of a dowry (*cīr*); literally, "gift that brings fame, glory, beauty" (cf. *strī dhanam*).

cīr varicai (Tm): affinal prestation of clothing and household items as part of dowry (*cīr*); literally, "rows of fame, glory, beauty."

Cōla (Tm). See *chōla.*

Collector (AI): chief administrative officer in an Indian district, also holding magisterial powers.

contakkārar (Tm): kin.

conta tavaṇai paṇam (Tm). See *sontha thavanai panam.*

crore (Hn): a unit of 10 million; 100 lakhs.

curul (Tm). See *cīr.*

cutcherry, kachahri (Ur): headquarters or central office of *zamindari* administration.

Deepavali (Hn): festival of lights in late October or early November.

dēvam (Tm). See *teyvam.*

devastānam (Sk): a place or establishment of the gods; thus, property of a temple.

dēvata (Tm). See *teyvatā.*

dharma (Sk): 1. moral code for an individual, righteousness. 2. the proper order of the universe.

dharma kartā (Sk): protector of a temple, executive officer.

dharśan (Sk): 1. a form of worship. 2. an auspicious sight; literally, a "glimpse."

dharśan huṇḍi (Tm): "sight" *hundi,* demand draft (cf. *naduppu huṇḍi*).

dṛṣṭārtha (Sk): visible, tangible goal of action.

dubash (Tel): Indian middleman for European traders in eighteenth- and nineteenth-century Madras; literally, a person who speaks two languages (*dobashi*).

eṭṭi (Tm): title for an important merchant during Tamil classical (Sangam) period.

fasli, fusli (Ur): the harvest year, beginning July 1st; add 590 to the *fasli* year to approximate the year Anno Domini.

gōmasta (Ur): 1. clerk-accountant. 2. a native accountant in the Revenue Department. 3. an officer employed by a Zamindar to collect rents.

gōpuram (Tm). See *kōpuram.*

gōtra (Sk): typically Brahman, exogamous clan.

Goundar (Tm): Veḷḷālar subcaste, traditionally comprising cultivators and landowners and residing primarily in Coimbatore and Salem.

grāma deyvam (Tm): village deity.

grāmam (Tm): village.

guṇa (Sk): humoral essence, quality (synonym: *kuṇam*).

guru (Sk): religious preceptor.

hoozoor, huzur (Ur): 1. the presence; the presence of superior authority such as a judge or a collector. 2. a place of authority such as an office or court.

huṇḍi (Ur): bill of exchange (synonym: *teep*).

huṇḍial (Tm): temple donation box.

īnām (Ur): tax-free land given for services to king or temple. There are many kinds of *īnām* including a *māniyam* (for a village servant), a *savaram* (for a revenue officer), an *agraharam* (for Brahmans), and a *dēvadasi inām* (for temple prostitutes).

jajmāni (Hn): a village system of rights and obligations for different status positions connecting landowning village patrons (*jajmāns*) with clients who perform services for a share of the crop.

jāti (Sk): 1. caste. 2. category, kind, species, etc.

jāti varalāṟu (Tm): caste history.

jīvikā (Sk): occupation, livelihood (synonym: *toḻil*).

kaḍai (Tm): shop.

kaḍai kaṇakku: demand deposit account similar to a checking account; literally, "shop account."

Kaikkōḷar (Tm): Tamil caste of weavers.

kaimāttu paṇam (Tm): undocumented loan between local Nakarattar bankers; literally, "hand money."

kalam (Tm): a measure of grain; half a bag; in the case of paddy, about 63.7 lbs.

Kaḷḷar (Tm): during the precolonial era, a Tamil caste of warriors and, according to colonial classification, robbers; now primarily cultivators.

kalutturu (Tm): gold necklace presented to Nakarattar bride by groom's family.

kalyāṇam (Tm): marriage.

kaṇakku (Tm): account.

kandu kisti (Tm): small loan advanced to petty traders with interest charged in advance.

kāni (Tm): land measure, about 1.33 acres.

kāṇiyācci (Tm): hereditary right to land or office.

kāṇiyāccikkārar (Tm): one who holds *kāṇiyācci* rights.

kanji (Tm): rice porridge.

karai (Tm): Pudukottai Kallar lineage; literally, "river bank, boundary, border" (cf. *paṭṭappeyar*).

karma (Sk): 1. action. 2. fate resulting from action.

karmam (Tm). See *karma*.

Kārtikai (Tm): November–December.

kāryakkārar (Tm): temple trustee; literally, "doer."

kaṭai (Tm). See *kaḍai*.

kaṭai kaṇakku (Tm). See *kaḍai kaṇakku*.

kaṭṭaḷai (Tm): endowment.

kāṭṭu kaṇakkuppiḷḷai (Tm): "field staff" of Nakarattar banking agency ("*kāṭṭu*" may be an AI spelling of *kāṭu* [Tm], for country or uncultivated land; cf. *nāṭu*).

kāvaṭi (Tm): shoulder pole used to carry religious offerings on a pilgrimage.

Kavuntar (also *KavuNTar*: Beck 1972). See *Goundar*.

kīḻivāram (Tm): landowner's (*raiyat's*) share of the land's produce after taxes; literally, "lower share" (cf. *mēlvāram*).

kirāmam (Tm). See *grāmam*.

kirani (reportedly): court clerk.

kitangi (Tm): Nakarattar bank office; cf. *aṟai*.

kiṭṭanki (Tm). See *kitangi*.

Komati Chetti (Tel): Telugu merchant caste.

Kōṉār (Tm): Tamil caste of cattle herders and shepherds, residing partly in Chettinad.

kōpuram (Tm): temple tower.

kōvil (Tm): 1. temple. 2. palace.

kōvil paṇam (Tm): accounting category for deposits from temples.

kōvil pankāḷi (Tm): member of Nakarattar temple clan; literally, "shareholder in the temple."

Kshatriya (Sk): second ranked *varna* category, traditionally kings and warriors.

kula (Sk): lineage.

kulam (Tm). See *kula*.

kula teyvam (Tm): 1. family deity. 2. lineage deity.

kumbāpiṣēkam (Sk). See *kumpāpiṣēkam*.

kumpāpiṣēkam (Tm): consecration and purification ceremony for a temple.

kuṇam (Tm): humoral essence, quality (synonym: *guṇa*).

kuppam (Tm): a sub-*nāṭu* or territorially bounded subdivision of Pudukottai Kaḷḷar lineages (*karais*), possibly related to *kuppal*, meaning "heap, crowd, or company" (cf. *teru; vaṭṭakai*).

kuṛippu (Tm): an account book for daily cash transactions.

kūṭṭam (Tm): meeting; crowd; assembly.

kūṭṭikkiṟa pankāḷi (Tm): Nakarattar maximal lineage segment; literally, "shareholders who are brought together" (i.e., for ritual observances).

kuttomb (Tm). See *kuṭṭam*.

kuṭumpam (Tm): family.

Labbi (Tel). See *Lubbai.*

lakh (Hn): a unit of 100 thousand.

Lakshmi (Sk): Vishnu's consort; goddess of wealth.

Lubbai (Tel): Telugu Muslim itinerant trading caste.

Māci (Tm): February–March.

māhāṇam, māhānāḍu (Tm): a small revenue division, similar to a *tālūk.*

makimai (Tm): 1. religious tithe. 2. tithe paid to Nakarattar rest house (*naka-raviṭuti*).

māṉiyam (Sk): tax-free land given for services to king or temple (cf. *inam*).

maṇṭakappadi (Sk): right to organize a religious ritual.

maṇṭapam (Sk): an open pavilion where religious rituals are performed.

Maṟavar (Tm): in the precolonial era, a Tamil caste of warriors residing in Ramnad, now comprised primarily of cultivators.

Māriammaṉ (Tm): important village and regional goddess in South India, strongly associated with smallpox, drought, and blindness.

Mārkaḻi (Tm): December–January.

maṟṟavaṉ nampikkai (Tm): trust.

maruntu kuṭital (Tm): ritual performed during pregnancy, involving drinking of sacramental water (synonym: *tīrttam kuṭittal*).

maryātai (Sk): honor; literally, "boundary."

maṭam (Sk): monastery, seminary (synonym: *āṭīṉam*).

Meenakshi (Tm): the goddess of Madurai, an incarnation of Parvati.

mēlāl (Tm): agent of a Nakarattar banking firm.

mēlvāram (Tm): an agricultural tax in kind; literally, "upper share," meaning the king's or government's share (cf. *kīlvāram*).

mēmpanan (Tm): Nakarattar bank's liabilities, deposits other than proprietor's; literally, "surplus funds."

mirāsi (Ur): hereditary privileges including shares in land and in temple rituals.

moi (also *moy*: Dumont 1957b) (Tm): wedding gift from anyone who attends a wedding, registered in a special book (*moippaṇa eṭu*) with reference to kinship distance.

moippaṇa eṭu (Tm): a book that registers gifts of *moi.*

mōkam (Tm). See *mōksa.*

mōksa (Sk): release of soul from cycle of rebirths.

moturpha (Ur): a tax on trade.

muchalika (Ur): legal agreement.

mudal paṇam (Tm): the proprietor's own capital investment in his firm.

mudalal (Tm): first assistant to the agent (*mēlāl*) of Nakarattar firm.

mudali (Tm): principal or proprietor of Nakarattar firm.

Mudaliar (Tm): Veḷḷālar subcaste; literally, "first ones."

Mudukkulattūr (Tm): collective name for three warrior castes of Tamil Nadu: the Kallar, Maravar, and Agamudaiyar.

muṟai (Tm): 1. affinal gifts from wife's family to groom's family, given on a regular basis for the life of a marriage alliance. 2. obligation, turn.

Murugan, Murukaṉ (Tm): Siva's second son, Skanda; other names: Velayuda, Arumukan.

mutal paṇam (Tm). See *mudal paṇam.*

mutalal (Tm). See *mudalal.*

mutali (Tm). See *mudali.*

Mutaliar (Tm). See *Mudaliar.*

nadappu huṇḍi (Tm): interest-bearing bill of exchange that functioned like a check (i.e., it was payable on demand); literally, "walking hundi."

nadappu vaṭṭi (Tm): rate of interest between Nakarattars on demand deposits.

Nadar (Tm): a Tamil caste of traders and toddy-tappers, residing primarily in Kanyakumari, Tirunelveli, and Ramnad during the precolonial and colonial periods; presently, its members work and live throughout Tamil Nadu in all walks of business.

nāḍu (Tm). See *nāṭu.*

Naganādu (Tm): original legendary home of Nakarattar caste.

nagaram (Tm). See *nakaram.*

Nagarathar (Tm). See *Nakarattār.*

nagaswaram (Tm). See *nakaswaram.*

naivettiyam (Sk): an offering of food, one of sixteen rites of daily worship to a deity.

nakarakkōvil (Tm): 1. Nakarattar clan temple. 2. Nakarattar temple-clan.

nakaram (Tm): 1. medieval merchant guild. 2. city.

Nakarattār (Tm): major merchant-banking caste of South India.

nakaraviṭuti (Tm): Nakarattar pilgrim rest house (cf. *viṭuti*).

nakaswaram, nakasuram, nakasvaram (Tm): reed instrument played at special functions and rituals.

nāṇayam (Tm): trustworthiness.

Nangudi Veḷḷālar (Tm): a Veḷḷālar subcaste residing in Tirunelveli.

Nāṭṭār (Tm): generally, the leaders of a *nāṭu;* contrasts with unusual Chettinad usage having just the opposite sense, namely, any non-Nakarattar caste in Chettinad.

naṭṭukkal (Tm): stone marking the site of a deity who protects a specific residential neighborhood.

Nattukottai Chettiar (Tm). See *Nakarattār.*

nāṭu (Tm): 1. a unit of territory. 2. an agricultural tract. 3. the dominant kin group of a (territorial) *nāṭu;* e.g., a clan or subcaste among Pudukottai Kaḷḷars.

Nayak (Tel): 1. title of a noble or chief; derived from "deputy," i.e., of an emperor. 2. a Telugu caste of warriors.

nērttikkaṭaṉ (Tm): payment for something given.

ōlai (Tm): palm leaf; page from a palm-leaf manuscript.

orē kutumpam (Tm): a joint family; literally, "one same family" (cf. *valavu*).

paḍaippu (Tm). See *paṭaippu*.

paise (Ur): a copper coin valued at 4 to the anna and 64 to the rupee.

pāḷaiyakkārar (Tm): Tamil military chief or "little king" (cf. *pāḷaiyam*).

pāḷaiyam (Tm): a domain or "little kingdom" with a military chief.

paṇam (Tm): 1. a coin. 2. a deposit.

panchāyat (Hn): traditionally, a group of five elders who met to resolve disputes or make decisions that affected the welfare of a village or caste.

Paṇḍaram (Tm): Tamil caste of non-Brahman priests and temple officiants.

Pāṇḍya (Tm): name of classical and medieval Tamil kingdoms.

Pāṇḍyanāḍu (Tm): the Pandyan kingdom; literally, "land of the Pandyas."

pangāḷi (Tm). See *pankāḷi*.

Panganeri Kaḷḷar (Tm): Kallar subcaste living near Sivaganga.

Panguṉi (Tm): March–April.

pankāḷi (Tm): member of agnatic descent group; co-parcener; literally, "shareholder."

pankāḷis (a composite term, formed from the Tamil root and the English plural morpheme). See *pankāḷikaḷ*.

pankāḷikaḷ (Tm): 1. members of an agnatic descent group. 2. the descent group itself.

panku (Tm): share.

paricam (Tm): "bride price" in some castes.

paripālakkar (Sk): royal protector.

parivara (Sk): joint family.

Parvati (Sk): Siva's wife (see *Meenakshi*).

paṭaippu (Tm): rite of ancestor worship.

paṭṭa (Tm). See *paṭṭayam*.

paṭṭappeyar (Tm): Pudukottai Kaḷḷar lineage (literally, "deed name"), used instead of *karai* when referring to lineages for purposes of marriage.

paṭṭāyam (Tm): deed.

pēkki pustakam (Tm): ledger of outstanding debts.

peṇ (Tm): woman.

pērēdu (Tm): an account book, specifically a general ledger or compilation of subsidiary ledgers.

pērētu (Tm). See *pērēdu*.

periya (Tm): large, important, older (cf. *ciṉṉa*).

peshkash (Ur): 1. land tax. 2. tribute.

pēṭṭai (Tm): 1. a fortified market town. 2. a Nadar caste organization.

peṭṭiyaḍi paiyaṉ (Tm): errand boy.

peṭṭiyaṭi paiyaṉ (Tm). See *peṭṭiyaḍi paiyaṉ*.

pey (Tm): ghost, demon.

Piḷḷaiyār (Tm): elephant-headed son of Siva; other names: Vinayakar, Ganapati, Ganesh.

pirantu iṭattukkōṭi (Tm): funerary *vēvu*: a gift of unbleached cloth and ceremonial items for the funeral pyre presented to the decedent by his or her *tāyātis* (i.e., in the case of a deceased man, presented by his wife's father or brothers, and in the case of a deceased woman, by her own father or brothers).

pirasātam (Tm). See *prasād*.

pirātu (Tm): honor, emblem.

pirivu (Tm): segment or division of Nakarattar lineage (*kūṭṭikkiṟa pankāli*).

poligar (AI). See *pāḷaiyakkārar*.

pollam (AI). See *pāḷaiyam*.

Pongal (Tm). See *Ponkal*.

Ponkal (Tm): 1. new year festival in January. 2. sweet rice porridge.

Pramalai Kaḷḷar (Tm): a Kaḷḷar subcaste living west of Madurai; their name is probably derived from Piranmalai located east of Madurai on the western border of Chettinad.

prasād, prasādam (Sk): sacramental food offered to a deity and redistributed to devotees.

pratiloma (Sk): in an unnatural order; as applied to marriage, an intercaste marriage in which the husband is a member of a lower-ranking caste than the wife (cf. *anuloma*).

pūcai (Tm). See *pūja*.

Pudukottai Kaḷḷar (Tm): a Kaḷḷar subcaste residing in Pudukottai.

pūja (Sk): worship; religious ceremony.

puḷḷi (Tm): Nakarattar conjugal family; literally, the dot used for reckoning a quantity of goods.

puḷḷi pārkka (Tm): to estimate.

puḷḷi vari (Tm): a temple tithe, *puḷḷi* tax.

purāna (Sk): history (synonym: *varalāṟu*).

Purattaci (Tm): September–October.

Purusha (Sk): Hindu mythical first man.

putumai (Tm): rite of first birthday.

raiyat (Ur): landowner, "peasant."

rishi, ṛṣi (Sk): seer, Vedic sage.

ryot (AI). See *raiyat.*

sahukar (Ur). See *soukar.*

sāmi (Tm): god.

sāmi aṟai (Tm): shrine in a household.

sāmi āṭi (Tm): person possessed by a god.

sangam (Tm): 1. gathering, convocation. 2. a mythical gathering of poets at Madurai.

śāstras (Sk): sacred Sanskrit texts.

saukar (Ur). See *soukar.*

Sētupati (Tm): title of the Raja of Ramnad.

shaṣṭiaptapūrti kalyāṇam, shaṣṭiaptapūrti śānti kalyāṇam (Sk): rite of a man's sixtieth birthday.

shreshti (Sk): merchant.

shroff (Ur): non-European merchant and semi-independent guarantee officer for a Ceylon bank.

Śiva (Sk): the great deity of Saivite Hindus; the creator and destroyer.

sontha thavaṇai paṇam (Tm): accounting category for deposits from the proprietor's relatives; literally, "relative's resting money."

soukar (Ur): native moneylender.

stāṉikar (Sk): priestly temple manager.

sthula (Sk): gross.

strī dhanam (Sk): dowry; literally, "woman's property"; often mistranslated as *cīr tāṉam.*

Śūdra (Sk): the fourth *varna,* traditionally comprising servants.

suksma (Sk): subtle.

suppiṭi (Tm): boy's coming of age ceremony.

tāhsildār (Ur): administrator of a *taluk.*

Tai (Tm): January–February.

takeed, takid (Ur): administrative or government order.

tāli (Tm): marriage pendant.

tālūk (Ur): a revenue subdivision of a district.

tāṇatu muṟai paṇam (Tm): 1. deposits from business proprietor's agnatic relatives including his lineage (*kūṭṭikkiṟa pankāḷi*) and clan (*kōvil*). 2. deposits from both agnatic kin and unrelated Nakarattars from a business proprietor's own and neighboring villages. 3. umbrella term for all deposits from relatives including *accimar panam* deposits from inlaws.

tank (AI): a reservoir for water; an artificial lake.

taṇṇīr pandal (Tm): shed for distributing water to pilgrims.

tavaṇai huṇḍi (Tm). See *thavaṇai huṇḍi.*

tavaṇai kaṇakku (Tm). See *thavaṇai kaṇakku.*

tavaṇai vaṭṭi (Tm). See *thavaṇai vaṭṭi.*

tāyāppillaikaḷ (Tm). See *tāyātikaḷ.*

tāyāti (Tm): 1. member of Nakarattar mother's brother's *kūṭṭikkiṟa pankāḷi.* 2. Nakarattar member of a lineage segment that was once allied by marriage with one's lineage. 3. among some castes, either descent group of an affinal kindred.

tāyātikaḷ (Tm): 1. members of Nakarattar mother's brother's *kuṭṭikkiṟa pankāḷi;* the *kūṭṭikkiṟa pankāḷi* itself. 2. members of any lineage that had once been allied by marriage to one's own lineage or members of such lineages.

tāyātis (composite term formed from Tamil root and English plural morpheme). See *tāyātikaḷ.*

teep (Ur). See *huṇḍi.*

teru (Tm): 1. street. 2. a royal lineage (*kuppam*) among the Pudukottai Kaḷḷar.

teyvam, teyvatā (Tm): village deity.

thanadumaral paṇam (Tm). See *tanatu muṟai panam.*

thandu morai paṇam (Tm). See *tanatu muṟai paṇam.*

thavaṇai (Tm): term to maturity of a deposit; literally, "period of rest."

thavaṇai huṇḍi (Tm): interest-bearing bill of exchange with a minimum specified term to maturity that functioned like a certificate of deposit.

thavaṇai kaṇakku (Tm): short-term deposit account of two, three, or six months; literally, a "resting account."

thavaṇai vaṭṭi (Tm): compound rate of interest paid between Nakarattars on term deposits.

tīrttam kuṭittal (Tm). See *maruntu kuṭittal.*

tiruvātirai (Tm): girl's coming of age ceremony (cf. *suppiṭi*).

tiruviḻā (Tm): religious festival.

toddy (AI): fermented sap of the palmyra palm.

toḻil (Tm): occupation, livelihood (synonym: *jīvikā*).

toḻil vilācam (Tm): Nakarattar firm name or firm initials.

Toṇḍaimāṉ (Tm): title of Pudukottai king.

toranam (Tm): leaf-decorated archway used to mark ceremonial occasions.

upachāra (Sk): offering or service that is part of worship (*pūja*).

ūr (Tm): village.

uraviṉ muṟai (Tm): right to renew a marriage alliance between two families.

urimai (Tm): inherited right.

urimai peṉ (Tm): the woman a man has a right to marry; literally, "rightful woman."

ūr vilācam (Tm). See *vīdu vilācam.*

utsavam (Sk): religious festival.

Vaikaci (Tm): May–June.

vaikai (Tm): "circle" or "division" of a large *kūṭṭikkiṟa pankāḻi* (cf. *vaṭṭakai*).

vairavi (Tm): temple servant.

Vaiśya (Sk): third *varṇa* category, traditionally comprising merchants and farmers.

vaḷavu (Tm): 1. Nakarattar joint family or minimal lineage segment. 2. architectural feature of Nakarattar house: the central courtyard and surrounding residential apartments for the conjugal families of a joint family. 3. a house.

vaḷḷaṉ (Tm): generous person.

vaḷḷaṉmai (Tm): generosity.

varakan (Ur): unit of money, Rs. 3.50 (also called a *pagoda*).

varalāṟu (Tm): history; a text in which myths and other traditions are preserved (synonym: *purāna*).

varavu (Sk): debit or expense entry or account (cf. *adhaya*).

varṇa (Sk): name of the four major status subdivisions of Hindu society; literally, "color."

vaṭṭakai (Tm): 1. endogamous subregion of Chettinad (cf. *kuppam*). 2. a subdivision of a large lineage (cf. *pirivu*); literally, circle.

vaṭṭi (Tm): interest.

vaṭṭi chiṭṭi (Tm): memoranda showing calculated interest.

vayan vaṭṭi (Tm): simple interest rate paid by Nakarattars on deposits of non-Nakarattar clients.

vayan vaṭṭi kaṇakku (Tm): accounting category for a deposit from a non-Nakarattar client on which Nakarattars paid simple interest at a fixed rate.

Vēlāyuda (Tm): Lord of the Spear, a manifestation of Murugan.

veḷḷaikkāraṉ paṇam (Tm): accounting category for deposits from foreigners (Europeans).

Veḷḷālar (Tm): high-ranking Tamil caste, traditionally comprising cultivators and landowners.

vēṇṭutal (Tm): something needed.

vevu (Tm): special ceremonial *muṟai* given on occasion of life-cycle rituals.

vīḍu (Tm). See *vīṭu*.

vīḍu vilācam (Tm). See *vīṭu vilācam*.

Vijayanagar (Tel): a city and empire of South India, 1300–1650 A.D.

vilācam (Tm): initials of a name.

Vināyakar (Tm). See *Pillaiyar*.

Vishnu (Sk): supreme deity of Vaishnavite Hindus; the Preserver.

vīṭu (Tm): 1. household. 2. house.

viṭuti (Tm): pilgrim rest house (synonym: *choultry*; cf. *Nakaraviṭuti*).

vīṭu vilācam (Tm): family name, initials of family name (synonym: *ūr vilacām*; cf. *toḻil vilācam*).

vivaram (Tm): detail.

yajamān (Sk): sacrifier (in contrast to sacrifier), that is, one who offers the sacrifice (in contrast to a priest who performs a sacrifice).

yāttirai (Tm): pilgrimage.

zamin (Ur): a type of landed estate.

zamindar (Ur): title-holder of a *zamin*.

zamindari (Ur). See *zamin*.

References

The bibliography is arranged under the following heads:

Government Records
1. India Office Library
2. Tamil Nadu Archives
3. Madras High Court, Record Room

Official Publications (Except Manuals and Gazetteers)
1. Government of Great Britain
2. Government of India
3. Government of Madras
4. Government of Burma
5. Government of Ceylon

Newspapers, Periodicals, and Commercial Annuals
Published Books, Articles, Pamphlets and Dissertations

GOVERNMENT RECORDS

1. India Office Library

Erskine Papers, vol. 5, Mss Eur D 596.
Government of Madras, Education Proceedings
1928–29 Report on Public Instruction.
Government of Madras, Law (Legislative) Department
1928 Government Order (G.O.) 365, August 28, 1928.
1928 G.O. 305, December 21, 1928.
Madras Board of Revenue
1783 Proceedings, May 24, 1783.
1793 Proceedings, September 23, 1793: 5518–5519.
1793 Proceedings, August 8, 1793: 4887–4889
1828 Board's Consultation, April 14, 1828, back number 47.

Madras Country Correspondence
1752–1757 Political and Country Correspondence (Records of Fort St. George, Country Correspondence, 1752–1757).

2. Tamil Nadu Archives

Government of Madras, Land Revenue Reports
1880–81 "Statement showing prices of foodgrains." *In* Land Revenue Reports for Fasli 1290 (1880–81).
1925–26 "Statement showing prices of foodgrains." *In* Land Revenue Reports for Fasli 1335 (1925–26).
Government of Madras, Local Self Government Department, Proceedings
1922 Government Order (G.O.) 783, May 3.
1922 G.O. 811, May 9.
1923 G.O. 1462, February 26.
1923 G.O. 1462, June 20.
1923 G.O. 1984, September 7.
1925 G.O. 104, January 9.
1926 G.O. 4139, September 25.
1927 G.O. 4905, December 11.
1930 G.O. 704, February 22.
1930 G.O. 4833, December 16.
Madura District
1830 Records, Serial No. 4678.

3. Madras High Court, Record Room (Appellate Side)

Madras High Court of Judicature
1876 Regular Appeal No. 80.
1923 Appeal No. 72.

OFFICIAL PUBLICATIONS

1. Government of Great Britain

Parliamentary Papers
1832 Report of the Select Committee of the House of Commons, Appendix No. 109.
1903 Statement Exhibiting the Moral and Material Progress and Conditions of India during the year 1901–1902. Parliamentary Papers, vol. 44. His Majesty's Stationery Office.

2. Government of India

Indian Industrial Commission
1919 Report of the Indian Industrial Commission (1916–17), Minutes of Evidence, vol. 5. Calcutta: Government of India.

3. Government of Madras

Kasinathan Chettiar, C. A. C.
1930 Evidence of Nattukottai Nagarathars' Association. MPBEC 1930 I: 101–118.

Madras Provincial Banking Enquiry Committee (MPBEC)
1930 Vol. I, Report. Vol. II–IV, Written and Oral Evidence.
Nattukottai Nagarathars' Association
1930 Evidence of Nattukottai Nagarathars' Association. MPBEC 1930 I: 101–118.
Nicholson, F. A.
1895 Report Concerning the Possibility of Introducing Agricultural Banks in the Madras Presidency. 2 vols. Madras.
Pillai, A. Savarinatha
1930 Monograph on Nattukkottai Chettis banking business. MPBEC 1930 I: 1170–1217.
Raghavaiyangar, S. Srinivasa
1892 Memorandum on the Progress of Madras Presidency During the Last Forty Years of British Administration. Madras.

4. *Government of Burma*

1887 Report on the Administration of Upper Burma during 1886. Rangoon.
Burma Provincial Banking Enquiry Committee (BPBEC)
1930 Report of the Burma Provincial Banking Enquiry Committee. Vol. I, Banking and Credit in Burma. Vol. II, Written and Oral Evidence. Rangoon.

5. *Government of Ceylon*

Ceylon Banking Commission (CBC)
1934 Report. Colombo.
Ceylon Banking Enquiry Committee (CBEC)
1934 Report. Colombo.
Colonial Office
1870–1881 Ceylon Blue Book Statistics. Colonial Office Report. Ceylon.
1913–1929 Ceylon Blue Book Statistics. Colonial Office Report. Ceylon.

NEWSPAPERS, PERIODICALS, AND COMMERCIAL ANNUALS

Asylum Almanack and Directory of Madras and Southern India
1909 Madras.
Ceylon Mercantile and Planting Directory
1891–92 Colombo.
Colombo Journal
1832 Colombo.
Contributions to Indian Sociology
1989 (n.s.) 23 (1)
1990 (n.s.) 24 (2)
Dhanavanikan
1930 Kottaiyar.
Dhanavanikan
1933–35 Rangoon.

Dhana Vysia Ooliyan
1921–22 Karaikudi.
Economist
1932–34 London.
Ferguson's Handbook & Directory and Compendium of Useful Information
1870–81 Colombo.
1891–92 Colombo.
Hindu
1921–36 Madras.
Journal of Asian Studies
1976 Vol. 35, no. 4 (August).
Kumari Malar
1968–72 Madras.
Nakarattar Malar
1970–80 Madurai.
Madras Mail
1920–28 Madras
Oolian (or Ooliyan)
1925–26 Karaikudi.
1935–37 Madras.
Report of the Committee and Correspondance of the Burma Indian Chamber of Commerce
1925–26 Rangoon.
1926–27 Rangoon.
1928–29 Rangoon.
Swadesa-Mitran
1896 Madras.
1905–1908 Madras.
Vysiamitran
1911–21 Devakottai.

PUBLISHED BOOKS, ARTICLES, PAMPHLETS, AND DISSERTATIONS

Abraham, Meera
1988 Two Medieval Merchant Guilds of South India. New Delhi: Manohar Publications.
Adas, Michael
1974 The Burma Delta: Economic Development and Social Change on an Asian Rice Frontier, 1812–1941. Madison: University of Wisconsin.
Aiyar, R. Sathyanatha (*See* Sathyanatha Aiyar)
Aiyer, K. V. Subrahmanya (*See* Subrahmanya Aiyer, K. V.)
Allen, G. C. and A. G. Donnithorne
1957 Western Enterprise in Indonesia and Malaya. London.
Andrus, J. Russell
1948 Burmese Economic Life. Stanford: Stanford University Press.

Annamalai University
1965 Dr. Raja Sir Muthiah Chettiar and Rani Lady Meyyammai Achi Sixtieth Birthday Commemorative Volume. Annamalainagar: Annamalai University.

Anonymous
1941 "Raja Sir Annamalai Chettiar of Chettinadu, a memoir." *In* Raja Sir Annamalai Chettiar Commemorative Volume, B. V. Narayanaswamy Naidu, ed., pp. 1–15. Annamalainagar: Annamalai University.

Appadorai, A.
1936 Economic Conditions in South India: 1350–1750 A.D. Madras: University of Madras.

Appadurai, Arjun
1974 "Right and left hand castes in South India." Indian Economic and Social History Review 11(2–3): 216–259.
1981a Worship and Conflict under Colonial Rule: A South Indian Case. Cambridge: Cambridge University Press.
1981b "The past as a scarce resource" Man, n.s. 16(2): 201–219.
1981c "Gastro-politics in Hindu South Asia." American Ethnologist 8: 494–511.
1983 "The puzzling status of Brahman temple priests in Hindu India." South Asian Anthropologist 4(1): 43–52.
1985 "Introduction: Commodities and the politics of value." *In* The Social Life of Things: Commodities in Cultural Perspective, A. Appadurai, ed., pp. 3–63. Cambridge: Cambridge University Press.
1986a "Putting hierarchy in its place." Cultural Anthropology 3(1): 36–49.
1986b "Theory in anthropology: Center and periphery." Comparative Studies in Society and History 28(2): 356–361.

Appadurai, Arjun, and Carol Appadurai Breckenridge
1976 "The South Indian temple: Authority, honor and redistribution." Contributions to Indian Sociology, n.s. 10(2): 187–211.

Appell, George N.
1983 "Methodological problems with the concepts of corporation, corporate grouping and cognatic descent group." American Ethnologist 10: 302–311.
1984 "Methodological issues in the corporation redux." *In* Social Structure and Social Relations [Special issue]. American Anthropologist 11: 815–817.

Arasaratnam, Sinnappah
1964 Ceylon. Englewood Cliffs, N.J.: Prentice-Hall.
1966 "Indian merchants and their trading methods (circa 1700)." Indian Economic and Social History Review 3: 85–95.
1967 "Dutch commercial policy in Ceylon and its effects on Indo-Ceylon trade." Indian Economic and Social History Review 4: 109–130.

1968 "Aspects of the role and activities of South Indian merchants c. 1650–1750." *In* Proceedings of the First International Conference Seminar of Tamil Studies. Vol. 1. Kuala Lumpur.

1970 Indians in Malaya and Singapore. Oxford.

1971 "The politics of commerce in the coastal kingdoms of Tamil Nad 1650–1700." South Asia 1: 1–19.

1978 "Indian commercial groups and European traders, 1600–1800: Changing relationships in Southeastern India." South Asia, n.s. 1(2): 42–53.

1979 "Trade and political dominion in South India, 1750–1790: Changing British-Indian relationships." Modern Asian Studies 13(1): 19–40.

1980 "Weavers, merchants and company: The handloom industry in South-Eastern India, 1750–1790." Indian Economic and Social History Review 17(3): 257–282.

1986 Merchants, Companies and Commerce on the Coromandel Coast 1650–1740. Delhi: Oxford University Press.

Arooran, Nambi

1980 Tamil Renaissance and Dravidian Nationalism, 1905–1944. Madurai: Koodal Publishers.

Ayyah, Chockalinga (*See* Chockalinga Ayyah)

Ayyar, Sadhavadanam Subramaniyam (*See* Subramaniyam Ayyar, Sadhavadanam)

Babb, Lawrence

1975 The Divine Hierarchy: Popular Hinduism in Central India. New York: Columbia University Press.

Bagchi, A. K.

1972 Private Investment in India 1900–1939. Cambridge: Cambridge University Press.

Baker, Christopher John

1975 South India: Political Institutions and Political Change, 1880–1940. Delhi: Macmillan Company of India.

1976 The Politics of South India, 1920–1927. Cambridge: University Press.

1984 An Indian Rural Economy, 1880–1955. Oxford: Oxford University Press.

Baker, Christopher John, and David Washbrook

1975 South India: Political Institutions and Political Change, 1880–1940. London: MacMillan Press.

Barnett, Stephen Alan

1973 "The process of withdrawal in a South Indian caste." *In* entrepreneurship and Modernization of Occupational Cultures in South Asia, M. Singer, ed., pp. 179–204. Durham, N.C. Duke University.

Bastianpillai, B.

1964 "From coffee to tea in Ceylon: The vicissitudes of a colonial plantation economy." Ceylon Journal of Historical and Social Studies 7(1): 43–66.

Basu, Susan Neild
1982 "The dubashes of Madras." Paper presented at the Thirty-Fourth Annual Meeting of the Association for Asian Studies, Chicago, April 2–4.
1984 "Pachaiyappa Mudaliar: The 'Great Philanthropist' redefined." Paper presented at the Annual Meeting of the Association of Asian Studies, Washington, D.C., March 23–25.

Bayly, C. A.
1978 "Indian merchants in a 'traditional' setting: Benares 1780–1830." *In* The Imperial Impact: Studies in the Economic History of Africa and India, A. Hopkins and C. Dewey, eds., pp. 171–193. London: Athlone Press for the Institute of Commonwealth Studies.
1983 Rulers, Townsmen, and Bazaars: North Indian Society in the Age of British Expansion, 1700–1870. Cambridge: Cambridge University Press.
1989 "Pre-colonial merchants and rationality." Cambridge. Manuscript.

Beck, Brenda
1972 Peasant Society in Konku: A Study of Right and Left Subcastes in South India. Vancouver: University of British Columbia Press.
1976a "Centers and boundaries of regional caste systems: Towards a general model." *In* Regional Analysis, C. Smith, ed., Vol. 2: 255–288. New York: Academic Press.
1976b "The symbolic merger of body, space and cosmos in Hindu Tamil Nadu." Contributions to Indian Sociology, n.s. 10(2): 213–241.

Benedict, Burton
1968 "Family firms and economic development." Southwestern Journal of Anthropology 24(1).

Bloch, Maurice, and Jonathan Parry
1989 "Introduction: Money and the morality of exchange." *In* Money and the Morality of Exchange, pp. 1–32. Cambridge: Cambridge University Press.

Boissevain, Jeremy
1968 "Second thoughts on quasi-groups, categories and coalitions." Man, n.s. 6: 468–472.

Bourdieu, Pierre
1977 Outline of a Theory of Practice. Cambridge: Cambridge University Press.

Breckenridge, Carol Appadurai
1976 The Sri Minaksi Sundareshvarar Temple: Worship and Endowments in South India, 1833–1925. Ph.D. dissertation, University of Wisconsin, Madison.
1977 "From protector to litigant: Changing relations between Hindu temples and the Raja of Ramnad." Indian Economic and Social History Review 14(1): 75–106.

1983 "Scale and social formations in South India, 1350–1750." Paper presented at the Meeting of the Society for South Indian Studies, Madison, Wisconsin, November 2–4.

Breman, Jan
1974 Patronage and Exploitation: Changing Agrarian Relations in South Gujarat, India. Berkeley and Los Angeles: University of California Press.

Brennig, Joseph J.
1977 "Chief merchants and the European enclaves of seventeenth century Coromandel." Modern Asian Studies 11(3): 321–340.

Brohier, R. L.
1964 "Chronological catalogue of letters and reports on Ceylon affairs (1795–1800) in the Madras Record Office." Journal of the Royal Anthropological Society (Ceylon), n.s. 9 (Part 1).

Brown, D. E.
1976 Principles of Social Structure. London: Duckworth.
1984 "More on corporations." *In* Social Structure and Social Relations [Special issue]. American Anthropologist 11: 813–815.

Buchanan, Francis H.
1870 "A journey from Madras through the counties of Mysore, Canara and Malabar." *In* A General Collection of the Best and Most Interesting Voyages, John Pinkerton, ed. Madras: Higginbotham.

Burkhart, G.
1978 "Marriage alliance and the local circle among some Udayars of South India." *In* American Studies in the Anthropology of India, S. Vatuk, ed. New Delhi: American Institute of Indian Studies.

Capper, John
1877 Old Ceylon or Sketches of Ceylon Life in the Oldest Times. Colombo.

Carrithers, Michael, Steven Collins, and Steven Lukes (eds.)
1986 The Category of the Person: Anthropology, Philosophy, History. Cambridge; New York: Cambridge University Press.

Carroll, Lucy
1978 "Colonial perceptions of Indian society and the emergence of caste(s) associations." Journal of Asian Studies 37: 233–255.

Carter, Anthony
1973 "A comparative analysis of systems of kinship and marriage in South Asia." Proceedings of Royal Anthropological Institute, 31–54.

Cave, Henry W.
1900 Golden Tips: A Description of Ceylon and Its Great Tea Industry. London: S. Low Marston.

Chandra, Bipan.
1966 The Rise and Growth of Economic Nationalism in India. New Delhi.

Chandrasekhar, S.
1980 The Nagarathars of South India: An Essay and a Bibliography on the Nagarathars in India and South-East Asia. Madras: Macmillan Company of India.

Chandravarkar, Rajnarayan
1985 "Industrialization in India before 1947: Conventional approaches and alternative perspectives." Modern Asian Studies 19(3): 623–668.

Chaudhuri, K. N.
1965 The English East India Company: The Study of an Early Joint-Stock Company, 1600–1640. London.
1978 The Trading World of Asia and the English East India Company, 1600–1760. Cambridge: Cambridge University Press.
1985 Trade and Civilization in the Indian Ocean: An Economic History from the Rise of Islam to 1750. Cambridge: Cambridge University Press.

Chaudhuri, K. N. (ed.)
1971 The Economic Development of India under the East India Company, 1814–58. Cambridge: Cambridge University Press.

Cheng, Siok Hwa
1968 The Rice Industry of Burma, 1852–1940. Kuala Lumpur: University of Malaya Press.

Chettiar, A. V. Ramanathan (*See* Ramanathan Chettiar, A. V.)

Chettiar, M. Ramanathan (*See* Ramanathan Chettiar, M.)

Chettiar, S. M. Lakshmanan (Somalay) (*See* Lakshmanan Chettiar, S. M.)

Chettiar, Vr. L. Chinnaiya (*See* Chinnaiya Chettiar, Vr. L.)

Chettiar Chamber of Commerce
1963 "Ilangayal Nagaratharakalin Theyva Thriupani." *In* Sri Kasi Nattukkottai Nakarachattiran Natrandu Vila Malar (Tamil), S. M. Lakshmanan Chettiar, ed. Madras.

Chinnaiya Chettiar, Vr. L.
1941–42 Nattukkottai Nakarattar Sarittiram (Tamil). (Reprint of Subramaniyam Ayyar 1895). Tirunelveli: South India Saiva Siddhantha Works Publishing Society.

Chockalinga Ayyah
1919 Nattukkottai Nakarattar enum Makutatana Vaicyarin Marapu Villakkam. Karaikudi.

Claus, Peter
1978 "Oral traditions, royal cults and materials for a consideration of the caste system in South India." Journal of Indian Folkloristics 1(1).

Cochrane, Glynn
1971 "Use of the concept of the "corporation": A choice between colloquialism or distortion." American Anthropologist 73: 1144–1150.

Cohen, Abner
1969 Custom and politics in Urban Africa: A Study of Hausa Migrants in Yoruba Towns. Berkeley and Los Angeles: University of California Press.

Cohn, Bernard S.
1960 "The initial British impact on India: A case study of the Benares region." Journal of Asian Studies 19(4): 422.

1962 "Political systems in eighteenth century India: The Banaras region." Journal of the American Oriental Society 82: 312–320.

1983 "Representing authority in Victorian India." *In* The Invention of Tradition, E. J. Hobsbawm and T. Ranger, eds. Cambridge: Cambridge University Press.

1987 "The Census, social structure and objectification in South Asia." *In* An Anthropologist among the Historians and Other Essays, pp. 224–254. Delhi: Oxford University Press.

Commander, S.

1983 "The jajmani system in North India: An examination of its logic and status across two centuries." Modern Asian Studies 17: 283–311.

Conlon, Frank F.

1977 A Caste in a Changing World: The Chitrapur Saraswat Brahmans, 1700–1935. Berkeley and Los Angeles: University of California Press.

Cooper, Chester L.

1959 Money-Lenders and the Economic Development of Lower Burma: An Exploratory Historical Study of the Role of Indian Chettiars. Ph.D. dissertation, American University, Washington, D.C.

Crawfurd, John

1971 [1837] "A sketch of the commercial resources and monetary and mercantile system of British India, with suggestions for their improvement by means of banking establishments." *Reprinted in* The Economic Development of India under the East India Company 1814–58, K. N. Chaudhuri, ed. Cambridge: Cambridge University Press.

Curtin, Philip D.

1984 Cross-cultural trade in world history. Cambridge: Cambridge University Press.

Daniel, E. Valentine

1984 Fluid Signs: Being a Person the Tamil Way. Berkeley and Los Angeles: University of California Press.

Darling, Sir Malcolm

1947 The Punjab Peasant in Prosperity and Debt. Bombay: Oxford University Press.

Das, Veena

1976 "The uses of liminality: Society and cosmos in Hinduism." Contributions to Indian Society 10(2): 245–263.

Das Gupta, Ashin

1967 Malabar in Asian Trade, 1740–1800. Cambridge: Cambridge University Press.

1970 "Trade and politics in 18th century India." *In* Islam and the Trade of Asia: A Colloquium, D. S. Richards, ed., pp. 181–214. Oxford: Bruno Casirer.

1979 Indian Merchants and the Decline of Surat, c. 1700–1750. Wiesbaden: Franz Stein Verlag.

Das Gupta, Ashin, and Michael Pearson (eds.)

1987 India and the Indian Ocean, 1500–1800. Calcutta.

David, Kenneth

1973 "Until marriage do us part: A cultural account of Jaffna Tamil categories for kinsman." Man, n.s. 8: 521–535.

1977 "Hierarchy and equivalence in Jaffna, North Sri Lanka: Normative codes as mediator." *In* The New Wind: Changing Identities in South Asia, K. David, ed., pp. 179–226. The Hague: Mouton.

Davis, Marvin

1976 "A philosophy of Hindu rank from rural West Bengal." Journal of Asian Studies 36(1): 5–24.

Day, David H.

1972 "The Nattukottai Chettiars of Tamilnadu: Explorations in the economic history of an entrepreneurial community." *In* South Asian Varia, pp. 65–77. Syracuse University Occasional Paper Series, No. 1. Syracuse, N.Y.: Syracuse University.

Derret, J. Duncan

1976 "Rajadharma." Journal of Asian Studies 35(4): 597–610.

Deyell, John S.

1970 "Numismatic methodology in the estimation of Mughal currency output." Indian Economic and Social History Review 13: 375–392.

Dirks, Nicholas B.

1976 "Political authority and structural change in early South Indian history." Indian Economic and Social History Review 13(2): 125–157.

1979 "The structure and meaning of political relations in a South Indian little kingdom." Contributions to Indian Sociology, n.s. 13(2): 169–204.

1983 "The royal Kallars of Pudukottai." Ann Arbor. Manuscript.

1987 The Hollow Crown: Ethnohistory of an Indian Little Kingdom. Cambridge: Cambridge University Press.

1989 "The invention of caste: Civil society in colonial India." Social Analysis 25: 42–52.

Dobbin, Christine

1972 Urban Leadership in Western India: Politics and Communities in Bombay City 1840–1885. London: Oxford University Press.

Dumont, Louis

1953 "The Dravidian kinship terminology as an expression of marriage." Man 53: 34–39. (Reprinted in Dumont 1983.)

1957a Une Sous-Caste de L'Inde du Sud: Organisation Sociale et Religion des Pramalai Kallar. Paris: Mouton.

1957b "Hierarchy and marriage alliance in South Indian Kinship." Occasional Papers of the Royal Anthropological Institute, No. 12. London: Royal Anthropological Institute. (*Reprinted in* Dumont 1983.)

1958 "A. M. Hocart on caste—Religion and power." Contributions to Indian Sociology 2: 45–63.

1959 "A structural definition of a folk deity of Tamil Nad: Aiyanar the Lord." Contributions to Indian Sociology 3: 75–87.

1961 "Marriage in India: The present state of the question. Part 1: Marriage alliance in S.E. India and Ceylon." Contributions to Indian Sociology 5: 75–95.

1962 "The conception of kingship in ancient India." Contributions to Indian Sociology 6: 48–77.

1964 "A note on locality in relation to descent." Contributions to Indian Sociology 7: 71–76.

1975 Dravidien et Kariera: l'Alliance de mariage dans l'Inde et en Australie. Ecole des Hautes Etudes en Sciences Sociales, Textes de Sciences Sociales, 14. The Hague: Mouton.

1977 From Mandeville to Marx. Chicago: University of Chicago Press.

1980 [1970] Homo Hierarchicus: The Caste System and Its Implications. Chicago. University of Chicago Press.

1983 Affinity as a Value: Marriage Alliance in South India with Comparative Essays on Australia. Chicago: Chicago University Press.

1986 Essays on Individualism: Modern Ideology in Anthropological Perspective. Chicago: University of Chicago Press.

Dutt, Romesh Chunder

1950 The Economic History of India in the Victorian Age. London: Routledge and Kegan Paul.

Elayathakudi Devasthanam (*See* Ilayathakudi Devastanam)

Emeneau, M. B.

1941 "Language and social forms: A study of Toda kinship terms and dual descent." *In* Language, Culture and Personality: Essays in Memory of Edward Sapir, L. Spier, A. I. Hallowell, and S. S. Newman, eds. Menasha: Sapir Memorial Publication Fund.

Evans-Pritchard, E. E.

1940 The Nuer: A Description of the Modes of Livelihood and Political Institutions of a Nilotic People. Oxford: Clarendon Press.

Evers, Hans-Dieter

1972 "Chettiar moneylenders in Southeast Asia." *In* Asie Du Sud: Traditions et Changements, pp. 635–645. Paris: Colloques Internationaux du Centre National de la Recherche Scientifique, No. 582.

Fabian, Johannes

1983 Time and the Other: How Anthropology Makes Its Object. New York: Columbia University Press.

Fabricius, J. P.
1972 Tamil and English Dictionary. 4th edition. Tranquebar: Evangelical Lutheran Mission Publishing House.

Fanselow, Frank
1986 Trade, Kinship and Islamization: A Comparative Study of the Social and Economic Organisation of Muslim and Hindu Traders in Tirunelveli District, Tamil Nadu. Ph.D. dissertation, London School of Economics, London University.

Fortes, Meyer
1954 "The structure of unilineal groups." American Anthropologist 55: 17–41.

Fox, Richard G.
1969 From Zamindar to Ballot Box: Community Change in a North Indian Market Town. Ithaca: Cornell University Press.

Francis, W. F.
1906 Gazetteer for Madurai. Madras: Government of India.

Freeman, J. D.
1961 "On the concept of the kindred." Journal of the Royal Anthropological Institute 91: 192–220.

Fried, Morton H.
1957 "The classification of corporate unilineal descent groups." Journal of the Royal Anthropological Institute 87(1): 1–29.

Frykenberg, Robert Eric
1965 Guntur District, 1788–1848: A History of Local Influence and Central Authority in South India. Oxford: Clarendon Press.

Fuller, C. J.
1979 "Gods, priests and purity: On the relations between Hinduism and the caste system." Man, n.s. 14: 459–476.
1981 "The government and the temple: The Madurai Minaksi Temple priests, 1937–1980." Paper presented at the Seventh European Conference on Modern Asian Studies, London, July 7–11.
1984 Servants of the Goddess: The Priests of a South Indian Temple. Cambridge: Cambridge University Press.
1989 "Misconceiving the grain heap: A critique of the concept of the Indian jajmani system." *In* Money and the Morality of Exchange, M. Bloch and J. Parry, eds. Cambridge: Cambridge University Press.
1992 The Camphor Flame: Popular Hinduism and Society in India. Princeton: Princeton University Press.

Furber, Holden
1951 John Company at Work. Cambridge: Harvard University Press.

Furnivall, J. S.
1956 Colonial Policy and Practice. New York: New York University Press.

Gadgil, D. R.
1959 Origins of the Modern Indian Business Class. New York: International Secretariat of the Institute of Pacific Relations.

Gallager, J., Gordon Johnson, and Anil Seal
1973 Locality, Province and Nation: Essays on Indian Politics, 1870–1940. Cambridge: Cambridge University Press.

Geertz, Clifford
1963 Peddlers and Princes: Social Change and Economic Modernization in Two Indonesian Towns. Chicago: University of Chicago Press.
1973 "Thick description: Towards an interpretive theory of culture." *In* The Interpretation of Cultures, pp. 3–33. New York: Basic Books.
1979 "Suq: The bazaar economy in Sefrou." *In* Meaning and Order in Moroccan Society: Three Essays in Cultural Analysis, Clifford Geertz, Hilda Geertz, and Lawrence Rosen, eds. Cambridge: Cambridge University Press.

Glieck, James
1987 Chaos: Making a New Science. New York: Viking Press.

Good, Anthony
1982 "The actor and the act: Categories of prestation in South India." Man, n.s. 17: 23–41.
1991 The Female Bridegroom: A Comparative Study of Life-Crisis Rituals in South India and Sri Lanka. Oxford: Oxford University Press.

Goodenough, Ward H.
1970 Description and Comparison in Cultural Anthropology. Chicago: Aldine.
1971 "Corporations: Reply to Cochrane." American Anthropologist 73: 1150–1152.

Goody, Jack
1958 The Developmental Cycle in Domestic Groups. Cambridge: Cambridge University Press.

Gopal, Surendra
1976 Commerce and Crafts in Gujarat, 16th and 17th Centuries: A Study in the Impact of European Expansion on Precapitalist Economy. New Delhi: People's Publishing House.

Gough, Kathleen
1981 Rural Society in Southeast India. Cambridge: Cambridge University Press.

Gould, Harold
1964 "The jajmani system of North India: Its structure, magnitude and meaning." Ethnology 3: 12–41.

Grant, James
1918 [1784] "Political survey of the Northern Circars." *In* Fifth Report from the Select Committee of the House of Commons on the Affairs of the East India Company, W. K. Firminger, ed., Volume 3. Calcutta.

Greenough, Paul R.
1983 "Indulgence and abundance as Asian peasant values: A Bengali case in point." Journal of Asian Studies 44: 831–850.

Gurney, J. D.
1968 The Debts of the Nawab of Arcot 1763–1776. Ph. D. dissertation. Oxford University.

Habib, Irfan
1960 "Banking in Mughal India." *In* Contributions to Indian Economic History, T. Raychauduri, ed., Vol. 1. Calcutta: K. L. Mukhopadhyay.
1969 "Potentialities of capitalistic development in the economy of Mughal India." Journal of Economic History 24(1).
1973 "The system of bills of exchange (hundis) in the Mughal Empire." *In* Proceedings of the Indian History Congress, 33rd Session, Muzatarppur, 1972, pp. 290–303. New Delhi.
1980 "The technology and economy of Mughal India." Indian Economic and Social History Review 17: 1–34.
1982 "Monetary systems and prices." *In* Cambridge Economic History, T. Raychauduri and I. Habib, eds. Vol. 1, c. 1200–1750. Cambridge: Cambridge University Press.

Habib, Irfan, and Tapan Raychaudhuri
1982 Cambridge Economic History of India. Vol. 1. Cambridge: Cambridge University Press.

Hall, Kenneth R.
1980 Trade and Statecraft in the Age of Colas. New Delhi: Abhinav Publications.

Hardgrave, Robert L., Jr.
1969 The Nadars of Tamilnad: The Political Culture of a Community in Change. Berkeley and Los Angeles: University of California Press.

Harper, Edward B.
1959 "A Hindu village pantheon." Southwestern Journal of Anthropology 15: 227–234.
1964 "Ritual pollution as an integrator of caste and religion." *In* Religion in South Indian, E. Harper, ed. Seattle: University of Washington Press.

Harriss, Barbara
1981 Transitional Trade and Rural Development: The Nature and Role of Agricultural Trade in a South Indian District. New Delhi: Vikas Publishing House.

Harriss, John
1982 Capitalism and Peasant Farming: Agrarian Structure and Ideology in Northern Tamil Nadu. Bombay: Oxford University Press.

Haynes, Douglas E.
1991 Rhetoric and Ritual in Colonial India: The Shaping of a Public Culture in Surat City, 1852–1928. Berkeley and Los Angeles: University of California Press.

Hazelhurst, Leighton W.
1966 Entrepreneurship and the Merchant Castes in a Punjabi City. Duke University Program in Comparative Studies on Southern Asia, Monograph and Occasional Paper Series, No. 1. Durham: Duke University.

Hobsbawm, E. J., and T. Ranger
1983 The Invention of Tradition. Cambridge: Cambridge University Press.
Hocart, A. M.
1950 Caste: A Comparative Study. London: Methuen.
Hubert, Henri, and Marcel Mauss
1964 Sacrifice: Its Nature and Function. Chicago: University of Chicago Press.
Ilayathakudi Devastanam
1939 Administration Report of the Elayathakudi Devastanam. Karaikudi: Chettinadu Press.
1963 Ilayattakudi Manmiyum. Ilayattakudi.
Inden, R. B.
1986 "Orientalist constructions in India." Modern Asian Studies 20(3): 401–446.
1991 Imagining India. Oxford: Basil Blackwell.
Inden, R. B., and R. W. Nicholas
1977 Kinship in Bengali Culture. Chicago: University of Chicago Press.
Inglis, Stephen
1985 "Possession and Pottery: Serving the Divine in a South Indian Community." *In* Gods of Flesh, Gods of Stone, J. P. Waghorne and N. Cutler, eds. Chambersburg, Pa: Anima.
Irschick, Eugene F.
1969 Politics and Social Conflict in South India: The Non-Brahman Movement and Tamil Separatism, 1916–1929. Berkeley and Los Angeles: University of California Press.
Ito, Shoji
1966 "A note on the business combine in India, with special reference to the Nattukkottai Chettiars." Developing Economies (Tokyo) A: 367–380.
Kane, P. V.
1941 History of Dharmasastra, Vol. 1. Poona: Government Oriental Series.
1946 History of Dharmasastra, Vol. 3. Poona: Government Oriental Series.
Kannangara, D. M.
1960 "Formative influences in Ceylon's banking development." Ceylon Journal of History and Social Studies 3(1): 82–95.
Kay, Paul
1965 "A generalization of the cross/parallel distinction." American Anthropologist 67: 30–43.
1967 "On the multiplicity of cross/parallel distinctions." American Anthropologist 69: 83–85.
Khare, Ravindra S.
1970 The changing Brahmans: Associations and elites among the Kanya-Kubjas of North India. Chicago, University of Chicago Press.

Kochanek, Stanley
1964 Business and Politics in India. Berkeley and Los Angeles: University of California Press.
Kopytoff, Igor
1986 "The cultural biography of things: Commoditization as process." *In* The Social Life of Things: Commodities in Cultural Perspective, A. Appadurai, ed., pp. 95–109. Cambridge: Cambridge University Press.
Kramrisch, Stella
1946 The Hindu Temple. Calcutta: University of Calcutta.
Krishnan, V.
1959 Indigenous Banking in South India. Bombay: Bombay State Cooperative Union.
Krishna Rao, M. V. G.
1964 "Salt industry in the Circars: From 1776–1805." Journal of the Andhra Historical Society 29(3–4): 71–82.
Kumar, Dharma
1965 Land and Caste in South India. Cambridge: Cambridge University Press.
Lakshmanan Chettiar, S. M. (Somalay)
1953 Chettinadum Tamilum (Tamil). Madras.
1963 Calcutta. *In* Sri Kasi Nattukkottai Nakarachattiram Natrandu Vila Malar (Tamil), S. M. Lakshmanan Chettiar, ed. Madras.
Lakshmanan Chettiar, S. M. (ed.)
1963 Sri Kasi Nattukkottai Nakarachattiram Natrandu Vila Malar, SKNNNVM (Tamil). Madras.
Lamb, Helen
1959 "The Indian merchant." *In* Traditional India: Structure and Change, M. Singer, ed., pp. 25–34. Philadelphia: American Folklore Society.
Lansing, Stephen J.
1993 "Emergent properties of Balinese water temple networks: Coadaptation on a rugged fitness landscape." American Anthropologist 95(1): 97–114.
Leach, Edmund
1960 "Introduction." *In* Aspects of Caste in South India, Ceylon and Northwest Pakistan, Edmund Leach, ed. Cambridge Papers in Social Anthropology, No. 2. Cambridge: Cambridge University Press.
1961 [1951] "The structural implications of matrilateral cross-cousin marriage." *In* Rethinking Anthropology, pp. 54–104. London: University of London Press.
Leonard, Karen I.
1978 Social History of an Indian Caste: The Kayasths of Hyderabad. Berkeley and Los Angeles: University of California Press.
1979 "The 'great firm' theory of the decline of the Mughal empire." Comparative Studies in Society and History 21(2): 151–167.

Lévi-Strauss, Claude
1969 The Elementary Structures of Kinship. Boston: Beacon Press.

Lewandowski, Susan
1976 "Merchants, temples and power in the colonial port city of Madras." Paper presented at the Comparative Conference on the Colonial Port City, Santa Cruz, Calif., June 14–16.

Ludden, David
1978 Agrarian Organization in Tinnevelly District, 800 to 1900 A.D. Ph.D. dissertation, University of Pennsylvania, Philadelphia.
1985 Peasant History in South India. Princeton, N.J.: Princeton University Press.

Macfarlane, Alan
1987 The Culture of Capitalism. Oxford: Basil Blackwell.

MacKenzie, Sir Compton
1954 Realms of Silver: One Hundred Years of Banking in the East. London: Routledge and Kegan Paul.

Madan, T. N.
1962 "Is the Brahmanic gotra a grouping of kin?" Southwestern Journal of Anthropology 18: 59–77.

Mahadevan, Raman
1976 The Origin and Growth of Entrepreneurship in the Nattukottai Chettiar Community of Tamilnadu, 1880–1930. M.Phil. thesis, Jawaharlal Nehru University.
1978a "Immigrant entrepreneurs in colonial Burma: An exploratory study of the role of the Nattukottai Chettiars of Tamil Nadu, 1880–1930." Indian Economic and Social History Review 15(3): 329–358.
1978b "Pattern of enterprise of immigrant entrepreneurs: A study of Chettiars in Malaya, 1880–1930." Economic and Political Weekly, Jan. 28–Feb. 4: 146–152.

Mahalingam, T. V.
1967 South Indian Polity. 2nd edition. Madras: Madras University.

Maine, Sir Henry S.
1931 Ancient Law. London: Oxford University Press.

Maloney, C.
1970 "The beginnings of civilization in South India." Journal of Asian Studies 29: 603–617.

Manickam, V. Sp.
1963 Nakarattar Arappattayankal. Devakottai.
1978 "Ancient history of the Nagarathars (from BC 2898 to AD 1800)." *In* Collected Papers, V. Sp. Manickam, ed. Karaikkudi: Centre for Tamil Development and Advanced Research.

Marriott, McKim
1976 "Hindu transactions: Diversity without dualism." *In* Transaction and Meaning: Directions in the Anthropology of Exchange and Symbolic Behavior, B. Kapferer, ed. Philadelphia: Ishi.
1990 "Constructing and Indian sociology." *In* India Through Hindu Categories, M. Marriott, ed. New Delhi: Sage Publications. (*Also in* Contributions to Indian Sociology, n.s. 24, no. 2 [1990]: 1–39.)

Marriott, McKim, and Ronald Inden
1974 Caste systems. *In* Encyclopedia Britannica, 15th edition. Chicago.

Marriott, McKim, and Manuel Moreno
1990 "Humoral transactions in two South Indian Cults." *In* India Through Hindu Categories, M. Marriott, ed. New Delhi: Sage Publications. (Also in Contributions to Indian Sociology, n.s. 24, no. 2 (1990): 149–169.

Marshall, Peter
1976 East Indian Fortunes: The British in Bengal in the Eighteenth Century. Oxford: Oxford University Press.

Masters, Allene
1957 "The Chettiars in Burma: An economic appraisal of a migrant community." Population Review 1 (Jan.).

Mauss, Marcel
1954 The Gift: Forms and Functions of Exchange in Archaic Societies. Translated by Ian Cunnison. Glencoe: Free Press.

May, Linda
1985 "Marriage negotiations in Tamil Nadu: A Dravidian marriage rule in action." Paper presented at the Fourteenth Annual Madison South Asia Conference, Madison, Wisconsin.

Mayer, Adrian C.
1958 "The dominant caste in a region of central India." Southwestern Journal of Anthropology 14: 407–427
1960 Caste and Kinship in Central India: A Village and Its Region. Berkeley and Los Angeles: University of California Press.
1966 "The significance of quasi-groups in the study of complex societies." *In* The Social Anthropology of Complex Societies, Michael Banton, ed., pp. 97–122. New York: Frederick A. Praeger.

Meister, Michael W.
1983 Encyclopedia of Indian Temple Architecture. New Delhi: American Institute of Indian Studies; Philadelphia: University of Pennsylvania Press.

Mencher, Joan P.
1978 Agriculture and social structure in Tamil Nadu: Past origins, present transformations, and future prospects. Bombay: Allied.

Mendels, Franklin F.
1972 "Proto-industrialization: The first phase of the industrialization process." Journal of Economic History 32: 241–261.

Michell, George
1988 The Hindu Temple: An Introduction to Its Meaning and Forms. Chicago: University of Chicago Press.

Michie, Barry H.
1978 "Baniyas in the Indian agrarian economy: A case of stagnant entrepreneurship." Journal of Asian Studies 37(4): 637–652.

Miller, Eric J.
1954 "Caste and territory in Malabar." American Anthropologist 56: 410–420.

Mines, Matison

1972 "Tamil Muslim merchants in India's industrial development." *In* Entrepreneurship and Modernization of Occupational Cultures in South Asia, M. Singer, ed. Durham, N.C.: Duke University Press.

1984 The Warrior Merchants: Textiles, Trade and Territory in South India. Cambridge: Cambridge University Press.

Moore, Melinda

1990 "The Kerala house as a Hindu cosmos." Contributions to Indian Sociology, n.s. 23(1): 169–202.

Moosvi, Shireen

1980 "Money supply and the silver influx in the Mughal empire: A fresh attempt at quantification." Paper presented at the Forty-first Session of the Indian History Congress. Bombay: Aligarh Muslim University Volume.

Moreno, Manuel

1981 "The god of healing poisons: Thermic complementarity and exchanges in two South Indian pilgrimages." Chicago. Manuscript.

1984 Murugan, a God of Healing Poisons: The Physics of Worship in a South Indian Center for Pilgrimage. Ph.D. dissertation, University of Chicago.

Morgan, Lewis Henry

1870 Systems of Consanguinity and Affinity of the Human Family. Smithsonian Contributions to Knowledge, No. 218. Washington, D.C.: Smithsonian Institution.

Morris, Morris David

1965 The Emergence of an Industrial Labor Force in India: A Study of the Bombay Cotton Mills, 1854–1947. Bombay: Oxford University Press.

1969 "Trends and tendencies in Indian economic history." Indian Economic and Social History Review 5(4): 366–368.

Mudaliar, C. Y.

1974 The Secular State and Religious Institutions in India: A Study of the Administration of Hindu Religious Institutions in Madras. Wiesbaden: Franz Steiner Verlag.

1976 State and Religious Endowments in Madras. Madras: University of Madras.

Murton, B.

1973 "Key people in the countryside: Decision makers in interior Tamilnadu in the late eighteenth century." Indian Economic and Social History Review 10(2): 157–180.

Musgrave, P. J.

1978 "Rural credit and rural society in the United Provinces, 1860–1920." *In* The Imperial Impact: Studies in the Economic History of Africa and India, G. Dewey and A. R. Hopkins, eds., pp. 216–232. London: University of London.

Nadarajan, M.
1966 "The Nattukottai Chettiar community and South-East Asia." *In* Proceedings of the First International Conference-Seminar of Tamil Studies, Xavier S. Thaninayagam, ed., Vol. 1. Kuala Lampur: International Association of Asian Research.

Naidu, B. V. Narayanaswamy
1941 "The Nattukkottai Chettiars and their banking system." *In* Raja Sir Annamalai Chettiar Commemorative Volume, B. V. N. Naidu, ed., pp. 457–472. Annamalainagar: Annamalai University.

Narayan, R. K.
1952 The Financial Expert: A Novel. London: Methuen.

Narayana Rao, Velcheru
1986 "Epics and ideologies: Six Telugu folk epics." *In* Another Harmony: New Essays on the Folklore of India, S. H. Blackburn and A. K. Ramanujan, eds. Berkeley and Los Angeles: University of California Press.

Natarajan, B.
1941 "Origin of Burmese competition in Madras rice market." *In* Raja Sir Annamalai Chettiar Commemorative Volume, B. V. N. Naidu, ed., pp. 309–319. Annamalainagar: Annamalai University.

Neale, Walter
1957 "Reciprocity and redistribution in the Indian village: Sequel to some notable discussions." *In* Trade and Market in Early Empires: Economics in History and Theory, K. Polanyi, ed. Glencoe: The Free Press.
1969 "Land is to rule." *In* Land Control and Social Structure in Indian History, R. E. Frykenberg, ed., pp. 3–16. Madison: University of Wisconsin Press.

Needham, Rodney
1962 Structure and Sentiment: A Test Case in Social Anthropology. Chicago: University of Chicago Press.
1986 "Alliance." Oceania 56(3): 165–180.

Nicholson, F. A.
1895 Report Concerning the Possibility of Introducing Agricultural Banks in the Madras Presidency. 2 vols. Madras.

Nisbet, John
1901 Burma under British Rule and Before. 2 vols. London: Archibald Constable.

Orenstein, Henry
1962 "Exploitation and function in the interpretation of jajmani." Southwestern Journal of Anthropology 18(4): 302–315.

Ostor, Akos
1984 Culture and Power: Legend, Ritual, Bazaar, and Rebellion in a Bengali Society. Beverly Hills, Calif.: Sage Publications.

Owen, T. C.
1881 The Cinchoma Planters' Manual. Colombo: A. M. and J. Ferguson.
Palaniappan, T. R.
1989 "Chettinadu housing." Architecture and Design 5(4): 105–113.
Paramasivam, K. (trans.)
1981a "The six Nakarattar deeds of gift." Manuscript.
1981b "A translation of Nattukottai Nakarattar Varalaru by Vr. L. Chinnaiya Chettiar." Manuscript.
Parry, Jonathan
1982 "Sacrificial death and the necrophageous ascetic." In M. Block and J. Parry (eds.) Death and Regeneration of Life. Cambridge: Cambridge University Press.
Pearson, Michael
1976 Merchants and Rulers in Gujarat. Berkeley and Los Angeles: University of California Press.
1987 The Portuguese in India. Cambridge: New York: Cambridge University Press.
Periakarrapan ("Tamil Annal")
1977 Nakara-k-kovil (Tamil). Madurai: Nakara Malar.
Perlin, Frank
1983 "Proto-Industrialization and pre-colonial South Asia." Past and Present 98: 30–95.
Pillai, A. Savarinatha (*See under* Government of Madras)
Pillai, B. Bastian (*See* Bastianpillai)
Playne, Somerset
1914–15 Southern India: Its History, People, Commerce and Industrial Resources. London: The Foreign and Colonial Compiling and Publishing Company.
Prakash, Om
1976 "Bullion for goods: international trade and the economy of early eighteenth century Bengal." Indian Economic and Social History Review 13: 159–187.
Prakash, Om, and J. Krishnamurty
1970 "Mughal silver currency: A critique." Indian Economic and Social History Review 7: 139–150.
Presler, Franklin A.
1987 Religion under Bureaucracy: Policy and Administration for Hindu Temples in South India. Cambridge: Cambridge University Press.
Price, Pamela G.
1979 Resource and Rule in Zamindari South India, 1802–1903. Ph.D. dissertation. University of Wisconsin.
Raghavaiyangar, S. Srinivasa (*See under* Government of Madras)
Raheja, Gloria Goodwin
1988 The Poison in the Gift: Ritual, Prestation, and the Dominant Caste in a North Indian Village. Chicago: University of Chicago Press.

Raja Rao
1978 [1939] Kanthapura. Madras: Oxford University Press.
Rajaratnam, S.
1961 "The growth of plantation agriculture in Ceylon, 1886–1931." Ceylon Journal of Historical and Social Studies 4(1): 1–20.
1964 "The Ceylon tea industry, 1886–1931." Ceylon Journal of Historical and Social Studies 4(2): 169–202.
Rajayyan, K.
1964–65 "Revenue and judicial administration of the Nawabs of the Carnatic." Journal of the Andhra Historical Research Society 30: 143–154.
1974 History of Madurai, 1736–1801. Madurai.
Raju, A. Saruda (*See* Saruda Raju)
Raman Rao, A. V.
1958 Economic Development of Andhra Pradesh (1766–1957). Bombay: Popular Book Depot.
Ramanathan Chettiar, A. V.
1953 Nattukkottai Nakarattar Varalaru (Tamil). Madras.
Ramaswamy, Vijaya
1985 Textiles and Weavers in Medieval South India. Delhi: Oxford University Press.
Rao, A. V. Raman (*See* Raman Rao, A. V.)
Rao, M. V. G. Krishna (*See* Krishna Rao, M. V. G.)
Rao, Narayana (*See* Narayana Rao)
Rao, Raja (*See* Raja Rao)
Ray, Rajat Kanta
1979 Industrialization in India: Growth and Conflict in the Private Corporate Sector, 1914–47. Delhi: Oxford University Press.
Raychaudhuri, T.
1962 Jan Company in Coromandel, 1605–1690. Caravenge.
Robert, Bruce
1983 "Economic change and agrarian organization in 'dry' South India, 1890–1940: A reinterpretation." Modern Asian Studies 17(1): 59–78.
Roberts, Michael
1982 Caste Conflict and Elite Formation: The Rise of a Karava Elite in Sri Lanka 1500–1931. Cambridge: Cambridge University Press.
Rocher, Ludo
1975 "Caste and occupation in classical India: The normative texts." Contributions to Indian Sociology, n.s. 9(1): 139–151.
1981 "Notes on mixed castes in classical India." Adyar Library Bulletin 44–45: 132–146.
Rudner, David
1985 Caste and Commerce in Indian Society: A Case Study of Nattukottai Chettiars, 1600–1930. Ph.D. dissertation, University of Pennsylvania, Philadelphia.
1987 Religious gifting and inland commerce in pre-colonial South India. Journal of Asian Studies 46(2): 361–379.

1989 "Banker's trust and the culture of banking among the Nattukottai Chettiars of colonial South India." Modern Asian Studies 23(3): 417–458.

1990 "Inquest on Dravidian kinship: Louis Dumont and the essence of marriage alliance." Contributions to Indian Sociology 24(2): 153–174.

Rudner, Richard S.

1966 Philosophy of Social Science. Englewood Cliffs, N.J.: Prentice-Hall.

Rudolph, Lloyd, and Susanne Hoeber Rudolph

1967 The Modernity of Tradition: Political Development in India. Chicago: University of Chicago Press.

Sadasivan, S. T.

1939 Three hundred years of banking in Madras. The Madras Tercentenary Commemoration Volume. Madras.

Sahlins, Marshall

1961 "The segmentary lineage: An organization of predatory expansion." American Anthropologist 62(2): 332–345.

1966 "On the sociology of primitive exchange." *In* The Relevance of Models for Social Anthropology, Michael Banton, ed. London: Tavistock Publications.

Said, Edward W.

1978 Orientalism. New York: Vintage Books.

Samaraweera, Vijaya

1972 "Ceylon's trade relations with Coromandel during early British times, 1796–1837." Modern Ceylon Studies 3(1): 1–17.

Sandhu, K. S.

1969 Indians in Malaya: Some Aspects of Their Immigration and Settlement (1786–1957). Cambridge: Cambridge University Press.

Sarada Raju, A.

1941 Economic Conditions in Madras Presidency, 1800–1850. Madras University Economic Series, No. 5. Madras: University of Madras.

Sathyanatha Aiyar, R.

1924 History of the Nayaks of Madura. Madras.

Scheffler, Harold W.

1971 "Dravidian-Iroquois: The Melanesian evidence." *In* Anthropology in Oceania: Essays Presented to Ian Hogbin, L. R. Hiatt and C. Jayawardena, eds., pp. 231–254. Sydney: Angus and Robertson.

1972a "Kinship semantics." Annual Reviews in Anthropology 1: 309–328.

1972b "Systems of kin classification: A structural typology." *In* Kinship Studies in the Morgan Centennial Year, P. Reining, ed. Washington, D.C.: The Anthropological Society of Washington.

1984 "Markedness and extensions: The Tamil case." Man, n.s. 19: 557–574.

Seal, Anil

1973 "Imperialism and nationalism." *In* India: Locality, Province and Nation, J. Gallagher, G. Johnson, and A. Seal, eds. Cambridge: Cambridge University Press.

Service, Elwyn
1985 A Hundred Years of Controversy: Ethnological Issues from 1860 to 1960. Orlando, Fla.: Academic Press.

Sharma, V. A. Seshadri
1970 Nattukkottai Nakarattar Varalaru (Tamil). Madras.

Siddiqui, A. M.
1956 History of Golconda. Hyderabad: Literary Publications.

Siegelman, Phillip
1962 Colonial Development and the Chettiar: A Study in Political Economic Ecology of Modern Burma. Ph.D. dissertation, University of Minnesota.

Singer, Milton
1972 "The Hindu ethic in the spirit of capitalism." *In* When a Great Tradition Modernizes. New York: Praeger Publishers.

Sjoberg, Gideon
1970 The Pre-industrial City. New York.

Skeen, George
1906 A Guide to Colombo. Colombo.

Smith, M. G.
1974 Corporations and Society. London: Duckworth.

Somalay (*See* Chettiar, S. M. Lakshmanan)

Southall, Aiden W.
1956 Alur Society: A Study in Processes and Types of Domination. Cambridge: W. Heffer.

Spellman, John W.
1964 Political Theory of Ancient India: A Study of Kingship from the Earliest Times to circa A.D. 300. Oxford: Clarendon Press.

Spencer, George W.
1968 "Temple money-lending and live-stock redistribution." Indian Economic and Social History Review 5(3): 277–293.

Spodek, Howard
1976 Urban-Rural Integration in Regional Development: A Case Study of Saurashtra, India, 1800–1960." Chicago: University of Chicago.

Srinivas, M. N.
1952 Religion and Society among the Coorgs of South India. Oxford: Clarendon Press.
1959 "The dominant caste in Rampura." American Anthropologist 61: 1–16.
1962 Caste in Modern India and Other Essays. Bombay: Asia Publishing House.

Stein, Burton
1960 "Economic functions of a medieval temple." Journal of Asian Studies 9(2): 163–176.
1969 "Integration of the agrarian system of south India." *In* Land control and Social Structure in Indian History, R. E. Frykenberg, ed. Madison: University of Wisconsin Press
1977 "Temples and Tamil country, 1300–1750 A.D." Indian Economic and Social History Review 14(1).

1980 Peasant State and Society in Medieval South India. Delhi: Oxford University Press.

Stokes, Eric
1978 The Peasant and the Raj: Studies in Agrarian Society and Peasant Rebellion in Colonial India. Cambridge: Cambridge University Press.

Subrahmanya Aiyer, K. V.
1954–56 "Largest provincial organizations in ancient India." Quarterly Journal of the Mythic Society, n.s. 45: 29–47, 70–98, 270–286 and 46: 8–22.

Subrahmanyam, Sanjay
1990 The Political Economy of Commerce. Cambridge: Cambridge University Press.

Subramaniyam Ayyar, Sadhavadanam
1895 Tanavaiciyar akiy Nattukottai Nakarattar Saritiram (Tamil). Tanjavur: Desabimani Press.

Sundaram, Lanka
1944–45 "Revenue administration of the northern Sirkars." Journal of the Andhra Historical Research Society 25(1,2,3,4).

Suntharalingam, R.
1974 Politics and National Awakening in South India, 1852–1891. Tucson: University of Arizona.

Tambiah, S. J.
1973a "Dowry and bridewealth and the property rights of women in South Asia." *In* Bridewealth and Dowry, J. Goody and S. J. Tambiah, eds., pp. 59–167. Cambridge: Cambridge University Press.
1973b "From varna to caste through mixed union." *In* The Character of Kinship, J. Goody, ed., pp. 191–230. Cambridge: Cambridge University Press.
1984 The Buddhist Saints of the Forest and the Cult of the Amulets. Cambridge: Cambridge University Press.

Thapar, Romila
1966 A History of India. Vol. 1. Baltimore, Md.: Penguin Books.

Thiagarajan, Deborah
1983 "The symbolic and social significance in the traditional Nagarathar house." Philadelphia. Manuscript.
1992 "Doors and woodcraft of Chettinad." Marg 43(2): 53–72.

Thomas, P. J.
1941 "Nattukkottai Chettiars: Their banking system." *In* Raja Sir Annamalai Chettiar Commemorative Volume, B. V. Narayanaswamy Naidu, ed., pp. 840–854. Annamalainagar: Annamalai University.

Thorner, Daniel
1960 "Emergence of an Indian economy." *In* Encyclopedia Americana, vol. 15, pp. 12–19.

Thurston, Edgar
1909 Castes and Tribes of Southern India. Vols. 1–5. Delhi: Cosmo Publications.

Timberg, Thomas A.
1978 The Marwaris: From Traders to Industrialists. New Delhi: Vikas Publishing House.

Trautmann, Thomas
1981 Dravidian Kinship. Cambridge: Cambridge University Press.

Tun Wai, U.
1962 Burma's Currency and Credit. Rangoon: University of Rangoon, Department of Economics.

Tyler, S.
1966 "Parallel/cross: An evaluation of definitions." Southwestern Journal of Anthropology 22: 416–432.

Vakil, C. N., and S. K. Muranjan
1927 Currency and Prices in India. Bombay and London.

van Gennep, Arnold
1909 The Rites of Passage. London: Routledge and Kegan Paul.

Varahamihira
1864–65 The Brhat Samhita of Varaha-Mihira. Dr. H. Kern, ed. Calcutta: Baptist Mission Press.

Wallerstein, Immanuel
1976 The Modern World System: 1. Capitalist Agriculture and the Origins of the European World-Economy in the Sixteenth Century. New York: Academic Press.
1980 The Modern World System: 2. Mercantilism and the Consolidation of the European World-Economy, 1600–1750. New York: Academic Press.

Washbrook, David
1973 "Country politics: Madras, 1880–1930." *In* Locality, Province and Nation: Essays on Indian Politics, 1870–1940, J. Gallagher, G. Johnson, and A. Seal, eds. Cambridge: Cambridge University Press.
1975 "The development of caste organization in South India, 1880–1925." *In* South India: Political Institutions and Political Change, 1880–1940. C. J. Baker and D. A. Washbrook, eds. Delhi: Macmillan Company of India.
1976 The Emergence of Provincial Politics: The Madras Presidency, 1870–1920. Cambridge: Cambridge University Press.
1981 "Law, state and society in colonial India." *In* Power, Profit and Politics: Essays on Imperialism, Nationalism and Change in Twentieth Century India, C. Baker, G. Johnson, and A. Seal, eds. Cambridge: Press Syndicate of the University of Cambridge.
1982 "Ethnicity and racialism in colonial Indian society." *In* Racism and Colonialism, Ronald Ross, ed. The Hague: Martinus Nijhoff Publishers.
1984 "Tamil nationalism, Dravidianism and non-Brahminism." Paper presented at the Conference on Caste, Class and Dominance: Patterns of Politico-Economic Change in Modern India, Philadelphia, Pa., May 3–11.

1988 "Class conflict, resistance and popular culture in colonial India." Paper prepared for India-China Seminar, John Fairbanks Center for East Asian Research, Harvard University, Cambridge, Mass., May 29.

Weber, Max
1947 The Theory of Social and Economic Organization. A. Henderson and T. Parsons, trans. New York: The Free Press.
1958 The Protestant Ethic and the Spirit of Capitalism. New York: Charles Scribner and Sons.

Weersooria, W. S.
1973 The Nattukkottai Chettiars: Merchant Bankers in Ceylon. Dehiwala, Sri Lanka: Tisara Prakasakayo.

Whitehead, Henry
1921 The Village Gods of South India.

Wiser, William H.
1936 The Hindu Jajmani System. Lucknow: Lucknow Publishing House.

Wiser, William H., and Charlotte Wiser
1969 Behind Mud Walls, 1930–1960. Berkeley and Los Angeles: University of California Press.

Wolf, Eric
1955 "Types of Latin-American peasantry: A preliminary discussion." American Anthropologist 57: 452–471.

Yalman, Nur
1971 Under the Bo Tree: Studies in Caste, Kinship, and Marriage in the Interior of Ceylon. Berkeley and Los Angeles: University of California Press.

Index

Abraham, Meera, 3, 189, 193
Accimar panam. *See* Deposits
Account books, 95–99, 189, 195; *kurippu*, 97, 118; *pekki pustakam*, 97, 117; *peredu*, 96–99, 115, 117; press copy book, 97; *vatti chitti*, 97, 103
Accounting, 70–73, 82–84, 95–99, 100–103; between affines, 174, 176–178, 180; by temples, 195, 209–210; lack of evidence for Nakarattar double-entry bookkeeping, 96
Adas, Michael, 5, 7, 80–81
Adathi ("parent banker"), 24, 77, 92, 108, 116–117, 119–124, 189, 214, 217, 230. *See also* Nakarattar elite
Adathi kadai panam. *See* Deposits
Adathi list, 77, 230
Adrstartha. *See* Hinduism
Aduthal, 118–119
Affinal gifts and prestations, 174–175, 179–180, 217; *cir*, 164, 174–179, 183, 186, 217, 218, 219; *cir tanam*, 164, 171–172, 175–177, 179; *cir varacai*, 172, 175–177, 179; cost of, 170–174; internal and external, 172, 179–180, 186, 219 (see also *cir*; *moi*); *mamiyar caman*, 171–172; *moi*, 175–177, 179, 219; *murai*, 127, 177–179, 183–186, 217; *piratu itatukkoti*, 179; *revei*, 175; source of funds for, 173; symmetric and asymmetric, 179–180, 187; *tali*, 178; *vevu*, 168, 179
Affinal kindred. *See* Nakarattar kin groups. *See also* Territorial division: *vattakai*
Affines: in contrast to kin, 161, 180–184, 208; definition of, 160–163, 180–183; perpetual and one-shot, 163, 181–183, 186; terminological, 217; virtual and perfect, 180–184. *See also* Affinal gifts and prestations: *murai*
Affinity. *See* Affines: virtual and perfect; *see also* Marriage alliance
Agraharam, 195
Agricultural zones, 25–26, 31, 65
Aiyar, R. Sathyanatha, 55
Allahabad, 42–43
Allen, G. C., and A. G. Donnithorne, 86–88
Ancestor worship, 199–201. *See also* Worship (puja): *pataippu*
Annamalai Mandram. *See* Tamil Music Academy (Raja Annamalai Mandram)
Annamalai Music College, 149
Annamalai University, 149–150, 153, 155, 215–216
Anpu. *See* Values: devotion (*anpu*)
Anti-Brahman movement, 45, 147. *See also* Tamil Renaissance
Appadurai, Arjun, 10, 45, 47, 138–140, 142–143, 214–215, 228, 235

Compositor:	Impressions
Text:	10/13 Aldus
Display:	Aldus
Printer and binder:	Edwards Brothers